Folklore Matters

Folklore Matters

Incursions in the Field, 1965–2021

BRUCE JACKSON

SUNY PRESS

Cover art: Bruce Jackson recording prisoners clearing live oak grove.
Ellis Unit, Texas Department of Corrections, 1965. Photographer unknown.
Courtesy of the author.

Published by State University of New York Press, Albany

© 2024 State University of New York

All rights reserved

Printed in the United States of America

No part of this book may be used or reproduced in any manner whatsoever without written permission. No part of this book may be stored in a retrieval system or transmitted in any form or by any means including electronic, electrostatic, magnetic tape, mechanical, photocopying, recording, or otherwise without the prior permission in writing of the publisher.

For information, contact State University of New York Press, Albany, NY
www.sunypress.edu

Library of Congress Cataloging-in-Publication Data

Name: Jackson, Bruce, 1936– author.
Title: Folklore matters : incursions in the field, 1965–2021 / Bruce Jackson.
Description: Albany : State University of New York Press, [2024]. | Includes bibliographical references and index.
Identifiers: LCCN 2023019225 | ISBN 9781438496160 (hardcover : alk. paper) | ISBN 9781438496177 (ebook) | ISBN 9781438496153 (pbk. : alk. paper)
Subjects: LCSH: Folklore—United States. | Folklore—Field work—United States. | Folk music—United States. | African Americans—Folklore.
Classification: LCC GR105 .J27 2024 | DDC 398.20973—dc23/eng/20230725
LC record available at https://lccn.loc.gov/2023019225

10 9 8 7 6 5 4 3 2 1

Folklore is a body of traditional belief, custom and expression, handed down largely by word of mouth and circulating chiefly outside of commercial and academic means of communication and instruction. Every group bound together by common interests and purposes, whether educated or uneducated, rural or urban, possesses a body of traditions which may be called its folklore.

Into these traditions enter many elements, individual, popular, and even "literary," but all are absorbed and assimilated through repetition and variation into a pattern which has value and continuity for the group as a whole.

—B. A. Botkin (1938)

The term "American folklife" means the traditional expressive culture shared within the various groups in the United States: familial, ethnic, occupational, religious, regional; expressive culture includes a wide range of creative and symbolic forms such as custom, belief, technical skill, language, literature, art, architecture, music, play, dance, drama, ritual, pageantry, handicraft; these expressions are mainly learned orally, by imitation, or in performance, and are generally maintained without benefit of formal instruction or institutional direction.

—From the American Folklife Preservation Act,
Pub. L. No. 94-201, 94th Congress (1964)

Folklore and Folklife Publications by Bruce Jackson

Books

The Story Is True: The Art and Meaning of Telling Stories, Second Edition, Revised and Expanded (State University of New York Press, 2022; first edition, Temple University Press, 2007)

Voices from Death Row, Second Edition, with Diane Christian (State University of New York Press, 2022, revised edition of *Death Row*, Beacon Press, 1980. French edition, *Le Quartier de la mort*, Editions Terre Humaine, Plon, 1985; second French edition with additional photographs, 1986; third French edition with new postface, 2011)

Terlingua Necropolis (Synergistic Press, 2017)

The World Observed: Reflections on the Fieldwork Process, coeditor, with Edward D. Ives (University of Illinois Press, 1996)

The Centennial Index: 100 Years of Journal of American Folklore, coeditor, with Michael Taft and Harvey Axlerod (American Folklore Society, 1988)

Fieldwork (University of Illinois Press, 1987)

Teaching Folklore, editor (American Folklore Society and Documentary Research, 1984; second edition, 1989; also a publication of the Modern Language Association)

Doing Drugs, with Michael Jackson (St. Martin's, 1983)

"Get Your Ass in the Water and Swim Like Me": Narrative Poetry from Black Oral Tradition (Harvard University Press, 1974; Routledge, 2004, with new CD)

Wake Up Dead Man: Afro-American Worksongs from Texas Prisons (Harvard University Press, 1972; second paperback edition, with additional photographs and new introduction, University of Georgia Press, 2000)

In the Life: Versions of the Criminal Experience (Holt, Rinehart and Winston, 1972: French editions with title *Leurs Prisons*, preface by Michel Foucault, Editions Terre Humaine, Plon, 1975, and with new signature of photographs, 1978)

A Thief's Primer (Macmillan, 1969, paperback title *Outside the Law*)

The Negro and His Folklore in Nineteenth-Century Periodicals, editor (American Folklore Society and University of Texas Press, 1967; most recent reprint, 2014)

Folklore and Society, editor (Folklore Associates, 1966)

Booklets

Folklore/Folklife, coeditor and coauthor with Judith McCulloh and Marta Weigle (American Folklore Society, 1984)

American Folklore (Empire State College, 1973)

Articles

Antioch Review, American Anthropologist, Atlantic Monthly, Folk Music, Harper's Magazine, Listen, Sing Out!, Boston Broadside, Journal of American Folklore, Nagyvilág, New York Folklore, Western Folklore, Southern Folklore Quarterly, Foxfire, Folklore Forum, Texas Monthly, Maledicta, First of the Month, among others

Films

Out of Order, with Diane Christian (89 min., 1983)
William August May, with Diane Christian (18 min., 1982)
Death Row, with Diane Christian (60 min., 1979)
Afro-American Worksongs in a Texas Prison, with Pete, Toshi, and Dan Seeger (30 min., 1966).

Plays

Get Your Ass in the Water and Swim Like Me, directed by Kate Valk, presented by the Wooster Group, in collaboration with Eric Berryman (2023)
The B-Side: "Negro Folklore from Texas State Prisons"; A Record Interpretation, directed by Kate Valk and first presented by the Wooster Group (2017)

Recordings

No More Good Time in the World for Me: J. B. Smith, Dust-to-Digital, two CDs (2015)
"I'm Troubled with a Diamond": Texas Prison Songs Vol. 1, Curlew (London), 1990, tape cassette (Library of Congress List of 50 Outstanding Folk Recordings, 1991)
Old Rattler Can't Hold Me: Texas Prison Songs, Vol. 2, Curlew (London), 1990, tape cassette (Library of Congress List of 50 Outstanding Folk Recordings, 1991)
Get Your Ass in the Water and Swim Like Me, Rounder (LP 1976, CD 1998)
Wake Up Dead Man: Afro-American Worksongs from Texas Prisons, Rounder (LP 1975, CD 1994)
Negro Folklore from Texas State Prisons, Elektra (1975); Moochin' About (London) (2019)
Ever Since I Have Been a Man Full Grown, Takoma (1965)
Eugene Rhodes, Folk Legacy (1962), reissued as CD by the Smithsonian Institution (2022)

For Ben Botkin, with enduring gratitude

Contents

Introduction: Getting Here — 1

Part I. Scenes

1. Prison Folklore — 9
2. In the Valley of the Shadows — 29
3. In the Arctic with Malaurie — 52

Part II. Outside the Law

4. From *In the Life* — 81
5. From *A Thief's Primer* — 125

Part III. The Folksong Revival

6. The Folksong Revival — 143
7. Skip James: "Skippy been places..." — 153
8. Liner Notes: Phil Ochs — 161

Part IV. Black Studies

9. The Glory Songs of the Lord — 171

10.	The Other Kind of Doctor: Conjure and Magic in Black American Folk Medicine	183
11.	Foreword to Lydia Parrish, *Slave Songs of the Georgia Sea Islands*	199
12.	Introduction to *The Negro and His Folklore in Nineteenth-Century Periodicals*	211
13.	Prison Worksongs: The Composer in Negatives	223
14.	What Happened to Jody	255
15.	The Afro-American Toast and Worksong: Two Dead Genres	267

Part V. People

16.	Benjamin A. Botkin (1901–1975)	283
17.	Remembering Alan Lomax (January 31, 1915–July 19, 2002)	289
18.	Legman: The King of X700	297
19.	In Prison with Pete Seeger	309

Part VI. The Folklore Business

20.	Things That from a Long Way Off Look Like Flies	315
21.	Folkloristics	335
22.	Arctic Silence: Icy Terror in the Heart of the Smithsonian	345
23.	"Only the Sailor Knows the Archipelago"	351
24.	From the Editor: The Humanities at Risk	361
25.	From the Editor: Dead Soldiers and the Arctic Night	365
Index		369

Introduction

Getting Here

The essays in this collection are some of the things I wrote about folklore and folklore study over more than a half century: articles, book introductions, reviews, field studies, and more. Sometimes I wrote for academic journals or in scholarly books, and sometimes I wrote for a wider audience. My writerly voice varied accordingly.

I like all the articles and excerpts here, though not for the same reasons. There was a period when I would use phrases like "one thinks" and "it is rather like . . ." The only time I use "one" now is as a number, not as a pronoun, and the only time I'd use "rather" now is when I'm making a comparative statement, such as "I'd rather eat worms."

I also seem to have gone through a phase when I was dropping a lot of psychological jargon. It did not, fortunately, last long. I think that came about when I was spending a lot of time with folklorist Roger D. Abrahams. Then I noticed that every few years Roger seemed to shift to a different vocabulary. I realized he wore it like an everyday coat: he'd use those words until he came upon a set driven by an idea he liked better, so he'd move on to that one. When I realized that, I started examining my own writing to be sure I wasn't doing the same kind of thing. I dislike jargon and try not to use it, save when I'm quoting someone else. Several articles I liked back in the day I can't bear reading now because of the psychobabble or academic jargon, so I'm not going to resurrect them here.

Even though I've published a lot of folklore work, I've never considered myself an academic folklorist. Folklore was one of the things that interested me and some of the field's theories and techniques fitted the work I wanted to do.

I had only one folklore course—a summer seminar on fieldwork with Richard M. Dorson at Indiana University in 1962. I took it under duress: my friend Judith McCulloh had gotten the ethnomusicologist George List, director of IU's Archive of Traditional Music, to hire me for the summer. The archive was under the Folklore Department, which Dorson then chaired. I found that odd because, so far as I could tell, Dorson had little or no interest in folk music. I'd already done a considerable amount of music and talk recording in Indiana State Prison and Missouri State Penitentiary, which Dorson knew. He insisted I register for his class as precondition to allowing George List to put me on the payroll.

I learned nothing about fieldwork in that class, but I learned something else that had a huge impact on my subsequent career. Dorson railed, again and again, against what he called "fakelore." That word connoted work that used the word "folklore" but didn't submit to the academic standards Dorson thought should undergird any work using that word. "Folklore" was what he, his colleagues, and his students did; "fakelore" was like what Benjamin A. Botkin and a few others did. It was Botkin he named most frequently. For Dorson, Botkin was the quintessential "fakelorist."

It was only later that I understood that Dorson was on a mission: he was trying to make folklore as respectable an academic field of endeavor as history or English or pharmacology. For that, he needed a foil. I was, at the time, a graduate student in comparative literature. The whole thing seemed quite silly to me. It still does. Dorson's folklore/fakelore dichotomy is a perfect example of what someone who says, "That's meaningless; it's just academic," might have in mind.

Later that summer, the Folklore Institute had a meeting in Bloomington, part of which was a picnic in nearby Beanblossom. A car arrived with two older men. They were George Korson (who had done important collections of songs of coal miners) and Ben Botkin. People talked to Korson; hardly anybody talked to Botkin. Ellen Stekert, a graduate student in the folklore program, said to me, "Would you like to meet Ben Botkin?"

"Damned right I would."

She led me over to the picnic table where he was sitting and we fell into a two-hour uninterrupted conversation. None of the folklore graduate students were going to risk Dick Dorson seeing them in casual conversation with the Evil One.

Ben and I started corresponding. He suggested things I ought to read (he kept that up until shortly before his death). And he nominated me for a Junior Fellowship in the Harvard Society of Fellows. That gave me four years to study anything I wanted: no reports, no speeches, all expenses paid. It was like a young person's MacArthur. I had the exquisite luxury of doing things without an end in sight, of risking failure. Graduate students can't risk failure on their thesis project if they hope to get a PhD before the funding runs out; assistant professors can't risk failure on their first book project if they hope to get tenure before the seven-year clock runs out. At least a dozen of my books, all of my records, two of my films, and the two plays based on my work came wholly or partly out of research I did in those years, hanging out I did in those years, conversations I had in those years. All of it a result of a conversation in Beanblossom, Indiana, with someone everyone else (except Ellen Stekert) had to pretend was toxic.

I say more about Ben in one of the essays here, so no more about him for now. But the polarity between Dick and him set up the two playing fields of my own work: I was as comfortable writing for the folklore journals as for general magazines, as happy doing academic work as being a director of the Newport Folk Festivals or helping set up the music program for the 1968 Poor People's Campaign, teaching a seminar or running in the Democratic primary as an antiwar candidate. From where I was, it was all seamless. The only thing I couldn't do is come up with a short, simple answer when someone asked, "What's your field?" I still can't. The closest I get is "To bear witness," but that's not an academic department so I don't tell it to very many people.

Now, all these years later, I think the primary difference between Dick Dorson and Ben Botkin about folklore had to do with their sense of time. Dick looked at folklore as data that validated the past; Ben looked at folklore as data that informed the present.

The boundaries between fields always blurred for me. I don't think I've ever identified as "folklorist" or "criminologist" when I was surrounded by folklorists or criminologists. Since I came to Buffalo, I've always been based in the English Department, but I've given seminars in the Law School, the School of Architecture and Planning, the Library School, and departments of Media Study, Sociology, and Art. My sociologist friend Howard S. Becker maybe put it best when he introduced me before a talk: "Bruce isn't a sociologist. But he's not *not* a sociologist, either."

I hadn't thought my books *A Thief's Primer* and *In the Life: Versions of the Criminal Experience* as folklore books until I read a few things by Richard M. Dorson, then the most prominent academic folklorist, referring to them as folklore books. Yeah, they are. I don't use academic folklore jargon in those books but they go after the same kind of answers folklorists seek: How do people narrate their lives? How do they learn crafts not taught in schools or in books? How do they perceive the communities they inhabit and, at least in part, let them identify who and what they are? How does the past inform their future?

I've grouped the articles, reviews, prefaces, and extracts here under six rubrics.

- "Scenes" is a group of articles about folklore and communities, one published in a folklore journal, one a sociology journal, and one an anthropological journal. The way I looked at and engaged people in Pikeville, Kentucky, when I was there on assignment from *Harper's Magazine*, and Nome, Alaska, when Jean Malaurie asked me to join him on a trip there looking around is no different from how I looked and listened in the southern plantation prison farms and Texas Death Row years earlier.

- "Outside the Law" consists of extracts from two of my books, *A Thief's Primer* (based on the career of one criminal) and *In the Life* (based on conversations with dozens of them).

- "The Folksong Revival" consists of one article about the popular folk music movement in the 1960s and articles about two musicians I was involved with at the time, the blues musician Skip James and the singer-songwriter Phil Ochs.

- "Black Studies" consists of some of the articles, reviews, introductions, and essays about what has long been one of my primary concerns in folklore research.

- "People" is about four friends in the folklore research and presentation worlds: Ben Botkin, Alan Lomax, Gershon Legman, and Pete Seeger.

- "The Folklore Business" deals with issues in and about academic folklore studies, some of my editor's comments for *Journal of American Folklore*, public presentation of folk material, and my own engagement with all of that.

I think all the essays I've included here have current interest, but some are grounded, at least in part, in time. "Prison Folklore" was written long before free-world gangs became the significant part of our prison culture they are now. Because of that, a current account of the structure of prison society would, for many institutions, look very different than what I encountered so many years ago. Our views and discourse on race, gender, and power have grown and changed significantly since much of this work was done.

I've tinkered with the text, but only a little. Articles and talks that did not have footnotes or endnotes in their original publication or presentation don't have them here. I got rid of a few then-trendy academic words, like *Weltanschauung*. I got rid of a few anachronisms. I also corrected a few errors that slipped in the first time around. That's it.

BJ

Part I
Scenes

1

Prison Folklore

(*Journal of American Folklore*, 1965)

A shorter version of this essay was presented in the Symposium of Urban Folklore at the 1964 annual meeting of the American Folklore Society in New York. Part of the research involved was supported by Harvard's Society of Fellows. Material was collected in the Indiana State Prison, the Indiana Reformatory, the Massachusetts Correctional Institution, the Missouri State Penitentiary, and the Texas Department of Corrections (the Ramsey, Retrieve, Ellis, and Wynne Farms, and The Walls).

∼

When a man enters prison for the first time, he may choose one of three modes of adaptation: he may go stir-crazy; he may encapsulate himself in a mental shell of one kind or another; he may adjust. Most men choose the third mode. They learn the ways of prison life, the factors that make for an independent world: the language and code, the stories and sayings, and, sometimes, the songs. They learn to be afraid of new things and to forget old ones. These involve the materials of folklore.

Until the new convict is immersed in the prison milieu, he is like the immigrants described by Oscar Handlin: They "could not locate themselves; they had lost the polestar that gave them their bearings. They would not regain an awareness of direction until they could visualize themselves in their new context, see a picture of the world as it appears from this perspective."[1]

In the free world, mores, values, and folkways are determined in varying proportions by geography, society, and occupation. "The central feature of total institutions," says Erving Goffman, "can be described as a breakdown of the barriers ordinarily separating these three spheres of life."[2] The urban equivalent of this condition exists in the slum ghetto, occasioned by a combination of ethnic and social insularity with economic disability.

Prison folklore exists symbiotically with free world folklore, a relationship that survives because the prison material satisfies certain needs the outside material cannot satisfy and because the influences operating on the prison folklore are all internal. Prison folksong, for example, has not been subject to the commercial refertilization (and contamination) that has so greatly influenced free world folksong since the advent of phonographs and radios for everyone. Disc jockeys do not play the few recordings of prison songs (which I do not consider here, since more is known about this genre of prison lore than the following materials);[3] radio and TV comics and free world newspapers and magazines do not relate the homosexual and trade anecdotes and jokes. When outside, the convicts keep this lore to themselves: it has an indelible prison stamp on it, and prison is not the kind of former address one advertises. The songs, stories, and argot lack occasion and audience outside.

All folklore is intimately related to the life situation that produces and maintains it, but this relationship is particularly visible in prison because it is easier for us to analyze the dynamics of so circumscribed a world. We see here folklore not only as an expression of culture, but as a force operating upon it. This situation has been described by Melville and Frances Herskovits:

> The relation between a literature and the culture of which it is a part is reciprocal, and the artist is the medium through which these influences flow. The world of the story-teller is largely defined by his culture, and in composing his tale, whatever its form or length, he draws on the world he knows, whether as reality or fantasy (or one in which tradition has fused both) for setting, plot, characterization, and the sanctions that give these meaning. Yet by this very act he reinforces the existing body of custom, bringing to it the validating force of emotional response.[4]

Before writing this essay, I assumed certain differences in the urban and rural folklore in a prison; I no longer do. How can one say a particular verbal or musical *event* is urban or suburban or rural, particularly in a culture such as ours? All one can reasonably say is where something occurred, what it concerns, and what is its probable provenience. We must see prison folklore as both urban and rural, for the forces shaping it are the products of urban and rural cultures and the intellectual baggage the bearers carry reflects those cultures. The unifying factor, however, the force of the prison world, is an artificial one.

In this essay, then, I shall attempt to describe aspects of the folklore found in a special kind of folk community (by which I mean the kind of community defined by John Greenway: "an unsophisticated, homogeneous group living in a politically-bounded culture but isolated from it by such factors as topography, geography, dialect, economics, and race"[5]), one which we ourselves have made by building a wall and fastening some bars and barbed wire, one in which folklore plays a far greater role in the inhabitants' lives than it does when they are in the free world. One encounters various states of folklore in a maximum security prison: indigenous material of a particular institution, material indigenous to general prison culture, and material from criminal culture and other free world folklore. One sees these in various stages of transformation as free world and general prison folklore are adapted to a particular institution and adopted by a particular informant.

We must first consider who has the folklore. Nowhere does everyone have it all; in few places do many people have very much. There are folksayers who do most of the saying, folksingers who do most of the singing; only a few people in a community make home brew worth drinking. So I shall begin by describing briefly the prison world and its inhabitants.

Prison Society

For any complex social body in which there are various levels and kinds of social interaction, more than one workable model may be posited. The most satisfactory model for describing the relationships in the captive society that are of interest here is one in which the inmate population is seen as having three components: *noncriminal*, *thief*, and *convict*.[6] This is a drastic oversimplification, of course, and quite inadequate for prison administration—but it is useful for discussions such as this one.

The *noncriminal* group is composed of men under sentence for a crime, naturally, but whose attitude and orientation are directed toward the values and goals of a noncriminal society. A large proportion of the homicides fall into this category. These are inmates who have committed one crime, generally under extraordinary circumstances, but who are not likely ever to commit another. Sometimes the political prisoners are part of this group, though they may form a fourth group standing apart from the other three in order to proselytize among them, such as political prisoners in federal institutions, civil rights agitators in Southern prisons, and, in the past, labor unionizers in state penitentiaries.[7] These men have little to do with underworld society, inside or out. They often avoid the politics of inmate society and steer clear of the various prison rackets. They try to do their time as quietly as possible. Sometimes a member of this group may go over to one of the others, especially if he is on a long sentence. Such conversion, for reasons too involved to examine here, is much more difficult than one might suppose.

The *thief* culture is composed of the professionals. Numerically, it is probably the smallest of the three. Its members engage in a variety of illegal activities in the free world, from floating phony stocks to commercial assassination, but they do these things for the high profits, not for the style of criminal life. Members of this group often live in a nice section of town, have wives that belong to the PTA, and have few or even no criminal friends.

Alexander Berkman, sentenced in 1892 to twenty-two years for his attempt on Henry Frick's life during the Homestead Strike, wrote of a professional he met while in prison—"Lightning Al." Berkman was trying to understand this man, so different from most of the other inmates. "But you spend most of your time in prison," Berkman said to him. Al replied:

> Not by a long shot. A real good gun's always got his fall money planted,—I mean some ready coin in case of trouble,—and a smart lawyer will spring you most every time; beat the case, you know. I've never seen the fly-cop you couldn't fix if you got enough dough, and most judges, too. Of course, now and then, the best of us may fall; but it don't happen very often, and it's all in the game. This whole life is a game, Mr. Berkman, and every one's got his graft.[8]

The *convict* group, the one that supplies the largest portion of the recidivist population, is of greatest interest to us. "The hard core member of the convict subculture finds his reference groups inside the institutions and . . . seeks status through means available in the prison environment."[9]

The thief wants leisure time, "things that will make prison life a little easier.... The convict seeks privileges which he believes will enhance his position in the inmate hierarchy."[10] Members of the convict group frequently get into trouble immediately on release, for they are dependent on the double authority imposed by the administration and other convicts, and their goals are conceived in terms of the prison and cannot be fulfilled in the free world. For them, *scoring* for a sack of sugar (getting it illegally), whether they need it or not, provides a significant satisfaction; *flying a kite* (getting off an illegal letter) may be more important than communicating whatever it is the letter contains. There are often only incidental relationships between members of the thief and convict groups in a prison, for the thieves consider themselves of superior caste. Since many of the members of the convict subculture received their indoctrination in juvenile institutions, where the thief culture is virtually nonexistent, and the two groups have little to do with one another outside, we see there is little likelihood of the two cultures merging. It is the convict group that seems most likely to tell and appreciate the homosexual jokes and it is also that group that is most likely to engage in homosexual activity in prison. The men who manage to apprentice to traditional trades, such as lockpicking and forgery, are not members of this group. The thief and noncriminal groups will not use slang as extensively as the convicts, and they tend to remain aloof from homosexual affairs. Criminals themselves are perhaps more sensitive to the cultural fragmentation of prison society than have been many penologists. (This, of course, is a highly generalized statement, admittedly open to qualification.)

The Code

It is moot whether the Code[11] receives more reinforcement from prison exigencies or Burt Lancaster movies. An old inmate at the penitentiary in Huntsville, Texas, told me a man who followed the Code was called *convict* by the other inmates, and it was a term of respect, which is a rather interesting inversion. "Convict," he said, "means that you're supposed to be a good people. To the inmate body. Wherever you might meet 'em, inside or outside. If they call you convict, why that means it's qualified as you keep your mouth shut and tend to your own business and you're not a snitch and you don't meddle in other people's business or things like that."

Don't inform, don't meddle, don't bring heat—says the Code. "Though there is little group loyalty in total institutions," writes Erving

Goffman, "the expectation that group loyalty should prevail forms part of the inmate culture and underlies the hostility accorded those who break inmate solidarity."[12] This does not mean informing doesn't occur; it does mean that it generally occurs *in camera*. The members of this society got where they are by breaking laws, and only a few bother to distinguish between laws made by civilians and laws made by convicts, however much their movie and personal romances claim otherwise.

A folklore repertory accompanies the Code—stories illustrating it in action or the dire retributions visited upon violators. Many of the stories describing group retaliations are true, but the one-man retaliations often bear further inspection. One ancient killing, for example, was cited by several convicts as an example of assassination for informing, but a little investigation indicated that the real cause was jealousy in a homosexual romance.

The Code may be a joke to the noncriminals and thieves, but to many members of the convict subculture it is as venerable as motherhood. In Massachusetts Correctional Institution (Walpole), I was told of an inmate who was in solitary confinement when the one other man in that row of cells cursed the guard through the door. The guard assumed the first inmate, Joe, was the one who had shouted, and told him to stop. The second inmate did it again and Joe got an extra five days of punishment. He couldn't say, "It wasn't me," because that would have been informing by implication. On the other hand, there is a well-known story about a warden who broke up a dining hall riot by promising to come in there with all the *snitch-kites* (informing letters) he had received in the last month if the hall wasn't cleared in five minutes. Old-timers insist there is far more informing nowadays, that in the old days punishment was swift and sure. But every contemporary account I have consulted, going back over seventy years, says the same thing. The fact is that informing is now and always has been part of the *modus vivendi*. And the Code is as much a part of prison folklore as ever.

Prose Narrative

Stories about local characters, legendary escapes, stupid guards, and clever convicts abound in prisons everywhere. The specific stories are not, apparently, very migratory, but because of identical conditions and concerns there seems to be some polygenesis. Inmates in Texas tell of Bullin' Jack O'Diamonds, the meanest guard on Central Farm, a man so tough he had to be chained down to die. "If he catch you," one inmate said, "a dark cloud would go over." Jack O'Diamonds carried a Luger, which he liked to use, and he seems to have appropriated folklore badman Stagolee's mantle: they say he told Satan, "Stand aside, I'm gonna rule old Hell myself!" In Massachusetts, I was told about a stupid deputy warden, nicknamed "Alligator," who "looked like a retired hit man [killer]." He decided inmates were taking advantage of the pharmacy, so he stopped all drugs, no matter what the illness. One inmate needed Doriden, a light narcotic. The deputy refused. "But I've been getting heart palpitations," the inmate said. "Keep on taking those," said Alligator, "they're better for you than Doridens, believe me." They also tell there a cycle of stories about Harry Bedour, a clown who stars in a variety of impossible adventures, ranging from climbing a flagpole in January stark naked and refusing to come down until the warden promised him an airplane with a propeller, to his tricking a tough but dumb guard who had heard Harry had a tough reputation and wanted to try him out. Harry feinted the guard into the vegetable refrigerator, slammed and locked the massive door, then dropped the thermostat.

Here are three other guard stories:

> You know, these hacks around here, they's stupid as hell. I mean, it's no kidding, some of them are not intelligent enough to hold a job on the outside, so they come up here and get a job of being hacks. And they's several things that's illegal here, like you catch a couple a' these boys one a-screwing the other one, that's strictly illegal, you see, so they watch for that. Man been in here a long time, he's apt to do it. I heard one guy walk up to a hack one day and he says, "Did you notice when you passed cell so-and-so down there?"
>
> And he said, "Yeah," he said, "I noticed."
>
> He said, "Well, didn't you see them two guys in there, one a-screwing the other one?" And he said, "Hell! Is that what they was a-doing? I thought they was playing leap-frog!"
> (Indiana State Prison)

> We had a old boss here, in fact he's still on this farm, we was shelling peanuts. And every time a man turned in a' gallon a peanuts, he'd check his name off. Had a big barrel, a fifty-five-gallon barrel. And he'd get up there and pour his peanuts in there and check the name off. Warden MacAdams came down

there and asked him how many peanuts he had in there and, I don't know, he told him a hundred-ninety, eighty, anyhow, close to two hundred gallon a' peanuts in that barrel. "Well," he said, "you can't have that many in there, that barrel's not that big."

He said, "I know darn well I can because I been checkin' every one a' them off and every one a' them put a gallon a' peanuts in there." There was actually about twenty-five gallons a' peanuts in the barrel and he thought he had two hundred gallons in there. (Texas)

I used to patronize a cathouse all the time. Had the same gal, I'd see her every Saturday night. Man, she'd make three dollars off a me real regular. I went there one particular Saturday night and she wasn't there. So I asked where in hell she was at, and they said she was going to have a baby. I said, "Holy Christ! I didn't know whores had babies!"

They said, "Sure. Where do you think these prison guards come from?"[13]

There is a simple salutary effect to verbalization: saying doesn't "make it so," but it may make it easier to take. Articulation may dull or exaggerate a concept, it may stand as surrogate for action (narcotic dysfunction), or it may act as a buffer by bringing the elements in a situation to tolerable proportions.

The average inmate has not had extensive homosexual experience before his first imprisonment. Though many may have been picked up by homosexuals or joined with friends to rob them, few have ever been in a situation where homosexual activity completely supplanted the heterosexual. The vocabulary of the average first time inmate is laced with synonyms for homosexual, every one of which is pejorative: *fag*, *fairy*, *queen*, *fruit*, etc. In prison he learns two new words—*punk* and *wolf*—and that things have changed. The larger proportion of the inmate population, not sophisticated enough to think in terms of social relativism, tend to be rather solipsistic in their interpretations and evaluations of sexual activity. In general, the attitude is that *queens*, free world overt homosexuals, are all right, because they are honest, while punks, prison catamites, are not all right, because they are covert and weak. "They're not man enough to admit what they are," a free world homosexual said to me, not without irony, explaining why he and his friends had little regard for the punks in the institution. The large segment of inmate population that abstains from sexual relationships seems to share this view. Many inmates insist that anyone dealing with a punk is not himself homosexual, while anyone dealing with a queen is; other inmates reverse the equation. Prison authorities—in practice if not conviction—are equally divided. This confusing multiplicity of values leads, as one might well imagine, to a variety of logical and emotional differences. Many of these find expression in the humor dealing with prison sex. It is easy to make too much of sex in prison. Girlie magazines play it up, prison administrators play it down, and it is difficult to find out just how much activity actually goes on. Inmates in one institution estimated, each with a degree of assurance that would astonish the Kinsey people, the incidence of participation at 10, 20, and 95 percent. Most prison administrators find sex to be a cause of violence and therefore they punish men participating; a few states actually add time to a man's sentence for homosexuality in prison, treating the problem as if it were a free world crime, and thus indicating that society's attitude toward homosexuality is sometimes more barbaric than that of the inmates.

Some of the jokes dealing with the problem are simply outside jokes fitted with prison uniforms, such as the familiar "Whose turn in the barrel?" Another, requiring a slightly more prisonized point of view, is the following adaptation of a well-known Jesse James story that usually centers on an old maid:

> Jesse James was robbin' a passenger train. Jesse James taken up all the money. He say, "I'm gonna rob this train. I'm gonna fuck all the men."
> This lady got up, said, "Mister Jesse James: you mean all the women."
> And there's this punk on there and he got up and said, "Hey, lady, who robbin' this train, you or Mister Jesse James?" (Texas)[14]

Others require that one be quite familiar with the prison situation, as the next two:

> There was another captain, over on the Central [Farm], every time you asked for a lay-in, you know, say, "My head hurts," he said, "I do, too. Mine, too; me, too," you know. "I got a . . . my arm hurts, my leg hurts, my stomach hurts, I got a stomach ache," and he'll say, "Me, too." So one day a guy says, "I'm gonna get me a lay-in." So he said, "Captain, I want to

lay-in." "What's wrong with you?" He said, "I got the claps in the ass," He start to say—he said, "Lay in!" (Texas)

Did you hear about the guy did thirty years in prison? Finally went out, finally got a parole. Now, after thirty years, everything changes, you know. And he's kind of leery of the new way of life. And when he went in, they didn't even have a streetcar, a bus, or anything like that. So he's standing one day by the prison gate with a suitcase, you know, with his five dollars, and he says, "Gee, what am I gonna do now?" you know. So he sees this civilian coming down the walk with a lunchpail, you know. So the con says to himself, "If I do what he does, how can I go wrong?" you know.

So the guy comes over and the civilian says, "Good morning."

The ex-con says, "Good morning." So they got talking, you know. Finally, the bus came and the civilian got on first. The con looks over his shoulder, you know, and he sees the guy take out a nickel and a dime. He puts it in the slot, so the con, he does the same, you know. So they sat down and got to talking. The bus took off, stopped, took off again. Finally, a nice-looking blonde came on.

Civilian looks at that and he nudges the ex-con. He doesn't know he's an ex-con. "Hey," he says, "look at the legs on that one," you know.

Ex-con says, "Yeah, nice. Very nice. But look at the ass on that bus driver." (Massachusetts)

Toasts

American Negro folklore has few narrative songs, but it does have a flourishing form of oral poetry, narrative in design and quasi-thematic in composition—the toast.[15] The Negro, in fact, is probably the last immigrant group in this land in which narrative poetry survives as an oral form. The toast's subject matter ranges over the entire catalog of western physical taboos, from sodomy to coprophilia, with more mundane exercises, such as sadomasochism, satyriasis, and nymphomania, sandwiched in between. Not all are obscene. Many are versions of narrative poems found in popular anthologies, others are drawn from hobo newspapers—"Blue Velvet Band," "The Shooting of Dan McGrew," "The Face on the Barroom Floor." Popular among urban and rural Negroes, many hobo jungle poems have found new breeding grounds behind prison walls.

Toasts are a particularly important genre in prison folklore. In addition to free world toasts, there are a number that are indigenous to prison. Moral poems, from the pulp anthologies, find wide currency, as do misogynistic poems. Some, such as "Jody the Grinder and G.I. Joe," can be pretty much dated by the slang they incorporate. Even in prison, where slang and argot are used extensively and modulate regularly, archaisms survive in verse. The following toast was recorded in Indiana State Prison from a white informant, who learned it from another white convict at Deer Lodge (Prison), Montana. I collected a substantially different version from a Negro informant in Texas.

> All you tough guys that thinks you're wise,
> take heed and avoid your downfall.
> For I'm a wise egg, I can lie, steal and beg,
> and I've traveled this whole world around.
> I been east and I been west and I been with the best
> when it come to covering ground.
> Why I juggled a tray in a New York cafe
> and I hopped hotel bells in Chi,
> and I've carried a pack down a B and O track
> and I've popped redball freights on the fly.
> Now, you know, all my life I've been a wanderer
> up and down that old cinder trail,
> and all the happy memories that I've got left
> are the few days I've spent out of jail.
> Why, I've laid in my cell and I've suffered like hell
> for the want of a shot of dope.
> I've prayed in despair to be sent to the chair
> or bumped off at the end of a rope.
> I have prayed without hope to the goddess of dope,
> to whomever with whom I have served—
> so just hark to the tale of the wanderer's trail,
> just look what it's done to me.
> You better stay out in the sticks with the rest of the hicks,
> that's a convict's warning from me.

Obviously this is a hobo narrative at heart. In George Milburn's *The Hobo's Hornbook*, we find a similar set of verses under the title "The Hobo's Warning." It begins:

> This is a tale of the wanderlust trail,
> Of a guy with his kick to the wall,
> So all you flip yaps ease up on your traps
> And take heed and avoid your downfall.

The remainder continues much as the prison toast above (omitting the lines about jail and dope) and concludes:

> Now all of you mutts 've heard me throw my guts,
> You can see how it's ending for me.
> Stay here in the sticks with the rest of the hicks—
> That's a hobo's warning from me![16]

The adaptation to prison here consisted merely of substituting "convict's" for "hobo's" and adding some lines about prison. Rarely is the genealogy so transparent.

In the Missouri Penitentiary I found far more whites knowing and telling toasts and "Playing the Dozens" than anywhere else. I discovered later that B Basement, the seclusion area where men were kept in lockup for extended periods, was not segregated and the cells had windowed doors facing a common hallway. I heard recently that this punishment has been abolished. Alfred Hassler, a World War II conscientious objector, writes of inmates playing the Dozens at Lewisburg Federal Penitentiary, where he was a prisoner in 1944:

> I have no idea what the origin of the name can be, but the idea is that the participants try to make each other mad by hurling epithets. The first one to lose his temper loses the game. I listened in on one, and it stood my hair on end. The players vie with each other in combining the most obscene and insulting accusations against not only the opponent himself, but anyone for whose reputation he might conceivably have some regard. Mothers, sisters, wives, children all come under the ban, and the players explore possibilities of degraded behavior, generally sexual, of the most revolting nature.[17]

In the Missouri Penitentiary the whites in seclusion learned toasts and Dozens by listening to the Negro inmates. But one Negro informant reversed the process. He celled next to a white man, who taught him the following toast. It deals with the problem of a criminal who did not have the one thing more important than a good alibi—money. Any convict who has spent much time in prisons can cite examples where the quality of justice has been considerably tempered by sufficient funds applied to paying off officials or hiring a good lawyer (who in turn may pay off officials); the cynicism reflected here is not atypical:

I was sittin' in the jail to do a stretch of time,
when through the door stepped two friends of mine.
I could tell by the look on their face, they didn't have a
   cocksuckin' dime.
So I took 'em over to the corner and sat 'em down
and pulled out my Country Gentleman and began to run it
   down [tell a story].
"Fellas, when you cross the street be prepared for your doom,
because there's some lousy motherfuckers in that silver court
   room.
Now, that judge looked at me like I was a roach on the floor,
and said he was gettin' tired a me dartin' in and out a' his
   goddamned door.
He said, 'Johnson, I'm gettin' tired a you fellas runnin'
   around here
doin' these nickel-assed crimes,
jumpin' up here before me and ain't got a cocksuckin' dime.'
I said, 'But your honor, I can truthfully say,
when the crime was committed I was miles away.'
Say, 'My people bought a home out in California, you know,
that's where I always be when I ain't got no dough.'
'Bout this time the prosecutor walked in
and my heart felt like a thousand dirty motherfuckin' pins.
He says, 'Your honor, that's old stick-high jivin' Johnson
playin' the part of a simp' [simpleton],
Say, 'if you let him out on the corner this evenin',
he'll be screamin' he's a motherfuckin' pimp.'
Say, 'If you let him out a' here talkin' that bunk,'
say, 'before sundown he'll have his arm full a that no-good junk.'

Prison Folklore | 21

Judge say, 'Yeah, I heard about you.'
Said, 'You been playin' these high-class broads, these broads
     a' the upper class.'
Say, 'I'm gonna see if you can't shake this quarter [25-year
     sentence] off your goddam ass.'
I say, 'But your honor, how 'bout my children, my sickly wife?'
He say, 'Contempt of court. Clerk, change that shit to life.'
Now they had me up, they had my ass and they had my feet
     off the floor,
they was draggin' me out the courtroom door.
Judge say, 'You know what, Willie, it's a damned shame,
but this time tomorrow, I won't know your cocksuckin' name.'"

Argot, Slang, Nicknames

Albert Guerard wrote, in another context, that "language groups are far more potent realities than are political units. Language is the only true frontier; the one that can not be altered by a stroke of the pen, nor ignored by airplane and radio, the one also that levies the heaviest toll on foreign goods. Community of language means even more than ease of communication: it implies a common background of education, common patterns of thought, a common cultural heritage."[18]

Argot and slang are components of language, and if their use is extensive, as in a prison, they fall within the scope of Guerard's literary comment. Such language is frequently far more connotative than ordinary language, and it is by these connotations that the outsider is usually kept outside. He perceives the denotations easily enough, but the connotations are embodied in the milieu that necessitates having an argot in the first place. It is not that members of an in-group plot so their words will be unknown to an outsider, but rather that these words obtain currency specifically because they express a particular aspect of reality not adequately handled by the more quotidian vocabulary. It is the situation that is incomprehensible to the outsider (which is, to skirt a circular statement, why he is an outsider), not the definition. A free world example might illustrate this most easily. In the 1940s and the early 1950s, the word *fay* or *ofay* (Pig Latin for *foe*) served a New York Negro as a suitable term of identification for a white man, carrying with it a contemptuous connotation, especially for slumming squares and roaming cops. With the increase in interest in jazz after the War and subsequent influx of whites to bars previously all Negro, the word slipped into more general usage. White musicians and their friends used it for whites who were not hip to Negro music, and blues fans used it to refer to squares and to one another (since that seems to be a group among whom degree of hipness is of special significance). So new words—*Whitey* and *Charley* among them—have assumed the old function. As H. L. Mencken put it, "Slang originates in the effort of ingenious individuals to make the language more pungent and picturesque—to increase the store of terse and striking words, to widen the boundaries of metaphor, and to provide a vocabulary for new shades of difference in meaning."[19]

One of the difficulties with this kind of language is that many of the words possess a variety of meanings. In Texas, the word *joint* means a marihuana cigarette, the penis, paraphernalia for injecting narcotics (obviously derived from the phallic usage), and the prison itself. *Jacket*, to the prison administration, means one's official records; to the inmates it means one's reputation; to some people, it is an article of clothing.

Not all inmates use the argot, but all know the meanings of the words. Highest currency is among members of the convict society. The thief culture is a bit wary of it. "I don't like to use slang," Lightning Al told Alexander Berkman. "It grows on one, and every fly-cop can spot you as a crook. It's necessary in my business to present a fine front and use good English, so I must not get the lingo habit."[20] A Midwestern inmate, who told me about his participation in over 150 holdups in two years, said, "I don't use slang. You want people to think I'm a crook?"

Northern prisons draw largely on the general body of underworld and prison slang, but Southern prisons develop extensive local vocabularies. The reasons for this are purely ecological (and illustrate again the concept of the folk community as an isolate). Population is more constant in a Southern prison than a Northern one. A Southern Negro or poor white is not so mobile as his Yankee counterpart. A crook in St. Louis or New York or Chicago has no difficulty getting into trouble in a neighboring state or relocating permanently, but a Houston hoodlum has to travel most of the day to reach a decent-sized city the other side of the Texas line. The recidivist population in most states tends to be local, but more so in the South. So there is continuity in the culture, not only of conditions but personnel as well.

Communications between penitentiary systems are poor. Few of the worksongs appear to be shared among prisons in Mississippi, Louisiana, and Texas. Everyone knows the song "John Henry," but no one in Louisiana seems to know that when a Texas convict hears that name he thinks the chow wagon is coming, and few Texans seem to know that when a Louisiana convict hears it he starts swinging his hammer or hoe (if he is an older man) or thinks of Uncle Tom (if he is a younger inmate).[21] Prison argot and slang deal with anything of local interest, and sex is high on the list. Donald Clemmer notes that a 1940 compilation of 1,000 slang and argot words from an Illinois penitentiary produced 116 with a sex reference—and over half of these had a homosexual reference.[22]

Here are some examples from Missouri State Penitentiary: *kite* is an illegal letter, *fly a kite* is to send an illegal letter inside the prison; *fly a kite by the birds* is to send one outside. An informer is a *snitch* or a *snake* (*squealer*, that derisive cry so essential to movie scripts, seems to be unused); a catamite is a *punk*; a catamite who is a prostitute is a *candy bar punk*. In Massachusetts, an *abnormal punk* is one who does it in prison only, while a *normal punk* is one who does it in the free world—which does indicate something about the attitude operative. In Texas, the scrip used for commissary purchases is called *cho-cho*. *Fire on the turnrow* means the warden is coming; *thunder on the turnrow* means the director of the system is coming; *Big bitch* is a life sentence under the habitual criminal act; *shake it, Jake* is a somewhat scatological call for rain. There is an entire vocabulary peculiar to the fieldwork done in the farms, including *turnrow* (the road forming the perimeter of a *cut* or single crop area), *sideline* (working up one side of a row), *flatweed* (working with a hoe), *catch up tight* (work closely together), and *don't leave a comeback* (get everything out of a row in one pass so that it is not necessary to work back up the other side of the row). The following story, told at Ramsey Farm, depends for its humor on the same turn as the story above of the ex-con on the bus:

> A man got out of prison and went to the barbershop for his first free world haircut. Well, when he sat down in the barber's chair, the barber, after looking this fellow's head over, asked him if he had been in prison. This fellow said no, he hadn't. And "Why do you ask that?"
>
> The barber said, "No reason in particular. Just wondered."
> The barber then asked this fellow how he wanted his hair cut.
> The fellow said, "Sideline the sides, flatweed the top, catch up tight, and don't leave a comeback."

Many of the expressions have collateral stories. Sometimes, in anger, the inmates will call *Strike him, lightning*, which is supposed to have started because of an incident some time ago: "One time on Retrieve, lightning struck a dog sergeant. Melted him, his horse, his dog, and his gun and everything else. That's their way of getting back." One old inmate wrote that *John Henry* was attached to the chow wagon because "the first dinner wagon was driven by an old man called John Henry and since that time meals carried to the men working have been called 'John Henrys.'"[23] An inmate on Ramsey said he heard another story from an official: "An inmate lost his head in the field. Somebody cut it off with an ax or a cane knife or something like that. So from that day in the field they called lunch in the fields 'John Henry.'"

The administration refers to a man by his surname or his number, the first-name usage in this society often implies a degree of friendship that few attain, so nicknames offer a useful middle ground. They also give inmates an opportunity to comment upon one another and their guards. They may describe a personality trait or echo a favorite saying of the bearer, as these three from Massachusetts: *Willie the Bungler, Back Home Murphy*, and *Odd Shape Walsh*. In Texas, some inmates were taking up a collection for a colleague being released after serving twelve years. The man taking up the collection found no one knew Roger Allen, but when he gave the man's nickname, *Hucklebuck*, the kitty swelled. Some nicknames for guards in Texas are *Two-Gun, I Killem Kelley* ("His initials were I. K. and he did kill a few, so they named him 'I Killem'"), *Hollywood* ("One a' those pretty-boy bosses. Came down with this Hollywood Wild West—two guns on, all dressed up, see. He's a big shot cowboy, so they hung 'Hollywood' on him"), *The Craw, Boss No-Socks, Belly, Robber, Captain Easy, Beartracks, Grizzly Bear*, and *Jesse James*. Inmate nicknames are even more various (since there are more of them): *Retus* ("Some used to call him *Arthritis* [a pun on his name] and *Retis* comes from that"), *Prune Heat, Sweet Pea, Lipstick* (a queen name; others are *Ruby Lips, Bubbles, Bambi, Dixie, Peaches*), *Chinaman, Mullet, Big Lucile, Korea, Creeping Jesus, February 14th*, and *Bacon and Porkchop*.

Material Folklore

One could easily do a separate study of the material folklore produced by prison society. Production is related to local needs and everywhere one finds a variety of ingenious responses to an environment dedicated to the suppression of such manufacture, as well as the attitude behind it.[24]

Most knives are made in the license plate plant by shearing a piece of sheet steel at a diagonal. There are regional varieties. Knives are cut differently if they are to be hidden in jacket linings or taped to a leg or carried in a pocket. Haywood Patterson writes of inmates carrying knives in the extra fold of cloth over the trousers' zipper, a place the guards did not pat when searching them.[25] Sometimes one comes across more elaborate knives with carved handles and shaped blades, but these are rare because one wants such a weapon to be difficult to trace; they have no ornamental value. In prisons where there are no tag plants, knives may be hammered from spoons. In Missouri, knives are identified by size and shape as *shank*, *shiv*, *shotgun*, and *mutton*. Far more inmates own knives than would ever consider using them. One inmate in Missouri Penitentiary had had his knife for five years and said he would feel naked without it; the instrument was so flexible and dull one could neither cut nor butter toast with it.

Indiana inmates are permitted to purchase jars of instant coffee from the commissary, but not devices with which to boil the water, so they fashion a device called a *hotstick*, made of a foot or two of electrical wire with a male plug at one end and a short-bared loop at the other, which will boil a glass of water in a few seconds (similar devices, with UL blessing, may be purchased in hardware stores). A narcotics runner gave me a stainless-steel belt buckle he had made in the machine shop; it has a secret compartment in which one may hide several caps of heroin and two or three folded bills. In some institutions a man wanting revenge without wanting to risk a violent encounter may drop a spoonful of croton oil in his enemy's coffee. The oil is a violent cathartic and, with the very starchy prison diet, is said to induce violent abdominal convulsions and often internal hemorrhaging.[26] Less grim liquid exercise is involved in the manufacture of booze and beer. Done everywhere, it was most developed as an art, in my prison experience, in Texas, where it is called *chock*, and produced by fermenting anything in anything from a swamp boot to an unused commode; it is reported to have a variety of flavors.

Traditional arts are maintained and crafts are learned. I met one expert lock and safe man (who would be regarded as a master locksmith were his penchant for opening doors predicated on the owner's request rather than his absence) who displayed an array of about fifty carefully machined and filed picks and twists designed to open any lock. These were machined in a fashion explained in no book and utilized in an occupation advocated in no lecture hall. As we walked around the prison, he demonstrated by opening doors and boxes with ease. He had broken out of every prison in which he had ever been placed (unfortunately he is much better at breaking out than staying out), and only by investing him with trusty ground privileges have his current captors been able to keep him in tow. He is a general handyman in the prison and has at least one student apprenticing lockpicking and safecracking techniques. Surely such a master of the old school is in the great tradition of American folk craftsmen.

∼

Because prison society is so naked, we can obtain there a more coherent view of certain kinds of folklore than we can in the confusion of the free world community where any man may at once be a member of several distinct subcultures. There is a range in the kind and style of folklore one finds in prisons, just as there is such a range outside, and in both cases the character of the lore is determined in part—but only in part— by geographical location and population distribution. There is also in circulation in prison society a large body of lore indigenous to prisons or a particular prison, assimilation of which is an essential element in the process sociologists call prisonization—the adjustment to the terms of the artificial world behind those very real walls.

Notes

1. Oscar Handlin, *The Uprooted* (Boston, 1951), 94–95.
2. Erving Goffman, *Asylums: Essays on the Social Situation of Mental Patients and Other Inmates* (Garden City, New York, 1961), 6.
3. Recordings of prison songs, generally with useful notes, are published by the Music Division of the Library of Congress, Folkways, Folk-Legacy, Folk-Lyric, Tradition, and Elektra record companies.
4. Melville J. and Frances S. Herskovits, *Dahomean Narrative* (Evanston, Illinois, 1958), 70.
5. John Greenway, *Literature among the Primitives* (Hatboro, Pennsylvania, 1964), ix.
6. See John Irwin and Donald Cressey, "Thieves, Convicts, and the Inmate Culture," in *The Other Side: Perspectives on Deviance*, edited by Howard S. Becker (New York, 1964), 225–45. I have freely incorporated their analysis into my own.
7. Archie Green pointed out to me the way political prisoners may serve as this fourth group.

8. Alexander Berkman, *Prison Memoirs of an Anarchist* (New York, 1913), 198.

9. Irwin and Cressey, 233.

10. Irwin and Cressey, 236.

11. See Donald Clemmer, *The Prison Community* (New York, 1958), 152–64, for a discussion of the Code in an Illinois penitentiary.

12. Goffman, 61.

13. Brendan Behan, in *Borstal Boy* (New York, 1959), has one character say, "Ever 'ear of the screw married the prostitute? 'E dragged 'er down to 'is own level" (40).

14. See Richard M. Dorson, *American Folklore* (Chicago, 1959), 241–42.

15. Roger Abrahams' *Deep Down in the Jungle . . . Negro Narrative Folklore from the Streets of Philadelphia* (Hatboro, Pennsylvania, 1964) discusses toasts and the Dozens extensively.

16. George Milburn, *The Hobo's Hornbook* (New York, 1930), 256–57.

17. Alfred Hassler, *Diary of a Self-Made Convict* (Chicago, 1954), 126–27.

18. Albert Guerard, *Literature and Society* (Boston, 1935), 38.

19. H. L. Mencken, *The American Language* (New York, 1937, fourth edition), 300.

20. Berkman, 199.

21. Reported in conversation by Harry Oster.

22. Clemmer, 89.

23. "More about John Henry," *Texas Department of Corrections Newsletter*, I:8 (July 1, 1964).

24. Thelma James suggests that this sort of activity be called "folk ingenuity."

25. Haywood Patterson and Earl Conrad, *Scottsboro Boy* (New York, 1951, reprint), 52.

26. Berkman, 188–89, mentions that croton oil was used to disable and kill scabs, presumably in the Homestead Strike.

2

In the Valley of the Shadows

(*transAction*, 1971)

This essay has a fraught history.

It came about because Frederic "Fritz" Fleron, an assistant professor at the University of Kentucky, phoned to ask if I'd join him for a visit to Pikeville, a coal-mining town in the eastern part of the state. Buffalo, I told him, was more than five hundred miles from Lexington; surely he had friends closer to hand who could accompany him on the trip. It wasn't company he wanted, Fritz said, it was publicity: community organizers working with the rural poor on the problems of strip mining and labor exploitation were being harassed by local government officials and shot at and blown up by mine owners. He thought an article in a major magazine might do some good.

I had a meeting scheduled only a few days later with Willie Morris, who was then editor of Harper's Magazine. I told Willie about Fleron's call. He said it sounded like a good project. I said the piece might run a little long; Willie said length would not be an issue. He reminded me of Norman Mailer's piece on the October 1967 antiwar demonstration in Washington, which had occupied the entire February 1968 issue of the magazine.

I went to Lexington, spent a pleasant evening with Fritz and his wife, LouJean, and early the next morning Fritz and I headed out of the bluegrass country into the hardscrabble mountains. "In the Valley of the Shadows" is about what I saw there.

Curious things happened to it on the way to publication. I sent the manuscript to Willie Morris and didn't hear from him for a long time. I thought of it as at least partially an advocacy piece, one in which the clock mattered. Those people down there were on the line, and it mattered that word of what they were doing and what was happening to them got out while it still might do them some good. I wrote Willie, but got no answer. I phoned him, but he wasn't ever in.

Then an edited manuscript arrived from Harper's. It had been cut by about a third. Writers are used to editors who want to make things shorter; writers want space to explore things or to display feathers and editors want to conserve space so they can have as many explorers as possible in the pages at their disposal. But what happened there had nothing to do with ordinary editorial shrinkage or tuning. The copyedited manuscript I got back had been turned into gibberish.

It didn't make journalistic, sociological, or editorial sense. From the marginal notations, I inferred that Midge Decter and two other editors had read the manuscript and someone else had combined the suggestions of all three without noting their mutual incompatibility, and had slashed and cut as had been instructed.

I withdrew the article and kept the payment for rent. Willie said he thought that was fair. (I learned later that Willie had nothing to do with the overkill editing; for personal reasons he'd not been around the Harper's office during the months I'd been trying to call him, and not long after he resigned the job, went home to Mississippi, and began writing again himself.)

I sent the manuscript to Bob Manning, editor of Atlantic. Bob said he liked it, but they had just scheduled one of Robert Coles's fine essays on Appalachia and didn't want to run another one on the same geographical area so soon. The tone of the piece wasn't right for the New York Times Magazine. It was now more than a year since I'd mailed the manuscript to Harper's, and I guess I lost heart about getting it placed anywhere.

Not long after that, Fleron took a job here in Buffalo. "I was glad that piece never got published," he said when we met on campus one day. I asked him why. "Because you didn't nail those bastards to the wall the way I wanted you to." I told him that nailing them to the wall wouldn't have been very objective or informative or even honest, that things weren't so black and white. "Yes," he said, "but what I wanted was for you to nail them to the wall and you didn't do that." I asked why he'd never told me that, indeed, why he never said anything when I'd shown him a draft of the manuscript. "Didn't matter," he said, which I've never understood.

When I told Diane Christian about the conversation she said, "You should try transAction with it." I sent it, along with a dozen photographs, to Irving Louis Horowitz, editor of transAction, who accepted the piece immediately. Several months later it appeared, but instead of my photos there was one terrific full-page photo by Bruce Davidson and several small *photos by Jill Kremetz. But none of Kremetz's photos were from Pikeville; they were collateral illustrations rather than integral parts of the piece. I called Horowitz in a rage. Why hadn't he told me he was using other people's photographs and why hadn't he used my photographs?*

He hadn't looked at them, he said.

"What do you mean, you haven't looked at them?"

"Everybody knows writers can't take photographs," he said.

I said a lot of vile things, and he told me to call back whenever I felt up to it.

Sometime after that we had a conversation in which I allowed as I might have been kind of violent in my reaction to his failure to look at the photos, and he allowed as he might have been a little remiss in not looking at the photos. Shortly thereafter I sent him a portfolio of photographs from the Arkansas penitentiary, and Horowitz published them; I think it was the first time transAction published photographs that were not illustrating a text. Those photographs were the first publication from a large group of images that would comprise Killing Time: Life in the Arkansas Penitentiary *(1977).*

I'm still annoyed that transAction went with photos of generic people in those mountains rather than the real ones. Why wouldn't an editor opt for the real rather than the generic? Why do "any size fits all" when you've got the specific fit? I guess that's an academic question.

~

Along the roadsides and in backyards are the cannibalized cadavers of old cars: there is no other place to dump them, there are no junkyards that have any reason to haul them away.

Streambeds are littered with old tires, cans, pieces of metal and plastic. On a sunny day the streams and creeks glisten with pretty blue spots from the Maxwell House coffee tins and Royal Crown cola cans. For some reason the paint used by Maxwell House and Royal Crown doesn't wear off very quickly, and while the paint and paper on other cans are peeling to reveal an undistinctive aluminum color, the accumulating blues of those two brands make for a most peculiar local feature.

Winter in eastern Kentucky is not very pretty. In some places you see the gouged hillsides where the strip and auger mines have ripped away tons of dirt and rock to get at the mineral seams underneath; below the gouges you see the littered valleys where the overburden, the earth they have ripped and scooped away, has been dumped in spoil banks. The streams stink from the auger holes' sulfurous exudations; the hillsides no longer hold water back because the few trees and bushes are small and thin, so there is continual erosion varying the ugliness in color only. Most of the people around here live outside the town in hollers and along the creeks.

Things are narrow; the hills rise up closely and flatland is at a premium. A residential area will stretch out for several miles, one or two houses and a road thick, with hills starting up just behind the outhouse. Sometimes, driving along the highway following the Big Sandy River, there is so little flat space that the highway is on one side of the river and the line of houses is on the other, with plank suspension bridges every few miles connecting the two. Everting is crushed together. You may ride five miles without passing a building, then come upon a half-dozen houses, each within ten feet of its neighbor. And churches: the Old Regular Baptist Church, the Freewill Baptist Church, the Meta Baptist Church. On the slopes of the hills are cemeteries, all neatly tended; some are large and old, some have only one or two recent graves in them.

In winter, when the sun never rises very far above the horizon, the valley floors get only about four hours of direct sunlight a day; most of the days are cloudy anyhow. One always moves in shadow, in greyness. Children grow up without ever seeing the sun rise or set.

The day of the company store and company house is gone. So are most of the big companies around here. This is small truck mine country now, and operators of the small mines don't find stores and houses worth their time. The old company houses worth living in have been bought up, either as rental property or for the new owner's personal use; the company houses still standing but not worth living in comprise the county's only public housing for the very poor.

At the end of one of the hollers running off Marrowbone Creek, three miles up a road you couldn't make, even in dry weather, without four-wheel drive, stands an old cabin. It is a log cabin, but there is about it nothing romantic or frontiersy, only grimness. Scratched in the kitchen window, by some unknown adult or child, are the crude letters of the word "victory." Over what or whom we don't know. It is unlikely anyway. There are no victories here, only occasional survivors, and if survival is a victory it is a mean and brutal one.

Inside the cabin a Barbie doll stands over a nearly opaque mirror in a room lighted by a single bare 60-watt bulb. In the middle of the room a coal stove spews outrageous amounts of heat. When the stove is empty the room is cold and damp. There is no middle area of comfort. The corrugated cardboard lining the walls doesn't stop drafts very well and most of the outside chinking is gone. On one side of the room with the stove is the entrance to the other bedroom, on the other side is the kitchen. There are no doors inside the house. A woman lives here with her nine children.

If all the nine children were given perfectly balanced full meals three times a day from now on, still some of them would never be well. A 15-year-old daughter loses patches of skin because of an irreversible vitamin deficiency, and sometimes, because of the suppurations and congealing, they have to soak the clothing off when she comes home from school. Last month the baby was spitting up blood for a while but that seems to have stopped.

It might be possible to do something for the younger ones, but it is not likely anyone will.

The husband went somewhere and didn't come back; that was over a year ago. The welfare inspector came a few months ago and found out that someone had given the family a box of clothes for the winter; the welfare check was cut by $20 a month after that. When the woman has $82 she can get $120 worth of food stamps; if she doesn't have the $82, she gets no food stamps at all. For a year, the entire family had nothing for dinner but one quart of green beans each night. Breakfast was fried flour and coffee. A friend told me the boy said he had had meat at a neighbor's house once.

Bony Hills

This is Pike County, Kentucky. It juts like a chipped arrowhead into the bony hill country of neighboring West Virginia. Pike County has about seventy thousand residents and, the Chamber of Commerce advertises, it produces more coal than any other county in the world. The county seat, Pikeville, has about six thousand residents; it is the only real town for about 30 miles.

The biggest and bitterest event in Pike County's past was sometime in the 1880s when Tolbert McCoy killed Big Ellison Hatfield: it started a feud that resulted in 65 killed, settled nothing, and wasn't won by either side. The biggest and bitterest thing in recent years has been the War on Poverty: it doesn't seem to have killed anyone, but it hasn't settled anything or won any major battles either.

About seventy-five hundred men are employed by Pike County's mines: one thousand drive trucks, five hundred work at the tipples (the docks where coal is loaded into railway cars) and mine offices, and six thousand work inside. Most of the mines are small and it doesn't take very many men to work them: an automated truck mine can be handled by about eight men.

Some people work at service activities: they pump gas, sell shoes, negotiate contracts (there are about 40 lawyers in this little town), dispense drugs, direct traffic, embalm—all those things that make an American town go. There are six industrial firms in the area; two of them are beverage companies, one is a lumber company; the total employment of the six firms is 22 men and women.

A union mine pays $28–$38 per day, with various benefits, but few of the mines in Pike County are unionized. The truck mines, where almost all the men work, pay $14 per day, with almost no benefits. The United Mine Workers of America were strong here once, but when times got hard the union let a lot of people down and left a lot of bitterness behind. Not only did the union make deals with the larger companies that resulted in many of its own men being thrown out of work (one of those deals recently resulted in a $7.3 million conspiracy judgment against the UMWA and Consolidation Coal Company), but it made the abandonment complete by lifting the unemployed workers' medical cards and shutting down the union hospitals in the area. For most of the area, those cards and hospitals were the only source of medical treatment. There has been talk of organizing the truck mines and someone told me the UMW local was importing an old-time fire-breathing organizer to get things going, but it doesn't seem likely the men will put their lives on the line another time.

With Frederic J. Fleron, Jr., an old friend then on the faculty of the University of Kentucky in Lexington, I went to visit Robert Holcomb, president of the Independent Coal Operators' Association, president of the Chamber of Commerce, and one of the people in the county most vocally at war with the poverty program. His office door was decorated with several titles: Dixie Mining Co., Roberts Engineering Co., Robert Holcomb and Co., Chloe Gas Co., Big Sandy Coal Co., and Martha Collieries, Inc.

One of the secretaries stared at my beard as if it were a second nose; she soon got control of herself and took us in to see Holcomb. (Someone had said to me the day before, "Man, when Holcomb sees you with that beard on he's gonna be sure you're a communist." "What if I tell him I'm playing Henry the Fifth in a play at the university?" "Then he'll be sure Henry the Fifth is a communist too.") Holcomb took the beard better than the girl had: his expression remained nicely neutral. He offered us coffee and introduced us to his partner, a Mr. Roberts, who sat in a desk directly opposite him. On the wall behind Roberts' head was a large white flying map of the United States with a brownish smear running over Louisiana, Mississippi, and most of Texas; the darkest splotch was directly over New Orleans. The phone rang and Roberts took the call; he tilted back in his chair, his head against New Orleans and Lake Pontchartrain.

Holcomb was happy to talk about his objections to the poverty program. "I'm a firm believer that you don't help a man by giving him bread unless you give him hope for the future, and poverty programs have given them bread only." The problem with the Appalachian Volunteers (an antipoverty organization partially funded by Office of Economic Opportunity, now pretty much defunct) was "they got no supervision. They brought a bunch of young people in, turned 'em loose and said, 'Do your thing.' I think they have created a disservice rather than a service by creating a lot of disillusionment by making people expect things that just can't happen."

Expanding and Wrecking

He told us something about what was happening. The coal industry had been expanding rapidly. "Over the last eight years the truck mining industry has created an average of 500 new jobs a year." He sat back. "We're working to bring the things in here that will relieve the poverty permanently." He talked of bringing other kinds of industry to the area and told us about the incentives they were offering companies that were willing to relocate. "We know a lot of our people are not fitted for mining," he said.

(It is not just a matter of being "fitted" of course. There is the problem of those who are wrecked by silicosis and black lung who can do nothing but hope their doctor bills won't go up so much they'll have to pull one of the teenage kids out of school and send him to work, or be so screwed by welfare or social security or the UMW pension managers or the mine operators' disability insurance company that the meager payments that do come into some homes will be stopped.)

The truck mines play an ironic role in the local economy: half the men working in them, according to Holcomb, cannot work in the large mines because of physical disability. The small mines, in effect, not only get the leftover coal seams that aren't fat enough to interest Consol or U.S. Steel or the other big companies in the area, but they also get the men those firms have used up and discarded.

From Holcomb's point of view things are going pretty well in Pike County. In 1960 there were $18 million in deposits in Pikesville's three banks; that has risen to $65 million. There are 700 small mines in the county, many of them operated by former miners. "This is free enterprise at its finest," he said.

The next morning he took us on a trip through the Johns Creek area. As we passed new houses and large trailers he pointed to them as evidence of progress, which they in fact are. In the hollers behind, Fred and I could see the shacks and boxes in which people also live, and those Holcomb passed without a word. I suppose one must select from all the data presenting itself in this world, otherwise living gets awfully complex.

We drove up the hill to a small mine. Holcomb told us that the eight men working there produce 175 tons daily, all of which goes to the DuPont nylon plant in South Carolina.

A man in a shed just outside the mine mouth was switching the heavy industrial batteries on a coal tractor. The miner was coated with coal dust and oil smears. He wore a plastic helmet with a light on it; around his waist was the light's battery pack, like a squashed holster. He moved very fast, whipping the chains off and on and winding the batteries out, pumping the pulley chains up and down. Another mine tractor crashed out of the entrance, its driver inclined at 45 degrees. The tractor is about 24 inches high and the mine roof is only 38 inches high, so the drivers have to tilt all the time or get their heads crushed. Inside, the men work on their knees.

The tractor backed the buggy connected to it to the edge of a platform, dumped its load, then clanked back inside.

I went into the mine, lying on my side in the buggy towed by the tractor with the newly charged batteries.

Inside is utter blackness, broken only by the slicing beams of light from the helmets. The beams are neat and pretty, almost like a Lucite tube poking here and there; the prettiness goes away when you realize the reason the beam is so brilliant is because of the coal and rock dust in the air, dust a worker is continually inhaling into his lungs. One sees no bodies, just occasional hands interrupting the moving light beams playing on the timbers and working face. Clattering noises and shouts are strangely disembodied and directionless.

Outside, I dust off and we head back toward town in Holcomb's truck.

"The temperature in there is 68 degrees all the time," he says. "You work in air-conditioned comfort all year 'round. Most of these men, after they've been in the mine for a while, wouldn't work above ground." (I find myself thinking of Senator Murphy of California who in his campaign explained the need for bracero labor; they stoop over better than Anglos do.) The miners, as I said, make $14 a day.

"When you see what's been accomplished here in the last ten years it makes the doings of the AVs and the others seem completely insignificant. And we didn't have outside money." The pitted and gouged road is one-lane and we find ourselves creeping behind a heavily loaded coal truck heading toward one of the tipples up the rod. "We think welfare is fine, but it should be a temporary measure, not a permanent one. And any organization that encourages people to get on welfare is a detriment to the community." The truck up front gets out of our way. Holcomb shifts back to two-wheel drive, we pick up speed. "These poverty program people, what they tried to do is latch on to some mountain customs and try to convince people they have come up with something new."

He believes business will help everybody; he believes the poverty program has been bad business. He is enormously sincere. Everyone is enormously sincere down here, or so it seems.

So we drove and looked at the new mines and tipples and Robert Holcomb told us how long each had been there and what its tonnage was and how many people each mine employed and how many mines fed into each tipple. One of his companies, he told us, produced 350,000 tons of coal last year and operated at a profit of 15.7 cents per ton.

Hospital death certificates cite things like pneumonia and heart disease. There is no way of knowing how many of those result from black lung and silicosis. The mine owners say very few; the miners and their families say a great many indeed. A lot of men with coated lungs don't die for a long time, but they may not be good for much else meanwhile. Their lungs won't absorb much oxygen, so they cannot move well or fast or long.

"This is a one-industry area," Holcomb had said, "and if you can't work at that industry you can't work at anything." Right. And most of the residents—men wrinkled or contaminated, widows, children—do not work at anything. Over 50 percent of the families in Pike County have incomes below $3,000 per year. Like land torn by the strip-mining operations, those people simply stay back in the hollers out of sight and slowly erode.

We talked with an old man who had worked in the mines for 28 years. He told us how he had consumed his life savings and two years' time getting his disabled social security benefits.

"See, I got third-stage silicosis and I've got prostate and gland trouble, stomach troubles, a ruptured disc. Now they say that at the end of this month they're gonna take the state aid medical card away. And that's all I've got; I've got so much wrong with me I can't get no insurance. I've had the card two years and now they say I draw too much social security because of last year's increase in social security benefits and they're gonna have to take my medical card away from me after this month. I don't know what in the hell I'm gonna do. Die, I reckon."

"Yeah, yeah," his wife said from the sink.

"It don't seem right," he said. "I worked like hell, I made good money and I doublebacked. Because I worked a lot and draw more social security than lots of people in the mines where they don't make no money. I don't see where it's right for them not to allow me no medical card."

He opened the refrigerator and showed us some of the various chemicals he takes every day. In a neat stack on the table were the month's medical receipts. He said something about his youth, and I was suddenly stunned to realize he was only 51.

"You know," he said, "sand's worse than black lung. Silicosis. It hardens on the lung and there's no way to get it off. In West Virginia I worked on one of those roof-bolting machines. It's about eight, nine-foot high, sandstone top. Burn the bits up drillin' holes in it. And I'd be there. Dust'd be that thick on your lips. But it's fine stuff in the air, you don't see the stuff that you get in your lungs. It's fine stuff. Then I didn't get no pay for it."

"You got a thousand dollars," his wife said.

"A thousand dollars for the first stage. They paid me first stage and I just didn't want to give up. I kept on workin', and now I got third stage . . . I just hated to give up, but I wished I had of. One doctor said to me, 'If you keep on you might as well get your shotgun and shoot your brains out, you'd be better off.' I still kept on after he told me that. Then I got so I just couldn't hardly go on. My clothes wouldn't stay on me."

The woman brought coffee to the table. "He draws his disabled social security now," she says, "but if he was to draw for his black lung disease they would cut his social security way down, so he's better off just drawing his social security. There's guys around here they cut below what they was drawing for social security. I don't think that's right."

It is all very neat: the black lung, when a miner can force the company doctors to diagnose it honestly, is paid for by company insurance, but payments are set at a level such that a disabled miner loses most of his social security benefits if he takes the compensation; since the compensation pays less than social security, many miners don't put in their legitimate claims, and the net effect is a government subsidy of the insurance companies and mine owners.

Mary Walton, an Appalachian Volunteer, invited Fred and me to dinner at her place in Pikeville one night during our stay. It turned out Mary and I had been at Harvard at the same time and we talked about that place for a while, which was very strange there between those darkening hills. Three other people were at Mary's apartment: a girl named Barbara, in tight jeans and a white shirt with two buttons open and zippered boots, and two men, both of them connected with the local college. One was working with the Model Cities project, the other worked in the college president's office; one was astoundingly tall, the other was built like a wrestler; they all looked aggressively healthy. Barbara's husband worked for the Council of the Southern Mountains in Berea.

The fellow who looked like a wrestler told me at great length that what was going on in Pikeville wasn't a social or economic attack on the community structure, but rather an attack on the structure of ideas and only now was everyone learning that. I asked him what he meant. He said that the poverty workers had once seen their job as enlightening the masses about how messed up things were. "We were ugly American's that's all we were. That's why we weren't effective. But now we've learned that you don't change anything that way, you have to get inside the local community and understand it first and work there."

I thought that was indeed true, but I didn't see what it had to do with the structure of the community's ideas; it had to do only with the arrogance or naïveté of the poverty workers, and that was awfully solipsistic. He hadn't said anything about his clients—just himself, just the way his ideas were challenged, not theirs.

The apartment was curiously out of that world. On the walls were posters and lithos and prints and pictures of healthy human bodies. The record racks contained the Stones and *Tim Hardin No. 3* and a lot of Bach. Many of the recent books we'd all read and others one had and the others meant to, and Mary and I talked about them, but there was something relative, even in the pleasantness, as if it were an appositive in the bracketing nastiness out there.

When we got back to the car I took from my jacket pocket the heavy and uncomfortable shiny chrome-plated .380 automatic pistol someone had once given me in San Antonio. I put it on the seat next to Fred's .357 revolver. They looked silly there; real guns always do. But people kept telling us how someone else was going to shoot us, or they recounted the story of how Hugh O'Connor, a Canadian film producer down in the next county the year before to make a movie, was shot in the heart by a man with no liking for outsiders and less for outsiders with cameras and it did seem awfully easy to be an outsider here.

We went to see Edith Easterling, a lifelong Marrowbone Creek resident, working at that time for the Appalachian Volunteers as director of the Marrowbone Folk School. "The people in the mountains really lives hard," Edith said. "You can come into Pikeville and go to the Chamber of Commerce and they'll say, 'Well, there's really no poor people left there. People are faring good.' Then you can come out here and go to homes and you'd just be surprised how poor these people live, how hard that they live. Kids that's grown to 15 or 16 years old that's never had a mess of fresh milk or meats, things that kids really need. They live on canned cream until they get big enough to go to the table and eat beans and potatoes."

She told us about harassment and red-baiting of the AVs by Robert Holcomb, Harry Eastburn (the Big Sandy Community Action Program director, also funded by OEO, a bitter antagonist of any poverty program not under his political control), and Thomas Ratliff, the commonwealth's attorney (the equivalent of a county prosecutor).

Some of the AVs came from out of state, especially the higher paid office staff and technical specialists, but most of the 14 field workers were local people, like Edith. Since becoming involved with the poverty program Edith has received telephone threats and had some windows shot out. The sheriff refused to send a deputy to investigate. Occasionally she gets anonymous calls; some are threats, some call her "dirty communist." She shrugs those away: "I'm a Republican and who ever seen a communist Republican?"

Changing a Way of Life

The Appalachian Volunteers began in the early 1960s as a group of students from Berea College who busied themselves with needed community band-aid work: they made trips to the mountains to patch up dilapidated schoolhouses, they ran tutorial programs, they collected books for needy schools. The ultimate futility of such work soon became apparent and there was a drift in the AV staff toward projects that might affect the lifestyle of some of the mountain communities. In 1966 the AVs decided to break away from their parent organization, the conservative Council of the Southern Mountains. The new, independent Appalachian Volunteers had no difficulty finding federal funding. During the summers of 1966 and 1967 the organization received large OEO grants to house hundreds of temporary volunteer workers, many of them VISTA and Peace Corps trainees. According to David Walls, who was acting director of the AVs when I talked with him, the organization's mission was to "create effective, economically self-sufficient poor people's organizations that would concern themselves with local issues, such as welfare rights, bridges and roads, water systems and strip mining."

It didn't work, of course it didn't work; the only reason it lasted as long as it did was because so much of the AV staff was composed of outsiders, people who had worked in San Francisco and Boston and New York and Washington, and it took a long time before the naïveté cracked enough for the failure to show through.

The first consequence of creating an organization of the impoverished and unempowered is not the generation of any new source or residence of power, but rather the gathering in one place of a lot of poverty and powerlessness that previously were spread out. In an urban situation, the poor or a minority group may develop or exercise veto power: they can manage an economic boycott, they can refuse to work for certain firms and encourage others to join with them, they can physically block a store entrance. It is only when such efforts create a kind of negative monopoly (a strike line no one will cross or a boycott others will respect) that power is generated. When that negative monopoly cannot be created, there is no power—this is why workers can successfully strike for higher wages but the poor cities cannot get the police to respect their civil liberties enough to stop beating them up; if everyone refuses to work at a factory, the owner must cooperate or close down, but there is nothing anyone can refuse a policeman that will remove the immediate incentive for illegal police behavior. The poor in the mountains cannot strike—they are unemployable anyway, or at least enough of them are to make specious that kind of action. Even if they were to get something going the UMW would not support them. The poor cannot start an economic boycott: they don't spend enough to hold back enough to threaten any aspect of the mountain coal economy. (There have been a few instances of industrial sabotage—I'll mention them later on—that have been dramatic, but pitifully ineffective.) One of the saddest things about the poor in the mountains is they have nothing to deny anyone. And they don't even have the wild hope some city poor entertain that something may turn up; in the mountains there is nothing to hope for.

Another problem with organizations of the very poor is they do not have much staying power: the individual participants are just too vulnerable. So long as the members can be scared or bought off easily, one cannot hope for such groups to develop solidarity. In Kentucky, where welfare, medical aid, disability pensions, and union benefits all have a remarkable quality of coming and going with political whims, that is a real problem. Edith Easterling described the resulting condition: "These people are scared people, they are scared to death. I can talk to them and I can say, 'You shouldn't be scared, there's nothing to be scared about.' But they're still scared."

"What are they scared of," Fred asked her, "losing their jobs?"

"No. Some of 'em don't even have a job. Most of the people don't have jobs. They live on some kind of pension. They're scared of losing their pension. If it's not that, they're scared someone will take them to court for something. 'If I say something, they're going to take me to court and I don't have a lawyer's fee. I don't have a lawyer, so I'd rather not say nothing.' When you get the people to really start opening up and talking, that's when the county officials attack us every time with something."

Publicity and Revenge

For someone who brings troublesome publicity to the community, there are forms of retaliation far crueler than the mere cutting off of welfare or unemployment benefits. One poverty worker told of an event following a site visit by Robert Kennedy a few years ago: "When Kennedy was down for his hearings one of his advance men got in contact with a friend of ours who had a community organization going. They were very anxious to get some exposure, to get Kennedy involved in it. They took the advance men around to visit some families that were on welfare. He made statements about the terrible conditions the children there in two particular homes had to live under. He wasn't indicting the families, he was just talking about conditions in general. These were picked up by the local press and given quite a bit of notoriety—Kennedy Aide Makes the Scene, that sort of thing. After he left, about three days later, the welfare agency came and took away the children from both of those families and put them in homes. This is the control that is over people's lives."

The group with the potential staying power in the mountains is the middle class, the small landowners. They have concrete things to lose while the poor (save in anomalous atrocities such as the one with the children mentioned above) have nothing to lose, they only have possible access to benefits that someone outside their group may or may not let them get. There is a big difference in the way one fights in the two situations. Something else: it is harder to scare the middle class off, for it has not been conditioned by all those years of humiliating control and dependency.

One Appalachian Volunteer, Joe Mulloy, a 24-year-old Kentuckian, realized this. He and his wife decided to join a fight being waged by a

Pike County landowner, Jink Ray, and his neighbors, against a strip-mine operator who was about to remove the surface of Ray's land.

Rights for Pennies

The focus of the fight was the legitimacy of the *broadform* deed, a nineteenth-century instrument with which landowners assigned mineral rights to mining companies, usually for small sums of money (50 cents per acre was common). When these deeds were originally signed no landowner had any thought of signing away all rights to his property—just the underground minerals and whatever few holes the mining company might have to make in the hillside to get at the seams.

In the twentieth century the coal companies developed the idea of lifting off all the earth and rock above the coal, rather than digging for it, and since the broadform deed said the miner could use whatever means he saw fit to get the coal out, the Kentucky courts held that the miners' land rights have precedence over the surface owners'—even though that meant complete destruction of a man's land by a mining process the original signer of the deed could not have imagined.

The strip miners are legally entitled, on the basis of a contract that might be 90 years old, to come to a man's home and completely bury it in rubble, leaving the owner nothing but the regular real estate tax bill with which he is stuck even though the "real estate" has since been dumped in the next creek bed. First come the bulldozers to do the initial clearing (a song I heard in West Virginia, to the tune of "Swing Low, Sweet Chariot," went: "Roll on, big D-9 dozer, comin' for to bury my home / I'm getting madder as you're getting' closer, comin' for to bury my home"), then they roll in the massive shovels, some of which grow as large as 18.5 million pounds and can gobble 200 tons of earth and rock a minute and dump it all a city block away.

Such a machine is operated by one man riding five stories above the ground.

On June 29, 1967, Jink Ray and some neighbors in Island Creek, a Pike County community, blocked with their bodies bulldozers that were about to start stripping Ray's land. With them were Joe and Karen Mulloy. The people themselves had organized the resistance; the Mulloys were simply helping.

With the strip-mining fight on the mountain, the AVs were for the first time involved in something significant. It was also dangerous: the members of the Island Creek group were challenging not only the basis of the local economy, but the federal government as well: the big mines' biggest customer is the Tennessee Valley Authority, and the Small Business Administration supports many of the smaller mine operators. The poverty program and other federal agencies were moving toward open conflict.

What happened was that the poverty program backed down and the local power structure moved in. Eleven days after Governor Edward Breathitt's August 1 suspension of the strip-mine company's Island Creek permit (the first and only such suspension), Pike County officials arrested the Mulloys for sedition (plotting or advocating the violent overthrow of the government). Arrested with them on the same charge were Alan and Margaret McSurely, field workers for the Southern Conference Educational Fund (SCEF), a Louisville-based civil rights organization. McSurely had been hired as training consultant by the AVs during the spring of 1967, but the real reason he had been hired was to restructure the cumbersome organization.

One of the first things he did was get the AVs to allow local people on the board of directors; he was fired in a month and went to work for SCEF. They even arrested Carl Braden (SCEF's executive director) and his wife, Anne. Anne Braden had never been in Pike County in her life; the first time Carl Braden had been there was the day he went to Pikeville to post bail for McSurely on the sedition charge.

In Washington, the response to the arrests was immediate; Sargent Shriver's office announced that AV funds would be cut off; no funds previously granted were taken away, but no new money was appropriated after that.

The Pike County grand jury concluded that "A well-organized and well-financed effort is being made to promote and spread the communistic theory of violent and forceful overthrow of the government of Pike County." The grand jury said also that "Communist organizers have attempted, without success thus far, to promote their beliefs among our school children by infiltrating our local schools with teachers who believe in the violent overthrow of the local government." Organizers were "planning to infiltrate local churches and labor unions in order to cause dissension and to promote their purposes." And, finally, "Communist organizers are attempting to form community unions with the eventual purpose of organizing armed groups to be known as 'Red Guards' and through which the forceful overthrow of the local government would be accomplished."

Untouchable Volunteers

The AVs came unglued. The Mulloys became pariahs within the organization. "We spent that whole summer and no AV came to see us at all in Pike County," Joe Mulloy said. "Once they came up to shit on us, but that was the only time. Then the thing of our getting arrested for sedition was what just really flipped everybody . . . This was a real situation that you had to deal with, it wasn't something in your mind or some ideological thing. It was real. Another person was under arrest. I think that the feeling of a number of people on the staff was it was my fault that I had been arrested because I had been reckless in my organizing, that I had been on the mountain with the fellas and had risked as much as they were risking and I deserved what I got, and that I should be fired so the program would go on; that I was now a detriment."

That fall, a special three-judge federal court ruled the Kentucky sedition law unconstitutional so all charges against the Mulloys, the Bradens, and the McSurelys were wiped out. But the AVs were still nervous. "After the arrests were cleared away," Mulloy said, "things started to happen to me on the staff. I was given another assignment. I was told that I couldn't be a field man anymore because I was a public figure identified with sedition and hence people would feel uneasy talking to me, and that I should do research. My truck was taken away and I was given an old car, and I was given a title of researcher rather than field man. It took away considerable voice that I had in the staff until then."

Karen Mulloy said that she and Joe really had no choice. "If we had organized those people up there, with possible death as the end result for some of them—fortunately it was kept nonviolent—and if we weren't with them they wouldn't have spoken to us. We took as much risk as they did. We said to them, "We're not going to organize something for you that we won't risk our necks for either. An organizer can't do that."

"These people have gone through the whole union experience and that has sold them out," Joe said. "And a great number of people have gone through the poverty war experience and that hasn't answered anybody's problems, anybody's questions. Getting together on the strip-mining issue—if there was ever one issue that the poverty war got on that was good, that was it. It all fell through because when we started getting counterattacked by the operators the poverty war backed up because their funds were being jeopardized. The whole strip-mining issue as an organized effort has collapsed right now and the only thing that's going on is individual sabotage. There's a lot of mining equipment being blown up every month or so, about a million dollars at a time. These are individual or small group acts or retaliation, but the organized effort has ceased."

(Later, I talked with Rick Diehl, the AV research director, about the sabotage. He described two recent operations, both of them very sophisticated, involving groups of multiple charges set off simultaneously. The sheriff didn't even look for the dynamiters: he probably wouldn't have caught them and even if he had he wouldn't have gotten a jury to convict. "And that kind of stuff goes on to some degree all the time," Diehl said. "There's a growing feeling that destroying property is going to shut down the system in Appalachia. The people don't benefit from the coal companies at all, 'cause even the deep mines don't have enough employees. The average number of employees in a deep mine is 16 people. So, you see, there is nothing to lose. It's that same desperation kind of thing that grips people in Detroit and Watts.")

Organizing Outrage

Even though the sedition charges were dropped, the Mulloys and McSurelys weren't to escape punishment for their organizing outrages.

One Friday the 13th Al McSurely came home late from a two or three day trip out of town, talked with his wife a little while, then went to bed. Margaret went to bed a short time later. "I wasn't asleep at all," she said, "but he was so tired he went right to sleep. I heard this car speed up. Well, I had got into the habit of listening to cars at night, just because we always expected something like this to happen. And sure enough, it did. There was this blast. The car took off and there was this huge blast, and glass and dirt and grit were in my mouth and eyes and hair, and the baby was screaming. So I put on my bathrobe and ran across the street with the baby."

"The state trooper was pretty good," Alan said, "he gave me a lecture: 'The next time this happens call the city police first to they can seal off the holler. They can get here much faster than I can.' I said, 'I'll try and remember that.'"

Joe Mulloy was the only AV with a Kentucky draft board; he was also the only AV to lose his occupational deferment and have his 2-A changed to 1-A. Mulloy asked the board (in Louisville, the same as Muhammed Ali's) for a rehearing on the grounds of conscientious objection, and he presented as part of his evidence a letter from Thomas Merton saying he was Mulloy's spiritual adviser (the two used to meet for talks in Merton's cabin in the woods) and could testify to the truthfulness of Mulloy's C.O. claim. The board refused to reopen the case because, they said, there was no new evidence of any relevance or value. In April 1968 Mulloy was sentenced to five years in prison and a $10,000 fine for refusing induction.

He was fired immediately by the Appalachian Volunteers. Some wanted him out because they honestly thought his draft case would be a major obstacle to his effectiveness with the oddly patriotic mountain people. (In the mountains you can be against the war, many people are, but if your country calls you, you go. It would be unpatriotic not to go. The government and the country are two quite independent entities. The government might screw up the poverty program, run that bad war, work in conjunction with the mine owners and politicians, but it isn't the government that is calling you—it is the country. Only a weirdo would refuse that call. But once you're in you are working for the government, and then it is all right to desert.) Others on the AV staff objected to Mulloy's getting involved in issues that riled up the authorities. The staff vote to get rid of him was 20 to 19.

What the AVs failed to admit was that the changing of Mulloy's draft status was an attack on them as well: the only reason for the change was the strip-mine fight. The draft board had joined the OEO, the TVA, the mine owners, the political structure of the state, and the UMW in opposition to effective organization of the poor in the mountains.

I asked Joe how he felt about it all now. "I don't know if I can really talk about this objectively," he said. "I feel in my guts as a Kentuckian a great deal of resentment against a lot of these people. And some of them are my friends that have come in and stirred things up and then have left. The going is really tough right now. I'm still here, all the people that have to make a living out in those counties are still there with their black lung. I don't think anything was accomplished. It's one of those things that's going to go down in history as a cruel joke: the poverty war in the mountains."

The two bad guys of the story, I suppose, should be Robert Holcomb, spokesman for the mine owners in the county, and commonwealth's attorney Thomas Ratliff, the man who handled the prosecution in the sedition and who was (coincidentally, he insists) Republican candidate for lieutenant governor at the time; Ratliff got rich in the mine business, but is now into a lot of other things. Like most bad guy labels, I suspect these are too easy. I'll come back to that.

I rather liked Ratliff even though there were things I knew about him I didn't like at all. It is quite possible he really does believe, as he said he does, that the McSurelys and the Bradens are communist provocateurs; there are people in America who believe such menaces exist, though not very many of them are as intelligent as Ratliff.

He claims the defendants in the sedition case had "a new angle on revolution—to do it locally and then bring all the local revolutions together and then you got a big revolution. Now whether it would have succeeded or not I don't know. I think it possibly could have, had they been able to continue to get money from the Jolly Green Giant, as they call Uncle Sam. I certainly think with enough money, and knowing the history of the area, it was not impossible."

What seems to have bothered him most was not the politics involved but the bad sportsmanship: "The thing that rankled me in this case, and it still does, this is really what disturbed me more about this thing than anything else, was the fact that.... They were able to use federal money... to promote this thing. Frankly, I would be almost as opposed to either the Republican party or the Democratic party being financed by the federal money to prevail, much less a group who were avowed communists, made no bones about it that I could tell, whose objective was revolution, and forceful and violent overthrow of the local government and hopefully to overthrow the federal government, and it was being financed by federal tax money!"

Once Ratliff got off his communist menace line, I found myself agreeing with him as much as I had with some of the remarks Joe Mulloy had made.

Ratliff spoke eloquently on the need for a negative income tax, for massive increases on the taxes on the mine operators, things like that. (Whether he meant the things he said is impossible to tell; one never knows with politicians, or anyone else for that matter.)

"It's the reaction to this sort of situation that really bothers me," he said, "because—there is no question about it—there is some containment of free speech, free expression, when you get a situation like this. People become overexcited and over disturbed. And the laws of physics play in these things: for every action there's a reaction, and the reaction, unfortunately, is often too much in this kind of situation. You begin seeing a communist behind every tree. That's bad. Because there isn't a communist behind every tree, or anything like that.

"But I think they've accomplished one thing, not what they thought they would.... That's the tragic part of it, I don't think they've uplifted anybody. I think they have left a lot of people disappointed, frustrated... But I think they have scared the so-called affluent society into doing something about it. Maybe. I think there are people more conscious of it because of that."

It is so easy to write off Holcomb or Ratliff as evil men, grasping and groping for whatever they can get and destroying whatever gets in the way; for a poverty worker it is probably necessary to think such thoughts, that may be the mental bracing one needs to deal as an opponent.

But I think it is wrong.

Holcomb is an ex-miner who made it; uneducated and not particularly smart, he somehow grooved on the leavings in that weird economy and got rich. He thinks what he did is something anyone ought to be able to do: it is the American dream, after all. His failure is mainly one of a vision, a social myopia hardly rare in this country. From Holcomb's point of view, those people stirring up the poor probably are communist agitators—why else would anyone interfere with the "free enterprise system at its best"? If you tried to tell him that a system that leads to great big rich houses on one side of town and squalid leaky shacks on the other might not be the best thing in this world he'd think you were crazy or a communist (both, actually) too. And Thomas Ratliff is hardly the simple Machiavelli the usual scenario would demand.

Picking out individuals and saying the evil rests with them is like patching schoolhouses and then expecting the cycle of poverty to be broken. Even when you're right you're irrelevant. What is evil in the mountains is the complex of systems, a complex that has no use or place or tolerance for the old, the wrecked, the incompetent, the extra, and consigns them to the same gullies and hollers and ditches as the useless cars and empty Maxwell House coffee tins and Royal Crown cola cans, with the same lack of hate or love.

The enemies of the poverty program, malicious or natural, individual or collective, turn out to be far more successful than they could have hoped or expected. One reason for that success is the cooperation of the victims: groups like the AVs become, as one of their long-time members said, "top-heavy and bureaucratic, a bit central office bound. We are . . . worried about maintaining the AV structure, and responding to pressures from foundations and OEO, rather than from community people." The federal government, presumably the opponent of poverty here, plays both sides of the fence: it supports activities like the AVs (so long as they are undisturbing), but it also supports the local Community Action Program, which is middle class dominated and politically controlled; it created a generation of hustlers among the poor who find out that only by lying and finagling can they get the welfare and social security benefits they

In the Valley of the Shadows | 49

legitimately deserve; it strengthens the local courthouse power structures by putting federal job programs in control of the county machines and by putting the Small Business Administration at its disposal; it commissions studies to document the ill effects of strip mining and simultaneously acts, through TVA, as the largest consumer of the product.

The mood is much like the McCarthy days of the early 1950s: actual legal sanctions are applied to very few people, but so many others are smeared that other people are afraid of contagion, of contamination, even though they know there is nothing to catch. They avoid issues that might threaten some agency or person of power, they stop making trouble, stop looking for trouble, they keep busy, or they stay home—and no one ever really says, when faced by the complex, "I'm scared."

Everyone has something to do: busy, busy, busy. I remember a visit to the AV office in Prestonsburg. They had there what must have been one of the largest Xerox machines in the state of Kentucky; it was used for copying newspaper articles. Someone on the staff ran it. There was an AV magazine assembled by a staff member who, if some of the foundations grants had come through, would have gotten a full-time assistant. The mining went on; the acting director of the AVs, Dave Walls, went about hustling private foundations grants and being sociable and vague and disarming to visitors, and not much of anything really happened.

I visited eastern Kentucky again a short time ago. There were some changes. The weather was softer and some leaves were on the trees, so you couldn't see the shacks back in the hollers unless you drove up close; you couldn't see the hillside cemeteries and junkyards at all.

I found out that Governor Louis Nunn had blocked any new AV funds and most of the other money had gone, so there were ugly battles over the leavings, mixed with uglier battles over old political differences within the organization itself.

Edith Easterling was fired; she now has a Ford grant to travel about the country and look at organizing projects. Rick Diehl has gone somewhere else. Mary Walton is now a staff reporter for the Charleston (W.Va.) *Gazette*. The Prestonsburg AV office is still open—with a small group of lawyers working on welfare rights problems; that is the only AV activity still alive and no one knows how much longer there will be any money for that.

I ran into Dave Walls in a movie house in Charleston. The show was *Wild River* with Montgomery Clift and Lee Remick, and it was about how good TVA is and what a swell guy Montgomery Clift is and how honest and true a mountain girl Lee Remick is. Anyway, I saw Dave there and we talked a moment during intermission. He still draws a subsistence salary from the AVs, still lives in Berea, over in the bluegrass country far and nicely away from it all. He is going to school at the University of Kentucky in Lexington, doing graduate work in something. He looked just the same, no more or less mild. Someone asked him, "What's going on in the mountains now? What happened to everything?" He shrugged and smiled, "I don't know," he said. "I haven't gone to the mountains in a long time."

Well, for the other people, the ones who were there before, things are pretty much the same. That woman and her nine children still live in that shack in Poorbottom. The man who worked the mines for 28 years is still kept marginally alive by the chemical array in his refrigerator he still somehow manages to afford.

A Distrust of Strangers

I met Jink Ray, the man who faced down the bulldozers, on that recent trip. When we drove up he had just put out some bad honey and the bees were a thick swarm in the front of the house. We went into a sitting room bedroom where his wife sat before an open coal fire and each wall had one or two Christs upon it. We talked about the strip-mine fight. On one wall was a photo of him with Governor Breathitt the day the governor came up to stop the strippers. We went outside and talked some more, standing by the overripe browning corn standing next to a patch of corn just about ripe, the hills thickly coated and overlapping to form a lush box canyon behind him. He pointed to the hillside the other side of the road and told us they'd been auguring up there. "You can't see it from down here this time of year, but it's bad up there." The seepage killed the small streams down below: nothing now. And fish used to grow there before they went to the river. Not now." Suddenly his face hardened, "Why you fellas asking me these questions?" We told him again that we were writing about what had happened in Pike County. "No," he said, "that ain't what you are. I believe you fellas are here because you want to get stripping going again, you want to know if I'll back off this time." He talked from a place far behind the cold blue eyes that was just so awful. We protested, saying we really were writers, but it didn't work—it's like denying you're an undercover agent or homosexual, there's no way in the world to do it once the assumption gets made, however wrong. He talked in postured and rhetorical bursts awhile and it seemed a long time until we could leave without seeming to have been run off. Leaving him standing there looking at the yellow Hertz car backing out his driveway, his face still cold and hard, polite to the end, but . . . But what? Not hating, but knowing: he knows about strangers now, he knows they are there to take something away, to betray, to hustle, he knows even the friendly strangers will eventually go back wherever strangers go when they are through doing whatever they have come down to do, and he will be just where he is, trying with whatever meagre resources he's got to hold on to the small parcel of land he scuffled so hard to be able to own. He'll not trust anyone again, and for me that was perhaps the most painful symptom of the failure and defeat of the poverty program in the mountains.

The others: Joe Mulloy, after about two years in the courts, finally won the draft appeal he should never have had to make in the first place; Al and Margaret McSurely were sentenced to prison terms for contempt of Congress after they refused to turn over their personal papers to a Senate committee investigating subversion in the rural South. Tom Ratliff is still commonwealth's attorney, there in the county of Pike, in the state of Kentucky. And Robert Holcomb still has his mines, his collieries, his offices, and his fine and unshaken belief in the American Way.

3

In the Arctic with Malaurie

(*American Anthropologist*, 1988)

Bring Gloves

I came home one Sunday in mid-September 1997 to a message on the answering machine from Jean Malaurie suggesting I meet him in Nome a few weeks hence. He said I shouldn't bother calling back because he was leaving in minutes "to go with Chirac for a meeting in Moscow with Boris Nicolaevitch," after which he'd be going to St. Petersburg for work at the Polar Academy. He said he would call when he got back to Paris on the thirtieth.

For years, he'd been suggesting I come along on one of his trips to the Arctic. He'd say things like, "You'll love it. Everyone does. The people, the tundra, the Arctic night!"

Malaurie is best known for his magisterial *Les derniers rois de Thulé* (*The Last Kings of Thule*, expanded four times since it was first published in 1956 and now translated into twenty-three languages) and for Collection Terre Humaine, his 110-volume series of translations and original works of humanistic anthropology and sociology.

He began as a geomorphologist: he studied rocks and made maps. After an early trip to the Arctic, his first major work was in the Sahara. The rest of his career has been on the ice: northern Greenland, Alaska, northern Canada, and Siberia. After he saw the terrible impact on the Greenland Inuit of the secret American nuclear airbase in Thule in 1951, his concern incorporated not only the land, but also the people who inhabited it.

I once asked how he could go from the extreme heat of the desert to the extreme cold of the far North. "They're both deserts," he said, "places where very small changes in environmental conditions have huge consequences for the land and for the people and animals living there. The Sahara and the Arctic have the same rainfall. The only difference is one is hot and the other is cold. You dress for that."

When he made that telephone call from Paris in September 1997, he was seventy-four years old and retired from the university. He was still vigorous and engaged: he had a short time before completed the first edition of *Hummocks*, a thousand-page ethnographic and autobiographical work about his years in the Arctic; he continued to expand Terre Humaine; and he had been serving as president of the Polar Academy.

When he next called, he said the meeting with Yeltsin had been fruitful and the Academy was doing well. Then: "So are you meeting me in Nome?"

"Of course," I said. "What are we going to be doing there?"

He said there was to be an international conference at the Polar Academy in 1999 focusing on a wide range of social and economic problems and attempts to deal with them. He hoped to find people who might join the conversations.

"So, we'll look and see what we can learn. You're the sociologist, I'm the anthropologist. Together we're Colombo: we ask questions and maybe we can learn something useful."

I asked if his office was making hotel reservations for us. "Reservations? Bruce: we're adventurers. Adventurers don't need reservations. But there is one thing."

"What?"

"Bring gloves."

I found the Nome home page on the Internet. There seemed to be only two hotels: the Nome Nugget Inn, where each room had a phone and bathroom, and the Polaris, where the phone was in the lobby and bathrooms were in the corridor. I called the Nugget and made reservations for both of us. The clerk, whose accent was distinctive and who I would later learn was an Eskimo from Anchorage who had moved to Nome as a boy, asked how long we would be staying. "I'm not sure," I said. "Does it matter?"

"Not this time of year," he said.

Malaurie as a George Segal

Every morning before dawn, when I looked out the window of my room at the Nome Nugget Hotel, I would see Malaurie seated on the bench of the public deck atop the seawall. He would be there whether the day was clear, rainy, or snowing. From a distance, he might have been a George Segal sculpture of a man, or a man mostly frozen in place. If the wind was blowing that morning, the ear flaps of his fur hat would be down; if the air was calm, the flaps were up. Only his head and his right hand moved.

The head went up a bit, then down again, up a bit, then down again; the hand made small darting movements.

After twenty minutes at most, he would gather up his things from the bench or the four-foot diameter table, made of a heavy-cable core, cross the narrow puddled road paralleling the seawall, and enter the building. A few minutes later I would hear the door of his room—next to mine—open and close.

Sometimes he showed me the pastel he had done of that morning's Arctic dawn, sometimes he didn't. I have one of them.

The shoreline above which he worked was littered with a dazzling variety of driftwood: entire tree trunks, some of which seemed only recently freed of their bark skins, others of which seemed to have been in water for eons. When, days later, I drove deep eastward along Norton Sound, I saw that same variety of wood on the beaches everywhere. You could have built splendid houses with them, or created abstract sculptures of whatever size you wished.

Someone in a restaurant told me, "They get here on the currents. Some from down the Pacific coast, where there are trees. Some maybe from Siberia. Who knows?" She nodded toward the Bering Strait; Siberia was about a hundred miles away. "The only trees around here are in the mountains, nowhere near the water. None of that wood is from here."

After breakfast, our workday began: we met with people, visited agencies, looked at what was happening on the streets. Some places and people we visited together (such as the Kawerak Native corporation, the XYZ Senior Citizens' Center, the house of the Little Sisters of Jesus, the Battered Women's Shelter, three churches); others we visited independently (Malaurie went to the hospital and he had conversations with the two Mormon missionaries working the town; I went to the court and to Anvil Mountain Correctional Center).

My Shadow

I took nearly a thousand photographs while we were working in and around Nome, and one element of many of them was my shadow, or Malaurie's shadow and my shadow.

That time of year, the sun in Nome comes almost straight up in the morning. It does not rise very high. It moves almost laterally toward the sea, and then drops almost straight down into it.

So shadows of people, whatever their height and girth, are long and thin. They track you everywhere. My shadow moved ahead of me through the day, mine, but wholly unlike me. I am not tall; my shadow was tall. I was then very overweight; my shadow was thin as a rail. It began at the front of my boots, but it inhabited a different world.

It was, in a way, like memory: part of me, but constantly changing, wholly dependent on the moment. Shadows, like memory, have no physical substance and exist only in the present.

I usually try to keep my shadow out of photographs, because it is an intrusion on what I am photographing. But in the October Nome light, it seemed integral to it.

Flare

I also try to avoid flare. Flare is streaks of color or roundish shapes that have nothing to do with what is being photographed, but which are, rather, a result of light bouncing around inside the lens barrel. Modern lenses contain several elements, so extraneous light in there introduces to the image things caused by the lens itself. The light that causes flare also reduces image contrast.

Every professional quality lens has a shade specifically designed for its internal geometry. The purpose of that shade is to avoid or minimize flare.

Several of the images from Nome have flare. But I don't mind them. They are not only an artifact of the structure of the lens, but a function of the low path of the sun in the October sky. If you turn in place, you will, for at least a third of that rotation, have the sun in your field of vision. It does things to what you see. Colors wash out and people become silhouettes. And dust shimmers in the air.

Flare is the manifestation on film of that physical fact of life in the North. For that reason, rather than being a defect in the photographs, it is an essential part of them.

Driving to Teller

One Friday we drove to the village of Teller, on Point Clarence Bay, seventy-two miles northwest of Nome.

Just past the Sinuk River, Malaurie said, "Pull over. Let's walk on the tundra." The spongy surface was deceptive for me, but not for him. Not far below was permafrost, a world that was forever frozen. Your feet think they are sinking, as if in mud or quicksand, but very soon they stop. We'd passed some knee-high willow bushes a few miles back, but where we were, nothing grew more than a few inches above the ground.

"Look at this," Malaurie said. I saw nothing other than beige and brown vegetation. His index finger traced a widening pattern in the surface. I saw the pattern repeating itself in larger and larger forms, radiating beyond us. He told me it was caused by action of the deep permafrost. "From the air"—he pointed at two ravens heading toward the Kigluaik mountains to the east—"you can see it even better."

He looked at the distant peaks covered in snow, ahead along the gravel road we'd follow to Teller, west toward the Bering Strait, and then back to the ground again. "I love the tundra," he said.

Teller

We saw few people in Teller: two men walking down a dirt road; two others, pulling a small hunting boat onto land; a hunter who yelled at me because I was photographing his dogs and seal kill without having asked permission.

Malaurie wanted to show me the marker for Umberto Nobile, the Arctic explorer who piloted the first airship to reach the North Pole and who was, in 1926, the first person to fly an airship across the Polar ice cap from Europe to America. Nobile's intention in that latter flight was to land at Nome, but the weather was against him, so he set down in Teller. It really wasn't that far from Nome, but Nome was Nobile's plan and Teller was a compromise.

The marker wasn't where Malaurie remembered it having been the last time he'd been in Teller, maybe twenty years earlier. He was upset that the marker wasn't there. After a while, I understood that the purpose of our visit to the marker wasn't for Malaurie to let me see it, but rather for Malaurie to visit it. He was paying homage.

Like men who have fought in the same war, even though on different sides and maybe at different times, he felt a bond with Nobile. They had been on the ice. Those Arctic explorers risked death every time they went out, and, not infrequently, Death won. It got Roald Amundsen, who shared credit with Nobile for that 1926 flight across the Pole, and who died trying to save Nobile and his crew when their airship went down on the way back from a Polar trip in 1928.

(I got an immediate sense of that bond in Paris in 1997 at a symposium at the Muséum National d'Histoire Naturelle occasioned by the International Polar Year. Malaurie introduced us to his old friend Artur Chilingarov, a Russian polar explorer. Earlier that year, Chilingarov had been one of a party of six that planted a Russian flag under the North Pole; he was awarded the title of Hero of the Russian Federation for that. In 1985 he had been awarded Hero of the Soviet Union after he headed a rescue operation in the Antarctic Ocean. During the three days of that symposium, Chilingarov and Malaurie regularly fell into conversation. Sometimes it was about issues that arose from one of the papers; more often it was exchanging stories. Chilingarov was Russian to the bone—he was even a member of the Soviet Duma from 1991 to 2011—and Malaurie was French to the bone—walk around Paris with him and he narrates events that occurred in almost every building you pass—but both considered themselves citizens of the Circumpolar Arctic, a condition that transcended time and nationality. I got the same feeling when I was with Malaurie and two seal hunters from Thule, Greenland, a few years later.)

"Why don't you go take some photographs," Malaurie said. "I'm going to find out what happened to Nobile's marker." He walked off. I drove around with the Bronco. I still saw almost no one. I photographed the dogs and gutted seals. The seal hunter came out of his shack and yelled at me.

Then Malaurie appeared. "It's all right!" he said. "The marker is over there." He pointed at a public utility building. "They're fixing it. They'll put it back."

Raymond

As we were heading back to Nome late that afternoon, we picked up a hitchhiker. He told us his name was Raymond and that he was going to Nome where he would spend the night with friends before catching the early morning plane to Anchorage, 540 miles south. His sister was in the hospital there, dying of cancer, and he was anxious to see her one last time.

In the warmth of the car—heater on, windows closed—Raymond exuded a sour whiskey odor. He asked if he could smoke. Neither of us responded, so he said, "Just one?" Malaurie said, "Just one," and I asked Raymond to open his window. I opened mine as well.

Raymond and Malaurie tried their Inupiak dialects on one another. Malaurie had spent time with Eskimos in Alaska, but he'd spent far more time with Inuit in Greenland and northern Canada. The language, like varieties of Latin in the south of Europe, was everywhere around the Pole. The circumpolar world has a coherence not only in climate but in language, no matter which country to the south lays claim to whatever part of it.

Raymond and Malaurie each understood a good deal of what each other was saying in Inupiak and both reverted to English whenever neither of their dialects worked. After a while, the two sang a song they both knew and both laughed about it.

Beargotim

We passed a shack missing most of one wall. It was on a hill overlooking Teller. Earlier that day, Malaurie and I had explored the place. Not far away were some ugly holes where the land had been torn up by miners many years ago. In that area, damaged surface can take a century to repair itself, and junk lingered forever. The countryside was littered with abandoned shacks, sheds, pieces of houses, gold mining dredges, large rusted-iron objects of a hundred different shapes, and even, on the Council road, a train partly nosed into a river where it had been stopped for a century.

Malaurie pointed and asked, "A miner's shack?" "Yes," Raymond said.

"What happened to it?"

"Beargothim," Raymond said. It was one word with three syllables: *beargotim*.

"A bear wrecked the cabin?"

"The miner. Bear got him."

Arctic Water

For the next twenty minutes, we saw only one car heading toward Teller from Nome. I had to pay careful attention to the road because the surface had turned slick and treacherous in the afternoon sun.

When I next looked in the rearview mirror, I didn't see Raymond. I said, "Where are you?" He came up from below the seatback, looking a little sheepish, a cigarette in his mouth. He grinned and tossed it out the window.

As we approached the Tisuk River bridge, Malaurie said, "Let's get a drink of water." He turned to Raymond and said, "You want to get a drink of water?"

"Sure," Raymond said. "Why not?"

I stopped the white Ford Bronco. Raymond went down the steep embankment to the right of the bridge; Malaurie went down a longer but less precipitous path on the left. Raymond was back soon. He stood with me, smoking. We talked about salmon.

After a while, we crossed the road and looked for Malaurie. He was still down at the river, flat on his stomach, his hands in the water, his head just above the surface. He was splashing water on himself. After a while he got up, shook the water out of his hair, put his jacket back on, and climbed up to where we stood.

"Arctic water is the best water in the world," he said.

Raymond lit another cigarette, took two quick drags, and flipped it away as we got into the Bronco.

Front Street

About ten the next morning I was taking photographs on Front Street when someone said "Hello" over my shoulder. It was Raymond. "What are you doing here?" I said.

"I missed the plane. Somebody rolled me last night in the Polaris. Can you lend me ten dollars?"

"All right." I reached for my wallet.

"How about twenty?" he said.

"Ten."

"Okay. I'll pay you back sometime when I see you."

"Okay," I said.

Not many people were moving along Front Street on foot. The kids were in school. Trucks and vans (many with cracked windshields from the gravel roads) headed out toward the villages. Three men spent the entire morning and much of the afternoon unloading cases of beer from a yellow seaborne shipping container into the Bering Sea Saloon. (A day later, three men did the same thing at another bar a little further down the street.)

As the afternoon progressed, more and more people were walking on the street, many with that peculiar walk drunks have: it's a wooden kind of motion and if you watch it you get a sensation in your own knees of too much pressure being applied with each step. Drunk-walk lacks fluidity.

"Who's going to hold my hand?"

A woman of about fifty—I saw her every afternoon and evening on Front Street—always wore a green jacket, green cap, and black stretch pants. With one exception, she'd been slightly, moderately, or very drunk every time I'd seen her.

The exception was election day afternoon when she crossed over from the other side of the street a few yards ahead of me, walking more steadily than usual. She was with a man about her age and a girl in her early teens. "Who's going to hold my hand?" the woman in green said.

She looked at the man but he ignored her. "Who's going to hold my hand?" she said again. The man continued to ignore her but the young girl, without turning her head, reached out her hand. With her left hand the woman in green held the young girl's hand and she put her right hand in the back pocket of her stretch pants.

Late that night, long after the polls had closed and the bars had opened, I saw her walking with two men I hadn't seen before, their steps equally uneven and their balance equally tentative.

A Family Conversation

In the Board of Trade bar at 5:30 in the afternoon a woman said to the man standing next to her, "You can't tell me what to do. You can't tell me what to do. Who do you think I am, your sister? You can't tell me what to do."

Both of her elbows were on the bar. She lifted her bottle of beer from the bar and drank from it without moving her elbows.

The man next to her, who also had both his elbows on the bar, was silent for a while, then he said, looking into the bar mirror, "You *are* my sister."

She was silent for a moment, then said, "That's right, I'm your sister. I'm your fucken sister. I'm your sister. You can't tell me what to do."

Christian Darts

A woman who worked at the Battered Women's Shelter talked about the missionaries suppressing native language and customs:

Right now what they're saying is, "We're sorry we did what we did to you. We shouldn't have done that to you. We were wrong to believe and to think that there were certain things you had to stop doing. We are sorry we did that to you. We acknowledge that. We will no longer try to take away from you your culture anymore. We will not determine what's evil or not anymore." That's the approach that they are taking now . . .

This is what people in the village like to say: there was a map of the Bering Strait region and each church had a dart and they threw their darts and that's how they divided our region. There's a cluster of villages that are predominantly Lutheran, a cluster of villages that are predominantly Catholic, and a cluster of villages that are Protestant. Those are the three primary churches around here.

The Blonde Eskimo

"You ever hear about the blonde Eskimo?" a silver-haired woman who worked in the Senior Citizens' Center asked us. I thought she was going to tell a dumb-blonde joke, which had been all the rage in the lower 48 a few years earlier.

"No, I haven't," I said.

"It's me. My mother was half Danish and half Eskimo, my father was half Norwegian and half Eskimo. They're from the same village. That's how come I'm blonde. I'm the blonde Eskimo."

She had grown up in a village east of Nome on Norton Sound. When she was a child and came into Nome to go to the movies. In the 1940s, the Eskimos had to sit in the balcony, the half-Eskimos sat on the left side of the aisle, the whites on the right.

Sometimes she came in with her sisters or cousins and the ushers would tell her to sit on the right side of the aisle. "I'd say, 'No. I'm with them.' They'd say, 'But you have to sit over there.' I'd say, 'I'm an Eskimo.' They'd look at my hair and wouldn't believe me but it was true. I spoke Eskimo and I knew how to hunt roots."

Court

There were two courtrooms on the second floor of the New Federal building on Front Street. The big courtroom was for Federal trials and major state trials. To the left of the bench was a furled U.S. flag, to the right a furled Alaskan flag. On the wall over and behind the judge was an object probably unique to Alaskan courtrooms, perhaps unique to that one: a bleached walrus skull with two long tusks curving down toward the top of the judge's head.

The smaller courtroom in the back corner of the building—the district court presided over by Judge Bradley M. Gator—was where you met ordinary people having ordinary problems. Judge Gator's court handled arraignments, pleadings, hearings, and minor trials. Because the courtroom was so small, the judge's bench was at an angle in the corner to the right of the door as you come in.

While we were waiting for Judge Gator, I took out my cell phone. The prosecutor, who was sitting in the row in front of me, turned around and said, "That won't help you here, sonny. You want to use that, go to Fairbanks or Anchorage."

Every weekday afternoon at 1 p.m. a state police van pulled up at the side of the building with prisoners from the Anvil Mountain Correctional Center (which everyone in the area referred to as "AMCC") a few miles north of town. After the prisoners in their Day-Glo orange and mustard jumpsuits were brought up, seated in the jury box, and had their handcuffs removed, the district attorney and the lawyers arrived. The accuseds' lawyers were always public defenders because, just like Outside ("Outside" is a word many Alaskans then used for the lower 48) most people handled by this court were poor, and poor people cannot afford to hire lawyers.

One young man asked the judge to let him remain free while awaiting trial. His sister asked the judge to make it a condition of his release that he not visit his parents' house. The judge asked why.

"Because they're worse drunks than he is," the public defender said.

The next case concerned twenty-seven-year-old Jerry Bunhart, who was charged with second-degree murder because, while drunk, he killed thirty-year-old Russel Apatiki with his green Ford Bronco on East Front Street late Saturday night. Bunhart had several character witnesses, one of whom was both the mayor of Nome and a high official of the Alaska Gold Company, one of Nome's major employers. They told the judge that he was a reliable worker and never once showed up for work drunk.

Bail was set at $10,000. Bunhart and a young woman grinned at one another and hugged. The lawyer told the woman that Bunhart would go back to AMCC for processing, then would be released, and that she could pick him up there later that afternoon.

During all of this, the trooper who ferried the prisoners to and from AMCC sat without moving in a chair just to the right of the door. On her thick black leather belt was an enormous automatic pistol, two extra magazines of ammunition, a great ring of keys, and several closed leather cases. During one long colloquy between the judge and the attorneys, she opened an envelope that was on the chair next to her and took out a group of four-by-six-inch color photographs. She looked at them one by one, smiling from time to time.

After Bunhart and the other prisoners of the day were taken out, the public defender told me that alcohol or other drugs were a factor in about ninety percent of his cases. He said the dead man had been picked up twice on the streets earlier Saturday evening for being drunk. "If they'd locked him up like they're supposed to, he'd be alive now."

He was referring to the law that allowed police to put drunks in AMCC for twelve hours without formal charge. After the twelve hours were up, they'd be released. If there was a car going to town or if they had family with a car or if they had money for a taxi, they got to ride; otherwise, they would walk the three miles back to town.

AMCC is the only American prison I've ever seen that houses nearly every category of prisoner: men, women, people doing long sentences for major felonies, people doing short sentences for minor offenses, federal prisoners awaiting trial or sentencing, people awaiting arraignment or awaiting or undergoing trial, and ordinary falling-down drunks getting sober enough to be cut loose in the morning without being a danger to themselves or anyone else. The only two prisoner categories it doesn't have are prisoners under sentences of death (the State of Alaska never had a death penalty) and prisoners serving Federal time (there are no Federal prisons in Alaska).

The first case on Thursday, two days later, was a young man who wanted to be furloughed from AMCC so he could go to the funeral of his cousin in the village of Gambell on St. Lawrence Island. His lawyer told the judge that the cousin had been killed by a drunk driver on East Front Street Saturday night and the body was still in Anchorage where it had been sent for autopsy. The judge asked if the body would be in Gambell in time for the funeral. The lawyer repeated the question to his client.

The man said, "We don't know for sure when he's getting there."

The judge looked at the dossier and said that because of the man's record he wouldn't release him. The man looked puzzled through much of this. When everyone was quiet for a moment, the prisoner asked the public defender whether or not he was going to be released.

The lawyer said, "He says no."

"Why?"

"Because you've screwed up so much."
"Oh. Okay."

The Fire on the Beach

Early one morning, I saw from my hotel room firelight flickering through spaces below the public deck built atop the seawall. I could hear nothing over the surf and wind, but I could see what seemed to be the silhouettes of people moving between the flame and the stone. Later, I asked the blonde woman who was the daytime desk clerk about it. She seemed disinterested so I asked her a second time. "Probably people having a cookout," she said.

"At five in the morning?" I asked.

"Oh, they do that sometimes," she said and turned back to her papers.

Later that day, the state trooper in court said, "Have you met our homeless people yet?" I said I hadn't. "When the tide's out, go down behind the chainsaw sculptures in the park by the visitor's center, the other side of the seawall. You'll see them there. And further up the beach toward the Roadhouse, past where the seawall ends."

I told her about the flames in the early morning. "That was them," she said. I told her what the concierge said. "Yeah, they'd say that," the state trooper said. "They don't like to think about the homeless people."

I said that this must be a very difficult place to be without shelter in the winter. "It's worse than you could imagine," she said. She finished handcuffing her prisoners and led them down to the van with the state insignia on the door and drove them back to Anvil Mountain Correctional Center.

The Man Whose Father Could Fly

Malaurie and I went to a house where Nicky, a man Malaurie had known on Little Diomede Island in the Bering Strait twenty years ago, was living with one of his granddaughters. The house was on the eastern end of town, near the school. Like many houses in Nome, it was built a few feet above the ground. If you built a house with heating right on the ground, the permafrost would melt and the house would sink into it. None of the houses I saw had basements and nearly all the streets were unpaved.

This house had five steps up to the small porch by the front door. A woman in her twenties let us in. Four or five children and two other grownups were watching television. One of the women led us to a room in the back of the house.

Nicky was lying in bed. There were no lights on in the room and the shades were drawn. His wife, who sat in a chair at the foot of the bed, told us he was blind and deaf now.

Jean said hello and asked if Nicky remembered him; Nicky said of course he did.

He sat up and turned toward us. Jean introduced me. I put out my hand and Nicky shook it. I said I was pleased to meet him. He said it was nice to meet me.

Nicky and Jean talked about people in the village: who was alive and who was not, who was living in Nome and who was still on the island, what was still the same and what was not.

Nicky said to me, "They say there is one man who could walk on water but there were three." One of the three, he said, was his grandfather, who one time was returning with some other hunters on the ice and they got near the shore where the ice was soft and so his grandfather kept poking at it with his stick to make sure it was strong enough to support their weight. Then he got to a place—Nicky mimed the action with his hand—where the stick went deep into the water, which meant there was no ice there at all.

"But my grandfather kept walking anyway. He did that."

I never learned who the third man who could walk on water was because Nicky then remembered and told us about a time when his father and a friend were returning to their village. Nicky was ninety-one years old when we met, and at the time of the story his father and the friend were young men, so this happened long ago.

There was a river that had to be forded ten miles from the village. Ordinarily, if you knew where the stones and high places in the riverbed were, you could just walk across and the water in those places was never deeper than your boots. But that day, because of the spring rains and meltings, it was impossible to walk across even if you knew the location of every high place, every submerged boulder.

"My father," Nicky said, "he could fly, so it was okay."

"He what?" I said.

"My father, he could fly. That day he could. A wind came and it lifted him and his friend and it put them down just like *that* ten miles the other side of the river. So, he flew, my father did. On that wind. Other people, they had to walk those ten miles if they wanted to get from that place to the village, but my father, he flew it."

He paused, then said, "That was before the white man came. Things are different now."

He opened his shirt and showed us a lump over his left breast. "It's a good thing you're here today. Next week, I have to go on the airplane to Anchorage to get a new pacemaker. I've had this one fourteen years." He tapped it with vigorous confidence. I wanted to tell him that pointing would suffice.

His wife said, "They said it was only good for eight years, but he's had it in there for *fourteen*."

Nicky grinned. "Jesus is my pacemaker." He tapped his chest again. "Jesus is my pacemaker, right?"

"Right," I said.

"*Fourteen years!*" his wife said.

Contrails

Jean and I left a little while later and walked to the breakwater near the chainsaw sculptures. There are two figures, a prospector and an Eskimo. Between them is a horizontal carved sign saying, "Welcome to the city of NOME Alaska."

A boy came by on a bicycle and sped to the edge, almost as if he were going into the sea. He stopped at the last possible moment, and turned away.

The late afternoon sun danced on the waves and we talked about how the world had changed in Nicky's father's lifetime, in Nicky's lifetime, in our fathers' lifetimes, in our lifetimes.

I told Jean that in 1909, the year my father was born, there were only fourteen miles of paved road in all of the United States. He reminded me that he had been the first European to reach the magnetic North Pole on a dogsled, which was the only way to do it in 1951.

We sat there talking about Nicky while late afternoon contrails traced Great Circles forty thousand feet above us.

Job

Job was, when I met him in the XYZ Senior Citizens' Center, eighty years old. He had been born in Solomon, a fishing village on Norton Sound about thirty miles to the east of Nome. It is said that Job's grandfather killed a bear with his hands. He told me that, and so did several other people. Job's father wanted him to be a seal hunter.

When he was a boy he learned those ways, but, he told me, he knew those ways wouldn't last so he learned how to operate heavy machinery. In World War II he was a heavy equipment operator in the Air Force, stationed at an airbase in the Aleutians. "I'd watch the planes go out and I'd count them; then I'd watch them come back and I'd count them." His eyes filled with tears for the planes that didn't come back more than a half century ago. "There's a lot of dead men out there," he said, nodding toward the Strait.

A young schoolteacher said of Job: "The amount of change that Job has seen from when he was a teenager to now is incredible. He is a respected elder in Nome. I know that as an elder, he has seen through his eyes the transformation of a whole world. From dogsled to jets. From word of mouth to the cell phone to the Internet. The change from a subsistence lifestyle to depending on the western lifestyle of living, a cash economy. To the changes in religion. And there's many more changes. You put those all together that have happened in the last fifty to sixty years and what do you get? You get frustrated individuals, dysfunctional groups, because of all the change that's happened. And you're getting pressure from the religious side saying, 'No you can't do this, it's wrong for you to speak in your native tongue.'"

Job told me that he and a friend were going out that afternoon to hunt berries and gather roots. I asked if I might go with them. He shrugged. "There is only room in the pickup for two people."

I said I could sit in the trucked. Job shrugged, and said again, "There is only room in the pickup for two people."

Malaurie told me later, "That wasn't it. He and his friend have places where they pick berries and gather roots. Why would they show them to us? We would have to be here a long time before they'd take us with them when they went to the places where they go for berries and roots."

Shamans

Malaurie was having endless conversations with people and sometimes I wished he'd stop. My idea of fieldwork is *not* having conversations, but only seeming to have them. In fieldwork, we have to listen far more than we talk because we're there to learn rather than participate in or have an influence upon ordinary life. Participation and influence—those are other kinds of activity entirely.

68 | Folklore Matters

One day the director of the senior citizens' center said she had seen alcohol destroy people and that many people were in denial about it. She started to describe the denial, whereupon Jean started talking about something going on in Europe. She looked at him, puzzled.

Later, we were walking on Front Street and Jean said he was very bothered about what is happening in France now, that his conversations that day with several people had gotten him thinking about the long-term implications of the Euro negotiations.

I said, "You come here to find what's wrong with the Eskimo and you find what's wrong with *you*?"

"That's what the work is all about," he said. "We look at the other and we find ourselves." (He put it more elegantly in *Hummocks*: "L'étude d'un peuple est pour moi une aventure intérieure.")

That night, in the Mexican restaurant on Front Street run by a Vietnamese family from Saigon, he talked about the place of shamans in the world, about their place in the present world, about how they've been displaced by things that do not replace them.

"They need their shamans," he said, "they maybe don't know it, but they do. Shamans have a knowledge nothing has replaced."

At that moment, it occurred to me that my friend Malaurie was not simply scientist and observer, but also a participant in the world of the Polar Eskimo, and that his impassioned talks at moments when I would be professionally silent represented his refusal or inability simply to *observe*. He was a French academic, editor of one of the world's most honored ethnographic book series, recipient of honors from a dozen governments—but at heart, like his friend Chilingarov, like Nobile—it was the North that was his ultimate home.

The last time I saw him—in 2010, when Diane Christian and I spent a few days with him and his wife Monique at their home in Dieppe—he told me he wanted to be buried on Little Diomede Island in the Bering Strait. Little Diomede is in the United States; Big Diomede, two miles away, is in Russia. The international dateline, as imaginary as borders, is the only thing, other than water, that separates them. In winter, you can walk on the ice from one island to the other, from one continent to another.

When we made our visit to Nome in 1997, he was compelled to use what he had learned in his half century in the Arctic to help, to participate in that boreal world about which he feels so passionately, on behalf of these people he truly loves. He had started on the path when he returned from the ice in 1951 and saw how the American nuclear airbase at Thule had destroyed the balanced native world he had left only a year earlier.

It was that year on the ice and what he found at the end of it that led to *Les derniers rois de Thulé*.

He couldn't stop talking because there was so much he needed to say.

Losing It on the Road to Council

We had breakfast the morning after our conversation about shamans at the Lucky Swede, a coffee and trinket shop next to the Nugget (named in honor of the ethnicity of one of the three men said to have first discovered gold in Nome). I told Malaurie I was going to drive up to Council, an abandoned gold mining town on the Niukluk River northeast of town. He asked what time we were going.

"*I'm* going," I said.

"Ah," he said. "I'll walk in the tundra. I've been wanting to do that."

As we walked back to the hotel, he remarked on the two young women who had been at the table next to us in the Lucky Swede. He said they seemed very nice, but he wondered why they hadn't been in school at this hour.

"They're whores," I said. He looked puzzled. "Whores. Schoolgirls around here don't dress like that. They service the guys who work the Russian ships that come over here from Chukotka. They were having breakfast before going to sleep."

"I thought they were schoolgirls," he said.

"Well," I said, "I can't read the tundra and you can."

The road from Nome to Council is formally called the "Nome-Council Highway." It is two lanes, with a gravel bed. It runs seventy-three miles east along the Seward Peninsula beaches and wetlands, then veers north into high tundra.

The section of that road along the water passes fishing shacks and a few abandoned gold dredges that tilt along stream and riverbeds like beached Mississippi River steamboats.

Thirty-three miles east of Nome, just to the right of a bullet-pocked sign saying, "Bonanza Channel," three rusting railroad engines (which began life in New York City as part of the New York Elevated rail system) and some flatcars are embedded in the water and ground.

When I first saw them I thought, "I can't be seeing that." Steam engines in wetlands and tundra? But I was; they were real. I stopped the Bronco.

Local people call the whole rusting mess "The Last Train to Nowhere." It is what remains of the Council City and Solomon City Railroad, which operated from 1903 to 1907. It was originally supposed to be part of a network of rail lines connecting all the mining camps, Council (which at one time had as many as fifteen thousand residents), Nome, and other places. But it didn't pan out, and the rail line was abandoned. What remained of it was mostly destroyed in storms in 1913.

Not far from the ghostly steam engines, the road cuts away from the water and runs along some low tundra. Then there are hills. And then the hills are very high on the right and the valley floor drops very deep on the left.

And that is where I freaked out.

The two-lane gravel road shimmered in the morning sun. I couldn't tell if it was merely wet or if it was coated with a carapace of ice. My foot rose higher and higher on the accelerator until the car was barely moving. I went from thirty to twenty to ten to five miles per hour to two miles per hour. I thought: "It will take me forever to get to Council now. And how can I get back?"

I imagined hitting ice slick and the white Bronco veering off to the left, then plunging down the steep side into the flats below.

I had seen only one other vehicle in the past thirty minutes, and that was before I'd gotten up to the highlands. If I went off and were still alive when the car stopped, I couldn't use my cell phone to call for help. That prosecutor had said it wouldn't work in the Federal courthouse in Nome, so it surely wouldn't work on the downside of a mountain two-thirds of the way to Council. No one would find me unless some moose hunters wandered by and went to look at the rusting SUV hulk and found inside my bones—assuming the bears hadn't dragged me off, in which case they wouldn't find anything at all. Save my useless cell phone.

I stopped the car and cut the engine. I thought: there is nothing to my right but that mountain, and nothing to my left until you reach the North Pole. I knew it was quite crazy, but knowing what you are thinking is crazy does not help you stop thinking crazily. I knew I was experiencing agoraphobia, which I had never experienced previously. Again, knowing that was no help dealing with it. Putting a name on terror doesn't expunge terror; it just gives terror a name. The fact that it was almost two thousand miles from where I was to the North Pole and that there were lots of Eskimo and Inuit villages between where the Bronco was parked and the Pole did nothing to extinguish my vision of that rusted Bronco, down on the flat, upside down and wrecked, with or without what remained of me inside it.

Where the hell was the ever-talking Jean Malaurie? A human voice would have made that all go away in an instant, and I knew it.

After a long while, I got out of the Bronco. It was not easy getting out, at first. I turned in the seat and put both feet on the ground. Then I stood. Then I stepped away from the car and shut the door.

The ground was wet, not icy. There was no wind, no sound. I noticed for the first time that the hill rising to my right was covered by trees. These were the first living trees I'd seen since arriving in Nome. Around town, and on the way to Teller, I'd seen nothing taller than knee-high bush, and often not even that.

I looked across the other side of the road, beyond the large expanse of flatland below to a mountain range to the north, capped in snow. I saw a single raven flying below me, then rising higher, and finally rising out of sight. The raven's easy motion through that infinite expanse of air, the distant capped mountains, were, in the Arctic silence, breathtakingly beautiful.

I remembered Malaurie saying on the way to Teller, "The raven doesn't migrate. The raven is always here. Even in the darkest part of winter, the raven is here."

My heart stopped pounding in my chest, my breathing rate slowed; I was back in time, back in the world. I got back in the Bronco and drove on to Council.

When I got there, the road ended. A sign announced that. There was a small river, beyond which the road continued into the town. A chain on the other side denied entrance. I'd been told that some people summered there but no one lived there this time of year or in winter; there was no electricity and no telephone lines. The streets of Nome were framed and cluttered by power and telephone poles and wires everywhere: what lives underground in the lower 48 must be in the air in Nome because of the ever-present permafrost and water. But in Council there was nothing other than houses, the other side of that small river I did not know how to cross.

An SUV came up near where I had parked and, without pause, drove into the river. The SUV moved left and right, obviously following an underwater route its driver knew perfectly well, then came out where the road continued. The driver got out, undid the chain, and drove on. I had not a doubt that, if you did not know where to turn left and right while fording that small river, you would be in serious difficulty, even with a four-wheel-drive vehicle.

I got back into the Bronco and drove back to Nome, going fifty or sixty miles an hour the entire way. It was colder than when I'd come up, and the shiny spots on the road now probably were ice, but I knew that did not matter at all. The car could handle it perfectly well, as could I.

A Ferret

That night, Malaurie and I had dinner at the Fort Davis roadhouse, the closest thing to fancy you could find in Nome that time of year. Only a few other patrons were in the restaurant.

"You were angry this morning," he said, "but you're not angry now."

"I needed some quiet," I said.

"Did you find it?"

"Yes."

"On expeditions," he said, "you never want to go out by yourself; you can go crazy. But you don't want to go out with just two people either. Sometimes you have to, but you shouldn't. With two people, when anger starts it just gets worse. One of them maybe kills the other one. If there are three, two bond against one, they vent their anger, and then things are okay. But with two, sometimes bad things happen."

As he spoke, I sensed a motion on the periphery of my field of vision. I turned to look, but nothing was there except the salad bar twenty feet away. We continued talking and I again sensed the motion. I looked, and still nothing was there.

So, while Malaurie and I continued our conversation, I just kept on looking. After a few minutes, a ferret appeared at the base of the salad bar. It stood on its hind legs, looked left and right, then hopped up, grabbed something, and went off with it. It came back a few minutes later and did the same thing again.

I beckoned the waitress. "I think I just saw a ferret at the salad bar," I said.

She shrugged. "You did. We don't know how he gets in and out. We looked, but we just can't find it. He won't bother you. He never bothers anybody."

"He's here a lot?" I said.

"Every day," she said. "He likes the salad."

A School Meeting

Someone at the community center had said, while Jean and I were watching some of the elders playing drums and teaching kids how to do traditional narrative dances, "You're both schoolteachers. You should come to the school meeting tonight."

We did. No one seemed to mind that two strangers joined the kids and adults sitting in those little chair-desks, the desk part of which, fortunately, was hinged, hence could be moved out of the way.

I saw Job there, sitting alone in the back, and a few other people I'd met or seen around town. Maybe thirty-five people in all, ranging from Job's age down to very young kids. As they talked, I realized some of the adults were parents, some were teachers, some were school administrators, and some were all three.

They discussed class offerings, truancy problems, budget needs, and more. I thought the meeting was not unlike AMCC: a place in which things that Outside would be handled by a wide variety of agencies and groups was here being handled by one, and somehow, they all fit. The meeting was at once a school board meeting, a PTA meeting, a teachers' meeting, a student engagement meeting, a meeting between school officials and local politicians.

They took votes, sometimes argued, sometimes speechified. Malaurie made a speech about education and the modern world and traditional ways. If anyone was bothered by it or thought there was anything improper about a French outsider who had arrived in town a week or two before carrying on about the town's school system, I saw no evidence of it. If you were there, it was because you were concerned, so you could talk and people would listen.

After the last vote was taken, everyone got ready to go home. It wasn't winter yet, but it was cold. Mukluks and parkas were put on, gloves were put on, hats were put on. Adults and children stood up, started milling, began moving toward the door.

Then Job, who had not put on his boots, his jacket, his hat, or his gloves, said, in a voice no louder than ordinary conversation-level: "Now I will speak."

Without a word from anyone else—parent, child, teacher, administrator—the garments came off. Parkas were draped over the backs of chairs; mukluks stood empty on the floor. Hats and gloves were tucked into pockets.

Job said he thought the meeting had been a very good one, but there were two things he thought hadn't been completed, or hadn't been decided correctly. He wasn't telling them what they should do; he was only saying what he thought. The two issues—I no longer remember what they were—had both received extended discussion and a serious vote in the previous few hours. Job's voice remained even; I don't recall him making eye-contact with anyone in particular. He wasn't avoiding eye-contact; rather, he was addressing the room.

When he was done, a man who had introduced and argued passionately for one side of one of the issues Job raised said he wanted to introduce a new resolution. The resolution he introduced was exactly the opposite of the resolution he had introduced and for which he had argued a short while earlier. It was almost a perfect reformulation of what Job had just said.

They voted immediately: it passed without dissent. The same thing happened with the second issue.

When they were done, Job smiled, everyone else smiled, the kids got noisy again, and once again, the mukluks, parkas, hats, and gloves went on, only this time, everyone left the room, left the building, and went home.

Things I Wonder About

In the villages, the ones you can get to only by boat or small plane, people now use email. They learn and share things on the Internet. They visit with FaceTime. Jet planes take people like Nicky to distant cities where microelectronic devices are fitted inside their bodies and they continue to live a while longer. Television sets show programs from Outside. The village life as it was is gone and it will always be gone.

There are subsistence villages still, but they will never again be whatever they were before the white man came with technology, alcohol, Christianity, and the economies of gold and oil, and, more recently, the incessant flow of information.

Malaurie writes in *Hummocks*, "La vie est mouvement et contact." *Life is movement and contact.* There's no point mourning the new; it's as much a fact of life as the garnet gold-bearing sands on the Nome beaches, the huge, rusted dredge buckets that now serve as public petunia flowerpots all over town, and the radiating patterns in the tundra caused by action of the permafrost. Human cultures are always in a condition of change, a state of flux, a mode of adaptation. So is the world.

But what is the cost of losing a language that worked perfectly well for thousands of years? How can you say in a new language the important things that must be said or tell the stories that must be told? What is the cost of getting more stories from television than the voices of the storytellers? What happens when you move from cyclical time to chronological time, from the time of the stars and the seasons to the time of airlines and governments? What happens when you move from a world in which you get what you need from hunting, fishing, and bartering to a world in which you get what you need by working for money or from a government agency? What happens when there is no Job who is empowered to say, "Now I will speak" and people who will fall silent and listen? Where are shamans to do their work and the elders to provide their wisdom if there are no communities in which their work has meaning or their words have a forum? What is to be done about alcoholism and children who have learned to sniff anything volatile, even gasoline fumes?

Some things have been lost; some things have faded. But Eskimo culture is very much alive; it reinvents itself every day. It is vital and energetic. It is not what it once was, but what else is? Even the tundra is not what it was a mere few decades ago.

A Bear

At a dinner in Buffalo a decade later, Malaurie spoke of how, for the Inuit, everything is alive, even stones. When a whale or seal is hunted, and killed, he said, the hunter is successful not only because of his virtue and skill, but because the animal agrees to be caught, agrees to provide food and clothing and ivory to the people, which is why the hunter always returns part of the animal to the sea, so that it may go home and then return again. Nothing is unrelated, nothing is unconnected.

One time, Malaurie said, he was alone on the ice, but then he was not alone: a large bear was next to him. The two stood together a while, then they exchanged spirits: the bear was Jean Malaurie and Jean Malaurie was the bear. He stood there, feeling not his bones, but the bones of the bear. After a while, each spirit returned to its body, and then the bear went away.

He learned something from that experience, he said, that could not be expressed in words. That was, he said, because not all the things that could be known could be known in words.

Malaurie's Books

Jean Malaurie has written many books about the Arctic, about his experiences there and about the experiences of other outsiders there, but the most important remains the first, *The Last Kings of Thule: With the Polar Eskimos as They Face Their Destiny*. Each edition has grown larger and richer. It is an amalgam of scientific report, personal narrative, written history, oral history, folkways, ethnography, photographs, poetry, drawings by Malaurie, drawings by Inuit, information about the past, information about what was the present when the first edition was written, information that Malaurie has acquired in the years since, and projections into the future.

It is, in other words, a book that enacts what shamans do every day. It brings together all the available knowledge of this world and other worlds, this time and other times, and tries to say what is really going on. If Malaurie had time, I do not doubt that there would be more editions. It is a book, like the life experience he writes about, that cannot ever be completed. Nor should it be.

Curtains and Ribbons

The moon at midnight my last night in Nome was near the horizon, southwest and below Aquarius, leaking white rinsings across a flat sea.

The downtown part of Front Street is less than a mile long and the lighted houses and buildings give out not much beyond that. After the town bypass, there are no more lights except the Fort Davis roadhouse and occasional oncoming cars rounding the headland at Cape Nome eleven miles away. I turned left onto a dirt road, turned off the lights and engine, stepped out of the car and looked north.

Nome is a border town, a border of the whole world town.

The yellow-green and blue-white ribbon of light started in the northwest at Draco, crossed over both Bears, and ended just under Orion on the far eastern rim of the sky. For a while the ribbon arced north at both ends, as if it were trying to clasp the Pole in its arms, then the right end folded down toward me and undulated toward Cassiopeia in the middle. The left side dissolved entirely into the black sky and brilliant stars, then rebuilt itself, but this time as diaphanous sheets rising to the top of the world.

Malaurie and I had early meetings in the morning before my plane to Anchorage, so after a while I drove slowly back to town, picking out constellations over the sea: Cygnus, Lyra, Pegasus, Pisces. The sky was as clear as a stellar map; it lacked only the lines connecting the stars and the labels. Like all the outsiders who had come here looking for something, I saw with designs formulated elsewhere. All the names I had for stars and constellations are Roman and Greek. The Eskimos had lived here at least three thousand years; some say more than ten thousand years. Their names for the figures in the sky predate those of the Romans and the Homeric Greeks. The lines they imagined are older than any I knew.

I went to bed, but sleep did not come. I kept thinking about the diaphanous sheets and ribbons draping themselves around those undrawn lines. At 3 a.m. I dressed and went downstairs.

In the hotel lobby, the night clerk, an Eskimo from Anchorage who moved to Nome as a boy, told me that he had looked at the aurora in the night sky for as long as he could remember anything and he still loved to look at it as much as ever, finds it as tranquilizing and mysterious as ever. "You look up there and you imagine things, you know?" he said.

Even before I was out of the sodium-vapor light of Front Street I knew it was not going to be any good. I drove to the dirt road again and once again killed the headlights and engine, but the aurora was done for this night: it was just the stars now, maybe even more brilliant and numerous than before but it wasn't stars I was seeking in that dark hour.

As I drove back to town I saw that Pegasus and Aquarius and Pisces had all shifted south and the moon had disappeared into Siberia. On Front Street, all the bars were dark save one. Four people spilled from its door into the street, stumbling and shouting at one another. None of them looked to see if my car had slowed or swerved to avoid them.

Further on, glowing in the headlights of an oncoming truck, I saw Raymond walking unevenly toward the Polaris Hotel. The truck passed him and for a moment he was enveloped in a swirl of dust.

In the lobby of my hotel two drunks argued with the night clerk about something I could not understand.

Part II
Outside the Law

4

From *In the Life*

(1972)

When I was doing the prison work, I never fretted much about whether or not what I was documenting was folklore or anything else: I was just documenting what I encountered, what I later learned Walker Evans had called "the cruel radiance of what is." The categorization was for later, for other people. When I published these conversations in Texas Monthly *and my book* In the Life, *Richard Dorson, to my surprise and delight, wrote about them as significant contributions to the field of folklore. They were, but until Dick wrote that, I doubted any of the academic folklorists would get it.*

Big Sal

I had a whorehouse on Hardy Street in Houston. And I pushed dope, I had pills, I had weed. Anything you want, just come to Sal's. That was the rumor around town. But, hell, there was a dope connection on every corner, it wasn't nothing to have dope. So I run that whorehouse. It was a real big house on Hardy Street. I had nine girls. And I had a payoff. It was $125 a week.

I was real funny about that. The Federal man came down here when I got my time and tried to get me out and testify against the men that I had the payoff with. I told him, "I don't know what you're talking about." These same policemen had helped me get out of a lot of scrapes, because I did them a favor by saving their reputation as policemen. And what good would it have done me to send somebody, even a policeman, to the penitentiary?

I've never been bitter toward the police. Hell, if we didn't have police we'd have an animal world. Really. We've got an animal world anyway. Dog eat dog.

Whatever the girls made in that place, I took $2 off $5. If they lived there and paid room and board, they'd pay $10 a day and the same $2 off each $5 they made. But there were no $5 dates in my house. I lived by the railroad yard where the railroad men got paid twice a month and came down. It was a good go. Girls who walked the streets and wanted a room for an hour or two, whatever they made was theirs, they just paid me for the room. But there wasn't but two girls I'd rent rooms to like that. If any others come off the street, I didn't know what they was talking about. I wasn't allowed to. We had rules on my payoff. I had to operate in such a fashion and keep it like a family rooming house.

When I got the house, it *was* a boarding house. This old woman had died and her son had just kept the roomers there. They'd been having roomers there for years. The same ones. There was one gambler that knew me, and when I moved in, he said, "Sal, what are you up to?" He knew.

I said, "I'm fixing to open this sonafabitch up."

And he told me, "I thought so. Well, I can't stand the heat, baby."

And I told him, "I need your room anyway." It was understood. So he moved. He left the front room for my hustling parlor; that faced the street, which made it convenient. Upstairs I had six roomers. I got them all together in the parlor that night and I told them, "I don't know who's going to stay and who's going to stay and play, but it's going to be a playhouse from now on."

And this little bitty guy, I never will forget him, he was about 920 years old, he says, "Well, I can't play—I gotta work tonight." Just so serious. I told him, "Well, we're going to play every night, honey." And he told me, "Are you going to sell beer?"

I told him, "I don't have no license to sell beer."

He got mad and he said, "Have you got a license to run a whorehouse?"

I told him, "Honey, I'm not running a whorehouse. It's a playhouse. Don't you understand?"

We made friends before he left. The rest of them, they all said, "Well, if we want a girl we'll come back and see you." Laughing. I never did have no rumbles out of them.

They never did run and call the police like a lot of people would. I don't know, maybe it was the neighborhood. Around there, there was a colored house on one street and then another one that was all Mexican. And there was so many connections around there.

Even the drugstores—they sold pills. It was just a real regular whoretown, I guess, right in that vicinity. What made my place look good, I had my kids with me.

You know, that's why I think my kids turned out to be squares, both of them. The oldest one married a policeman's daughter. I don't know, they just don't want no part of that kind of life. They've seen it with me.

Webster

There's an old game called the American Services Association. Generally, the way it is, you get you a lot of pamphlets and things made up. Say you got an insurance policy and you have a pamphlet showing a lot of stores and businesses and things. You go, you knock on a door, a lady comes to the door and you say, "Good evening, madam." You start conning them. "Good evening, madam, is the lady of the house here?"

And she say, "Well, *I'm* the lady of the house here."

So first thing you did, you paid her a compliment, so she's already at ease almost. You give her some, you know, "Well, you sure look young to be the lady of the house," and so forth. And then you tell her, "Well, I'm with the American Services Association. We are in connection with the American Automobile Association and the NAACP, and I'd like to interest you in a project which will enable you to benefit yourself. I'm going to give you—" then you stop and say, "I'm not going to *give* you anything. I'm going to put you in the position to grab some of the goodness this organization has to offer." And you proceed to tell her how you get a discount on everything from a shoeshine to a hairdo. And you show her your pamphlets showing her all the stores and if she's a member of this club all the thing she can get. And you show her all the benefits that you can get from it and it only costs $37.50 a year. She can either pay all of it or half of it. Anything you get is a gift, you know, so you accept it. So now most of the time if you actually get them in this mood and show them all the facts that are connected with it, they'll pay the whole thing. So if they pay the whole thing you tell them, "If you pay the whole thing, the whole $37.50, you don't have to worry about any additional cost that comes in. You get a $500 bail bond certificate. You know, in most states if you have a wreck you can't be moved until the police officers arrive, but if you happen to be a member of this club and have a bail bond certification, then you can be moved right away."

You explain to them that if you're a member of this organization, then if you happen to have a wreck any bond that you would have to pay up to $500 you can get out without having to pay one penny. And then you explain to them that your lawyer for your organization is an ex-judge and he'll fight a traffic ticket if necessary. And if they have a gas war on, you get a percentage still for your gas. Anything, anything you can think of that there could be a percentage for it, you tell them they get a percentage if they're a member of this organization. And usually they pay the whole thing.

I'll tell you, most any game that's played, there's more than one way to play it. That's with the Drag Game—there's several different branches to it, and the Pigeon Drop, they're all different, and even the O'Grady. It all depends on who's got the game, who knows it, and how they play it. But mostly any game used can be used on white or colored, except that one I was just telling you about, the American Services Association thing. Mostly that is used only on colored because now there's this integrational crisis and you make sure you tell 'em, say, "Most white people already have this benefit, they been having it for years. But now, with the NAACP's official okay, the Automobile Association has banded together with several other millionaire businessmen to give the colored people the same benefit." Now this automatically gives a little boost.

How many of these can you make in day?

Usually we go to a project area. Like there's middle-class people, they all live in these government projects. They automatically looking for some help. You know this from the neighborhood. You make a door-to-door call. Sometimes I've seen in the run of a day where I've made as much as $600. All depends on how hard you're willing to work, if you're willing to go make these calls, just go from door to door. Some doors you might not make it, then next two houses you might make it. And you'd be surprised how those $37.50s run up.

Jack

I've never had a joint. I am a nickel-and-dime pimp who has been built up in the papers to be more than what I was. The only thing I've ever had was an apartment where I had three girls at one time. And that was a very short time. I mostly had one girl and that's it and I became strictly a pimp. I didn't write checks, I didn't rob. A lot of pimps are like burglars and they'll have an old lady, they'll send her to work only when they need bond money in the event they get busted trying to make a joint.

I've been called the vice lord of Harris County, I've been called the Lucky Luciano of South-Central Texas, and I've *never* had over three girls in my life. That really annoys me.

The only time I made good money is when a perfect square turned out and while I was with her she would make anywhere from $500 to $1,500 a week. We were only together for about a month because I was doing a jail sentence in Houston there for a while. I have had some girls who could make close to that for short periods, but most of them, it was between $300 and $450 a week, that's all.

Everybody thinks being a pimp is easy; it's not easy.

There is more headache in pimping and prostitution than you'd have if you were working on a space problem over at NASA. Probably you'd have less headaches at NASA because with the whores you've got their emotions to contend with.

And I've never had a dope fiend whore and never will, this is just regular whores I'm talking about. (Though they all eventually get on pills, on Nembutal or barbiturates of some kind, most of them that I've seen.)

I've had call girls and this is the best area. And I've had what I call "joint girls," and I'm one of the kind of pimps that over the years I've felt if a girl will be a good whore she will work in a joint. It's a test for me. If she's there working in one of those places when I come by, fine, and if she's not, fine. But I would, when I could, put a girl in a joint first. If I got a girl to start with, when I first got with her, that's my test.

In a joint you meet every kind of situation, perversion, and what have you, and if a girl's going to be a good whore, then before I put her on a phone or a trick book this is what I do. I don't know what others do.

A pimp in Texas, in my school of discipline, if you want to call it that, doesn't do *anything*. He just takes care of her in the sense of maintaining whatever needs to be maintained in the apartment, he makes sure that they have that. If you're working on the phone, he makes all the necessary business arrangements. He does make contacts, say, if you're on the phone, to different porters, hotel porters, key people that generally have use for that business.

Part of a pimp's job is protecting the girl from men who are giving her trouble. Did you ever have any?

Rumbles? Yes. This is what a pimp does, Texas-style. And I'm sure that this style does not just stay here. I know some pimps in California: same thing. Many times, over a period of ten, fifteen years, many times I've had this type situation.

One time in particular I got busted for. I was with Terry, she was in this hotel in Houston and it couldn't be worse. It was a skid-row area, but the hotel spot is not bad. Money-wise the spot is not bad, but the location of the hotel is terrible. And there was a rumble there and it happened to be a pimp.

He was just passing through and what he did is one I've played myself. A lot of times you'll go to a hotel or spot where you know you can make out with the gal, and you might even trick her and play the role of the square with the intent of stealing the whore. In other words, winning her affections, trying to get her to join up with you.

So Terry had the trouble with this dude in the room and she came back up to the room where I was at. I wasn't staying there but I was there that evening for a few hours. And she told me about it, so I go down there. I had my pistol and she had told me that it was a character, although she didn't know who it was, nor did I.

I go into this room and he's about half-juiced. And he opens the door. When he sees me—he's in his shorts, his undershirt or pants, and he had a bottle of beer I think in his hand—he tried to shut that door shut. Well, I took that pistol and, believe it or not, I just went like that, pointed it at him and pulled the trigger.

I don't know whether the bullet wasn't in the chamber or it didn't fire for some reason, but it did not fire. And after that, oh, man, about a week later, it shook the hell out of me. I actually got afraid, scared. I could have shot that guy.

Anyway, we tussled and I ended up whipping him over the head with the pistol and he took the bottle and he tried to hit me over the head—and may have. I don't remember. We all ended up in jail eventually because the manager—not the porter, the porter tried to cool it—he called the police while I'm up there cursing and carrying on and whipping on his head and all.

This is a trick of whores, you know. They'll rib you into these kind of positions. Many a pimp and many a character has been killed, shot and killed, because of some whore playing a trick like that.

It seems to me that some women thrive on that sort of thing. Some whores are nymphos, they say, I don't know. Some say they're frigid, some say they hate their father, I don't know. But some, I think, thrive on thrills, and they get some sort of bang out of getting their old man and another man feuding and they become the center.

So when I look back on this one particular case, I think maybe that's what she did. Anyway, we all went to jail and I got filed on. As I told you. there's a popular misconception—not that anyone is particularly interested, but it is a misconception—about pimps going and saying, "Say, buddy, you like my sister? Two pesos," or "How about spending the night with my old lady for a hundred." They don't do that. What they do is they make the contacts with porters and madams, people like that, they make contacts with people who set things up. They do not themselves call up the customers.

You may work a trick book. You may work that up yourself or you may buy it. In the trick book there are alphabetically listed different tricks, or customers, and these vary from $20 to $50, or there's one in Oklahoma that's $5,000. I know a girl who made a dude in Amarillo for $55,000 over one week's time. That man, the trick, is from Canyon, there's no sense mentioning his name, what matters is that tricks like that are rare.

You buy a trick book. You buy one in Chicago or you buy one in Dallas or you buy one in Hollywood. And these say who goes for what. Like the Hollywood trick book says that so and so goes for three girls, freaks, you know.

That's one of my kicks too. I'm sure there's a deep Oedipal complex involved, or some terrible side of me, but I became freaky in this sense myself. I just can't dig a kick with one girl.

In fact, that's what got me into trouble this last time. This girl made a pass at my woman, my old lady, which I don't mind, but the point was she didn't know it was my old lady. Secondly she wanted to get this stripper and they were going to some stag party and they would each make a hundred or so after the party. I know what that means and one thing led to another and I guess I got kind of brutal. I told her, "You want to play pimp, I'm gonna help you," and we got into a beef and that was it. I didn't want to let her go because of what would have happened when I let her go, but I couldn't keep her either. A real switch.

Bebop

I'm going to talk about dope, narcotics. Having been an addict I know something about it, one of the narcotics especially: heroin. Some people call it "the Big Boss: Horse." "Horse is Boss."

I've had several bands, been in several bands. I'm called a pretty good musician.

I'm a horn player. And I have known some of the greats. Some of them were junkies, they used dope. I've seen a lot of pictures, movies, and I've read a lot of books, but I haven't read one yet that actually told about dope like dope is. I don't know, I think that all of the people that are doing the research, they never put themselves in the position that a junkie or a dope user is usually in when he is using dope, so they really don't know.

I feel very strongly about this because I don't feel that dope was the cause of me coming to prison. I don't feel that dope has caused me to do anything that I didn't want to. I don't think that dope is the controlling factor.

I've heard it said that reefer, marijuana, makes people act different or peculiar. Well, so does whiskey. If a person is gonna steal something, if he's gonna rape somebody, if he's gonna take and beat somebody's brains out, he's gonna do that whether he has a reefer, horse, or whatever, because that's his nature. I don't feel that my nature is to kill a person, so I don't think I'd do it if I shot all the dope in the United States.

I've never seen people shoot dope and go completely crazy like they say. (I don't know about teenagers because I've never been around them.) I know heroin makes you soothed, it gives you a soothed feeling, you want to sit still and relax. I like to get high and listen to my record player, listen to music. There's no violence in it. I enjoy sitting listening to people talk and trying to analyze what they were saying.

I like to listen to music especially. That's my business and my joy. And if I follow one horn down one time through, maybe I'll listen to one record fifty times and listen to each individual instrument. I feel that dope, as you call it, enables me to center my mind, pinpoint it in other words. I could sit up and the whole band would be playing but I could hear any individual instrument that I wanted to hear, and hear it exact without all of the other distortion.

So I'm in complete disagreement with all of these doctors and all these reports.

These people don't know what they're talking about, I don't think.

I've met an awful lot of junkies. I know 'em from New York to Mexico, all through Mexico. I know fellows who steal much more and do all the crimes and they don't do nothing. Some of the worst people in the world, the sickest people I've seen in my life, were winos, drinking that fifteen-cent-a-quart wine. I've *never* seen junkies in that shape.

Most of the time a junkie will get up. If he has to go steal something to get that dope, he'll get up and do it. I've seen winos lay around so sick till they couldn't move. In bars in New York or by my home in Detroit, you can see them in every alley, sleeping out there. A junkie can't afford to sleep in the streets—you get chills when you get sick, and as the dope recedes your body and you need a shot you start having chills and your legs ache, your stomach turns over, you vomit, I don't know the technical term for vomit but you what we call puke your guts out. And your nose runs, your eyes run, and you can't afford to be out there, you would catch double pneumonia or something. A junkie is going to get him some money if there's any money. And there always is money.

I wouldn't sit here and say dope was detrimental to me. I will say this: Had I been a millionaire and had I accomplished in life what I wanted to—which is to become a good musician, I'm thirty-eight now and still have a few years left—but if I had had a million dollars and a place to be left alone with it, I would prefer shooting heroin and cocaine than drinking Scotch, Black and White or Black Label, what have you, or smoking reefers or any of it. I prefer it to any high there is because it treats me better. I don't wake up in the morning with a hangover, I don't wake up with all the nervousness, all the hassle.

I don't know. Were I saying this to some reformer or something I would talk a whole lot different, but I'm just talking, I'm speaking my mind . . .

On dope, when you don't have it, you don't sleep, you can't eat, you can't do much of anything, you're a nervous wreck. It won't let you lay still. It's just like butterflies or ants or something crawling around in your stomach. Your stomach turns over and over and over and a green type mucus comes out your nose, out of your mouth. Your eyes steadily run water. Well, you're just a nervous wreck, especially if you're hooked.

Sometimes you see guys beat their heads on the walls. Well, they're just weak lilies. If you pinch 'em they'd holler. You know, some people put on a show about anything. I've seen grown men out in the street actually hungry—I think little of a man like that. If he's grown and talking and he's asking for money to go and get him something to eat, why he's no man, he's *nothing*. And that's the way I feel about these fellas—they holler if you stick them with a pin, they hurt.

My wife used to go to bed for a cold and I never could understand it. Weakness in people. I don't know, my dad was so strong. I guess it was the way I was raised that caused me to feel this way. But I don't believe a person is supposed to show all of their emotions to everybody, you know.

Well, a junkie is a junkie. There is a true junkie, a person that just won't do without dope. I've known fellas that would die rather than give up dope, they'd rather be dead. It's a kick and it's pleasurable.

See, it's such a powerful thing until you never actually get completely rid of it.

You hear people make these statements about "I'm completely cured, I'm this, that, and the other about dope," but to me it is the greatest high in the world.

If it was just legal, like wine. I think wine is twice as detrimental. I'm no authority, I'm going only by what I have seen. My brother is an alcoholic, the only brother I have, and I've seen him go completely blind at the wheel of his car just because of alcohol. Completely blind, driving his car fifty miles an hour! Now I've never seen a junkie do anything like that in my life, and I've been around all types of junkies—women, men, and whatever.

I know a bunch of women prostitutes, whores I call them, that are junkies. But I've never known one yet that was a junkie when she started or that she started in the business because she wanted to get some dope. They say that. But I know women that will do anything to prove that they love you, I mean women that are old women, middle aged and on up, that have never used dope, there's nothing that they wouldn't do to prove to me right now . . . There's several women in this country that I could get in touch with and tell them to turn tricks all the way up here from California and bring me whatever they made and they would jump up there if I would promise them we'd be together after that. So it isn't the dope, I don't think, that makes those women get into prostitution.

Most of the girls that use dope that I've talked to have used it because it was a kick. And they find that they can turn tricks and center their minds on their man and believe that it's him. You see they make believe—as I said in the beginning—I'm able to pinpoint things much clearer, even when I smoked marijuana, it enables you to pinpoint.

When I'm playing, I stand on the bandstand, if I'm tired, I've traveled maybe 300 miles that day and I'm tired, it's the same thing over and over every night, you play the same tunes and things, so I'm just beat. It isn't a big town, there isn't a bunch of friends there, bunch a people you don't know is all, so you feel let down, you need something to give you the lift because you've got to put on a good show. And you know if you drink a bunch a that whiskey you're not going to be able to drive on that next 300 or 400 miles that same night. You'll likely have to leave right after the gig, which lets out about two, and drive on through today or maybe ten or eleven o'clock before you'll get a chance to rest. So I want something to keep me up, to keep me spry. So I get me a couple of benny tablets, I know I'll be woke then. Then I got to get something to lift me, not to get high.

Juice [alcohol] will make me sluggish, I'll go to sleep. I take me a little heroin, mix it with a little cocaine, and it's *such* a lift.

When I hear people—get around reformers, whatever—talking that talk: "That dope really brought me down to this and it brought me down to that," well, then, I think they're just blaming their weaknesses on something else, they're just passing the buck . . .

Jack: "The criminal code is bullshit . . ."

To me the criminal code is bullshit. The very guys that promulgate it are the ones that violate it. If you're tough enough, if you're bad enough, whatever the individual does then is right, and that includes snitching. That's the biggest bunch of shit.

You ask the old-timers has the joint changed for ratting and snitching? Almost every one of them says, "Yes, you bet, boy, really changed." But this code is so much shit for the young ones, it just doesn't exist.

It exists to this extent: might makes right. In the convict context. I like to say I'm not a snitch. I probably have done some snitching, not to my knowledge directly, but I'm sure in the code it would be considered that. No one has ever come to the joint with me, I've always come alone, but you'll notice down here they always have a "fall partner" [partner convicted at the same time]. Some people must be doing some talking if they're always getting convicted together. I don't know, I've never quite understood that, but it occurs.

Now the way the Rangers carry on with you—I've had dealings with them twice, not for prostitution but other areas, robbery—the way they carry on with you you'd probably say your mother is a no good so-and-so and you boys just put her in jail. They are rather strong in their methods.

My first experience with the Rangers was when I was young, real young, I was seventeen, right before I went in the navy. It was in Houston. I used to box then, amateur fights, and I had won quite a few. We had gone out to Playland Park, it's an amusement park, and we got into a few cars. There were four other guys and three of them I knew through the fighting and they were characters.

So we all go to jail. This one guy who was a sergeant in the sheriff's department and two Rangers, they carried me out and took me to a place they called the Windmill. I was handcuffed, I was by myself then and I didn't know where the other guys were and it was at night, they were going to put me over this kind of wall they have there. They take a chain with a weight on it and put it over the wall and it pulls you off the ground. I had heard about this and I was scared to death of it. I don't care who knows that, I was frightened. I'm talking about *afraid*! I'm not talking about that big tough bullshit. I'm telling you, I was afraid. I was young then.

From *In the Life* | 91

Instead of doing that, they just went through all the motions of doing it. But this one guy, this sergeant—I say sergeant, I don't know that he was, but he acted like one—he had a blackjack in his hand and he kept hitting it into his palm. Instead of putting the weight over, what he did was he hit me up the side of the head with the blackjack. And I fell down, it knocked me down. And the Rangers started kicking me. I don't know if you've ever had boots in your butt or stomach or in your nuts, but *man*! It's very painful, I was still chained, and as I say I was extremely frightened.

But that's not all they did. A very good friend of mine, he's doing life now, they put a wire to the battery of a car and they put the other wire to his testicles.

How long did they have you there?

It seemed to me like forever, but I guess it was a couple of hours.

Did they bring you [make you say what they wanted you to say]?

Oh, yes, I admitted stealing it. You know: "Yes, sir!"

Sam told me, "I'm always a half-nut and I always used to say I can't be brought, but they brought me."

There isn't anybody that can't be brought, and that's what I mean about the inmate code: the bravado, the facade, call it what you want. It's so much shit.

The only thing I do say is that we're put in prison for violating laws, they are behind the shield and can do the very same things we are behind bars for. To criminals they can. I know they're not going to go up to *you* and hit you over the head or put a wire to your testicles, you know they just won't do it, but to people like *me* they will, to people in my element.

Richie: "You should use some finesse..."

I've been a pimp, drug addict, dope peddler, professional crap hustler. I turned out as a crap hustler, card hustler, drag games or bunko games as they are commonly known. I served my apprenticeship as a card mechanic; I was in the Federal penitentiary and practiced diligently for ten or twelve hours a day for about two years. I'm not as much a perfectionist with cards as I am with craps.

I specialize in manipulating legitimate craps, legitimate dice.

I do—and this is a divergence with what I just said—work with what they call a "bust-out" mob. Craps in conventions, picnics, things like that. There you work eight- or ten-handed. Oftentimes you have eight or ten men and they're within the group and all are capable of shifting. And in situations like that, you're working with "tops" or "bust-out craps."

Those are spotted, ace, trey, five, for example. A crap has ace, deuce, trey, four, five, and six on each crap. But on bust-out, there's no possible way to get a seven, so you just pass. You *can* crap, but you can pass anyway. You just keep on passing.

Don't people notice this?

That's where the professionalism comes in. When you switch the dice, there are about five basic moves, and in the event they should spill or there is any kind of mistake on your part the rest of the mob is there to cover up for you and not let the suckers get to you.

In terms of working with legitimate craps, that's where I depend on my skill against other gamblers. My skills to manipulate the craps. The other hustler knows that you may be in that situation, it's an understood thing, and it's a question there of who is the best, who had the most skill.

I should add that the fact that I turned out at a very young age was a great advantage. No one ever suspected I knew as much as I knew. I used to shortchange a lot. That was kind of a daily must because I could go out and make—without too much effort—$40 or $50 a day. There's a minimum of risk and it's a misdemeanor in the states I worked anyway, so there was really no risk at all. I usually did that during the day and gambled at night.

You have to have a place where they have a cashier. There are two systems, one is called "working forwards," and the other "working backwards." Probably what is most common is working with a $1 bill and a $20 bill.

A man will come in and pay with a $20 bill and when he receives his change, he'll go to put it back in his pocket and he finds that he has a one and he say, "Gee, you know I had a one all the time. I didn't mean to cash the twenty. Can you use some of this change?" And so he plops out the ten. "Can you give me a $10 bill for this change?" he says.

So they give him a $10 bill. He puts it in with the other money and counts down $9 and hands it to the cashier. Naturally the cashier will recount it before he puts it in the till and he looks at you and says, "You only have $9 here."

You say, "I'm sorry. Let's see: you have got nine and one more is $10. Here, take the $11 and give me my $20 back." You've got their ten in your pocket, right?

That may be a little crude. There are variations that depend on the individual, how he works.

From *In the Life*

Sometimes I've worked with other guys. Some of them use no finesse at all. I think, doing that sort of thing, you should use some finesse.

Bob: "I worked as a shill . . ."

I worked for a while as a shill at the Bowler Club. A shill is a man who works for the house. He works eight hours a day. You gather around a table and there'll be six—if the table's empty—six or seven shills will gather around. And each bets the same, they bet a dollar at a time, all on the pass line. If they pass, they pick up their dollar, leave the one down there; if they lose, they put down another dollar. The reason they all bet the same is they all get the same amount of money to start and that way the table boss can look around and make sure nobody's making any money off the house because they've each got the same amount of money in front of them.

I worked as a shill for about four months and I finally got a job after going through a short training period as a dealer on a regular draw poker table. At our poker table there were eight seats. The dealer don't play, all he does is deal, make change, cut the pot—normally 10 percent. But of the eight seats, only three are open. The five other seats are filled by house men. And most people don't realize this. The house men have certain rules they must play by. The house man can't open on draw poker if he's got anything less than two pair. If one house man opens and if I haven't got two pair beat and I'm working for the house, then I can't call. In other words, the only time I can call is if I have something better than two pair. And we never draw to a straight and we never draw to a flush. I've got to have three of a kind or two pair of face cards in order to call the bet. And if I call, the next house man in turn has to have something better than that. In other words, if he has had one house man open and another call, the third one has to have three of a kind in the face cards in order to call that bet, otherwise he drops. So you can probably see how much chance a sucker's got if he's playing it.

If the sucker opens, hardly anyone will call. If a sucker opens, the house has to have better than two pair to call. In other words, he's got to have at least three of a kind even to call the sucker's bet. We call *suckers* the three men sitting down there. The house figures they take an average of $200 an hour out of the poker game. Since they're only paying the five shills sitting there a dollar or two an hour, they're making pretty good money.

When I worked there, which was a few years ago now, you made $22.50 a shift for dealing. That's an eight-hour shift with work forty minutes and off twenty every hour. Which amounted to $132.50 a week on a six-day week. Now there are ways to subsidize your income down there which we were taught. Everybody wears French cuffs and the shirts are supplied by the house. They give you one new shirt each week because you wear the bottoms of your cuffs out on the green top of the table doing the dealing and dragging your cutter's percentage in. But the French cuffs are fake French cuffs, they're sewed on so there's no place you can stick anything in the cuffs.

But at novelty stores there they sell what they call "snap-backs." They advertise these things and sell them in those stores. A snap-back is nothing more than an alligator clamp–type affair on a long rubber band that you pin one end of the rubber band underneath the armpit of your shirt and the alligator band comes down to your watchband. There's a little unit that you put on your watchband and hook this little alligator clamp on. The alligator clamp is open and it's got a device like a mousetrap in it; when you touch that with a chip the clamp will automatically close and will loosen itself in the watchband and in turn the rubber band will snap it right back up under your arm again.

Chips in Las Vegas are as negotiable as green money. You can take them into any club and cash them in for money, for $5 or $10 or whatever it is. So all you've got to do is put a chip in the end of your fingers, turn your hand down like you're trying to touch your wrist, and you can comshaw—or steal—comshaw is a much better word—a $25 chip from a table.

They also got what they call false trousers. They call them "falsies" for short, but not falsies like you wear in a brassiere. They're a unit made in Las Vegas and they fit under your trousers, under the belt. The top part of them is made of metal and they're about six inches long. You strap them around you like a money belt. Only they're a sack about fifteen inches long that goes down your pants leg. The top of the unit is held open a quarter of an inch. The metal is stiff for that quarter inch, but it's got joints in it which are flexible and concur with your waist. When you're standing at a table or when you're getting up from a table, if you palm a chip and stand up and rub your trouser top, rub your hand across your belt like you were checking your belt, the chip will automatically go into this open slot, which is held open by the metal, drop down into the sack in your leg. And that's the way you can steal some more from the club. Usually, if you're careful, you can make anywhere from $20 to $50 a day with a few chips. At night or whenever it is you're off, you cash them in at a club.

I got caught and was fired. There's no penalty for it. They don't take you to court for stealing, they just fire you and put out what they call a blacklist, and that blacklist is sent out every month to every club in Nevada. Come hell or high water, if you get on it once you won't get a job there again. Of course, if you figure the price is worth it you do it anyway. I know people there that's gotten away with it for years and never been caught.

There are other devices, but those are the only two I'm familiar with because they are the only two that I tried, but they do work and they are very effective.

I'll tell you about a little scheme that was, to my knowledge, used to defraud one of the big hotels in Las Vegas out of some money on a false arrest suit.

The way it all started was two gentlemen got together—we'll call them Number One and Number Two for clarity. Number Two goes to the bank in Los Angeles and opens a checking account for $10,000 there in the name of Number One. After opening this checking account, Number One goes to this hotel in Las Vegas and registers in his own name and goes to the cashier's window and requests that his checking account be approved so he can cash checks in Las Vegas.

The setup there was they fill out a card on you. You don't fill it out yourself—they fill it out with information on your bank, the amount of money you have in your account, how much you want to cash, and how many checks you want to cash, things like that.

Number One man in Vegas, he tells them that he would like to cash checks for no more than $500 each and no more than ten checks in the time he's going to be there. That's $5,000. He goes on up to his room and the hotel checks on his account and finds out he's clear for that amount of money and approves his checking account. Next morning, Number One comes downstairs with a checkbook.

This checkbook has been made out by Number Two in Los Angeles—only not every check. The first check is left blank, the second check is filled out, the third check is left blank, the fourth check is filled out, etc., all the way through the book. They know the dates they're going to cash the checks and that's all filled in prior to coming to Las Vegas. The only thing left blank is the "Pay to" line, that's because all the hotels in Las Vegas use a stamp rather than making you write in on the "Pay to" line.

Number One takes this checkbook to the cashier's window on that second morning and requests to cash a check. They ask him to fill out a check. He takes out his checkbook in front of the man and when he

96 | Folklore Matters

comes to "Pay to" he asks the man, "Who do I make it out to?" They tell him to leave it blank, they have a stamp for it. He continues filling out the rest of the check with the amount—$500—the date, and he signs his name and he picks up the $500. *But* instead of tearing out the check he's just filled out, he takes out Number Two's check, he tears that one out—remember, that one has been filled out prior to this by Number Two in Los Angeles—and hands that one to the cashier. The cashier will stamp his check in the "Pay to" column and stamp the back of the check and give him his $500. Which he, in turn, either keeps with him or sends back to the man still in Los Angeles.

In the meantime, in the first day, the man in Los Angeles goes to his bank and closes out his checking account, he takes out the $10,000. Then he leaves the city, going to some predesignated spot. But the man in Las Vegas continues cashing a check every morning for $500 until the first check bounces from Los Angeles.

When this check bounces in Los Angeles, the bank in Los Angeles will automatically phone the hotel in Las Vegas to tell them they have a check for $500 in a certain name drawn on an account closed. That used to take approximately nine days—it's probably somewhat less now that they're computerized. The man in Las Vegas, Number One, on the eighth day gets rid of his checkbook and all evidence of a checkbook. He tears it up, flushes it down the commode, or whatever he wants to do to get rid of it. Even the pen he writes with he gets rid of. So they can't identify a pen. The hotel will come and arrest him for cashing checks on an account that's been closed. They figure that he must have flown back to Los Angeles and pulled the money out. It's only a short flight from Las Vegas.

The man that's arrested makes no statement. He does not deny it, he does not admit it, he makes no statement of any kind. He submits to arrest and goes to jail. He gets himself a lawyer. Usually, of course, the lawyer has been arranged beforehand. Within fifteen days, normally, in Las Vegas, they'll take you to court. They're not slow about that whatsoever.

In court they try the man for cashing checks on an account that's closed, which is fraud, or robbery, stealing, whatever you want to call it. And he pleads not guilty. The evidence they have is the checks, plus the cashier's positive identification that he watched the man write out the check. In examination and cross-examination it is brought out that the cashier witnessed the man writing out the check, watched the man tear the check out of the book, hand the check to him, that he stamped it and he will identify the check by his initials and stamp on the back. The defense calls a handwriting expert. They take the man's driver's license out of his wallet, his registration card from the hotel, and check the handwriting: they're not even similar. With it being proved that the checks weren't made out by this man they've got no evidence. The only thing they have is the man's statement that he witnessed Number One making out the checks and that has to be a mistaken identity, somebody that looked like you, because then it's his word against yours. The evidence is thrown out of court, and they will throw the case out too for nonsufficient evidence.

At which time the lawyer for the defense jumps and says he does not want the case thrown out for nonsufficient evidence, he wants an acquittal. That's legal. So the court will have to acquit the man because of insufficient evidence.

The lawyer then sues the hotel for false arrest.

I think you'll find that 99 percent of the people in Las Vegas, the hotels and gambling houses, they will settle out of court. This particular scheme worked for about $20,000 that time. That's in addition to the $5,000 for the checks.

What if the clerk asks for sufficient identification and checks the signature?

Ah. I think if you'll ever cash a check in Las Vegas, after you get the check card made out and approved, you'll find that the formality of asking for additional information, especially if you are registered in the hotel as a guest, is something they consider embarrassing and they don't do it. For a one-stop item they might. But I think you'll find that at your better hotels, where you check in and pay when you leave, that if they see you come up there and your account is approved and you're living at the hotel, there really is no need for any more identification. Because they've got you right there. They won't ask you for any more identification. And to forestall that, if necessary a duplicate set of identification with the signatures of the man still in Los Angeles could be brought along and that could cover any such problem.

But as far as I know they never asked the people involved in this deal for any identification, and it worked fine.

Rice: "I've seen them eat plumb up by the dogs . . ."

We had a clown named Slew Davis, he used to clown in the rodeo. He was on the Retrieve the night Ernest Jones cut Redwine's head off. They had an exceptionally good pudding, which is unusual in the penitentiary, we didn't have sweets much in those days. Slew Davis was sitting pretty close and he wanted that pudding. But, he said, he just couldn't fade [handle] it looking at that head. Them eyes was blinking, he said. He wanted to eat that pudding, but he finally had to leave it go.

Why did this happen?

Ernest and Redwine had had a beef. And they fought in the building. Redwine made the mistake of telling Ernest, "Don't come back in the building. If you do, I'm gonna kill you." Ernest worked in the dining room, he was flunkey there. So when he came out there he got old Bill Garrett to sharpen a cane knife. They use them to cut bread in there. Jack Bronson took it back there and got Bill Garrett, a butcher, to sharpen it. And he gave it to Ernest. Ernest went out there and told Redwine, "Redwine, let's talk this over. Hell, I've got to come back in that building, man, I live in there."

And Redwine said, "You come back in that building I'm goddamned sure going to kill you."

And so Ernest just stepped back and took that cane knife and whoosh, cut his head off. The head just bounced over the table and Redwine had a Lucky Strike cigarette standing just like that, it never did leave his finger, just kept burning. His body never did move.

And Slew Davis, he said, "I wanted that pudding, goddamnit, but I couldn't fade it."

What happened to Ernest?

Nothing. That gave him five years to run CC [concurrent] with the five he already had. That was in 1948. Redwine already had a pretty bad reputation, you see.

He and I had just got shot off a roof on the Eastham. We cut a hole through the roof and was up there. There was a boss up there that was a dead shot with a rifle—I always swore I'd never give him a shot at me—name of Gus Morgan, and I didn't know he was up there. He was up on the high part and we were on the low part with the light shining down on us.

We weren't really intending leaving then, but I was showing Redwine how best to knock out the lights when we do leave. Redwine must have saw his hat or something because he started scuttling for that hole. And Gus Morgan shot. He shot right in front of him, right in front of his stomach, and punctured his stomach with all them rocks and everything from the rock and tar roof.

Goddamn, I thought they done stopped up the hole with him. I looked at the hole and there was Redwine laying there and I jumped all around. Course Gus Morgan kept shooting. I told him afterwards I didn't believe he was shooting to kill me 'cause I knew he's a better shot than that. He'd always shoot just where I'd been. Every time. Finally I saw the hole was open and I dove in it. Old Redwine, he was wounded pretty bad. Rocks done went into the hollow of his stomach because of that lead from the .30-30. And he already had some pretty bad escape records against him and everything. So he's paid for it. Back in those days two or three killings now and then didn't amount to anything. They didn't hardly get any time over it.

Except Clay Whittles. Ankles we'd call him. He got the electric chair for killing old Kelly on the Eastham. Now he didn't have no business killing Kelly. I don't believe Clay would have had the guts to kill him if he'd been sober, but he was drunk.

I was a witness to the killing and everything. But I walked away from there to keep from being a witness. We just had a killing a few days before that and the guy had killed him on my bed. I told 'em I never went back to my bed. Told the district attorney and everything. So when this killing occurred I walked on away.

I knew Ankles was drunk, but I really didn't think he had the courage to kill Kelly. There was a pistol sent in by old Tom Norris sometime before, is what it was about. Any time Ankles got drunk he would jump Kelly out about that. Kelly didn't run in no clique or anything, he was just a man by himself.

When he walked up behind Kelly, we was just fixing to go out to go to work. I was sitting up in the barber chair. A boy came up and started playing with me. I said, "Look out, man, old Ankles is fixing to kill old Kelly." I really didn't think he'd kill him because he stood up behind him with that knife a long time. Kelly wasn't paying him no attention, he was just there waiting for the door to open. He finally shoved the knife on in, right in his spleen. Kelly looked around, he didn't say anything, he just looked around right quick and stepped in the corner. By this time the boss throwed a lever on the door and Kelly jerked the door open, and went on out. He died in a few minutes.

Ankles had already done a lot of broadcasting in the building.

And just before that, Ankles and I had had a little fight in there. What it was, I had lined some of them up and I was mad because they had run over [beat up] a boy. Him and a couple of other boys. They'd run over another boy in the building and I thought they just done it because he was some old rum [powerless]. I told him, "You'd better not be going down this alley"—I was half drunk myself—"unless you fight me."

They said, "All right, we'll fight you."

I said, "You all fight me one at a time." They said, "Yeah."

So I said, "All right. Come on back. I'll start fighting Ankles first."

While I'm fighting Ankles, somebody creeps in, cops a sneak on me, and knocks me out.

So Ankles, I figured, didn't have the courage to come right out with anything.

So when he killed Kelly we went on out to work. We just sharpened up a cane knife and figured when we get in, we'll just kill old Ankles. He had no business killing Kelly, so we're just going to administer justice ourselves because it really was a killing that wasn't called for.

They had him locked up by the time we got back and they wound up giving him the electric chair.

Of course I wasn't a witness nowhere on the case. They called me up and asked me did I know anything about the killing, and naturally I told them no, I didn't even see it, or I wasn't nowhere around there. They made me say that under oath before a notary public. And therefore Ankles couldn't use me for a witness. I wouldn't be a witness for him, but I wouldn't have been a witness against him either. That's the sort of thing we'd settle ourselves back in those days.

About that gun. We escaped, Gene Paul Norris come and took us off the Ferguson Farm. And Tom Norris had sent the pistol back to a truck driver. This truck driver had sold it to Ankles and a couple of boys. They had showed me the pistol when I came in right after they brought me back off of escape. They captured me pretty quick after escape. I told them I don't want nothing to do with it. I said, "When we want to show a pistol in the building, if we don't use it right then you'd better get away from it. I don't want anything more to do with it." And that's what happened. We wound up fucking around and getting that boy killed. And nobody ever used the pistol either.

Since 1934, I've been on a lot of escapes. I escaped in 1936 off the Darrington. I escaped in 1937 off the Eastham by grabbing a guard. In those days times were different. It was tough then. You'd either escape or get killed in the penitentiary. They put you on the spot [set you up to be killed] in the penitentiary in those days. When you done anything to put any heat on the state of Texas, why you're sure to be put on the spot when you're brought back. So it's either shoot your best stick and get away, or die out in the field. I've seen a lot of men killed in the building, I've seen men killed in the field.

Back in the early thirties the toughest farm was the Retrieve. Warden there was I. K. Kelly, assistant warden was named Benjie Tower. It was brutality plus on that farm then. You see guys at the Walls with their left hand cut off where they'd cut them off with a cane knife or a hoe or something like that, just to get off that farm, get out of the work. They'd cut their feet, cut their heel string [Achilles tendon]. They wasn't cutting heel strings so bad then, they was cutting their feet plumb off, and cutting their hands plumb off. That's just how bad it was.

I've seen them sit down twenty and twenty-five at a time and cut their heel strings. Course at that time they thought cutting that heel tendon was a pretty bad thing, they thought they couldn't walk or anything. But hell, I've seen 'em cut their heel strings, cut both of them, and in less than thirty days they'd be carrying a row [working in the fields] out there. Just depended on how scared they'd make them. They put a man like Rob Parker—this was a real killer—down here and put him to carrying them and they'd carry that row.

The penitentiary changed a lot from what it used to be. This place used to be wide open. You take a warden on a unit like the Ramsey, he was God. He butchered his own meat and he done as he pleased. If a man got killed, he probably wouldn't notify the Walls or anything for two or three months unless they asked about him. There wasn't no board or anything then. It's just a hell of a lot different now. Clyde Barrow and Bonnie Parker was well thought of down here, you know, because they was criminals. I knew Clyde, I knew Bonnie. That break they had off the Eastham was just before I got there, but I left right after that. That was when Clyde came down after Raymond Hamilton and Joe Palmer.

Clyde had a BAR [Browning Automatic Rifle] sawed off. He drove down this Calhoun Ferry Road when they was clearing that land there. They had already smuggled two .45s in to Joe Palmer and Raymond Hamilton. When he heard the axes falling on these trees where they was clearing land, he just stepped out of his coupe—he knew the squads were at work—and started shooting through the treetops with this BAR. That was the signal for Raymond and Joe that everything was ready, so they came out with their .45s and started shooting. That's when they killed Major Crowlson, one of the guards carrying them. Raymond and Joe and Hilton Bybee all ran, got in the car, and they drove them right on through. Went right into Dallas. Then old Baldy Wallis started hauling them around on various deals. They went on up the country and were squabbling all the time. Old Bybee told me that. We went over the same territory right after that when we escaped. He's telling me they're squabbling all the time. Never making any money or anything. They finally robbed a little old bank up there and split up. Bybee came down and got busted in Amarillo.

I believe about the toughest man I ever saw down here was old Buddy Barret. I guess he was about half crazy. He's in Rusk [State Hospital]; he finally went crazy.

They brought him down from Amarillo along about 1938 or 1939 and put him in the south building. That was on Eastham Farm, which at that time was for incorrigibles. They put Buddy in there. And I believe he is about the toughest damn man I have ever seen. I've seen him whip five or six convicts in there, and still go right out.

I've seen convicts that will fight other convicts, but still go out and take anything from a guard, convicts that will take stuff off of a guard, but still wouldn't take anything off of a convict. Buddy wasn't scared of nobody. Guns or anything.

He was on the lead row [first worker in a squad] and I was on the push row [second worker in the squad] for three or four years down at the south building. Buddy had those epileptic fits. He'd been an amateur fighter sometime or the other, and he had a fever when he was in Kansas City. Maybe it was Chicago. Where they have those Golden Glove fights. And that's when Buddy had that fever, and it made him start having epileptic fits. I don't know what brought them on.

One time a highway patrolman captured me over there close to Round Rock. We'd escaped out of the building down on Eastham and they asked me if I knew Buddy Barret. He's from that area up there, around Amarillo. I told them, "Yeah."

And he asked me, "What makes him have those fits?"

And I remembered Buddy breaking his arm one time, and right after he broke it he had two or three of those epileptic fits. The only thing I could think of was a shock, you know, so I told him, "Well, shock, I guess."

He said, "Hell, I don't know anything that'd ever shock him." Told me he's the toughest man they ever saw up there. I believe he's the toughest man I've ever seen in the penitentiary, and I've been with some tough ones.

Hilton Bybee was about one of the coldest-blooded men I've ever run with. He's the one Clyde Barrow and Bonnie Parker come down here and got in 1934. He left with Joe Palmer and Raymond Hamilton. Right after that, they captured Bybee and brought him back. We happened to be on the same plow squad on Eastham. The high rider had an excuse to bring a man from the hoe squad over to the plow squad, and when he was taking this other man from the plow squad to bring him back to the hoe squad it got him out of our sight for a few minutes. I grabbed this guard. He wasn't very alert, he was what you call a dead head, he's a dead head for the plow squad, he carried a shotgun and a pistol. I grabbed him and held him while Bybee took his shotgun.

Bybee started to kill him and I told him, "Man, don't kill him. We don't want that much heat on us." But Bybee, he wanted to kill him. He's really a cold-blooded killer. And on all our plays after that I believe he's about the cold-bloodest man I have ever been with as far as shooting a man down. He would explain to him what he wanted, but if a man didn't comply he would shoot him down in cold blood. It happened in Oklahoma, it happened in Missouri, it happened in Iowa, and it happened in Arkansas.

He's dead now. He got killed in that last gunfight we had there in Monticello, Arkansas. We just robbed a bank there and we'd come back. We'd cased another bank and one of the boys with us had got picked up. We'd told him to go and take a car out for us. He's supposed to follow us, but he picked up the sheriff, which he shouldn't have done, and we had to turn around and take him away from the sheriff. Then we got in a little gunfight there and got on away.

But we come back. Since we already spent the money casing this bank we was going to go ahead and rob it. We run into the same posse, it was out a week before us, and that's where Bybee got killed. Old Charley Frazer, I guess he's about one of the coolest men. I believe Harry Roberts is as cool as Charley Frazer. Charley Frazer's escaped from Louisiana penitentiary and killed a captain and a guard down there, and they brought him down here. Then they released him to Louisiana—they figured they'd electrocute him. I believe he is the coolest man in a gunfight outside of Harry Roberts.

Harry Roberts was with us in Arkansas. He killed a deputy sheriff in Breckenridge when the sheriff arrested Hilton Bybee. Harry went down to stop him at the bottom of the stairs. This guy was a crack pistol shot, he was champion of that area. And he was evidently trying to shoot Harry's gun from his hand or something, 'cause he shot Harry through his coat sleeve and under his coat sleeve and through his right knee. But Harry shot him between the eyes. And so, that's why I say he's awful cool in a gunfight. We had several gunfights and little escapades after we escaped from down here.

Did you specialize in banks?

No. Anything where there's money. Back in those days it was just wildcat hijacking. The only thing I found that'd really pay off would be bottling works. If they got four trucks, you know they've got as much as

$400. If four trucks has come in, you can figure $100 to the truck. We specialized in those bottling plants mostly. Banks weren't much good then, you couldn't get over $5,000 or $6,000 out of a bank back in those days. 1936 or '37. Of course they were a lot easier to rob—except in Texas. Texas still had that $5,000 reward for dead bank bandits then. Not live ones, dead ones. Maybe it's still in effect.

We had a building tender on the Retrieve at one time, Lee Smith, an ex–Texas Ranger. What he was sent down here for, he had sent some Mexicans into a bank, and when they're coming out, he killed them, you see? Figuring he'd get the $5,000 reward. And they wound up giving him life in the penitentiary.

Up until recent years they wouldn't dare put a man who had ever been a convict guard in some other penitentiary, like Arkansas, in a line with these convicts. They'd kill him before he'd pass the fourth bunk. I can remember the time on that Eastham over there, on Number One, which was the incorrigible farm, that any man that walked in that door, if he'd been any kind of a convict guard or a snitch ever and anybody knew it—and somebody in there would, because it was all second- and third-timers in there—he wouldn't get past the fourth or fifth bunk. There'd be three or four knives stuck in him.

I've seen killings in that Eastham building and 300 men could go by that district attorney and the warden one at a time and not a man would know anything about it. It may have taken the guy fifteen or twenty minutes to kill the other one and not a man would know anything about it. That's how close they were at one time.

That's all over with now. For one thing, the overtime [good behavior time] changed it. They had a different commutation law then. And the segregation program [for first offenders].

A young guy comes in the Walls now, they don't indoctrinate him like they used to. An eighteen-year-old boy used to come in the Walls and them old heads would get ahold of him and they'd teach him what to do and what not to do. He'd go on down to the farm and finish his time in the penitentiary under that impression. They'd teach those youngsters to kill all the snitches and everything like that.

What other things would they teach him?

Whatever they could, according to how weak he was or how strong he was.

You know, for my first twelve or fifteen years in here, all I ever thought of was escape. And any man that thought anything else I didn't even want to talk to him. As far as homosexuality and stuff like that is

From *In the Life* | 105

concerned, I wasn't even interested in it. I thought a man that would interest himself in that, I'd think, "Hell, this guy he's institutionalized or something." If a man would order a feather pillow from home—he used to could order stuff like that—I'd think, "Goddamn, he just wants to stay in the rest of his life or something." I never walked out the door expecting to come back that night my first fifteen years down here.

There was a lot more of the homosexuality then. Now the officials let you know you can come to them and get some kind of help. In those days you couldn't. If a boy was lined up on and eighteen or twenty men lined up and fucked him and he goes out there and tells that warden, "There's twenty of them lined . . ." He says, "Hell, there's three hundred of them trying to fuck me every damned day! Get on out of my office!" That's the kind of reception you got, see? But nowadays a boy knows he don't have to do anything like that unless he wants to. You don't see much of it now.

In those days you associated in certain cliques. The hijackers and bank robbers and characters, they'd stay in one bunch, the others would stay in their bunch. They didn't associate with one another at all. That's changed to a certain extent. You never know now. You're liable to be talking to a good friend of yours, you know him and you know he's a hijacker and a character, maybe a safe burglar, but he may have a good friend of his that's sleeping right beside him who's a rape fiend. That's something that used to be strictly out, a rape fiend was never any good down here. Nobody would associate with a rape fiend. Hijackers and bank robbers and first-class safe burglars, they were the elite in the penitentiary, they were the characters. The lowest were the rape fiends, nobody wanted to associate with a rape fiend.

Why do you think that changed?

I don't know, to tell you the truth, I just don't know. It's just a matter of putting everybody on an equal basis around here. I don't know how it came about. Mr. Ellis changed it some way when he took this penitentiary over. He changed so damn many things. I didn't think he could do it, but he changed this penitentiary just opposite to what it was. O. B. Ellis. It didn't take him long. Four or five years it began changing. He took over in '48 and it had changed pretty much by '52. Dr. Beto's the same way. Before them we didn't have educated men in here running this penitentiary. We had Lee Simmons.

I believe he was about the most cold-blooded general manager they've ever had down here. They say he was a good general manager and he might have been, but from the convicts' point of view he wasn't. He had the penitentiary on a paying basis, not only self-sustaining but paying.

That's unheard of for a penitentiary. He done it with pure blood. Many a convict lost his life and many a convict cut his hand or foot off under Lee Simmons. 'Cause he was really bloodthirsty. It's common talk among the convicts that he'd tell a guard—see, there'd been a lot of escapes till then—that when a man escapes you go after him and if you don't bring back blood instead of the convict, you're fired. He was really tough.

He sanctioned all. They used to put a lot of people on the spot down here, convicts. I do know that they used to kill a convict on each farm along in the spring and along in the fall. In the field or in the building. Maybe get the building tenders to kill him or shoot him down in the field. That'd tighten the field up, which it will, you know. Bunch of men get to talking—they don't want to be bothered or nothing, so they'll go ahead and work hard.

There were more gangs in the prison in those days. A lot of times if there weren't enough real men on the farm, these kid gangs would form. They can be vicious, these youngsters. A new man will come in, they'll take his shoes and belt away from him and stuff like that. Just flaunt it in front of him and the guy can't do nothing with everybody wearing a big knife. I was always protesting anything like that. Generally on the farms that I was on there was always enough men to stop that kind of stuff because we didn't appreciate it. That just brought heat on the farm. All we had in mind was escaping. We didn't believe in none of those gangs at all.

How many times did you attempt escape?

Tell you the truth, I don't know.

How many did you make?

Three or four times for long periods.

Did you ever get caught by the dogs?

Oh, yeah. But them dogs don't bother me none. I just catch the dogs. One night there was five packs caught up with me. That's about fourteen or fifteen dogs. We'd gone out a window. There was four of us—me and this Ernest Jones that killed old Redwine, Jack Bronson and Carl Hudson. They kept telling me, "You're going back toward camp, you're going back toward camp." When we went out that window they was shooting at us from every angle. It was real dark and you couldn't see anything. I always heard the thick bark and moss on a tree is always on the north side, so I told them, "No, man. Feel of this tree. You know we're going north." And we'd feel of the tree—you couldn't see a tree, you had to feel it. We kept going and along about midnight the first pack of dogs got on us. We split then, Bronson and Jones went one way and Hudson and I went the other way. First thing I know, we're running in an open field and no trees

From *In the Life* | 107

there to get up on, and I see two dogs running on each side of me. I told Hudson, "Hell, man, you might as well quit. The dogs done passed me."

They were real good bloodhounds. They weren't vicious. So we let that go along for a while and we walked along. The dogs just thought we was dog boys, I guess. I got to thinking about dog boys, how they train dogs. They can't make one-man dogs out of them, it's got to be dogs that any dog boy can handle. So pretty soon we get another pack behind us. They're real fresh, we can tell from the way they bark. And a pretty big pack, and there wasn't no trees to get up then either. There was just one little old sapling and I tried to climb up it. Old Hudson grabbed me by the belt and dragged me down. He wanted me to stay there with him. Finally the dogs caught up with us and we just squatted down. Made the mistake of putting my hand out to pet them. You don't want to do that ever, 'cause them dogs will damn sure eat you up, that's what they're trained to do. I snapped then, they're used to that dog boy fighting them with his hand and a switch. So I just put my hand between my legs. Then they just come in to be petted. Five packs caught us that way that night and we still got away the next morning. We had every dog. We had to lift them over barb-wire fences. The dogs can't get through and if you go ahead they'll start howling and if they do finally find an opening to come through he'll pick up your trail and bark on it again. That noise was tearing me up, I couldn't stand it, so I just picked them up and threw them over the fence every time. We had fourteen or fifteen dogs.

You don't ever want to try to kill a dog. If you do kill one, them other dogs will go crazy. They'll eat you up. They'll eat the dog up you're trying to kill. So I know better than that. I tried that once before. So we just decided we'd keep them with us. They won't tear you up if they catch you by yourself and you put your hands between your legs. Don't act scared or anything. But if you ever stick your hand out, one dog'll see the other one get a bite and he's going to get a bite. First thing you know they'll tear you all to pieces. I've seen men with their nuts and everything eat up. All this leg muscle torn out. I've seen them eat plumb up by the dogs.

Ray: "The hole. Oh, the hole"

The camps at Angola [Louisiana state prison farm] are separated and of course they're completely segregated, black from white. They also segregate the first-timers from the second-, third-, fourth-timers, and lifers. I was in the first offenders' camp.

I still can't figure out why they call it a penitentiary. It's nothing but a huge farm as I recall it, some 13,000 acres. The biggest part of it is planted in sugarcane. There's a sugarcane refinery there where they do their own refining. The place is really pretty much self-contained. They grow all their own vegetables, they have a large dairy farm, do their own butchering. I understand that the yearly cane crop is quite a big thing, money-wise, for the state.

Things have changed a great deal since I was there, they're supposed to be better now. I heard when I was there that they were better than they'd been before that, so that must have been quite some place in the old days.

When I was there, they had convict guards. I mean that the men that guarded the convicts, the men who carried the shotguns and rifles, were convicts the same as we were. I believe Arkansas has the same arrangement and a few other southern states did too. I guess they found it a lot cheaper than hiring guards.

Most of the men who did that were men with a great deal of time. It always seemed odd to me, but there was little instance of any of them running off, although they had plenty of chance to. But when we went out in the field to work they set up what was called a guard line with anywhere from four to ten guards, all armed with rifles and shotguns and all of them convicts as we were. They had their own living facilities, their own dining room and all. They never mixed with us at all.

Occasionally, to use the slang that was used down there, when one of them did "fall"—in other words, he broke a rule of some sort while a guard—he'd very seldom be put in the same camp where he'd been guarding. I know of one or two instances where it did happen, and in one instance the man was dead within less than a week after he came back on a regular job.

I know that even in other penitentiaries today, even up North, when an ex-convict does come in and they find out that he has been a guard in one of these southern penitentiaries he's told not to say anything about it to the other men, they try to keep it under cover as much as possible because of the circumstances.

Were those convict guards harder on the men than free world guards?

I would say very much so. I guess it's probably a mental thing in our society, they are pretty sure that what they are doing is wrong. The only reason they're doing it is, well, it's not for money, because if I remember correctly, they only paid the convict guards there $10 a month. Of course their food was better and their living conditions were quite a bit better. The quarters were better. The only other distinction was in clothing. When

From *In the Life* | 109

I was there we still wore big stripes, the kind you see in the cartoons; the guards got to wear khaki uniforms. But I believe the so-called square guard or the freeman guard is much more lenient, is much more inclined to go along with you than the convict guard ever would be.

Out of the 250 men in the particular camp I was in, there was only two free people working there. Sometimes there was three, but usually just the two: the captain of the camp and the particular freeman who was in charge of the fieldwork. Everything else was taken care of by convicts. Even the clerical work.

The camp I was on had two square men. They were brothers. One of them was in charge of what we call the main line, which is the line that works out in the fields in our camp; the other one was in charge of a similar line at the second offenders' camp. They had both worked at the farm for some forty years. One of them, it was the only job he had ever had; the older brother had worked a little while in Texas at one of the farms out at Huntsville. All that time they had worked colored camps until just a year before I got there and they had been called "Mas," Big and Little Mas, which I found out later was a shortening for "master."

We were told, all of us as we came in, that that was what they wanted to be called. We were told when we entered the field, "Don't call me 'mister,' you sonofabitch. I'm Mas. It's short for master and that's the way I want it to be." Consequently, that's the way it was.

We would be marching down the road going to work while it was still dark. When we brought in our tools at night it was dark. During the summer months we worked six days a week. When it came time to cut the cane we worked seven days a week in rain or shine. Cane has to be in when it's ready or it will sour in the ground, so it's work just as long as you can go.

The physical work is hard, but like anything physical, it's not anything you can't get used to. I think really the worst part about it is the change, the attitude, the mental change that comes over a person in a situation like that. From the beginning you're not treated in any way like a human being, and you're continuously cursed. The first two or three weeks the object seems to be whether or not they can break you. If they can, they proceed to do so just as fast as they can. If not, they finally reach the point to where they finally let up on you and they find that you can take it and you can make it.

Sometimes they're pretty easy to get along with, and after a year or so I got to where I could more or less pick my job as far as the Man, the boss, was concerned. I did just as much as I pleased. There were several of us that way.

But for a lot of guys it's not. You've heard of cutting the heel strings, things of that nature. I've seen it done time and time again. There's one man that's in here now that I did time with in Louisiana who is slightly crippled now as a result of cutting his own heel tendon.

I guess it reaches the point, the work, where you finally feel, what the hell. And the food! I could go on for days about the conditions of the food.

The main diet consisted of rice and gravy or rice and red beans or hominy grits and gravy. I never in the thirty months there saw any beef, and I remember chicken about twice. Although they had a huge dairy we never saw any milk in the dining room. I'm a pretty good-sized man, I'm over six foot one and I weigh about 170; when I left there, I came out weighing 147 pounds.

There was food to be purchased in the commissary. There wasn't any limit to the amount of money you could have, but of course, as in any penitentiary, the money always seemed to be limited to a certain few.

I know of instances where arms and legs were broken in an afternoon's work—anything to be able to get into the hospital. You couldn't just check into the sick line and say, "I'm sick, I want to go to the hospital." You had to have something very definitely wrong with you, and you had to be able to prove that you were running a high fever, you had to be able to prove in some manner that you were too weak to be able to stand up and do the work. Or else it had to be something you could go right to the Man and show him, such as a cut heel string or a broken arm or leg, something of that nature.

I remember one time, we went out across the levee right down into the Mississippi with the object of bringing whole trees and logs floating in the river to land, let them dry, cut them up, and use them for that winter as firewood. All the boilers were wood-burning boilers at that time. I don't know if you've ever seen the levee of the Mississippi that far south, but it's quite a thing, quite a construction by itself. If you can imagine it in rainy weather, trying to carry whole trees and huge logs on your shoulders and back to the top of the levee to be loaded into buggies and taken back into camp with the men not even being able to stand up under the weight, maybe reaching halfway up or further, one of them stumbling and two or three of them rolling all the way down to the river, only to be told to get up again and start again.

There were two or three of us at the time. We were trimming dead limbs and all off the trees before they were loaded. We were somewhere a way off from the main work gang and one of the boys happened to wander over and say, "Boy, the last time I fell, I sure wish I'd broken a leg. I wouldn't have to put up with this. Get into the hospital."

We were joking about it and one of us said, "Well, you want your leg broken?"

"Yeah."

"Well, we can take care of it for you."

And he thought for a minute, then he said, "I'm serious. Can you break it?"

We laid the lower part of his leg from the knee down over two logs and then dropped another one in the middle.

Word got around. Before the day was over, we'd done away with something like a half dozen arms and even more legs.

Finally the Man decided to take the whole bunch of us in before we crippled the whole field. The Man knew what was going on, but there really wasn't anything he could do about it.

I told you about how it was dark when we went to work and dark when we came back in at night. I remember time and time again when I'd eat and flop down on my bed and be covered with mud from my knees down, after working at cleaning and digging out draining ditches or even just hoeing after a particularly rainy day. Well, I'd say to myself, "I'll just lay here a minute and then I'll get down and take that shower and clean up." And next thing I'd know they'd be ringing that big bell the next morning and I'd still be laying there with the muddy pants and the muddy shoes and muddy socks still on. I'd have to pick it up and go out to work the same way. All you could do at times like that was grab your sleep when you could and try to keep going.

Of course there were what they'd call the political jobs, working in the laundry and the hospital, clerk or some particular little job on the yard, like maybe in the tailor shop or maybe something like that. But these were so few. The penitentiary's main income was derived from the cane, and therefore that's where the biggest work went into. And there was a lot of it. I've walked all over that 13,000 acres from one end to the other, going to and from work.

I couldn't tell you much about the colored camp because we were completely segregated. We were, of course, also completely segregated from the women's camp. The women's penitentiary was right on the same grounds as the men's. The women made all of our uniforms, mattress covers, and things of that nature. But I can remember one particular colored incident that might tell you something how they were there.

Any time a man tried to escape we'd be brought in immediately from the field and locked in the dormitory so that the extra guards could be sent out with the dogs. And this particular day we heard the dogs circling back. A bunch of us ran to the end of the building and looked out the windows. We could see the figure of a man, still in his stripes—you could spot those black and white stripes for twenty miles—and we couldn't see the dogs or horses yet. He ran into a patch of cane maybe four or five hundred yards from camp. One of the guard towers spotted him, and when the other guards did come in sight he yelled to them and motioned to where he'd gone into the cane and they threw a guard line around the patch of cane.

And I cannot recall, honestly, hearing anyone call in to him, asking him or telling him to come out, saying they had him surrounded and knew where he was. But I saw four get off their horses, go into the cane patch, heard the shots, and then I saw the four men drag his body out. And, as I say, I cannot recall, and couldn't at the time, hearing them tell him to come out, they were going to come in after him and . . . they just went in and shot him.

About the worst incident I can recall: I happened to be out in the yard, not working this particular day because I had blood poisoning in my left hand. I was laying around the yard when they brought a group of men over from Camp E, the second and third offenders' camp, to the hospital. The hospital was right next to the camp I was in. They were lined up at the gate waiting for the guard to unlock the gate and let them in. Just to the left of the line was a guard tower; it stood immediately above the line of men. And about a city block or so away, in the corner of the building, was the other guard tower.

The guard tower nearest them, the one right behind the gate, was harassing two or three men in the line. What they said I don't know, I was just laying in the grass in front of the building. I could hear the voices and I heard a commotion, and when I looked up one fellow had already started up the steps to the guard tower. When he got about halfway up the steps, the guard got out. Now the guards at the point, the ones in the corner of the square, had 30-30 rifles, and the guards in the gate tower carried twin double-barreled shotguns.

Well, he stepped down when the fellow started up the stairs and shot him in the face and chest with both barrels of that double-barreled shotgun.

From *In the Life* | 113

He made his mistake when he emptied *both* barrels before the other guard could get to him and summon help. Even though he was shooting right into the middle of the whole bunch of them, there were some twenty-five or thirty of them, the whole bunch charged right up the stairs, drove the guard down the stairs, and beat him to death right in front of the hospital.

He made his mistake, as I said, when he emptied both barrels, because then he didn't have anything to hold the others off with.

There was one old-timer there, I'll call him Charlie but that's not his real name. He came from what I understand was a pretty good old Louisiana family and got in for bank robbery and had escaped six different times and each time he was eventually brought back. When I met him, whenever he went anywhere—to the hospital or to the administration building or somewhere else—he never went with any of the other convicts, just himself and four guards. They were a little bit worried about Charlie.

He told me about the time when he was working in the fields and one of the convicts jumped a pusher. Now a pusher was a convict too although he wore a guard's uniform. The object of his job was to go up and down the line and make sure that everybody was continually working as fast as he could. Anyway, one of the convicts jumped this pusher and gave him a pretty good beating and then he ran into the cane field.

The freeman didn't want to have the guards go in after him, so he gave the pusher a cane knife and said, "Go in and get him yourself. Bring him out." He took all the other workers out and had them standing out on the row and Charlie said he heard a couple of shots fired, heard some yelling, and then they went back. He looked down into the drainage ditch and the convict who had attacked the pusher had the pusher down in the ditch and was drowning him. Putting his head under water and drowning him. And the guards were shooting at him and had evidently hit him a couple of times because the water was bloody. But it wasn't doing any good, he was hanging on pretty well.

So the man came over and got off his horse and drug him back up. And he had been hit twice. Instead of doing anything for him or sending him to the hospital and then trying him in a court as they do these days—I think most penitentiaries now have some sort of a disciplinary court—he just proceeded to beat hell out of him right there in the field, then put him up under a water wagon and let him lay there. And the man just died. He just bled to death from the two wounds.

The thing of cutting heel strings goes back years and years. I was back in the Los Angeles county jail two or three years back and I ran into

114 | Folklore Matters

an old friend and he'd been in there again and he'd also been in Texas at one of the farms out in Huntsville, on some cotton farm. And we got to talking and he mentioned a few people and did he know them, did I happen to know them, that sort of thing.

He was sitting on the top bunk and when he got down from the bunk—you've never seen such a sight in your life! One foot went one way and one foot went the other. He'd cut either his left three times and his right five times, or vice versa. Each time they caught it—it seems that if they catch him in time they can pull the tendon back down, but if not, if they wait too long and the tendon jumps back up past to the muscular part of the leg, then the man's gonna be a cripple for the rest of his life. But they had caught him, although he still had the bad scars, and he was only slightly crippled. I mean, he could get around by himself. He had done something like twelve years in Texas and six or eight in Louisiana and, as he said, this time he was going to try the West Coast joints, he'd had enough of those down South.

Remember I was mentioning Mas, the square man we had running our field gang down there? Now he worked down there for forty years. It was the only job he'd ever had and to my knowledge the only schooling he'd had was very little, very little.

When I first went to work for him, he comes on with this kick one day, asking where I was from. I consider California my home, but my father's living in New Mexico and I'd come directly out from New Mexico, so I said, "New Mexico."

"One of them goddamned greasy Mexicans," he said. I said, "No, New Mexico's in the States."

"I know where New Mexico is, you sonofabitch. Don't tell me where goddamned Mexicans come from."

And you know, in thirty months I could not convince that man that New Mexico is in the United States, part of the continental USA. He had me below that river and I was going to stay there. Talk about stubborn.

I had a nickname while I was down there, the whole time, it was "Senator." It all happened with Mas again. He kept asking me my name which I would tell him, but he couldn't pronounce it and it's not that difficult to pronounce. But he kept calling me "Bilbo." There was a senator in Mississippi, a very well-known senator, named Bilbo. One day after all this I just got sick and tired of correcting him over and over again. We were cleaning out shit ditches and I laid down my shovel and I crawled out up on top and I said, "Now, Mas, my name is not Bilbo. It's spelled—" And I spelled it out for him.

From *In the Life* | 115

"You get your ass back in that goddamned shit ditch!" he said. "Don't you tell me what your name is. You know it: Bilbo it is. If it's good enough for a United States senator, you sonofabitch, it's good enough for you!"

So from there on, man, it was Senator. That's all you could hear across the field: "Hey, old Senator, get your ass over here."

He was, I guess, completely illiterate. They'd give him his work orders for the day written on a sheet of paper. You know, what cuts we were supposed to take care of, things like that. He'd either call me, or Whitey the waterboy, or somebody, over and say, "I forgot my goddamned glasses. Here, read this off for me." So off we'd go and we'd read his orders for him.

He had false teeth, Mas did. Both uppers and lowers. And to give you an idea of the kind of gentleman I was working under, that was supposed to be my superior: Mas chewed a little tobacco, snuff, stud, anything he could get ahold of. Just as long as it would chew, Mas chewed. But when he got through with his cud and threw it out, he'd just walk over to the nearest ditch, draining ditch or anything else, and he'd take out his false teeth, swish them around the water a little bit, wipe 'em off with his old handkerchief he had tied around—we were very festive down there—with the old handkerchief he had tied around his neck. Why he'd just plop them back in his mouth and go on his merry way.

He had a new Buick at this time, it was in good condition anyway. The driver's side of that car was just mottled, just spotted. It looked like it came from a paint job that way, and it was from him chewing all the time and spitting out the window. He never washed the car and the whole one side of it was completely covered with tobacco juice. It was the damnedest-looking thing you ever saw. He was something else.

I never will forget that car and him taking those teeth out and washing them in that canal. He was *clean*.

We had a camp captain at one time. He stood about six foot four, I guess. Must have weighed 260 or 270 pounds if he weighed an ounce. And he was a pill head. He was constantly on pills, usually Benzedrine. Occasionally when he got a feeling too much up in the air why he'd bust loose with a barbiturate of some kind to kind of bring him down. I saw him high every night.

We had mail call right after chow, after evening chow. We'd gather round before we went up to the dormitories and they'd call out the mail. And Captain Naba is standing there and he is so high he's rocking back and forth from toe to heel. He's so high he's trying to put his hands in his pockets and he can't find his pockets, and I tell you, he broke up the whole congregation. Everybody stopped what they were doing to watch him just try to get his hands in his pockets. Big old belly sticking out, and he just can't make it.

Another time this fool, he gets all high on pills and I think he'd been drinking too, he smelled like it. At this time, I was on the yard with a bad hand. So he called down—there wasn't any trusty on the yard—and tells me, "You SOB, go down to the barn and get my goddamned horse. And you'd better not get on him, you walk him back up here."

So they let me out the gate. I wandered down to the barn and I got his horse for him. I got it all saddled, brought it back up. He was going to ride out to the field and inspect the field. And he couldn't get on that horse and he got mad at me because he couldn't get on the horse. He took a couple of swipes at me. I ducked out of the way. I let him get a couple of easy swipes in, you know, but nothing to bother me, and he's just giving me hell.

"You SOB, come over here and hold this horse." So I held the horse for him. And for about fifteen minutes this goes on. Finally, he just gives up in despair and tells me to take the goddamned horse back down, and he stomps back into the office.

Pretty soon he comes out again. I'm standing over in the yard watching him. He comes out and he's got this Stetson pulled over his eyes. He looked around. Just higher than a kite, boy, I wish I'd a been as high as that man was that day. He was feeling no pain, just having himself a ball. So he looks over at me and sees me standing there and says, "You SOB, where's that goddamned horse?"

So I had to go back down and get it for him and this time he made it.

At the time they had done away with the old whipping post. They hadn't done away with the post; they'd done away with the whipping. So they would tie you to the post and leave you there for a day or two while they constantly fed you mineral oil, Epsom salts, and stuff like that. And left you there.

But actual floggings and beatings, no. Just the occasional bump on the head or thump across the shoulders. The guards and freemen still carried long sticks when I was there, and they never hesitated to use them. But the day of the really brutal beating is gone.

A group of fellows hit the yard one day when everybody was on the yard and they had some Molotov cocktails all made up. Gasoline in the bottles, stuffed with rags at the top, you know. They came down under the tower in the left-hand corner of the yard down there and they cut loose with their cocktails and they set the guard tower on fire. The guard was so excited that instead of jumping out on the outside of the wall he jumped in with the convicts, and he took off across the field and headed for the guard shack.

They had a rope all fixed up. They throw the rope over and one of them goes up, and then the next one. If they'd gone over one by one, as they were supposed to, they would have made it because way down at the end where the other guard tower was, there was one guy who was completely dumbfounded as to what was going on, and he probably couldn't hit the broad side of a barn if he had one to shoot at with what was happening there.

But as one guy almost reached the top another one jumped on the rope and in the anxiety to get over, a third one grabbed on.

And blooey, the whole thing gave and they all dropped back on the inside.

There wasn't much else happened after that. They completely gave up and said the hell with it.

It was pretty funny, especially to see that guard jump down in the middle of the yard and take off running.

Talking about breaks. In Angola we lived in dormitory type places, all upstairs. Two-story buildings. The downstairs had a kitchen, a couple of lobbies, a library, a barber shop, whatnot, a little dispensary. And the whole thing was surrounded by a twelve-foot fence, a Cyclone fence with three strands of barbed wire facing in. And guard towers on each of the four corners, and along the length of the fence there were two towers in between.

Some of the fellows decided that they were going to go. I don't know why they were going to go over the fence. I mean, what the hell, everyday you're outside the fence working, all you got to do is sneak across the cane cut, take a chance on getting past one guard, and hit it. If there *was* any place to go. There wasn't any place to go.

But they decided they were going to be very spectacular about the whole thing and go over the fence in broad daylight. So half a dozen or so got down to the very corner underneath the guard tower, which is no-man's land. You just aren't supposed to get under there where the guard can't see you.

They proceeded to have a little fight, a little sham battle. The guard jumped down and he's standing over or leaning over them, trying to break all this up. One of these characters, a pretty good-sized boy from Houston, he runs up and grabs ahold of the barbed wire with his bare hands and three of them go up over him, they just use him as a scaling ladder. He drops back on the inside.

This so confused the guards in the four towers that could see them that they just stood there and they looked, and they looked, and we kept waiting. And the suspense got so bad that all of us felt like shouting, "Shoot at them, you silly sonofabitch," but they just set there and they looked. And finally, when those three guys are almost down to the barn, a good quarter of a mile or so away, they finally decided to cut loose on them.

They get to the levee. The only thing left is what they call "running the levee." You try to make it to Baton Rouge along the Mississippi levee. It's been done about two or three times. I couldn't get you the exact distance. I'd say something like about sixty miles. But it has to be done ahead of the dogs, and only a couple of them have made it. Both of them colored guys. It's quite a little jaunt.

Each camp had its own dog house, its own group of bloodhounds. The real bad bunch was up at the administration building and the only thing you could call them is killer dogs. When they brought them out you knew they were really hot after somebody. They decided they were going to use those dogs.

Those guys decided to run the levee and they made the mistake of taking the long way around the levee. I think they thought that if they could get around to the back gate—that was nothing but a ferry landing for a ferry to cross the Mississippi—they could make it that way. For the men in that part of the state who had to bring prisoners into the joint, they came across the ferry instead of going all the way around. It was big enough for one car or a pickup truck. And these guys decided they'd commandeer that ferry and take off.

They got down to the ferry and, of course, there's a couple hundred guards already there. There's no hope for them there. So they swing back and they cut all the way through the farm, they cut right across it. And they bypass the administration building and they head up into the hills. If they can get across the other side of these bluffs in through there and across the river they'd be in Mississippi.

They get up into the hills, and they hunt for them the rest of that day and that night. You could hear the dogs. All of a sudden, word came the next day for us to go out to work. We figured they'd caught them. Somebody said, "No, they didn't catch them, they gave up on them." We couldn't figure why in hell they gave up, because the place is surrounded on three sides. It's in a horseshoe bay on the Mississippi River. There's only one way out by land, that's through the main gate. Well, where in hell are those hoosiers? They gotta be somewhere.

From *In the Life* | 119

We're walking down the road and we go past the garden gang—they took care of the vegetable garden. Most of them were older men. We're walking along and I looked down across there by the garden and I looked down there, I look again, I take a third look. I nudge this sonofabitch and I said, "Look at that sonofabitch, that's one of the guys that ran off."

"That couldn't be."

And we looked again and we kept on walking.

You know, those silly SOBs worked all day out there with the garden crew. And even the guard on the garden crew didn't realize it. They come back in the gate at night, they checked in, and ate. The guards didn't find out they were back until they made the bed check that night about eleven o'clock. They thought they'd gotten away and here they just come back in the joint. They gave up and just came back in. And had worked all day with this guard and with this crew. That garden crew didn't have a square man with them, all they had was this one guard, and he didn't know who he had working for him.

I had told that guy, "I know that's one of them over there," and it was, bigger than hell.

We had a food riot. There was one down there about every month or so that never amounted to anything. But things got really bad down there one summer. Oh, the food was just terrible. We had been living for two or three weeks on nothing but syrup and cornbread.

We decided we'd had enough of this nonsense, so we called for a little general strike, like Castro. Well, it didn't come off. Everybody said, "Oh yeah, yeah, we're with ya, we're with ya," and the time came and I looked like a fool standing out there by myself. So I sidled off in line with the rest of them.

Finally I decided we're going to have to do something with these fools.

We were on the yard for dinner one day. When we got through eating in the summer they'd let us stay in from noon till about two o'clock, during the hotter part of the day. So everybody's in one of the two lobbies, playing cards or laying on the floor asleep, something like that. Like here right now. So we proceeded to lock the doors and bolt them so they can't get out. They've gotta join us now.

The Man come in. The law claimed that they can't come on the yard with guns, they could come in with sticks or axe handles or things like that, but no guns. Well, the Man wouldn't even come on the yard. He stands in front of the gate and he yells in to us, "What's the trouble in there?"

"We gotta have some food. We can't work the way conditions are."

"Goddamn, we're feeding you sonofabitches good. You're living better than you were outside." All that nonsense.

"That may be, but we can't make it. We can't work every day on this kind of food."

He gets all hot at us and he takes off. We ask to see the warden. The warden wasn't there, or so we were told. A few of the people were getting kind of restless and we had to bang a few heads to calm everybody down. We were in there two hours when the Man comes back out again. He wants to talk to us.

So loudmouth me, I gotta speak up, and he knew there was a Yankee talking somewhere in there. He knew there was a Yankee talking and he could eliminate them on one hand. So finally he said, "Nothing's going to get settled right now. Come on out, have supper, and we'll take care of it tomorrow."

"No, we're going to stay right here till we see the warden and something gets settled."

We stayed there all night long and hadn't anything to eat. Finally, the next morning, the warden comes down and he says, "Well, I know it's been bad, the vegetables are getting ripe, fresh vegetables and everything, food is gonna get better, and I'll give them orders to slaughter a couple of hogs and we'll have some pork chops. Now I won't say it'll get better all the time, but I'll do my best for you right now. So you can come out."

Everybody's getting hungry about this time. Somebody yelled out, "Are we going to get into any trouble over this?"

"No, absolutely no trouble for anybody. We'll just forget about it."

Yeah. So the ones of us that really instigated the thing, there were six of us, we got in among everybody else and filed out. And I'll be damned if they didn't slaughter a couple of hogs. Had some pretty nice pork chops and a pretty decent supper.

The next morning we come down and lined up to go out for work. I'm standing there waiting, thinking that things will be getting better. All of a sudden they start reading off these names, six of us. Somebody snitched us out, and we never did find out who it was.

Somebody snitched us off because they had just exactly the right people. Not even one over or one less or anything, just exactly the right people. They talked about taking us outside to try us, and then they decided not to because there might be a bit too much publicity, the New Orleans *Times-Picayune* was looking for a reason to come on the joint anyway at the time. The food did get better, but the Man, almost any time anything happened, I don't care what it was, whether it was a fight in the showers when the six of us were still out working in the field, we six got rapped for it. He found himself six fall guys, and every time something happened there that he couldn't account for, he knew all he had to do was tell the warden it was the six of us. So every time we turned around we were headed for the sweatbox or solitary. It made it easy for him.

The hole. Oh, the hole.

Each camp had its own sweatbox, usually three sweatboxes. Our particular camp had three. They were about four by four by four, and sitting right in the middle of the whole thing was a toilet stool. You couldn't stand up, you couldn't curl up on the floor because of the toilet stool, and what you could do was sit there on that toilet, that's all, But the law allowed them to keep you there only three days, no longer than seventy-two hours. Of course, they could let you out for six, then put you back in for another seventy-two. So they never actually broke the law in any way.

The main form of punishment for infraction of the rules was what they called the "red hats." The name still held, although the way of running it had changed a lot over the years. In years before, the disciplinary crews had been forced to work at the worst type of work on the farms, such as cleaning drainage ditches behind the hospital and things like that. And to show that they were a strictly disciplinary group they'd been forced to wear red hats and they had a special guard line.

When I was there they didn't work anymore, but they had their own building which is still called the red hat building. If you were sentenced there, it was for no less than thirty days. I was in it twice. The last time was when I was supposed to be one of six who instigated that food riot for lack of food. We weren't out of the cell once in thirty days. We never had a shower, we never shaved in that thirty days. We had a meal every three days. Twice a day we received bread and water.

The last time I was in was during the month of August and part of September which, if you know the South, you know how hot this time of year can be and what the humidity is. When I finally got out, they took us out about ten o'clock in the morning and a truck was waiting for us. None of us could make it to the truck ourselves, they had to help us into the bed of the truck. And when we got there, myself and two or three of the other fellows were completely covered with heat rash—I've never experienced anything like it since or even seen anything like it since. I had heat rash even on my eyelids and on the insides of my ears and my nostrils. From not being able to bathe, from the constant perspiration, the sweating.

I went right back to work that afternoon. These shades I wear, they're prescription lenses, they're not sunglasses alone. But because of that particular incident alone that's why I have to wear them, all during the daylight hours I have to wear sunglasses. That afternoon, when I went out after having been in the hole for thirty days, I went out three separate times with heat prostration and each time I was back on my feet and sent back to work. Right after that, the headaches and all that started and I still have to watch myself in hot days, especially hot sunny days and such, I have to be pretty careful. Make sure I get in someplace out of the sun when I feel I'm getting a little ill.

5

From *A Thief's Primer*

(1969)

A Thief's Primer is a book that happened because a place I was doing fieldwork in the mid-1960s—Ramsey prison farm, about forty miles southwest of Houston—was so hot and muggy that when I took photographs I had to get the shot off immediately, before my eye blurred from the sweat running into it.

The prison was segregated then: Ramsey 1 was for White prisoners; Ramsey 2 was for Black prisoners. I did all of my outdoor work on Ramsey 2 (my primary project was the Black convict worksongs), and I recorded interviews and conversations at both.

The entire prison, Ramsey 1 and Ramsey 2, had, as I now remember it, only two air-conditioned spaces. One was the warden's office, out front; the other was the dentist's office, inside the locked down part of Ramsey 1. Some days, after recording in the tanks of Ramsey 1 or recording and photographing in the tanks and fields of Ramsey 2, I was so worn down by the heat and humidity I took refuge in the air-conditioned space closest to hand: the dentist's office.

Three people ran that space, one of them a free world dentist who visited once a week or once a month, one of them a former free world dentist doing time for narcotics violations, and the third a convict dental assistant, a former check forger, and safecracker. The prisoner dentist could do everything the free world dentist did but prescribe sedatives. The convict dental assistant did everything dental assistants in the free world do, plus things neither of the real dentists wanted to bother with, like drilling and filling teeth. He took to the craft just as he'd taken to the craft of safecracking. He could drill with precision, too.

Most of the times I took refuge in that cool space, he was the only one there. I'd sit in the patients' chair and we'd talk. He'd talk about Ramsey, about people he knew I'd interviewed, about his own life. It was too much for me to remember, so one day, I said something like, "Okay if I record this?" It was fine with him.

So I put my Uher on the round tray where dentists' instruments are usually arrayed. And our conversations continued. At first, I thought they'd help me with a lot of other things I was hearing. Then, back in Cambridge, looking at the transcripts, I realized they were their own story.

At the time, I was writing for Atlantic Monthly, so I submitted the manuscript to Atlantic, Little Brown, their publishing arm. It consisted of transcripts from the tapes, with commentaries on those transcripts by Texas cops and crooks I knew, and me.

I got a contract, with an advance. There was one problem: their reader said something like: "The stories are interesting but Bruce is a much better writer than Mac. Bruce should rewrite what Mac told him from his point of view."

That was my first trade book, and I really wanted it to happen. But I thought that reading and subsequent editorial demand that I rephase what Mac said missed the point of what the book was about. Mac's voice, his perception, and presentation of things were as much a part of what the book was showing as whatever was described or postulated in them.

Many years later, our quondam University at Buffalo English Department colleague John Coetzee was here for dinner and said, "Those men you and Diane interviewed and filmed on death row, how can you know when they were being self-serving and how can you know what truth is in what they say?" I replied, "I never know when they're telling the truth. But I do know that at that moment in that place, that is what they said. There is the truth of utterance."

Same here with Mac. What's of interest and importance is not just what he says, but how he says it and the fact that he is the one saying it. Those conversations happened. That's what makes these passages folklore or ethnography, rather than fiction. There are facts we get from utterance, and there are facts in the utterance itself. All poets know that.

～

When I came down here to prison the first time, I heard so much about safes. When I got out, I was bumming around, gambling around, and finally I got off in a trap where I owed a bunch of money, and I decided I'd put some of what I'd learned in prison and the contacts I'd made there to some use.

You just find somebody that's busting safes if you want to learn it and you need the money. What happened to me was I was drove up and I needed a lot of money. It got so I didn't have any place to gamble and I didn't have any bank roll to gamble with. I had just gotten out of jail on that two-year deal and I called a friend of mine and told him I needed to find somebody to make some money with. He asked me how I wanted to make it and I told him I didn't give a shit, any way is all right.

He told me about this boy who was in town from Fort Worth and he'd known him a long time, knew one of his uncles, and the boy was all right. So we made a meet and messed around together a couple of weeks I guess. And things still hadn't gotten any better. He loaned me five or six hundred dollars during that time. So whenever he got ready to go, well, I was ready too. I owed him that money and I wanted to pay off.

And I got in a big switch. I wasn't even involved in it, but I got rapped for it and I had to pay the bill. There was a big party at a motel and they filed charges on me. But I was just at the party. They knew they'd never get the money any other way than by trapping me. I could have gone to court and beat it, but making bonds and paying those lawyer fees—the lawyer wanted $5,500 to defend me—it just wasn't worth it. It's easier to pay it off and forget about it, mark it up to experience, and the next time I see the people, just take a pistol and get my money back. But I never did see them. It was just one of those deals.

So we started out.

I guess I'm kind of funny. Whenever I start stealing, boy, I dig a hell of a charge out of it. I dig a fantastic charge! At night, whenever we'd go out, if we'd got some places cased out, before we made the first one, I'm scared, I'm scared to death. But after I get in there and make the first one, all my fear leaves and I get maybe too careless. Then I think I'm invincible, and I'd walk up in broad daylight if I wanted to do something.

But he wasn't that way. It took them about sixteen years to ever bust him. And that is a fantastic run of luck those sixteen years. The thing about it is, they knew that he was a safe man. They had his MO, everything, and whenever he'd bust a safe, they'd know. But he's a lucky guy.

For instance, we went up to San Marcos, Texas, and they have an aqua show, an underwater thing. We went in and the guy has a tough safe, but he forgot to put the money bag in the safe. He'd carried it into his office and left it there beside the safe and gone out. He'd gotten busy and just left. So when we went in, we didn't have to touch the safe, the money was already out. That's just this guy's luck.

And a supermarket in Beeville. We went in there and I just reached over and flipped it and it was on day lock. We just opened the safe, took the money, and walked out. In there about thirty seconds. But that's this guy's luck, you know.

Then he and I split up. He got hold of this Mexican whore and her old man got after him, so it got down to where it's going to be a killing and he just took the gal and left. Another boy, a kind of friend of both of ours, he cut in and we had been working a threesome for a while, so when Jack left, this other boy, my fall partner, we worked together. We kept going until we got busted on this case. We never implicated Jack in any way, and he continued until about a year and a half ago, when he got filed on in Fort Worth. He had three or four burglary cases up there, a couple of supermarkets I think.

Jack showed me a lot, but you have to remember that when you're learning, you're in a building with the police maybe breathing down your neck and you're uptight and you're trying to get the money, and so you haven't got time for a man to say, "Now you see this tumbler? When you do this, then over here something happens." You haven't got time for all that. You just have to stand there and watch him. You can't talk, it's all too fast. You see what he does and what it looks like; then after you get home, you say, "What did you do here?" And he would draw you some diagrams and you could learn something.

I guess that's about the way I got into it. It seemed like the most natural thing in the world. It seemed like that's what I'm supposed to be. I'm sure that deep down I have a fear of failure, and none of my family is a failure.

∼

Safes are good. You know, you can't knock a safe, man. If you can find the place that's got the money, if you've got somebody that can spot it for you, it is good. There's no problem making the safe, there's no problem at all. The problem is to find the safe that has the money in it. As far as getting into the safe, anybody can get in. Hell, children get into them all the time; twelve- and thirteen-year-old kids, they bust safes. There's no problem beating a safe, the only problem is finding the one with the money in it. But with a check, the money is already there, you know it's there, you just have to go in. You don't get as much at a time, but at the end of the day you've got a lot more money.

Something else: they don't get *mad* at you for checks. I've never even been touched; I've never been forced to sign a confession with checks. The police take the attitude that if people are crazy enough to give money for a piece of paper, then they ought to be beat. And they just do not worry about check writers because they are too numerous. Hell, half the housewives, they're always floating bad checks.

~

We consider a score what a particular proposition brings. If it's a check score, then it's that series of checks from that town. You go in that town, and although you might be there two weeks putting out checks, that's all just one score because it's all one operation. And if you get busted on it, it's all one bust.

Checks are the most lucrative. They're head and shoulders above anything else in the world. After a while though, it's hard to get down anymore. If you're around that part of the country, they look you up every time something comes up. The police consider a safe burglar a dangerous person because they figure that he is armed and if he gets jumped up on, he's going to hurt somebody. Say the man in the store leaves something there and comes back for it, then, they figure, he's dead. And probably he is. More than likely, with some people. Myself, I'd just hit him in the head or make him go lay down over there. If he came to, it would probably be a godsend, because I could make him open the safe and I wouldn't have to do any work. But the police do consider you dangerous.

Do you carry a gun when you're working?

All the time. The police, they shoot at you without warning. They don't say, "Give up," or something. They just start shooting. And if they're trying to kill you, well hell. I've had some awful good friends who were handcuffed when they died. I'm not going to take that kind of a chance.

~

This is when we were cracking safes.

I called my lawyer and had him meet me down in the garage of his office building. He came down to the garage and I had a couple of thermos bottles of coffee and we sat there and had a cup of coffee and I told him where we were planning on working. Of course, he knew that if we found something along the way, we would probably work it too.

At this time, we're giving him $500. Two hundred fifty dollars a week, $500 every two weeks. This $500 was to make any bonds. Fees, if we had to go to court later, that was all extra. The $500 was if we got busted, for him to get there and keep us from getting killed.

You know, they got a law that they can't whip a confession out of you; they won't accept it in court anymore, it has to be given with counsel present. Well, son, when they got confessions in the past, it didn't make any difference how they got them: they were good. They never overruled one in the state of Texas.

But, anyway, that was the purpose of that visit.

We went off on this beef, on this job, made three or four places, and got to running. We checked into a motel, and I called into Corpus and told him where we were working. We looked around and decided that we wanted to get it the next day. We had heard about it, and we had just been putting it off.

It was in Harlingen, Texas; it's a big drugstore, right in town. We went by and looked at it, and it had a regular old wooden house door! I mean, you can take anything—you can take a nail or a pocketknife or a pair of nail clips or anything to open it. It's just one of them old spring locks; all you do is barely get something in there and you pull. It's absolutely nothing. I'd rather not have a door.

We saw it and it looked real good. We went in and looked, and the safe was sitting back in the office by itself, so we decided we'd go ahead and make it. And there was a big feed store there we'd heard was good, and we wanted to make that too.

First we went to the feed store and made it, but someone else had made it the night before and there was just a busted safe sitting there.

We went back to the drugstore and made it. Coming out, the police ran up on us. The trunk of the car was open and we were putting the tools and money and dope in the back, and so I just told the chief of police—he was in that police car, "Goodnight, sir." Then we got in our car and we drive off.

That chief lost his job on account of it. He testified at my trial and they busted him to a patrolman.

We headed back to Corpus. We knew that he had got our license number. And we had been in a hurry and didn't change license plates, so we knew there was going to be some heat on the car. He had followed us a little ways, and we knew he got our license and everything. We took off down the highway and we knew he would go back and check that

130 | Folklore Matters

drugstore—it's the only thing of value there. When he did, then we cut and went cross-country, got off the main highway.

We had a real good stealing car that we had bought. A De Soto. It was a 1957 De Soto and we had brand-new tires on it, new engine, everything. It was equipped for that, nothing else. It was kind of a big car and yet it's kind of a small car, and people can't recognize De Sotos. They call them Chevrolets and Fords and Cadillacs and everything, because people just don't know a De Soto. And we got it in this neutral color, an old green color, with black tires, and we had it all fixed up with a police radio in it.

We took off running about 120. We beat the roadblocks back to Corpus. I called there and told these girls—we had a couple of whores there—to clean up the house and get everything out that wasn't bought and paid for, anything that was taken out of a burglary.

You know, we had a lot of little old stuff that we took. I wanted to get it out of there just to be sure. Actually, if they found it, they couldn't make a case on it because it was stuff that all drugstores handle and you could have bought it anywhere. So we got in to the place and I told my fall partner, "Let's go, man, everything's packed."

He said, "I don't want to go. They can't do anything to us." I said, "They goddamn sure can. If the Rangers get you, they're going to get a confession."

He said, "I can fade 'em." He's supposed to be a hog, you know.

I told him, "Well, I'll tell you what: I can't. Now you do what you want, but I'm leaving. If you want to stay here and fade the beef, as soon as you get picked up, get the people upstairs to let me know and I'll get the lawyers on it and try to make your bond. But don't forget now, when the Rangers get you, they're gonna take you off and hide you. It's liable to be a week before the lawyers can find you."

He said, "Okay."

Down here, the Rangers are all the law. They can just pack you up, put you in a car, carry you from town to town, from city to city, just anywhere they want to carry you, and nobody questions it.

I went and checked into a hotel. This girl I had at my place, I left her at the apartment too. If they're going to stay, she might as well stay there and answer that phone and make some money.

When I left the house, I took about eight or nine hundred dollars in change we just hadn't gotten time to get rid of. A lot of times, when I first started, I wouldn't even take the change out of a safe, but then you take it out and it's a couple of hundred here, three or four hundred there, and after you make seven or eight safes, you've got a lot of change. So I made a deal down at the bank. I'd send this girl down there, and they thought I was a coin collector, and she could just take it into the bank with no questions asked. At first, I let her take it and get more change in return. Then after that was over a couple of times, then we told them I had another outlet where I was getting change, and she just put it in the bank and got cash for it. This was just some of that change that had piled up. We was stealing every night, man; we was busting safes every night.

I went to the hotel and scored for another whore. I was walking down the hall after I got in there, and as soon as I saw her, I knew she was a whore. So I told her, "Boy, if I wasn't so tired, I'd buy some pussy."

She said, "Would a drink of Scotch wake you up?"

I told her, "Yeah." So, she went down and got a bottle, and we got to bullshitting and everything, and about two hours later I had all her money; I had her clothes in my car and everything. She was a hell of a broad; she was a beautiful girl, man.

Anyway, we went on and a friend called me at the hotel the following day and told me the Rangers had busted in and arrested all of them. I got the lawyers working on it, and they couldn't find them. Of course, they knew the Rangers had them, but they still couldn't find them.

I had another lawyer I used sometimes. When [he] couldn't get them out or even find them, I went to Roy Scott. He lives in a real nice motel and he's an old bachelor. He's dead now. Got a world of money. I went down to his motel and I asked him what the hell I could do. He told me, "I'm gonna have him in court at nine o'clock in the morning. They promised to produce him at nine."

I said, "Well, how much is the bond going to be? I'm going to go ahead and pay it and get it over with."

He said, "I don't know." It ended up with me giving him $2,500 down. At first, he just wanted to make the bond and I'd pay him later on, but I said, "No, I want to leave some of it now so I won't have that big old bill." I only gave him $2,500.

This girl I got at the hotel had $900. I got it from her, made out a deposit slip, and sent it to my bank.

Roy Scott, he told me, "The best thing for you to do is get out of town."

I told him, "Well, all right."

I was going to go to Houston with this girl. She's got an apartment . . . a good apartment, a $600- or $700-a-week spot. When I told

Roy, he said, "That's the best thing for you to do, go with that girl to Houston. You call me every day and we'll keep in touch." I told him what name I was going to register under in the hotel in Houston and to be sure and call me whenever anything comes up.

I went out to my stash in the country where I had some narcotics and dug me up a big bunch of Dilaudid; then I went back to the hotel and got that girl. We started out of town going to the airport and the police arrested me.

First time in my life I've ever been stopped by a policeman and just arrested! They took me down there on an old warrant that was about forty years outdated. But I thought it was this Harlingen deal, that somebody had cracked, because they had some gals with them and all of them are dope fiends. I figured somebody had cracked.

Well, it was just this old deal. I got them to call this district attorney, and the district attorney said, "Yeah, that case has been dropped." So, the police put me in a police car and carried me to the airport and put me on the airplane. While I was on the way to Houston, the Rangers had teletyped Corpus and said to pick me up. Corpus teletyped back and said that the Rangers had made a mistake, that the Sam they had in Corpus was a check man and wouldn't steal anything. So the Rangers thought that maybe they got the wrong one. They went back in and requizzed those other people. They think they've been given a bum steer.

In the meantime, I got off the plane in Houston. Well, I've got this broad with me and, like I said, she's a whore. This old boy that arrested me in Corpus, he's the chief of the check detail. He knows me real well, he knows my family real well. So he just put two and two together and figured that was where I probably was with that girl at her hotel. They arrested me there.

What had happened was, those people signed statements on me down at Palacios, which is where the Rangers had them. When they arrested me, they took me to Ranger headquarters and carried me on down to Bay City and on down to Palacios. When I got to Palacios, I hadn't told them anything. They had offered me all kinds of deals to sign a statement, and I wouldn't do it.

I remember when they was strumming my head, the sheriff there said, "Cut it out, you can't do that here," and I thought I was off the hook, but then he said, "Cut it out; if you have to do that, take him out in the country and do it."

Man, the last thing in the world I wanted at that moment was that nice country air.

From *A Thief's Primer* | 133

When I finally got there to Palacios, there's all my narcotics and the tools and all this stuff just sitting there. And there's my fall partner.

I walked over to the side where he was. My hunting knife was on the table. I was going to kill him. I was so mad, you know.

When I got right next to him, he said to me, "Don't worry about anything. I didn't sign any statements on anybody but just me and you."

Man, I just slumped. I didn't know what to do.

They whipped this girl that I had, the one that I left at the apartment with them.

There was a boy in the next cell to me. He had nothing to do with our case; he was there on a deal of his own. He told me his name through the ventilator and he asked me who I was. I told him and he said, "Man, you're in a world of trouble."

I said, "What's the matter?"

"Your fall partner's been signing statements against you all day in Corpus. They're carrying you down there for a lie detector test."

"Yeah," I told him. "I figured that. What about the girl?"

"She your old lady?"

"Yeah."

He said, "Man, she's something else. They worked that girl just unmercifully, and she wouldn't admit she knew you."

Remember, I didn't leave anything at the apartment. I took all my clothes and everything I owned with me when I left, just so they couldn't put me there. And they couldn't, not until those people told them.

Anyway, that gal never did admit that she knew me. A pretty good girl. They whipped her so bad and messed with her so bad that as soon as she got out of jail, her family checked her into a hospital. She came from a pretty wealthy family. She almost died; she had a mental collapse. She was in terrible shape because they mistreated her so bad. A lot of girls can't stand that.

But she did not tell them.

∼

Now checks, as I say, they're fabulous. You can go into a store with a pencil and a piece of paper, and that man just gives you his money. Just stop and think about it! There's a man behind the counter over there—he might be a college graduate, he might be worth $250,000,000—and you can walk in there with a fountain pen and an old raggedy checkbook and he is going to give you his money. He'll give you anything in the store.

Anything that you want, he'll give it to you for that piece of paper. It's fantastic. How can they be so stupid?

I read a few years ago that in Dallas they lost $1,740,000 in hot checks in the first three months of the year and it was way down. They were proud of it. Safecrackers wouldn't take that much in Dallas in twenty years. But they were proud of it. Checks are fantastic, you just have no idea. I've used them to buy loads of cattle and sheep and ranches and everything in the world. Just whatever I happen to want to buy, and I turn and sell it and get out of it before they clear the check. I even bought a whorehouse in Mexico once. I sold it back to the guy about four days later, before he had time to clear the check. Got cash for the money. He thought I was taking a loss on the deal, that he really put one over on this gringo.

Checks are the best if you can operate, but now, every time there's a bunch of checks put out in this part of the country, the first thing they do is take my picture over there. They don't never come to your house and roust you and take you down to be identified; all they do is just take your picture. And you can't hardly do it anymore, especially after you're known.

Which do you prefer, checks or safes?

Checks. You ask me why. Primarily because there's more money in checks than there is in safes.

∼

Now I'll tell you about the work.

The last set of equipment I had was given to me by a real good safe man in Fort Worth. I had two sets of tools: one set for the safe, the actual box tools, and then a set of roofing tools. For going through a roof you need hatchets and stuff like that. The two sets would run about $350. Not too much. If you have a pneumatic drill, something like that, that's extra. But you don't buy those things; you go steal them.

What they weigh depends on the box you're going after. I had an old army knapsack that rolls out; you hang the stuff on the side. I had one of those and I cut off part of the straps and put my stuff inside and rolled it up. It's a dark color and easy to carry. I could put my tools in there and it would weigh about thirty-five or forty pounds. Not too much that you can't climb with it. Roofing tools weigh a little bit more, and I had those in a larger knapsack.

I didn't fool with nitro because the possession of explosives is a federal offense. If you're driving down the highway and you happen to get a rumble, then not only the state but the federal can file on you too.

Until a few years ago Texas didn't have a tool law. You could drive down and they could catch you with all the burglary tools in the world and they couldn't file on you for having them. But in some states they could, and now they can in Texas too. But you have to have a drill. So if you're going to use a drill, you take two cars and you keep the drill in the other car.

I had boxes built for my tools. Say I was going to Oklahoma City to beat a safe. I'd put my tools on a Greyhound bus and I'd pick them up in Oklahoma City when I got there. That way I'm driving down the country and haven't got a thing in my car, not one thing. And when I get through in Oklahoma City, then I put my stuff on the Greyhound bus and I send it back. I never carried anything far. Sometimes if I was only going 150 miles, especially if I had been working in the area and I knew that the Rangers were looking for me, I would do that.

A well-known safe man like myself, when I go out, they know what kind of car I have. When I drive into a town and if the police see me, they don't arrest me. They notify the Rangers, and they tail me as I go around casing the stores; then they go around setting traps. That's common; I've sat in a Ranger car and listened to them. They know that we know they do that. But the things about it is, we just figure that we're smarter than they are and they don't know what kind of car we're in that night.

I'll tell you what I always try to do whenever I'm going off to do something like that. I always have some kind of square-john girlfriend someplace and I say, "How about letting me borrow your car? I'll have it tuned up for you and you can use mine." Then I use her car.

∽

There are a lot of those words you have to use just to say what you're talking about; there aren't any other words for some things.

There is one type of bar that's better than any other type of bar for getting into a building. We call it a jimmy-bar. Now there's many jimmy-bars, but the part of the country where I come from, the safe men around there call a jimmybar a multisided bar that has a nail puller on one end and a bill on the other; the bill turns slightly so you can put it in there and it gives you that leverage. They're very heavy-duty and real strong, and you can rack on them or beat with them or do whatever you want to do.

We don't call a safe a safe: we call a safe a *box*. A *squaredoor box* is an ordinary one-door box with the dial in the center and the handle usually on the left middle; it opens, looking at the safe, from your left to your right. We also have what we call a *double-door box*. Then you get into your *keisters*. A keister is, as anybody knows, an ass, and a keister stash is an asshole. Keisters are the asshole of the safe profession because they're so hard to get into. And safe salesmen, they call them keisters too. There are different types. You have a *square-door keister*, and you have a *round door keister*, and you have a *nigger-head* keister. A niggerhead keister is a large ball, just a round ball that's set in concrete.

I can't get in them. I have heard of people that could get in them, but I don't believe it. I had one one time, I had it on an island. I had a bunch of dynamite and I blowed that thing. I dug a big hole in the sand and buried it there and blowed it, and it would go up like a rocket. And finally I blowed it all the way out in the ocean. And I never did scratch it. I couldn't get in. I tried to cut them and I can't get in. That time, I knew I couldn't get in the safe, so I went in the building and took the safe with me. And I still couldn't get in.

Later on, I had guys tell me, "I heard about that safe you had, the keister that you had, and I wish I'd had it; I'd have got into it and split the profits with you." But I don't believe it. I don't believe that they can get into them.

Other slang we use: A *jigger* is used by a lot of people. It means a lookout, someone that you put on the point that notifies you in case the police are approaching. Not so much the police, because you're not so much worried about them—it's the old person out for an evening's stroll or straggling along in the street, someone just wandering around, they're the ones who give you the trouble. The police catch very few people. They always have someone who calls and tells them somebody's in the building. The chances of them catching you are outlandish if someone doesn't inform them. So you don't actually worry about the police—it's just the person strolling down by the store who hears the noise.

And then there is *punch* or *punching*. That is when you knock the numbered dial off. There's a pin in there, and that pin holds the tumblers in position. You knock the pin and the tumblers fall down and the door will open. One safe in Harlingen, Texas, a Trans-Texas Airline office: I went in and out in about four minutes. If a safe is punchable, then it's very easy. Nowadays they weld a plate in the back where you can't punch that pin through the metal, and the pin mushrooms on you and blocks the tumblers.

Peel—that means just what it says. You open them like a can of sardines without a key. You just get at the [upper-left] corner and whip it. You need a big cold chisel. You put the cold chisel up into the first layer of the door. Now a safe door is thick, but it's not all iron; it's hollow, and inside is asbestos fireproofing and cement and other stuff. It has just a small layer of steel—about one-quarter inch—on the outside. That depends on the price of the safe and the year it was made. I think L. C. Hall is the best single-door safe ever made; they were made in Cincinnati, and they stopped making them fifty or sixty years ago. Every time I run into one it's hell. Anyway, about the safe: if you just get into that first little ridge where that front plate is, then you drive your bar or chisel in there and just pry it loose. Then you get your jimmy-bar in there and just rip either the weld or the rivets that are in there. Once you get a start, it's just a matter of minutes. It's getting the start that's the problem. I've tried as high as ten hours to get a start on a safe and never did get it.

∽

Sometimes it's so nice. We were in a little town named San Marcos. They had a little square-door back in a pharmacy. The door going back to where the safe was was only a half door, one of those swinging gate sort of deals; it came halfway down so the pharmacist could look out without having to open the door. I put a big chisel in the top left-hand corner and just tapped it, and I guess the rivets were so old they had calcified—no, crystallized—and it just went *poppop-pop-pop-pop-pop* all the way down the side. I hit it once across and that was it. I guess it took maybe three or four minutes to get in the safe.

Why did you specify preferring the upper left-hand corner as a place to start?

On the upper-right side—this is looking at the safe—is where the safe's hinges are; on the left side there aren't any hinges. If you peel to where the hinges are, it's going to stop and it doesn't do you any good, you have to peel it all the way around. But you can get a start in the upper left-hand corner and without having to tear very much get you a start to where you can dig down or reach in there and get hold of the locking bars, or you can just come down the side if you want to. I would say that a hundred percent of the people that make safes who know that they're going to peel will start at the upper left-hand corner.

So, you peel most of the time. Why?

It takes less equipment than almost anything else. Blowing a safe makes a lot of noise and it carries a twenty-five-year sentence for the explosive if you're just caught driving down the road. If you drill, you have to lug that big old drill around with you and they've got tool laws for that. You can punch them. We always try that before we peel, but very few safes punch anymore. I hear people tell me about punching safes here and there, but I've only punched about two. They weld an extra plate on the back and the pin mushrooms. And something else: if it's a real good score, more than likely they're going to have tear gas in it. So it's better if there's any doubt to just go ahead and peel it.

How long would it take you to peel a safe?

Anywhere from ten minutes to never.

If you are going to use a cutting rig, they have one for $125 now that, my God, boy, it's something else! Hell, you can cut the cement off a keister; you can do anything you want to. I forget what temperature it gets; it has a new alloy cutting rod, the latest thing out. I was reading in the paper the other day that they're giving demonstrations at the welding shop, so you can go down and take lessons free.

But peeling is best all around. All it takes is two or three chisels and a couple of good mallets and you're in business.

∼

Safecracking is hard work; it is goddamned hard, man.

You don't know. You're cooped up in a little office, you can't turn on an air-conditioning machine because you can't turn the power on, and you're in a little bitty office, and you have got that physical exertion. I tell you, I have seen the floor in an office where I was working so wet with sweat it looked like it rained in there. People don't know how hard you have to work.

I have worked so hard on a safe I have had to lay down and rest before I could get out of the building. You work until you're completely exhausted. You're nervous anyway and that contributes to it. You have no idea. When you come out of a building, you are completely given up.

I have come home and slept the clock around, just absolutely exhausted. It's hard work. There's climbing fences and roofs and going through those roofs and chipping that cement out and all that. And you're working under a strain and you're looking over your shoulder all the time.

But there's one thing about safes: I think that it actually charges you.

There's only two danger points in burglarizing: your entrance and your exit. Your entrance is the most dangerous, and the reason for that is that if they see you go in, you're inside, and they've got you. But exiting, if they see you coming out, you don't have too much to worry about because you're already on your way. So, the entrance is more dangerous than the exit.

After I get inside a building, I consider myself absolutely safe. And you are. When you go in, you get yourself another exit; you know a couple of ways you can get out in case you get run up on or anything, and it is very seldom that they are going to send a force out to a building to surround it, as they say. Something else: that old policeman that drives up there—you know, he wants to live. And whenever he comes up there, he's going to be kind of cautious, and if there's any danger of him getting hurt, nine out of ten of them will let you go. I've had them pull up outside of a building on me, I'd stick my pistol out there and point it up in the air and shoot it, and they'd just get in the car and drive off down the road. Oh yeah, goddamned right! And I would too. Why would you want to run in there and get yourself killed? People don't realize those things, but they do happen.

Now after I get inside, all my fear more or less is gone, as I said. And you concentrate on the safe. Of course, you always know what kind of safe it is before you make your entrance. You go in, you've got your tools, and you can estimate what's in the safe. If it's a place that has delivery trucks, you can figure a couple of hundred per truck. That's the average for any kind of business, whether it be a beer truck or a dry-cleaning place.

But still and all: that jewel *might* be the one. It might be the guy that's beating the income tax, or it might be the guy that's booking all the big football payoff or layoff.

And there is no charge in the world like when you see that smoke. For instance, if you're punching it and you hear that pin hit the back of the safe—*clingggg!*—you know you're home free. If you're peeling it and you see that smoke come out—which is from that fire insulation in there—whenever you pop that door and see that smoke, you know that you've cracked the rivets and it's all yours. And when you pull that safe door open: it is a *charge*!

I think the most safes I ever made was six in one night. But that was four of them in one building, and you just go from safe to safe. But man, it never became less. It's not like fucking, where the first time it's pretty wild, then each time it tapers off; you get part of the same drive, the same action, but it's not like the first. Safes are not like that. Each time it's more so because you figure the odds are more in your favor of it being the big score.

Part III
The Folksong Revival

6

The Folksong Revival

(*New York Folklore*, 1985)

A folksong revival occurred in America twenty-five years ago. Like many revivals, it appealed primarily to individuals who celebrated traditions not their own. Blues were popular in the folksong revival, but the audiences were mostly whites; rural songs and performers were popular, but the audiences were mostly urban; labor songs were popular, but the audiences were mostly middle-class students. Many of the traditional performers were in their fifties, sixties, and even their seventies—but the audiences were primarily under twenty-five. Scholars were involved but it was not a scholarly revival. Topical and political songwriters figured prominently, but by and large the audiences were apolitical. Walt Whitman provided a century earlier what is perhaps the best approach to the revival: "Do I contradict myself? I contradict myself then. I contain multitudes."

Many writers and festival fans claimed the revival provided an opportunity for millions of modern Americans to better understand their country's musical roots, as well as an opportunity to honor the musicians who still represented those traditions. Others—often disparagingly referred to as "purists"—were certain the revival and its attendant commercialism would provide the death stroke for whatever fragile rural and ethnic traditions still survived.

In retrospect, the fears seem inordinate and the anxieties misplaced. On the whole, the movement was benign. I think the revival can be fairly characterized as romantic, naive, nostalgic, and idealistic; it was also, in small part, venal, opportunistic, and colonialistic.

I do not include in the revival most ethnic or regional folklore celebrations or performances that went on within the communities or regions that were the source of the materials. It is not, in my view, a revival when a group of Arkansas musicians in Arkansas sings Arkansas songs for fellow Arkansans—not unless these songs are self-consciously learned in order to put on such a performance. On the other hand, middle-class Italians in Buffalo, New York, using federal funds to hire Italian traditional singers from Philadelphia, Pennsylvania, to put on concerts for them, as happened recently, *are* part of the revival.

The same performer might have at once been both inside and outside the revival. Instrumentalist and ballad singer Hobart Smith participated in the Newport and other large folk festivals; he also sang with his family and friends in Saltville, Virginia. Blues performer Big Bill Broonzy performed for white students at the University of Chicago Folksong Club and, often on the same weekend, performed for Blacks in ethnic southside Chicago bars. When he performed in the Black clubs, he used an amplified guitar, but he used an acoustic guitar for the white university audiences because they let him know they thought the acoustic guitar more "folksy."

The complex of events called the Folksong Revival probably dates from 1958 and 1959. Like most social movements, the beginning boundary is soft and slightly arbitrary. The Weavers, an influential urban eclectic folksinging group, had hit records as early as 1950 and 1951, and even after they were blacklisted for being too far on the political left they continued for a while to perform on campuses. Their records were widely shared by folk music enthusiasts long after those records became unavailable in stores. But the great expansion in folksong activity happened toward the end of the decade.

Although university students and some faculty members were central to the revival, the revival had little direct impact on university teaching or research in the 1950s and 1960s. Many students, for example, who entered the Indiana University folklore PhD program in those years (it was the only PhD program in folklore in America at the time) were drawn to the field by their interest in folksinging, but that aspect of their lives was kept totally separate from their formal studies. Richard Dorson, who directed the program, was uninterested in music in general and he loathed in particular nonacademic popularization of folklore.[1] Nothing that went on in the Folklore Program gives any indication of the revival involvement by Bruce Buckley, Joe Hickerson, Neil Rosenberg, Ellen Stekert, Edward D. Ives, and many others.[2] Typical of such student singers was Roger D. Abrahams, who did his graduate work at the University of Pennsylvania: "I began to study the background of the songs which I was singing (this leading to a study of folklore in general)" ("Folk Songs . . ." 1966:12). Some faculty members at other universities took part in some of the folk festivals—University of California professors D. K. Wilgus, Bertrand Bronson, and Charles Seeger were all involved in the 1958 Berkeley Folk Festival—but so far as I know that enterprise was totally separate from any of their classes. It was like a mildly embarrassing hobby one tolerates in a friend who is otherwise virtuous.

Three commercial artists of the 1950s helped set the stage for the folk revival: Harry Belafonte (an actor who performed carefully arranged and orchestrated folk songs), the Kingston Trio (a slick group that took their songs completely out of context and sometimes parodied the traditions), and the Weavers. All were enormously popular, especially with white, middle-class audiences.

The folksong magazine *Sing Out!* began publication in 1950, but its circulation remained small for most of the decade. Like the Weavers, it was very much indebted to Pete Seeger's inspiration. In its early years *Sing Out!* was heavily political. It published words and music to traditional songs, but there were also anti–Korean War peace songs, civil rights songs, anti-draft songs, Ethel Rosenberg's death song, and songs from Soviet Bloc countries. Special issues were devoted to Paul Robeson, the Rosenbergs, Pete Seeger, IWW organizer Joe Hill, and the Progressive Party campaign. Toward the end of the decade, *Sing Out!*'s politics became less strident as its editors attempted to reach the large audience developing for folk music and topical songs. This audience seemed more willing to sing about political causes than it was willing to be involved in any of them. The first two issues of *Sing Out!* in 1959 had, in addition to many traditional and topical songs, articles on counter-tenor Richard Dyer-Bennet, commercialism and the folksong revival, folksongs and summer camp, and an article by Alan Lomax on "folkniks" with a reply by John Cohen. The revival had become self-conscious enough to begin looking at itself.

In 1959 and 1960, jazz concert producer George Wein and promoter Albert Grossman put on two commercial folk festivals at Newport, Rhode Island. The concerts featured what Wein and Grossman thought important stars of the revival, but both festivals were financial failures. The two promoters had missed the point: stars weren't enough to attract big audiences in this phase of the revival. Audiences were beginning to demand significant participation by traditional performers. The first University of Chicago Folk Festival, held in 1961, avoided name performers almost entirely in a conscious attempt to avoid the errors of Newport.

It is always, in cultural matters, difficult to separate causes and effects. How do we know if something starts a trend or is instead just an early representative of a trend already in motion? If an artist is spectacularly successful with something apparently new, we should assume that an audience was, for whatever reasons, ready to receive that something new, and that the "something new" fitted a slot or fulfilled a need already there.[3]

The Newport festivals *would* become central to the folksong revival, but not in the commercial form designed by Wein and Grossman and not before the occurrence of a spectacular and sometimes traumatic sequence of political and cultural events.

In 1959, the Cuban dictator Batista fled Havana and was replaced by Fidel Castro, then still a hero in America. In 1960, John F. Kennedy—young, charming, and literate—was elected president. In 1961, the Bay of Pigs fiasco occurred, the Berlin Wall was erected, the idealistic Peace Corps attracted thousands of volunteers, and the cult novels *Catch-22* and *Stranger in a Strange Land* were published and became bestsellers, especially on college campuses. Freedom riders trying to integrate buses in Alabama were attacked by racist mobs. In 1962 the Cuban Missile Crisis brought the world for the first time to the edge of nuclear war. William Faulkner, e. e. cummings, Eleanor Roosevelt, and Marilyn Monroe died. The hit songs were "Days of Wine and Roses," "Go Away Little Girl," and Bob Dylan's "Blowin' in the Wind." James Meredith was denied admission to the segregated University of Mississippi by Governor Ross Barnett and US marshals and 3,000 soldiers suppressed riots on the campus. In 1963, civil rights leader Martin Luther King was arrested in Birmingham and President Kennedy was obliged to call out 3,000 federal troops to restore order. Two hundred thousand people demonstrated against racism in Washington, DC. *The Spy Who Came in from the Cold*, a novel that demystified the romantic world of spies and delineated the cynical inhumanity of bureaucracies on both sides of the Iron Curtain, was a bestseller. The Guggenheim Museum in New York mounted the first major show of the antiestablishment pop art by Andy Warhol, Robert Rauschenberg, Jasper Johns, and others. *Dr. Strangelove* was one of the year's top movies. By year's end, 15,000 American advisers were in Vietnam, Diem and Nhu were overthrown and murdered in Saigon, and John F. Kennedy was murdered in Dallas. Lyndon Johnson became president, and the American Congress was about to pass the most sweeping welfare and civil rights legislation in the nation's history. The list of most popular singers in America included folk revival performers Joan Baez and Bob Dylan.

And the *new* Newport Folk Festival, which until the establishment of the Smithsonian Folklife Festival four years later would be the largest and most influential of the revival folk festivals, was born.

Once again, it was Pete Seeger who was instrumental in engineering what happened. Seeger knew about the financial disaster of George Wein's commercial folk festivals of 1959 and 1960. Seeger had the idea of starting over as a nonprofit foundation. Wein, Seeger, and actor/singer Theodore Bikel developed Seeger's idea of a Newport Folk Festival that would be a forum for folk music programmed and directed entirely by performers (they later added one scholar), a festival which was not grounded in profit. If all performers worked for the minimum, Seeger said, there would be enough money to invite more traditional performers than any other festival had so far been able to afford. The big names would draw the crowds which would then be able to hear the traditional musicians. The festival was to be as much an educational as an entertainment event. In addition to the usual large concerts on a center stage, there would be smaller workshops where performers could have more time to perform and audience members could get closer. (The number of workshops steadily increased during the seven years the Festival survived. In 1964, no more than three workshops went on simultaneously; the crowds were large and electrical amplification systems were necessary. In 1968, twenty-two workshops went on simultaneously and microphones were banned in order to keep the groups around the performers as small as possible.) Year by year the directors increased the proportion of traditional performers. In 1963, there were about twice as many urban as traditional and ethnic performers; in 1967 and 1968, it was just the other way around.

The largest audience for a single Newport concert was slightly over 18,000 people. The largest profit after all expenses was about $70,000. The festival used all its profits to sponsor fieldwork, produce regional concerts of folk music, and make grants that would be beneficial to what the directors thought were the revival's roots. Grants were awarded to the John Edwards Memorial Foundation, *Foxfire*, Highlander Research Center, Old Town School of Folk Music, the folklore program at UCLA, cowboy singer Glenn Ohrlin, public radio station WGBH in Boston, and other organizations and individuals. Newport profits paid for a Cajun festival in Louisiana (later credited with directly leading to a regional revival of Cajun music), a Georgia Sea Island Christmas Festival, Native American projects in New Mexico and Florida, and music programs for Resurrection City and the Poor People's Campaign. Newport profits bought guitars for blues musicians Skip James, Pearly Brown, and John Hurt, and Ampex tape recorders for the University of Pennsylvania for copying archive tapes.

Newport wasn't the earliest folk festival in the revival and neither was it always the biggest. But it was the best known and it had in abundance the virtues and faults of the revival.

By 1966, the revival was booming. *Sing Out!* doubled its page size and began newsstand sales for the first time. Its circulation reached 25,000. Other magazines reached wider and wider audiences. Robert Shelton, folk music critic of the *New York Times*, edited *Hootenanny: The National Folk Singing Magazine*, which started publishing in 1964. A nationally broadcast television show, *Hootenanny*, featured many folk performers (but not Seeger and others who were still being blacklisted).

Then political events overwhelmed the revival. By the end of 1967 nearly 500,000 US troops were in Vietnam and even the *Wall Street Journal* was predicting that the war could not be won. Riots erupted in the black ghettoes of Cleveland, Newark, Detroit, and other cities. Anti-war demonstrations were held all over the country. Many of the kids who had formed the audiences for the folk festivals became eligible for the draft as student deferments were lifted. The year 1968 brought the Tet Offensive, Eugene McCarthy's astounding near-victory in the New Hampshire primary, Lyndon Johnson's surprise announcement in March that he would not run for reelection, and the murders of Martin Luther King and Robert Kennedy. American troop strength reached 540,000 and there were hundreds of student riots across the country. The top performers were soul-singer Aretha Franklin and acid-rock guitarist Jimi Hendrix. The romantic idealism so much a part of the folk festivals was, I think, inappropriate in the climate of continually escalating violence. For many individuals who had formed a large part of the festival audiences, singing about social and political problems was no longer adequate. The late 1960s and early 1970s were years of increasing political activism.

The 1969 festival was a financial disaster from which the Newport Folk Foundation never recovered. Nor did many of the other large festivals. The big successful festival of 1969 was Woodstock, with well over a *quarter-million* fans jammed into the fields of a New York state farm. Woodstock starred rock groups such as Jefferson Airplane, The Who, Joe Cocker, Crosby Stills Nash & Young, and Jimi Hendrix, and former folk revival performers Canned Heat, Arlo Guthrie, and Joan Baez. The mixture wouldn't happen again: Woodstock was the only large rock festival in which folk revival singers were a major element.

With a single exception, all the big music festivals of the '70s were rock festivals. The exception was the Smithsonian Institution's Festival of American Folklife, directed by Ralph Rinzler.

Rinzler, in a far quieter and less public way, is to the federal festival what Seeger was to Newport. Rinzler was a member of an excellent revival group, the Greenbriar Boys, then he worked for Newport as a fieldworker, talent coordinator, and as a board member. In 1966 and 1967, Newport "lent" him to the Smithsonian to do fieldwork. He traveled the country seeking performers for both festivals. The job at first was temporary, then it became permanent.

The first Smithsonian Festival of American Folklife was in 1967. It was free, it was accessible, it was broadly conceived—and it was a smashing success. The folk festivals of the earlier phase of the revival had appealed primarily to younger people; the Smithsonian festival appealed to people of all ages, and it seems to have been especially attractive to vacationing families. Unlike all the other festivals, the Smithsonian's never had to turn a profit and it never had to find grants; it just had to continue to make political sense to the bureaucrats in the Smithsonian and the congressmen on Capitol Hill. It was the only festival, then, that could afford to ignore the usual marketplace demands, and it therefore became the most traditionally based and responsible of all the large festivals. The Smithsonian Festival of American Folklife could not have developed as it did without the groundwork laid by Newport and the other festivals. It has been able to afford a depth of representation and seriousness of concern none of the others could ever attempt.

The federal government, through the Folk Arts Program of the National Endowment for the Arts, controlled funding for many of the local festivals that went on in the 1970s and 1980s. Folk Arts was established in 1974 with Alan Jabbour as its first director. In 1975, the program awarded about a half million dollars in grants. That amount doubled the next year. In 1979, Folk Arts gave $1.33 million, in 1980 $2.27 million, in 1981 $3.1 million, and in 1982, a year in which many agencies were suffering the first of the drastic Reagan cuts to the arts, Folk Arts gave away $2.64 million.[4]

Rinzler directed the Smithsonian festivals until 1984. Alan Jabbour became the first director of the American Folklife Center in 1976. Since its third year, the Folk Arts program has been run by Bess Lomax Hawes, the daughter of John A. Lomax and sister of Alan Lomax. All Folk Arts grants are voted on by a panel, but Hawes selects all panel members herself. Federal folklore power, then, has been wielded by a small group of people for more than a decade. (Hawes, by the way, was a participant in the 1963 Newport Folk Festival.)

The Folksong Revival | 149

As federal involvement increased, the folk revival changed form. The large festivals gave way to many more smaller festivals. So far as I can tell, most of these are without politics except in the sense that the nostalgia they articulate reflects a kind of romantic conservatism. It is a kind strongly endorsed by the Folk Arts Program of the National Endowment for the Arts, which, as I noted earlier, provides funding for many of them.

I don't think the folksong revival of the 1960s died so much as it became ordinary. Much of the revival was fad or fashion, and it should be no more surprise that the youths went somewhere else than it was when disco came and went or when the recent fad of breakdancing is replaced by something else. The nice thing about the folksong revival is how much of it survived and became part of the general culture, how much of it is still accessible. I doubt that rock music would have developed the way it has were it not for the folksong revival. More folk festivals go on now than ever went on during the 1950s and 1960s, and many of them reflect real sensitivity and sophistication in programming. Many are directed by graduates of folklore PhD programs—men and women who themselves had often been in the audiences of the folk festivals of the 1960s.

One of the best assessments of the revival was written by B. A. Botkin in 1964, well before the popular phase had run its course:

> Every revival contains within itself the seed not only of its own destruction (in our mass entertainment the destruction proceeds from repetition and dullness as much as from catering to the lowest common denominator) but also of new revivals. Thus, the revival has already gone through British and native American balladry, gospel songs, and jug bands and has started on the blues, minstrel song and ragtime, and the popular songs of the twenties and thirties. What is being revived, in other words, or rediscovered, is not so much American folk music as the musical past of America, with the young folkniks running ahead of some of the professors who got stuck in the ballads, and behind other professors and scholars (Newman I. White, Robert W. Gordon, and Phillips Barry, for example) who were ahead of many of their colleagues in the diversity of their folksong interests. Any revival that can accomplish this kind of rediscovery has earned its name. (Botkin 1967:98)

There has been a great deal of journalistic writing about the folksong *revival*, but *very* little scholarly attention has been paid to it thus far. It did not fit the academic models of folkloric behavior fashionable in the 1950s, 1960s, and 1970s. Perhaps the revival was too closely linked to popular movements, perhaps it was too close to contemporary political and social events for the taste of American folklorists. One can read every issue of the *Journal of American Folklore* published between 1963 and 1983 and get no idea from them that the United States had for ten years in that period been engaged in a massive land and air war in Asia, so it is hardly surprising that what seemed a transient and popular phenomenon escaped scholarly notice.

Professor Alan Dundes has suggested that the folksong revival, since it consisted of performers and audience members who had little in common with one another outside the festival, wasn't a matter of folklore concern so much as it was an example of *folklorismus*.[5] I disagree. As the Broonzy anecdote I recounted earlier illustrates, the revival, over a period of years, developed aesthetics clear enough to influence performers from tradition. I would suppose that all the performers to some extent modified their presentations to fit their image of the festival context—a musical instance of what linguists call "code switching." The events involved three groups—performers, audience, organizers—but there was continuity in the membership of those groups over a period of years. I doubt that many performers, organizers, or audience members were simple-minded enough to think they were seeing and hearing folk music performed in an original context. But they *were* seeing and hearing folk music performed in a real context, a real community: that of the folk revival. Transitory as it may have been, the folk revival community was as real and as legitimate as any other based on shared interest and knowledge. Performers and audience members learned songs and performance styles from one another; they exchanged narratives about folk music, folk revival music, revival performers, and about the revival itself. If the folklorists' models cannot account for that kind of learning, and for that kind of tradition, the defect is in the model, not in the event.

The social vision of American folklorists is broader now, and it is more catholic, but the moment when direct observation of the revival might have occurred is long past. Folklorists can examine the revival as an historical event, but not, alas, as the vital season it in fact was.

Notes

1. According to Roger D. Abrahams, Sandra Dolby-Stahl, and Ralph Rinzler, Dorson's interest in and attitude toward revival folksinging, festivals, and popular-

ization changed significantly near the end of his life. He published a popularizing folklore collection targeted for a general audience (*America in Legend*, 1973), developed a few years after that an interest in the Smithsonian's Festival of American Folklife, and he began to enjoy parties where students performed musically.

2. Buckley subsequently became director of the graduate program at Cooperstown, Hickerson director of the Archive of Folk Culture in the Library of Congress, and Rosenberg, Stekert, and Ives became professors of folklore at Memorial University of Newfoundland, University of Minnesota, and University of Maine, respectively.

3. For an excellent recent study of the relationship between artists, technologies, audiences, and social and political contexts, see Howard S. Becker, *Art Worlds* (1982). For an involved participant's autobiographical observations on the revival, see Oscar Brand, *The Ballad Mongers: Rise of the Modern Folksong* (1962). *The American Folk Scene: Dimensions of the Folksong Revival*, edited by David A. DeTurk and A. Poulin, Jr. (1967), contains many contemporary articles about the revival by a wide range of critics and commentators.

4. Bess Hawes told me more funds were available that year, but they were not given out because she and the evaluation panel didn't find enough worthy projects.

5. Dundes' suggestion was made after the oral presentation of this paper at the "Culture, Tradition, Identity" symposium at Indiana University, 26 March 1984. The symposium, which took place in Bloomington 26–28 March 1984, was sponsored by the Joint Commission on the Humanities and Social Sciences of the American Council of Learned Societies and the Hungarian Academy of Sciences.

References

Becker, Howard S. 1982. *Art Worlds*. Berkeley and Los Angeles: University of California Press.
Botkin, B. A. 1967. "The Folksong Revival: Cult or Culture?" In DeTurk and Pulin, 95–100.
Brand, Oscar. 1962. *The Ballad Mongers: Rise of the Modern Folk Song*. New York: Funk & Wagnalls.
DeTurk, David A., and A. Pulin, Jr., eds. 1967. *The American Folk Scene: Dimensions of the Folksong Revival*. New York: Dell.
Dorson, Richard, M. 1973. *America in Legend*. Pantheon.
"Folk Songs and the Top 40—A Symposium." 1966. *Sing Out!* 16, no. 1 (February/March): 12–21.

7

Skip James

"Skippy been places . . ."

(*First of the Month, 2021*)

I'd written about Skip twice previously. The first was an article for Sing Out!, *"The Personal Blues of Skip James" (1965); the second was liner notes for the Vanguard album* Skip James/Today! *(1966). Parts of both are incorporated here.*

∼

Skip James sometimes stayed with us in Cambridge when he was performing nearby. The last time he visited, I gave him a dog, Dewey Decimal, a fyce I'd brought home from a trip to San Antonio a few weeks earlier. The fyce and my four-year-old son Michael didn't get along.

Skip said he'd be happy to take him home to Philadelphia. They bonded immediately. I next saw Skip at a blues session in the Smithsonian's annual Festival on the Mall. He was performing in it and I was doing the introductions. He and his wife said they and the fyce were doing just fine.

He died a year later—on October 3, 1969—of the cancer he'd been dealing with the entire time I knew him. We'd met in 1964. John Fahey brought him by a few times to record in my basement. The session I remember most was when John and Skip brought Mississippi John Hurt with them. We taped in the basement for a while, then Skip said that he really wished there was a piano around because there were songs he liked doing on piano more than guitar. I said there was a piano the previous tenant of my study in Harvard's Adams House had left. I didn't know how in tune it was. John Hurt and Skip both laughed at that: a slightly out-of-tune piano was hardly alien to them.

So we went to Adams House. We recorded blues, but the startling moment was when Skip and John began singing songs by 1920s country singer Jimmy Rodgers. Jimmy Rodgers was famous for his yodeling. Skip and John did those songs and they yodeled.

Skip James and John Hurt were, each in their own way, great musical artists. What I learned in that moment when they yodeled white country songs with that out-of-tune piano was, if you think you know who those guys were or what those guys knew on the basis of their classic records, forget it. They were all more complicated than you or I will ever know.

The first time I heard Skip perform had been two years earlier at the Saturday afternoon Blues Workshop of the 1964 Newport Folk Festival. It was called a "workshop" but there was a huge audience.

Newport that week was cold and damp. The wind and rain went on and off at irregular intervals. The cold stayed on just about all the time. When the music was good you could maybe forget it for a while, but rarely for very long. Some of the performers announced songs, then decided to do something else when they realized the coldness had gotten through to the bones and their fingers just couldn't respond the way they should.

For most of us, many of the people Sam Charters and Willis James introduced in that workshop had been names in books. A few were voices heard on friends' old 78 rpm records. One by one they came up, were introduced, made the foulness of the day go away for a few minutes: Mississippi John Hurt, Reverend Robert Wilkins, Robert Pete Williams.

And then Sam Charters introduced Skip James. I was sitting behind the small stage with Hammy Nixon. The name made us both look up. A thin, dark-suited man with a serious hat settled into the iron chair and we saw his back against the field of three thousand or so faces.

Then suddenly—I don't know quite how to describe it—Skip's incredible voice began the slow agonizing wail of "Devil Got My Woman Blues," and it wasn't a matter of competing with the weather at all, but instead one of those rare electric moments when things manage to connect and coalesce perfectly. Skip's precise tenor soared into the gray and careless cold and many of those young faces in that vast field were suddenly still as they listened, were taken up, and began to feel something of what it was all about.

If you can find it, listen to the Vanguard album *The Blues at Newport/1964/Part 2*, which has a recording of that performance. Imagine that hostile gray afternoon sky and Skip's voice splitting it open. Or listen to

Skip's best studio album, *Skip James/Today!*, and you'll get some more. *Today!* was Skip's third LP, the first that was well enough recorded to give some idea of his range and versatility. You'll never mistake another guitar or voice for his. Somehow within the quality that is his alone there is a sweeping range of techniques and styles. Each piece sounds as if it had been programmed to the last note, the last multiple hammer, but then you hear other recordings or make it to a live performance and you realize that it is not the specifics that characterize his musical personality but his skillful and completely idiosyncratic manipulation and juxtapositioning of them.

Nehemiah James ("Skippy" was bestowed by schoolmates as a comment on his dancing style) was born June 9, 1902, just outside Bentonia, Mississippi, a small town halfway between Yazoo City and Jackson on US 49. He spent parts of his youth in the Delta—to your right if you drive south out of Memphis on US 61 toward Vicksburg—an area rich in cotton and blues. The blues are one of American folk music's greatest indigenous products and the central and Delta Mississippi bluesmen have been its greatest exponents: Charlie Patton, Bill Broonzy, Willie Brown, Son House, Robert Wilkins, Robert Johnson, Skip James.

Skip's father, a Baptist minister, played organ and guitar. When he was seven or eight, Skip heard Henry Stuckey and Rich Griffith, two Bentonia musicians, and begged his mother to get him a guitar. It cost $2.50 and he couldn't put it down: "It was just in me, I guess, and I was just graftin' after it. I would just sit until . . . I didn't have sense enough to know how far to go and how hungry I'd get 'cause my mind was on the music, what I was trying to learn."

Learn: though music came naturally to him he always consciously tried to learn technique, always deliberately watched, studied, worked at his craft. A year or two later he went to Jackson to hear a musician who already had a growing reputation in the area, John Hurt. When he was about twelve, he started high school in Yazoo City and had his only formal musical training—two piano lessons at $1.50 each, which, he told me, he terminated because he decided it was too much for the family budget. In his mid-teens he traveled and worked, learning along the way: "I came to a place in the upper part of Mississippi, long about the middle of the Delta part. Rosedale, Mississippi. They had a good road camp there. And I worked a little while in that good road camp and there was a guy there, he could play guitar a little bit. Not very much. More than I could." He traveled through Texas, back to Mississippi, then to a sawmill job in a small town about fifty miles south of Memphis where he met a piano player, Will Crabtree, who worked both white and Black dancehalls. Crabtree, Skip said,

> was a professional musician, played piano and nothing but that for his living. Found out that I was so eager to learn music, he decided that he'd take a little interest in me. . . . 'Course, I always was reared up to be kind of malleable in respect to old people. And he just taken a liking to me. Well, at his rest periods, when he got up off the stool to go and take a recess or get him a drink or sandwich or something, soon as he'd get up, I'd sit right on the stool behind him. . . . And so he would give me an idea about some things, different notes and so on. Well, I stayed there two years and seven months. About four or five months before I left there, then I could kinda crawl a little bit.

As Skip's playing got better, Crabtree's breaks got longer. Skip went to Memphis, played music in a barrelhouse for a while, met a group of musicians there, then returned to Mississippi, where he met Little Brother Montgomery and some other bluesmen. Eventually, he settled in Jackson. He summed up his musical education:

> After I got that much from those, then I just used my own self: Skip. I don't pattern after anyone or either copycat. I may hear something, but if it's nice enough for me to get an idea about, I think I like a phrase or something, I may get it and put it in where it will be befitting in some of my pieces. But other than that, I don't. It's just Skip's music . . . I don't sing other people's songs, I don't sing other people's voices. I can't.

In 1931, he was rooming with Johnny Temple in Jackson. Temple and two friends persuaded Skip to apply at H. C. Spier's music company for a job. Skip says he was hoping to get a job playing in the store. (Son House told me similar stories of visits to Spiers' second-floor office.) Skip saw Spiers and was told to return the next day. When he arrived, the place was crowded with other performers who were hoping to audition. Skip played two stanzas of "Devil Got My Woman" and was suddenly stopped by Spiers, who told him he'd made a "terrific hit" with the judges, that he was the only performer that day to do so. Skip was signed to a two-year recording contract and told to get ready for a trip to the Paramount studios in Wisconsin.

He reached Grafton two days later at six a.m. on a frozen February morning. Arthur Laibley met him at the station and took him to a hotel, where he slept until noon, then got up for the afternoon's recording session. He cut about a half-dozen songs that day, and finished the next. He remembers recording twenty-six sides, most of them on piano. "Cherryball" was the last song he cut for Paramount. He said he wrote it that afternoon. "There was a tall slender girl standing right to the back of my chair. And quite naturally she was very cheery looking and glamorous to me. She had two big bowls of cherries over each shoulder. As I played I dedicated that piece to her. That was the first time I met her and I haven't seen her since."

Only a few of the Paramount sides were released and they do not seem to have been widely circulated. "I didn't do anything but play around for frolics in different places a little while, then I gave up music then, just quit it altogether until I organized me a quartet. A group of singers—went singing spirituals."

That lasted two years, then he went to Birmingham where his father was running a small school. Skip was ordained a Methodist minister about 1942, then was ordained again as a Baptist minister a year later. He worked in a mine in Birmingham, returned to Mississippi where he had a job cutting timber. Then he was "driving tractor, doing day work, and after they taken me off the tractor I was just overseer over the hands on a plantation."

He played no more music until 1964, when John Fahey, Bill Barth, and Henry Vestine appeared at his bedside in the Tunica hospital. He wrote a song about his hospital stay in Washington a few weeks later: "Washington, D.C., Hospital Center Blues." It is on *Skip James/Today!*

His songs were often a blend of traditional lines and his own comments on the life he was living. The threnodic "Cypress Grove" is based on feelings about a place where he used to cut timber in Mississippi. His "Hard Time Killing Floor Blues" ranks with Yip Harburg's "Buddy Can You Spare a Dime" as one of the three or four great Depression songs. The phrasing is odd, but never strained when Skip sings: "Hard times is here and every / where you go / times are harder / than ever been before." He wrote the song when, "back to Dallas, the people was on soup lines. You know, lines just getting soup, wasn't having anything, just what the government was giving us."

The only song he ever made any real money from—I think it was $10,000—was a children's song, "I'm So Glad." The money came not from one of his performances, but from royalties from Cream's cover (*Fresh Cream*, 1966). His own performance of "Hard Time Killing Floor" is on the soundtrack of Joel and Ethan Coen's film *O Brother, Where Art Thou?*; I assume his estate got something for that.

The best thing I've seen about Skip's work is Peter Guralnick's 1966 review in *Crawdaddy* of *Skip James/Today!* It reads, in part:

> This new Vanguard release is a great album. Of all the singers who have been rediscovered—indeed I would say of all the country blues singers—Skip James along with Robert Johnson initially possessed the greatest talent. And of all the rediscoveries, except perhaps for Furry Lewis, Skip James retains the most of the talent that he did have. Son House flails away at his guitar, and Bukka White grossly recalls the brilliant recordings he once made. Peg Leg Howell embarrasses us. But Skip James makes his music live now. While it has metamorphosed, while it is different from what it was, mellower, less harsh and more lyrical, the changes come together not to drain the music of its meaning but to make it live now, Today! as the album boasts. We are more suspicious of today's music because it does not stand still for us; but I think only an archaist would be able to find greater value in Skip James's 1931 recordings than in his present ones.
>
> One reason to say this is that Skip James more than almost any other blues singer is a conscious and brilliant artist. He is a sensitive, thoughtful man who attempts uniquely to bridge the gap between himself and an audience. "As I first said, it's a privilege and an honor and a courtesy at this time and at this age to be able to confront you with something that may go down in your hearings and may be in history after I'm gone. I hope to try to deliver and to promulgate some things and teachings for the students and those that are really eager and conscientious to try to learn some music, and my style especially. And I try to play it in a way some time so they can get ideas." Or he may introduce a song: "It was during Depression times that I recorded this number. Times was hard all over, and that's the title of this song, 'Hard Time Killing Floor Blues.'"

Peter's got it right (except perhaps for the Furry Lewis comparison).

I've seen Skip described as cold, aloof, moody, and difficult to deal with. Someone wrote me about him recently saying all of that. I never experienced him that way.

Skip James was a man of great dignity and seriousness. Not grimness—he could be very funny—but seriousness about his person and about his art. He was in the Mississippi blues tradition, but no other bluesman sang what he did, played the way he did, or sang how he did, and he knew it. He'd spent a long time learning the craft on the way to becoming the great artist he was. Little wonder that he didn't spring into immediate chumminess with people less than half his age expecting such a relationship simply because they liked the blues, or that he didn't like people telling him how he should perform. He'd spent too long and been through too much becoming the person and artist he was for that. The whole time he was part of that 1960s folk music scene—less than five full years—he had a cancer he knew was killing him.

Something that happened and something he said the first time I met him gets that better than I can.

The 1964 Newport Folk Festival was paradise for blues fans. In addition to Skip, there were at least a dozen great blues performers on the program: Mississippi John Hurt, Son House, Willy Doss, Reverend Robert Wilkins, Jesse Fuller, Robert Pete Williams, and more.

Many of them were housed in the same building. On the Saturday night of that weekend, going from room to room, you could open a door and another blues tradition was in process.

Skip was playing in one room and for a while a friend of mine named Al Wilson played harmonica along with him. (Al got famous for two songs he did with a group called Canned Heat: "Goin' Up the Country" and "On the Road Again." Al could play any instrument well. He died in 1970 at the age of twenty-seven of a drug overdose.) That night in the Newport mansion, Al played while Skip performed and then said, "How was that, Mr. James?"

Skip said, "It was okay. But why do you look like that?"

Al was generally pretty scruffy. That evening was no different from any other. Without a word, he got up, left the room, then came back a while later shaved, combed, and smelling better. He'd just gone into someone's room and cleaned up. Skip nodded and they played some more. No one asked: Whose razor did you use? Whose shirt is that?

The two did another song, one of Skip's 1931 Paramount recordings. When they were done, Al again said, "How was that, Mr. James?"

Skip looked at him a moment, nodded in approval for Al's performance on the harp, then said, "Skippy been places you ain't never gonna get to go."

I think about that sentence a lot: "Skippy been places you ain't never gonna get to go."

Skip James | 159

8

Liner Notes
Phil Ochs

(First of the Month, 2019)

A folklore professor from the Ivy League was scowling when he came up to me at the 1969 meeting of the American Folklore Society. He stabbed a finger in my direction and, without a hello, said, "There's one thing I can never forgive you for."

"What's that?" I asked.

"You wrote the liner notes for Phil Ochs' album."

"What's wrong with that?"

"That's not authentic folk music," he said.

"Who cares?" I said.

He obviously did. He arched an eyebrow and stalked off. Some academic folklorists were like that in those days. It was okay to write about a guy in a Kentucky holler who had a song he remembered or thought of, but it wasn't okay to write about a songster who'd been born in Texas, had gone to military school and then to Ohio State University. Academic folklorists wrote countless articles and books parsing such distinctions.

Phil and I met at the 1964 Newport Folk Festival. It was his second time there as a performer. His first album, *All the News That's Fit to Sing*, had come out to very good reviews a few months earlier. He was walking around tossing a baseball into the air and catching it with a well-used fielder's mitt. I had in the trunk of my car the fielder's mitt I'd had since I was a kid. We played catch until the leather thong that held the webbing in place in my mitt disintegrated, after which the mitt was useless, so we just talked.

I was then living at 28 Holden Green in Cambridge, a row house in a complex for Harvard graduate students and visiting faculty. It was cheap; two stories above the ground and a finished basement below. That basement was great: I could write deep into the night, playing music as loudly as I liked without bothering anyone, and, on other occasions, I could record visiting friends (like Phil and Skip James and Al Wilson) without any intruding sound from the world outside.

When Phil had a gig in the Boston area, he'd often sleep on our couch. Most of the times he visited, he'd have a new song, either one he'd written or one he was adapting, like Alfred Noyes' "The Highwayman" or Edgar Allan Poe's "The Bells." If it was a new song he'd written, he'd show me the words and ask what I thought of them as poetry, then he'd sing it and we'd talk about what worked and what maybe didn't. When he asked me to write the liner notes for his second album, *I Ain't Marching Anymore*, I was delighted. Phil was married then. I liked and admired his wife, Alice. They had been friends since they were students at Ohio State. They had a young daughter, Meegan.

Beatles '65 came out and they were all Phil could talk about. I was unsympathetic.

"That's just noise," I said.

"Have you listened to them?"

"I've heard them on the radio."

"Have you *listened* to them?"

"No. Why would I want to? It's just noise."

He came by with *Rubber Soul*. "Just listen to this and then we'll talk about it."

"No, I'm not gonna." He put the album on the kitchen table and left. Every so often, he'd ask me if I'd listened to the album yet. I'd say, "No," and he'd look at me as if I were an idiot.

Then, at least six months after Phil had left the album on the kitchen table, I listened to it. I listened to it again. I was incurably hooked. I talked about them to anyone I could get to listen.

One winter night, Phil turned up accompanied by a guy wearing a cowboy hat. "I brought Jack," he said. I was just home from a seminar I'd been teaching that semester with a psychiatrist friend, Norman Zinberg.

"Jack" performed under the name "Ramblin' Jack Elliott." I had two of his records. I'd seen him perform, but we'd never met. Jack had started out in life in 1931 as Elliott Adnopoz, son of a Brooklyn Eastern Parkway surgeon. I'd started out five years later and two miles away in a far less plush part of Brooklyn, Bedford-Stuyvesant. When Jack grew up, he decided he wanted to be a cowboy singer, so he gave himself a name that was a better fit. Every time I've seen him since—and in just about every photograph I've seen of him since—he's been wearing a cowboy hat, and, most times, a bandanna around his neck. I don't know if Jack has ever been near a cow.

Phil had a gig that winter night at the Unicorn in Boston, one of the two key folkie clubs in the area. The other was Club 47, in Cambridge. Jack was not part of the event; he and Phil were just hanging out at the time. When it got time for Phil to go to work, Jack said to me, "Are you going over there?"

"No," I said. "Not this time."

"Well," he said to Phil, "I think I'll stay here and rap a little while. I'll meet you later." Phil left and Jack said, "I hope you don't mind my staying." I said it was fine with me. "Good," Jack said, "because you're a psychiatrist and there's something I want to ask your opinion about."

"I'm not a psychiatrist," I said.

"But you *know* those people," Jack said, "and that comes to the same thing."

"No, it doesn't."

"Well, it's good enough for me."

"All right," I said.

"Do you think there's anything odd about . . ." I have to stop there. Jack talked without pause until Phil returned four or five hours later. He asked several interesting questions and told me several great stories, some of which I wrote down so I wouldn't forget them. I can't tell you any of them because of HIPAA. We psychiatrists, real or phony, play by the rules.

Jack came by early one Saturday before a gig he had in Boston. We talked a while about what had happened to whom since we last talked. He told me Phil and Alice had split up. Then we sang some songs. The songs were just going back and forth until he sang Dylan's "Don't Think Twice It's All Right" which, for several reasons, fit him so well and which he sang with so much pain and understanding and *mésure* that I sat there astonished and moved. Jack, I thought, was equally moved: things came together in that moment.

"You know something that's terrible," he said. "Nothing ever dies. You put it in the closet, but it's always *there*. And you know it's there."

"And," I said, "it's hard not to open the door once in a while just to make sure."

"Yeah. James Dean thought I was the only guy in Hollywood doing what he wanted to do, just strumming my guitar. I sang to him in a parking lot one night. He thought I was real cool. Of course, I wasn't."

He told me of a time after a performance when everyone was going to a party and he was to go but no one bothered to tell him where it was. So Jack found himself alone in the darkened club with only two of the service people there. He talked with them until dawn, then brought them up to his place in the hills where he gave them the bed and took himself out to the grass and went to sleep naked. He woke up with a vicious sunburn.

A few weeks later, Phil turned up at 28 Holden with a gorgeous companion who seemed to know nothing about anything, who got none of anyone's jokes, and responded to most questions in monosyllables. I didn't know what was going on, but it seemed a bad trade had taken place.

I next saw Alice at the Newport Folk Festival. She was adorned with Nikons and light meters. I said, "Hi, how you doing?" and she said, "Fine," and I said, "How's Meegan?" and she said, "Fine. We're both holding up." I asked if she'd seen Phil anywhere. She said she'd heard he was around and there was something she wanted to ask him about.

I said I hadn't seen him. I said, "You making it all right? Really? Money and everything?"

"Oh," she said, "That's no problem. I have enough of that."

I got into my car to drive across the field to check on the workshops. Alice yelled, "Bruce, wait!" I waited. She gave me a small beige card. The front said "Alice Ochs. Photographer." It had an address and phone number in smaller letters. "That's what I'm doing now in case you want to tell anyone." I still have the card.

The next time I saw Phil, he was living in a flat just off the corner of MacDougal and Bleeker in the Village, a few doors from the Rienzi. He was taking a crap when I got there. A young woman who said her name was Lana let me in. She was, she said, Australian. She told me that she never went out in the day. I said that was an interesting affectation. Lana said it wasn't an affectation at all: her visa had run out three months earlier and if she were picked up by anyone official for anything they'd ship her home immediately and she didn't want that. She said she was a singer, too, but she couldn't perform without a visa. She paused for a while, then said, maybe she would go home after all. She could apply for a new visa and then she could maybe get gigs. She wondered if I thought that was a good plan.

The toilet flushed and Phil joined us. We smoked and went out, leaving Lana behind. I forget the stops along the way, but we wound up in a joint where the waitress brought us a huge tray of bagels, lox, and mounds of cream cheese. She put the platter on the table and just stood there, hovering.

Phil said, "We just ordered beer."

She said, "I loved your album."

I would see Phil only twice after that. Both times were at Newport Folk Festival post-concert performer parties. I was one of the directors of the Festival by then. After the evening concerts, we would have, in one of the Newport mansions the Festival rented to house everybody, dinners and parties for all the performers and their families. People played instruments and sang deep into the night. There'd be country in one room, blues in another, Cajun in another . . .

One night, everyone cleared off an epically long dining room table so Junior Wells could dance from end to end, playing his harmonica, while his pal Buddy Guy wailed away. All the furniture was pushed back against the wall and the room filled with people. We kept urging the two of them not to stop. I can't imagine what the surface of that long antique polished table looked like in the morning light.

Another party evening I saw Janis Joplin sitting on the staircase, drinking out of a pint bottle of Southern Comfort. Those Newport performer parties were communal and she was the most alone person I ever saw at any of them. There was no way to say that. What I said instead was, "You look bored."

"I'm always bored," she said. I'd seen her on stage only a few hours earlier: no way she could have been bored during that electrifying event. Maybe the rest or the time—day to day life, parties, hanging out—but not on stage.

George Wein couldn't stand Janis on stage. He told me, when we were standing in the wings earlier that evening while she was performing, that he didn't like what she did to blues, but I don't think that was it at all: it was that George found her obscene. I argued with him a little, but not very much. Janis would have been less sexual on stage only if she had taken her clothes off, because then there would have been nothing left to suggest. What George couldn't accept, and what I didn't yet understand, was that it was, in all likelihood sincere: performance was for her the superfuck of all superfucks. Little wonder the rest of the time was boring.

There was always a logistical problem with those post-concert parties: we wanted all the performers and their families to have easy access and we wanted to keep crashers at bay. Year by year, more and more people found out about the parties. Nobody would go bonkers knowing that an Appalachian fiddler or a blues performer was there, but let word get out that Bob Dylan or Joan Baez or Janis Joplin or Peter, Paul and Mary might show up and there was an immediate crowd problem.

The directors set up a rotating-bully schedule. I don't know how else to describe it. We couldn't ask assistants to turn away People Who Mattered. So we took turns at the door doing it ourselves. Nobody who wasn't on the program or the family of someone on the program was to be let in.

I was at the door when Phil turned up with William F. Buckley, Jr. Phil (who was not on the program that year) said, "Bruce, you know Bill?"

I didn't know Bill. I knew who Bill was. I loathed everything he wrote and everything he said on TV. I hated his Yalie smirky smile. Maybe I said something like, "No, I don't. Why do *you*?"

I weakened and let them in. I wound up having an interesting conversation with Buckley, no part of which I remember.

In 1968, Phil did it again. This time, the crasher problem was more acute.

Pete Seeger or Oscar Brand had been on the door before me and when it got to be my turn, whichever one of them it was told me it had been awful: he'd had to turn away friends.

I got on the door. People who were on the program turned up: I waved them in.

People who weren't turned up: I waved them away. Then Phil, who wasn't on the program, turned up. His companion this time was Jerry Rubin. I hadn't met Rubin, but I knew who he was. I thought about my relationship with Phil and I thought about what Pete or Oscar had just said.

I said, "No. No crashers. Sorry, Phil. It's performers only. You know that."

"I'm with Jerry Rubin," Phil said.

"Yeah," I said. "It's only performers, Phil. Look in there: the place is jammed."

Phil called me a "cop" or something like that and they left. That was about the time when Jerry, Abbie Hoffman, Paul Krassner, Phil, and some other people were forming the Yippies, which would play such an important part in the devastating 1968 Democratic convention in Chicago.

In spring 1969, there was a big drug symposium in Buffalo. I wound up on a panel seated between Jerry Rubin and Abbie Hoffman. The symposium went as academic symposiums go. While a psychiatrist far up the table was talking, Jerry said, "I have the feeling I've met you."

"I don't think so," I said.

"Are you sure we haven't met?" Jerry said.

"I'm sure," I said, lying.

Things didn't go well for Phil after Chicago. He drank a lot. He developed the same bipolar problem his father had. He hanged himself in his sister's place in 1976. He was thirty-five.

A few years later, my daughter, Jessica, came home from school one day all abuzz with a singer/songwriter someone had turned her on to. "Phil Ochs. He's fantastic. You should listen to him." I went over to the record shelf, got the LP, and handed it to her. "How cool! You've got one of his records."

"Turn it over," I said. She looked at the back, then at me. "Look at who wrote the liner notes," I said. It took her a moment to get it.

"You knew him? What was he like?"

"I don't know," I said. "Listen to the songs."

Part IV
Black Studies

9

The Glory Songs of the Lord

(*American Folklore*, ed. Tristram Coffin III,
Voice of America Forum Lectures, 1968)

The term "spiritual song" was in use as early as the middle of the sixteenth century, when it meant, simply, a song that was not secular. It wasn't until the camp-meeting phase of the Great Revival, shortly after 1800, that the term took on the meaning we understand: a body of folksongs of a more or less religious nature, fairly loose in structure, generally designed for group responsive singing.

There are three main types of spirituals: those sung by the Pennsylvania Dutch, the newest and least known; those sung by the whites, the oldest; and those sung by the Negroes, the best known. The three types are intimately related yet are different enough to have caused violent disagreements that have lasted for three quarters of a century. Arguments have ranged over what belongs to whom, over whether or not the Negro created his spirituals, over how much borrowing went on from whom. Some have insisted that the promised land in the Negro spirituals was the traditional Christian afterlife; others insisted the slaves meant freedom from physical slavery; some said the spirituals' reports of battling against sin *really* meant warfare against the slaveholders; others say the spirituals meant just what they said, nothing more. On one side are those who have seen the spirituals as a sung code language through which the slaves, on their own initiative, managed to express political and sociological notions they were otherwise prohibited from expressing; on the other side are those who have seen the spirituals as religious activities, exactly the same in content, if not in style, as what certain whites were doing.

One of the reasons for the confusion is that the two contributing folklore contexts—African and early American—were not studied until long after the more didactic works on Negro spiritual singing had been completed and accepted. Another reason is that few of the early students were adequately equipped or sufficiently interested to relate the spirituals to the historical context in which they arose, a context quite distinct from the institution of slavery.

The religious roots go back to the middle of the eighteenth century, when John Wesley and his followers, reacting against the formalism characterizing permissible religious expression, preached of faith through inner emotional conviction. His followers were called the Methodists and their numbers grew rapidly as the century drew to a close. Compared with the rigorous and austere formalism of the Church of England, Wesley's mode offered an excitement that appealed to the lower and middle classes. Music was an important part of Wesley's approach; his brother Charles composed about sixty-five hundred hymns. Racially mixed services were not uncommon in the early nineteenth century, especially among the dissenter groups. Bishop Francis Asbury, leader of the Methodist missionaries to America, and Lorenzo Dow, who was also instrumental in the spread of Methodism in this country, both preached to mixed audiences.

Early in the nineteenth century there began a large-scale religious revival in America that has been called the "Second Awakening." According to folklorist Don Yoder, the "Second Awakening, using in part the materials created through the Great Awakening—the Evangelical Hymn, the new lighter tunes—but originating the 'chorus' which became the distinctive mark of its songs, created the camp-meeting spiritual. By the addition of the chorus to the Evangelical hymn-texts, through the use of folk and popular melodies rather than the antiquated psalmtunes and chorales of New England and the Middle Colonies, a new genre of religious folksong was created which was to hold its own into the 20th Century." Yoder sees the spirituals as having a natural appeal to the camp-meeting crowds. "The spirituals," he says, "were live, rather than literary. They were folk-dominated rather than clergy-dominated. Hymnbooks were discarded. Many of the frontiersmen were illiterate; besides, it was difficult to read the words of a hymn by a flickering torchlight at a night-session of the camp meeting—or when one had one's arms around a fellow 'mourner.'"

Because many of the whites could not read, the practice of "lining out" hymns was often adopted: the leader of the session, sometimes a minister and sometimes just a member of the congregation who had the "call," would read or call out two lines to be sung, then the congregation would sing them back to him; then he would call out the next two lines and they would sing those back. There were variations: he might sing or speak, he might do one or two lines at a time; interspersed might be a chorus that all knew, and sometimes the leader would sing out a verse line and the congregation would sing a burden, or chorus line, and the effect would be conversational or antiphonal. In the more formal expressions, the group only repeated after the leader or sang back a regular chorus, but in those situations that have been described as "wilder," there was much more freedom for everyone. Those who wanted to sing harmony could do so, those who wanted to shout could do that, too, because there were plenty of other people to carry the words; the preacher himself could vary both melody and text considerably if there were a chorus, because the audience knew the tune and acted as a sort of guide. This dovetailed nicely with the already existing Negro call-and-response tradition, which may have been in religious singing and which certainly was in such secular traditions as the work songs. The wilder songs in white tradition rarely found their way into print, but they continued to exist in the more isolated church groups. As the other church groups became more literate and middle class—in orientation if not in means—they more and more used hymnbooks into which the more presentable of these songs found their way. These books were often titled or subtitled "Hymns and Spiritual Songs."

It was the proselytizing of the Methodists and Baptists that caught the Negro spirit, but they did not work virgin soil. Almost from the beginning of slave-importing to this country there were attempts at religious instruction for the slaves. In the seventeenth century, slaves were baptized and taken into the Anglican Church; in the eighteenth century there was a more serious attempt to recruit the Negroes when the Church of England established its Society of the Propagation of the Gospel in Foreign Parts, an organization that trained Negro preachers and established missions along the Eastern seaboard. During the century, Negro religious identification was courted by other groups as well—Moravians, Presbyterians, Quakers, and Catholics among them.

But it was the mass appeal of the Methodists and the Baptists that proved most effective. The ministers and preachers were of the people, not the educated and alien preachers of other sects, and these men had a natural and mutual affinity with and for the people to whom they spoke. In the camp-meeting style of religious expression, simple and direct feeling was negotiable: it certified faith and was more important than textual proficiency, than literacy or formality.

"Beginning in 18th Century New England," says Don Yoder, the spiritual "passed southward through Pennsylvania to the Upland South, where it changed *color*, and the Negro spiritual was born. As the Negro and White spiritual came with the camp meeting to Pennsylvania at the time of the Second Awakening, the spiritual changed *language*, and the Pennsylvania (Dutch) Spiritual was born." The Dutch spiritual, at least at first, was "a German-language or Dutch-dialect copy of the White spiritual of the Methodists (and others) in early Americana."

Newman I. White, of Duke University, was probably the first serious scholar to establish the intimate relationship of the texts of the white and Negro spirituals. But it was George Pullen Jackson, of Vanderbilt University, who extended White's textual correlations to tunes, and in so doing presented what is still the most coherent picture of the spirituals' genesis and development. Jackson saw the songs others have called spirituals as existing in three categories: religious ballads, hymns, and spiritual songs. The religious ballads were songs for individual singing. As other ballads, they told a story, often drawing on Biblical sources, but many were also first- or third-person morality or conversion stories. One of the oldest of these is "Romish Lady," which begins:

> There was a Romish lady, brought up on popery
> Her mother always taught her, the priests she must obey.
> "O pardon me, dear mother, I humbly pray thee now,
> But unto these fake idols I can no longer bow."

Then, in what is an Inquisitional context, the girl is questioned and finally burned for her Protestant renunciation of Catholic artifacts and ikons in favor of the Bible itself.

The folk hymns, unlike the religious ballads which were not tied to any particular religious group or movement, were, according to Jackson,

> bound up genetically with the protestant evangelical activity which followed John Wesley's lead in England and then in America. The Wesleyan revival began as an ordered small-group affair and spread and developed ultimately into a movement whose aspects and practices were completely free-affairs of the uninhibited masses. In the same way the songs of that move-

ment, beginning with merely the taste of textual freedom offered by Watts and the Wesleys, and of musical freedom offered by those who furnished the melodies, spread ultimately far beyond the "allowed" tunes and hymn texts of the authorities until religious gatherings were musically completely liberated.

The words to these songs were penned by various eighteenthcentury religious poets and song writers, some of them, like Watts, quite well known; the tunes were often lifted directly from traditional secular songs, such as "Barbara Allen," "Lord Love!," "McAfee's Confession," "Three Ravens," "Wife of Usher's Well," "The Girl I Left Behind Me," and "Pretty Saro." The texts, in this stage—which Jackson dates around the last fifth of the eighteenth century—seem to have been fairly rigid; what varied were the tunes and styles of performance.

The camp meetings that occurred during the first part of the nineteenth century were large, boisterous affairs and the folk hymns didn't quite suffice for the spirit of the crowds. Jackson says,

> At the camp meetings it was not a question of inducing everyone to sing, but of letting everyone sing, of letting them sing songs which were so simple that they became not a hindrance to the general participation but an irresistible temptation to join in. The tunes of the folk-hymns were adequate. But the texts (Watts, Wesley and their schools) still demanded a certain exercise of learning and remembering which excluded many from the singing. The corrective lay in the progressive simplification of the texts; and it was in the main this text simplification which brought about and characterized the type of camp-meeting song which was called, in contradistinction to all other types, the spiritual song.

These songs were not taken seriously by scholars or publishers during the nineteenth century, but a few collections did find their way into print; one of the earliest of these was *The Christian Harmony*, published in 1805.

The Negro spiritual was discovered, for all practical purposes, by the Northern whites who went south in the early years of the Civil War to work with recently freed slaves. Some of these were military officers, like Colonel Thomas Wentworth Higginson, whose 1867 *Atlantic Monthly* article, "Negro Spirituals," was the first such collection ever to see print.

Others were involved in religious or educational activities, as were the editors of *Slave Songs of the United States*, published later in 1867, the first volume of real Negro songs published in this country. They presented their discoveries with the feelings of those who have found something new on the face of the earth.

How was it that the early discoverers of the Negro spiritual failed to recognize its relationship to white singing? Newman White says that "The Northern welfare workers who took up the spiritual in the eighteen-sixties as an instrument of propaganda were further away from the White spirituals than Southern White people were.... Thus they made the honest, characteristic mistake of assuming the fundamental originality of the Negro spiritual. They had to, or what would have become of their preconceived notion that the Negro spiritual was the 'sorrowsong' of slavery?" "What these sympathetic interpreters overlook," White says, "is that precisely the same imagery was common in the religious songs of White people during the early nineteenth century and down to the present day." And, "whatever they may have come to mean to some Negroes at a later time, they were never originally, or even generally, the expression of the Negro's longing for physical freedom."

Only one of the songs in *Slave Songs of the United States* can be taken as a direct reaction to slavery: "Many Thousand Go." The words are simple and striking:

> No more peck o' corn for me, no more, no more
> No more peck o' corn for me, many thousand go
> No more driver's lash for me
> No more pint o' salt for me
> No more hundred lash for me
> No more mistress' call for me

One of the very first Negro spirituals to reach white Yankees was "Roll, Jordan, Roll," which Lucy McKim, one of the editors of *Slave Songs*, included in an 1862 letter to the Boston publication *Dwight's Journal of Music*. In that letter, she said the songs expressed the character and life of the Negro race: they were wild and sad and reflected the misery of the slaves' current situation and faith in the future; she also said that the songs were adaptable to a variety of functions. Ironically, the song she picked to illustrate her theme was one that has a long and demonstrable existence in white tradition. At one time, the song celebrated an admiral's mid-eighteenth-century return to England in victory:

> He comes! He comes! The hero comes!
> Sound your trumpets, beat your drums!
> From port to port let cannons roar
> His welcome to the British shore.

Charles Wesley changed it to its spiritual form:

> He comes, he comes, the Judge severe, Roll, Jordan, roll.
> The seventh trumpet speaks him near, Roll, Jordan, roll.
> I want to go to heav'n, I do, Hallelujah, Lord
> We'll praise the Lord in heav'n above, Roll, Jordan, roll.
> His lightnings flash, his thunders roll,
> Roll, Jordan, roll;
> How welcome to the faithful soul, Roll, Jordan, roll.

When the song passed into Negro spiritual tradition it changed again. In *Slave Songs of the United States* it appears this way:

> My brudder sittin' on de tree of life
> And he yearde when Jordan roll
> Roll, Jordan, Roll, Jordan, Roll, Jordan, roll!
> O march de angel march, o march de angel march
> O my soul arise in heaven, Lord
> For to yearde when Jordan roll.
> Little chil'en, learn to fear de Lord,
> And let your days be long;
> Roll, Jordan, etc.
> O let no false nor spiteful word
> Be found upon your tongue;
> Roll, Jordan, etc.

For "My brudder" in the first stanza, other nouns could be substituted, expanding the singing time indefinitely. The editors of that early collection said: "This spiritual probably extends from South Carolina to Florida, and is one of the best known and noblest of the songs."

Publications such as *Slave Songs* and the Higginson article created so much interest that some Negroes decided to take practical advantage of the situation. Fisk University, a Negro college under white control, organized a choir called the Jubilee Singers, who sang the slave songs. They quickly adapted the rough and enthusiastic singing style of traditional singing to the tastes of the white music-hall audiences, still keeping some part of the original drive. They were enormously successful, and they raised a considerable amount of money for the school and sang to audiences on two continents. Hampton Institute, Tuskegee Institute, and other Negro colleges soon had choral groups out on tour, raising money for their schools. One of the accidental side effects of this was that it took nearly fifty years for anyone to notice that Negroes sang anything *but* spirituals; folklore collectors didn't document secular singing among Negroes for quite some time.

In the spirituals, the Negro ones especially, Biblical figures are seen as persona in a stanzaically intermittent sequence of dramatic scenes. These are no vague abstractions or metaphorical religious actors; they are real people, functioning in a world that is very much like this one. We find "Paul and Silas bound in jail," and we learn that "Fisherman Peter out at sea," though "he cast all night and he cast all day/he catch no fish but he catch some soul." Satan and Jesus have a horse race that one could hardly call otherworldly:

> I an' Satan had a race, Halelu, halelu
> I an' Satan had a race, Halelu, halelu
> Win de race agin de course . . .
> Satan tell me to my face . . .
> He will break my kingdom down . . .
> Jesus whisper in my heart . . .
> He will build 'em up again . . .
> Satan mount de iron grey . . .
> Ride halfway to Pilot-Bar . . .
> Jesus mount de milk-white horse
> Say you cheat my fader children . . .
> Say you cheat 'em out of glory . . .

And the kingdom of the afterlife is seen in terms of the pains and trials of this world that will be absent:

> No more rain fall for wet you, Halelu, halelu
> No more rain fall for wet you, Halelujah
> No more sunshine for burn you . . .
> No more parting in de kingdom . . .
> No more backbiting in de kingdom
> Every day shall be Sunday . . .

The themes of the spiritual may be otherworldly, but the referents are of this life. Trains, wheels, rivers, all figure prominently in the imagery; major Biblical figures are encountered in *vis-à-vis* situations; when death approaches, Jesus doesn't hover in some abstract theological background but instead prepares a bed that is quite corporeal:

> Oh, well, well, don't be uneasy
> Well, don't be uneasy
> Well, well, don't be uneasy
> Jesus gonna make up the dyin' bed.
> Oh, well, he's a dyin' bed maker
> Well, he's a dyin' bed maker
> Well, well, he's a dyin' bed maker
> Jesus gonna make up the dyin' bed.
> Oh, well.
> Well, in my time of dyin',
> I don't want my friends around
> Well, it's all I want my mother to do
> Is just to ease that pillow from under my dyin' head.
> Well, well, I'll be dyin' easy
> Well, I be dyin' easy
> Jesus gonna make up the dyin' bed
> Oh, well.
> He's a dyin' bed maker
> Well, he's a dyin' bed maker
> Jesus gonna make up the dyin' bed.

Devices familiar from other genres of folksong, such as the catalogue of relatives, are frequently employed. The loose style permits considerable play here. A one- or two- or three-verse sequence may be repeated over and over again, with the only change being the relation named, as in "Way Over in the Promised Land," which an informant of mine learned as a boy from his grandmother in Appaloosas, Louisiana:

> O lord, I wonder where is my mother
> Wonder where is my mother
> I wonder where is my mother
> Way over in the promised land.
> She sittin' down in God's kingdom . . .
> She's tellin' God 'bout her trials . . .

> Lord, one a these mornins I'm goin' meet her . . .
> Oh bye and bye I'm goin' meet her . . .

Then he sings,

> Lord, I wonder where is my father . . .

and goes through the entire sequence again. Then the same for "auntie," etc. The problem of sin is seen as traditional combat, not as a theoretical rule violation; Satan becomes as corporeal as the bedmaking Jesus:

> I shall not, I shall not be moved
> I shall not, I shall not be moved
> Just like a tree that's planted by the water
> I shall not be moved.
> On my way to heaven . . .
> Fightin' sinnin' Satan . . .
> Jesus is my captain . . .

For the island boatman, his craft becomes a metaphor for the transport to the promised land, a metaphor that retains all its realistic characteristics:

> Michael row de boat ashore, Hallelujah!
> Michael boat a gospel boat, Hallelujah!
> I wonder where my mudder deh . . .
> See my mudder on de rock gwine home
> On de rock gwine home in Jesus' name
> Michael boat a music boat . . .
> Gabriel blow de trumpet horn . . .
> O you mind your boastin' talk . . .
> Boastin' talk will sink your soul . . .
> Brudder, lend a helpin' hand . . .
> Sister, help for trim dat boat . . .
> Jordan stream is wide and deep . . .
> Jesus stand on t'oder side . . .
> I wonder if my maussa deh . . .
> My fader gone to unknown land.
> O de Lord he plant his garden deh . . .
> He raise de fruit for you to eat . . .
> He dat eat shall never die . . .

When de river overflow . . .
O poor sinner, how you land?
Riber run and darkness comin'
Sinner, row to save your soul . . .

Because of their moving quality and broad applicability, the spirituals have produced an excess of sentimentality from both Negro and white observers. James Weldon Johnson, in his *Book of American Negro Spirituals* (1925), manages to say that in the songs "you catch a spirit that is a little more than mere nobility; it is something akin to majestic grandeur. The music of these songs is always noble and their sentiment is always exalted. Never does their philosophy fall below the highest and purest motives of the heart." And, "the White people among whom the slaves lived did not originate anything comparable even to the mere titles of the Spirituals." And, "the Spirituals are purely and solely the creation of the American Negro." Miles Mark Fisher, displaying the same kind of sentimentality but a less excusable degree of ignorance, defines a spiritual broadly "as the utterance of an individual Negro about an experience that had universal application at whatever time that song was popular, "then, relying on internal evidence entirely, manages to infer that the songs were a kind of mystic musical cryptography: Biblical nouns are taken by him as code names for current socio-political figures; the journeys are into and out of slavery; sin and spiritual questions, with which the songs are so much concerned, play hardly any role at all in his elaborate structures.

Even at the present time there is a tendency to confuse, as ballad scholar D. K. Wilgus has said, "origin and essence. Early evidence is scanty and confused; the authority of print has been opposed to internal evidence; and both sources have been variously interpreted. In fact, the same evidence has nourished both sides."

Although these are a number of comments about *how* Negroes sang in the early nineteenth century, there is almost nothing to tell us *what* they sang. About the whites we know a great deal more, and what we do know suggests that what happened was, to quote Professor Wilgus again, "To America from Africa the Negro brought a song tradition differing from and yet in some respects resembling the European folk tradition (with which, in fact, it had some historic connections). From the songs of the Whites, the Negro borrowed what was congenial to him, and the Whites were debtors as well as creditors. The resulting hybrid [and in this we must include Don Yoder's Pennsylvania Dutch] is a folk music which sounds African in the Negro tradition and European in the White tradition."

10

The Other Kind of Doctor

Conjure and Magic in Black American Folk Medicine

(*American Folk Medicine*, ed. Wayland D. Hand,
University of California Press, 1976)

There is a remarkable account of conjure work in the *Narrative of the Life Adventures of Henry Bibb: An American Slave Written by Himself*, originally published in 1849. Bibb tells of slaves who adopted various techniques to avoid whippings. "The remedy is most generally some kind of bitter root; they are directed to chew it and spit towards their masters when they are angry with the slaves. At other times they prepare certain kind of powders, to sprinkle about their master's dwellings."[1] Bibb says he got into a scrape for slipping off one time. He expected to be flogged; so he went to a conjurer who gave him both a powder to sprinkle and a root to chew, and "for some cause I was let pass without being flogged that time."[2] The next week, encouraged by his apparent power over the master, Bibb stayed away most of the weekend and on his return talked back to the master. "He became so enraged at me for saucing him, that he grasped a handful of switches and punished me severely, in spite of all my roots and powders."[3] Bibb went to another conjure doctor who told him the first doctor was a quack; the second supplied him with a sneezing powder to sprinkle about the master's bed; it would, he said, turn feelings of anger to love. The only effect was the master and his wife both suffered violent sneezing fits. Bibb "was then convinced that running away was the most effectual way by which a slave could escape cruel punishment."[4]

His interest in flight was suspended for a while when he got interested in women. Even though he'd been ill served by conjure doctors before, he once again turned to them for help. "One of these conjurers, for a small sum, agreed to teach me to make any girl love me that I wished. After I had paid him, he told me to get a bull frog, and take a certain bone out of the frog, dry it, and when I got a chance I must step up to any girl whom I wished to love me, and scratch her somewhere on her naked skin with this bone, and she would be certain to love me, and would follow me in spite of herself, no matter who she might be engaged to, nor who she might be walking with."[5] One Sunday, Bibb saw a woman he liked walking with her lover. He "fetched her a tremendous rasp across her neck with this bone, which made her jump." It also made her rather angry. He went to still another conjure adviser, an old slave who told him to place a lock of his lady's hair in his shoes, an act which would "cause her to love me above all other persons." He was by that time interested in another girl, but she refused him the hair. "Believing that my success depended greatly upon this bunch of hair, I was bent on having a lock before I left that night let it cost what it might. As it was time for me to start home in order to get any sleep that night, I grasped hold of a lock of her hair, which caused her to screech, but I never let go until I had pulled it out. This of course made the girl mad with me and I accomplished nothing but gained her displeasure."[6]

To the modern reader, Bibb's experience must seem absurd on at least two major counts: How could he believe such devices would function? And after he saw they didn't help him, why didn't he learn from experience that the conjure doctor's advice was not only not helpful but sometimes downright dangerous to him?

We must change the logic a bit, shift the basic premises. What if we assume that events in this world are *causally* rather than *randomly* linked? What if we assume the world has a sense to it greater than accident and less than total divine plan? Then the only real problem is to find out how to influence the various operations. The *donnée* would be that the world *can* be influenced for good or ill, that both events and persons can be directed in significant ways. The various failures Bibb reports could then be viewed as resulting from incompetence on the part of the practitioners or some mistake on Bibb's part, but they do not themselves invalidate the theory, the process, the art.

The curious thing about the stuff so often referred to as "primitive" medicine or magic is that it is terrifically logical. It assumes the operation of the universe is causal, not gratuitous. The educated executive in New York may attribute his fall down a flight of steps to bad luck, his missing a plane to uncommon traffic congestion, but the so-called primitive would ask why he—rather than someone else—had the mass of cars in his way that afternoon and why he should have missed that top step he had always found in the past. The "logical" answer is that something caused it to happen.

A. B. Ellis, writing of Gold Coast folklore, said:

> To the uncivilized man there are no such deaths as those we term natural or accidental. All deaths are attributed directly to the actions of men or to the invisible powers. If a man be shot or his skull be fractured by another man, the cause of death appears to the uncivilized man obvious. Such and such an injury has been inflicted by So-and-so, and experience, either personal or derived, has shown him that death results from such injuries. But should a man be drowned, be crushed by a falling tree in the forest, or be killed by lightning, such an occurrence would not be considered an accident; and a man who met his death in one of these modes would be believed to have perished through the deliberate act of a malignant being. And such, to us, accidental deaths, prove to the uncivilized man both the existence and the malignancy of these beings. A man is drowned. Who has killed him? So-and-so, a local spirit of the sea or a river has dragged him down. . . .
>
> Thus far for violence and sudden deaths; but the same belief is held with regard to deaths which are really due to disease or old age. These are likewise attributed to the action of the invisible powers directly, or to witchcraft, that is to say, to the indirect action of the same powers; for it is from them that wizards and witches obtain assistance and mysterious knowledge.[7]

An extraordinary amount of folk culture is devoted to ways of dealing with what highly literate groups like to consider luck. If there are potent beings in the universe, they can do well or ill; if they exist, they can probably be influenced; if they can be influenced for good, they can be influenced for ill; if someone has caused an evil influence, perhaps someone else can cause a good one, or at least undo the evil. The world of folk magic and medicine, as many commentators have noted, assumes a total coherence in the operation of the world.

What has been assumed to be learned fatalism among lower-class American Blacks in the seventeenth, eighteenth, and nineteenth centuries wasn't fatalism at all: most *knew* quite well that whatever happened was *caused*. Some things were beyond their power of influence. That didn't mean it was beyond anyone's influence—only theirs, in that place at that time.[8]

If the magic didn't work, it meant either that it was done imperfectly or that someone else was working something stronger. It is curious that a high degree of learning is directed away from the "logical" and toward the gratuitous. But the random and gratuitous are far harder to accept and live with, far more fearful exactly because one cannot cope with them.[9]

In a recent article on folk medicine, Don Yoder writes:

> Of folk medicine there are essentially two varieties, two branches: (1) natural folk medicine, and (2) magico-religious folk medicine. The first of these represents one of man's earliest reactions to his natural environment, and involves the seeking of cures for his ills in the herbs, plants, minerals, and animal substances of nature. Natural medicine, which is sometimes called "rational" folk medicine, and sometimes "herbal" folk medicine because of the predominance of herbs in its *materia medica*, is shared with primitive cultures, and in some cases some of its many effective cures have made their way into scientific medicine. The second branch of folk medicine is the magico-religious variety, sometimes called "occult" folk medicine, which attempts to use charms, holy words, and holy actions to cure disease. This type commonly involves a complicated, prescientific world view.[10]

The important difference between the two kinds of folk medicine is that the first assumes a direct cause and effect between application of some substance to some somatic problem while the other attempts to influence some agent other than the doctor or patient or subject. The first is quite close to what we usually consider proper medical practice; the second is closer to what we consider religious manipulation.

In Old World Black culture, the two were often combined. The medicine man or voodun in Africa or Haiti would not only cure with herbs but would also act as intermediary with various divinities in the manipulation of a variety of situations. What is curious about the American situation is that the second aspect survived, but it survived without the theological framework upon which it was based. George J. McCall, for example, reports:

"Hoodoo" represents the syncretistic blend of Christian and Nigritic religious traditions in the United States, corresponding to *vodun* ("voodoo") and *obeah* in Haiti, *shango* in Trinidad, *candomble* and *macumba* in Brazil, *santeria* in Cuba, and *cumina* in Jamaica. In twentieth century hoodoo, however, Catholic elements are less prominent than in the other variants, and Nigritic collective rituals have largely disappeared. Instead, hoodoo has been assimilated to the bewildering variety of store-front spiritualist churches in its truly religious aspect, leaving a heavy residue of sorcery and fetishism as the remaining native elements.

As with sorcery among other peoples, the major foci of hoodoo sorcery lie in the realms of health, love, economic success, and interpersonal power. In all these cases, hoodoo doctors—after careful spiritual "reading" of the client—prescribe courses of action (which always include some hoodoo ritual) and gladly sell him the charms, potions, and amulets the ritual requires.[11]

At its most fully developed, as in Haiti and nineteenth-century New Orleans, voodoo is a system which explains the world; it has various deities assigned a variety of tasks, deities who may be supplicated or motivated in various ways. The voodoo doctors are trained in such manipulation. But rootwork, the more common form found in the rest of the United States, is only technique; much of the work done by root doctors and conjure men has to do with common folk remedies and with good luck (or bad luck for others) charms. The voodoo doctors sometimes engaged in simple medical work, but they originally did such work through the agency of a powerful outsider, a god.

The function of the voodoo doctor in the Haitian and Louisiana traditions is close enough to the function of African medicine man that we may cite John S. Mbiti's long description of the medicine man's work:

> First and foremost, medicine-men are concerned with sickness, disease and misfortune. In African societies these are generally believed to be caused by the ill-will or ill-action of one person against another, normally through the agency of witchcraft and magic. The medicineman has therefore to discover the cause of the sickness, find out who the criminal is, diagnose

the nature of the disease, apply the right treatment and supply a means of preventing the misfortune from occurring again. This is the process that medicine-men follow in dealing with illness and misfortune: it is partly psychological and partly physical. Thus, the medicine-man applies both physical and "spiritual" (or psychological) treatment, which assures the sufferer that all is and will be well. The medicine-man is in effect both doctor and pastor to the sick person. His medicines are made from plants, herbs, powders, bones, seeds, roots, juices, leaves, liquids, minerals, charcoal and the like; and in dealing with a patient, he may apply massages, needles or thorns, and he may bleed the patient; he may jump over the patient, he may use incantations and ventriloquism, and he may ask the patient to perform various things like sacrificing a chicken or goat, observing some taboos or avoiding certain foods and persons—all these are in addition to giving the patient physical medicines. In African villages, disease and misfortune are religious experiences, and it requires a religious approach to deal with them. The medicine-men are aware of this, and make attempts to meet the need in a religious (or quasi-religious) manner—whether or not that turns out to be genuine or false or a mixture of both. . . .

On the whole, the medicine-man gives much time and personal attention to the patient, which enables him to penetrate deep into the psychological state of the patient. Even if it is explained to a patient that he has malaria because a mosquito carrying malaria parasites has stung him he will still want to know why that mosquito stung him and not another person. The only answer which people find satisfactory to that question is that someone has "caused" (or "sent") the mosquito to sting a particular individual, by means of magical manipulations. Suffering, misfortune, disease and accident, all are "caused" mystically, as far as African peoples are concerned. To combat the misfortune or ailment the cause must also be found, and either counteracted, uprooted or punished. This is where the value of the traditional medicine-man comes into the picture.[12]

The most complex and highly structured voodoo work in this country apparently occurred in and around New Orleans because both the Black and white populations there had strong ties with Haiti. One of the most interesting descriptions of that scene is offered by Zora Neale Hurston. In the second half of *Mules and Men*, she describes how, while doing research as a Columbia graduate student, she was several times initiated as a voodoo doctor. She offers formulas for various influences: "Concerning Sudden Death," "To Rent a House," "For Bad Work," "Court Scrapes," "To Kill and Harm," "Running Feet," "To Make a Man Come Home," "To Make People Love You," "To Break Up a Love Affair"[13]; and she quotes some "Prescriptions of Root Doctors."[14] The tradition she describes is essentially Caribbean and African; it operates with the claimed mediation of deities and through the application of chemicals, and some of the practitioners claim temporary apotheosis as the source of their power. Luke Turner, descendant of famed voudooienne Marie Leveau, gives Hurston a long description of Leveau's work and says, "Marie Leveau is not a woman when she answer one who ask. She is a god, yes. Whatever she say, it will come so."[15]

Turner described in some detail Leveau's method of affixing a curse:

She set the altar for the curse with black candles that have been dressed in vinegar. She would write the name of the person to be cursed on the candle with a needle. Then she place fifteen cents in the lap of Death upon the altar to pay the spirit to obey her orders. Then she place her hands flat upon the table and say the curse-prayer.

"To the Man God: O great One, I have been sorely tried by my enemies and have been blasphemed and lied against. My good thoughts and my honest actions have been turned to bad actions and dishonest ideas. My home has been disrespected, my children have been cursed and ill-treated. My dear ones have been backbitten and their virtue questioned. O Man God, I beg this that I ask for my enemies shall come to pass:

"That the South wind shall scorch their bodies and make them wither and shall not be tempered to them. That the North Wind shall freeze their blood and numb their muscles and that it shall not be tempered to them."

There follows a catalog of bodily afflictions and diseases and infirmities that make the plagues of Exodus seem a mild sentence in comparison.[16]

It is difficult to estimate the actual spread of voodoo worship in Louisiana in the nineteenth century, but the practice was extensive enough to get wide contemporary coverage in popular magazines in other parts of the country. George Washington Cable, for example, told the urban readers of *Century Magazine* in April 1886 of the potency of voodoo worship:

> Whatever the quantity of Voodoo *worship* left in Louisiana, its superstitions are many and are everywhere. Its charms are resorted to by the malicious, the jealous, the revengeful, or the avaricious, or held in terror, not by the timorous only, but by the strong, the courageous, the desperate. To find under his mattress an acorn hollowed out, stuffed with the hair of some dead person, pierced with four holes on four sides, and two small chicken feathers drawn through them so as to cross inside the acorn; or to discover on his door-sill at daybreak a little box containing a dough or waxen heart stuck full of pins; or to hear that his avowed foe or rival has been pouring cheap champagne in the four corners of Congo Square at midnight, when there was no moon, will strike more abject fear into the heart of many a stalwart negro or melancholy quadroon than to face a leveled revolver. And it is not only the colored man that holds to these practices and fears. Many a white Creole gives them full credence.[17]

But outside of the curious situation in southern Louisiana, Black folk medicine on the mainland United States has in general lacked an overarching theory or any coherent organization of deities. Much of what Hurston's doctors do is simply the uttering of folk superstitions, many of which are common to European traditions. ("If you kill and step backwards over the body, they will never catch you. . . . If you are murdered or commit suicide, you are dead before your time comes. God is not ready for you, and so your soul must prowl about until your time comes. . . . Bury the victim with his hat on and the murderer will never get away.")[18] Her root doctor prescriptions cover common diseases—bladder trouble, rheumatism, swelling, blindness, lockjaw, upset stomach, loss of mind, poisons. Though some of the salves for swelling might work well enough, it is hard to see how some of the treatments for gonorrhea ("parch egg shells and drink the tea" or "fifty cents iodide potash to one quart sarsaparilla; take three teaspoons three times a day in water") or for syphilis ("ashes of one good cigar, fifteen cents worth of blue ointment; mix and put on the sores" or "get the heart of a rotten log and powder it fine; tie it up in a muslin cloth; wash the sores with good castile soap and powder them with the wood dust")[19] would help sufferers much. (Of course, the techniques of medical doctors at the time weren't any better for treating those diseases.)

Although there was—and still is in some rural areas—much belief in the efficacy of various magical practices and the potency of folk doctors and the existence of certain supernatural beings, that body of belief does not form a system so much as a great mass of techniques varying widely from place to place; and just about everywhere in this country, it is the technological, rather than the theological, aspect which is operative.

The most spectacular collection of Black folk medicine is Dr. Harry M. Hyatt's *Hoodoo-Conjuration-Witchcraft-Rootwork*.[20] The first four volumes of this projected five-volume work consist of almost thirty-eight hundred pages of interviews with hoodoo doctors and thousands of samples of techniques for various situations and afflictions. The fifth volume, an index being done under the direction of Wayland D. Hand, should make this enormous mass of rare data more easily accessible and approachable. At present, it is pretty much like wandering in a cataloged but unindexed archive, where we have the names and titles of performers but can only sense the holding by experiencing the entire collection. Dr. Hyatt is quite aware of his collection's value and limitations. "Though *Hoodoo* is full of magic rites and cures," he wrote me recently, "always I sought the professional operator, the *doctor*, his appearance, personal mannerisms, origin of his power, possible descent from a predecessor, activities, beliefs, methods and the atmosphere surrounding him. The latter also means a study of his clients. As you can see, *Hoodoo* is an archive, not a logical presentation of material or a *Golden Bough* trying to prove a theory; but a picture of living people, talking, demonstrating rites in front of you, 1,600 of us, asking study by the scholar."

The literature on Black folk medicine and magic, on conjure and such, is quite extensive.[21] In the nineteenth century, long before F. J. Child began his monumental library work at Harvard, gifted amateurs were already hard at work in the field collecting Negro folktales (Joel Chandler Harris's first Remus book was published in 1880)[22] and folk song (Thomas Wentworth Higginson's influential article "Negro Spirituals" was published in *The Atlantic Monthly* in June 1867, and the first book-length collection of Black American songs, *Slave Songs of the United States*, was published in the same year.)[23] There were numerous articles about Black superstition, magic, and medicine in the third quarter of the nineteenth century,[24] and when the American Folklore Society was organized in the late 1880s, its founders set forth as one of its areas of special concern the folklore of the Negro.

But there is another reason why there is so much material on Black folk medical and magical practices and customs: there was in fact a great deal of such material around. There were few other sources of power available to the slaves and ex-slaves; there was no justice in the courts for them and no regular source of financially reasonable medical aid from the white doctors in town. Because of custom and the policy of the controlling class, those practices among the folk survived long after they had become moribund in other groups. It is still difficult to know how much of that nineteenth-century material was African survival and how much was European material translated into Black idiom and style. Just as with spirituals, there remains something of both. But those things remained because they were necessary, because more sophisticated devices of control were absent. I think John Dollard expresses this as well as anyone else:

> There is another means of accommodating to life when it is not arranged according to one's wishes. This is the use of magic. Of course, one can think of magical practices among the Negroes as lagging culture patterns, which they are, but one can also think of them as forms of action in reference to current social life. Magic accepts the *status quo*; it takes the place of political activity, agitation, organization, solidarity, or any real moves to change status. It is interesting and harmless from the standpoint of the caste system and it probably has great private value for those who practice it. Magic, in brief, is a control gesture, a comfort to the individual, an accommodation attitude to helplessness. There is no doubt that magic is actively believed in and practiced in Southern town and county.[25]

I think it is clear that one of the reasons many of these practices have become rarer in the past three decades is that those lacks Dollard notes have become realities: there has been considerable "political activity, agitation, organization, solidarity, [and other] real moves to change status." But the remembrance of such times is still with us. Mrs. Janie Hunter told Guy and Candie Carawan in the early 1960s:

> We didn't go to no doctor. My daddy used to cook medicine-herbs medicine: seamuckle, pine top, epson molasses, shoemaker root, ground moss, peachtree leave, big-root, bloodroot, red oak bark, terrywuk. And you hear about children have worm? We get something call jimsey weed. You put it in

a cloth and beat it. And when you done beat it, you squeeze the juice out of it, and you put four, five drop of turpentine in it, give children that to drink. You give a dose of castor oil behind 'em. You don't have to take 'em to no doctor. . . .

All this from old people time when they hardly been any doctor. People couldn't afford doctor, so they have to have and guess. Those old people dead out now, but they worked their own remedy and their own remedy come out good.[26]

But it wasn't just for medical problems that people visited the folk doctors. Social affairs were just as much in their domain. There are many reports similar to the story told by Henry Bibb about people visiting hoodoo or conjure doctors to try to get help in managing the difficulties of simply getting on in the world. John Dollard wasn't the first observer to understand how such belief compensated for a sense of impotence or for a lack of other kinds of organization. Leonora Herron and Alice M. Bacon, writing in the *Southern Workman* in 1895, said:

Overt and natural means of obtaining justice being forbidden the Negro, was it surprising that, brought up in ignorance, and trained in superstition, he should invoke secret and supernatural powers to redress his wrongs and afford him vengeance on those of his fellows whom envy, jealousy or anger prompt him to injure?

The agent of this vengeance was usually the Conjure Doctor. This individual might be a man or a woman, white or colored, but was found in every large Negro community, where though held in fear and horror, his supernatural powers were still implicitly believed in. The source of these powers is but ill defined.[27]

As the source of power some of their informants cite the devil; some God; some, education. Basically, they say, "The conjure doctor's business was of two kinds: to conjure, or 'trick,' a person, and to cure persons already 'conjured.'"[28]

The conjure doctor is simply a library of folk beliefs and techniques in the areas of contagious and homeopathic magic. Many people know of these matters and can cite a limited number of cures or techniques, but he is the man (or woman) one goes to for the best technique for a specific situation. He is known by various names, but his functions are relatively constant.

Richard Dorson describes categories of such operators when he discusses the term *two-head*: "Although 'two-head' designates any person with esoteric gifts, the Southern Negro speaks of three separate kinds. The hoodoo doctor diagnoses and treats diseases caused by hoodoo evil. The fortuneteller, like renowned Aunt Caroline Dye of Newport, Arkansas, prophesies the future, and locates lost persons and property. The healer cures natural ailments that baffle doctors through his secret arts. Some of the most graphic stories told by Negroes involve these two-header practitioners."[29]

Dorson is no doubt correct that there are three separate kinds of practitioners in this area, but the boundaries dividing them are sometimes rather amorphous. Most of the reports in this century suggest that the practitioners assume a variety of functions which seem to depend as much on neighborhood needs as on professional divisions of labor.

Carl Carmer, for example, describes an Alabama conjure woman whose name is Seven Sisters. "It's a spirit in me that tells," she told Carmer, "a spirit from the Lord Jesus Christ. Used to be old voodoo woman lived next to my mammy's cabin. She tol' me how to trick. She say her mammy in Africa teached her. But she was a bad ol' woman—a voodoo conjure woman. I tricks in the name o' the Lord."[30] She offers recipes and techniques for various conjure acts. One will "keep your wife from flirting around; take a persimmon sprout about six inches long and bury it under the doorstep while her flirting spell is on." Other cures have to do with getting good crops, inflicting revenge on an enemy, knowing when you've been tricked by another conjurer, or curing warts. You can get a girl to sleep with you if you "steal something dirty from being next to her skin—a string from her drawers, moisture from under her right arm, best of all a menstruation cloth—stick nine pins in it and bury it under the eaves of the house" or "take hair from her head, make it into a ball, sew it up, and wear it under your right arm."[31] Norman Whitten, reporting on such practices in North Carolina, found a similar combination of activity. The conjurer, he said, "is the professional diviner, curer, agent finder, and general controller of the occult arts. Local synonyms for the conjurer are 'root doctor,' 'herb doctor,' 'herb man,' 'underworld man,' 'conjure man,' and 'goofuhdus man.' [This last is probably *gooferdust man*, referring to the graveyard dust such doctors sometimes use.] The principal function and role of the conjurer is to deal with and control the occult. This he does for a fee."[32] And Loudell F. Snow, reporting on a voodoo practitioner in Tucson, Arizona, says her informant will treat any sort of disorder: "I don't turn down nothin'," the practitioner said to Snow, "I don't care what's wrong with 'em, I just have confidence. I tell you what. I believe in God.

I believe God can do anything and everything. That is a high power, faith and the belief. I never lose faith, I never doubt myself. I know there's nothin' I can do *without* him, and I feel like He's with me at all times."[33]

This last is in many ways close to the white fundamentalist preacher who sometimes also assumes the power of healing; she is clearly a long way from the complex theological framework of the African slaves and New Orleans devotees of Haitian voodoo of the last century. It would be difficult to separate which of her techniques derive from European and white American tradition and which derive from African and Black American tradition. Clearly some significant melding has occurred, and many old contexts have disappeared. I don't think this informant is anomalous: although there are remnants of those older traditions still around, one would now be hard put to duplicate the monumental fieldwork of Hyatt or the important collection of Puckett.

But it isn't completely dead. Although these practices are not much in evidence in modern American cities (and the majority of America's population—white and Black—lives in urban centers now), there are occasional reports that suggest some of the old power is still there, that it still influences behavior in significant ways. Though fewer people may be involved in the various levels of practice than in previous years (as is the case with most rural folk traditions brought to the city), many still take them with as much seriousness as ever, with deadly seriousness. Both the folk remedies and the techniques for control still surface as significant elements in certain communities. Consider the following item, an Associated Press dispatch datelined Miami, February 12, 1974:

Court Refuses to Appoint Voodoo Doctor

> The court was bedeviled when a defense lawyer asked to have the defendant examined by a voodoo doctor or an exorcist.
>
> "What's a voodoo doctor?" Circuit Court Judge Dan Satin asked at a hearing Monday.
>
> "One who by training has learned about the powers of voodoo," replied defense lawyer David Cerf.
>
> Mr. Cerf pointed out that the defendant, Harvey Lee Outler, has been determined competent for the murder of his common law wife but the evaluating doctor said Outler believed he was under a curse. Mr. Cerf said Outler, 36, believed that Mable Young, 31, had put a curse on him. Police say Outler shot Mrs. Young with a pistol April 13.

"Your honor, a voodoo curse is just as deadly as a threat with a gun," Mr. Cerf said.

Judge Satin said: "I respect any man's rights. But if you think I'm going to appoint a voodoo doctor, you've got another think coming."

Mr. Cerf's motion was denied.

Notes

1. In Gilbert Osofsky, ed., *Puttin' On Ole Massa: The Slave Narratives of Henry Bibb, William Wells Brown, and Solomon Northup* (New York: Harper and Row, 1969), 70.

2. Ibid., 70.

3. Ibid., 71.

4. Ibid.

5. Ibid., 73.

6. Ibid.

7. A. B. Ellis, *The Tshi-Speaking Peoples of the Gold Coasts of West Africa: Their Religion, Manners, Customs, Laws, Languages, Etc.* (London: Chapman and Hall, 1887), 13.

8. See, for example, Norman E. Whitten, Jr., "Contemporary Patterns of Malign Occultism among Negroes in North Carolina," *Journal of American Folklore*, 75 (1962), 311–325; reprinted in Alan Dundes, ed., *Mother Wit from the Laughing Barrel* (Englewood Cliffs, N.J.: Prentice-Hall, 1973), 402–418. Whitten notes: "Everything has its antithesis. For instance, for every disease there is an antidote if man can only find it" (413). See also Ruth Bass, "Mojo," in *Scribner's Magazine*, 87 (1930), 83–90, reprinted in Dundes, op. cit., 380–387. Bass writes: "So far as I have been able to discover, there seems to be a trick for every kind of occupation and desire in life. To the swamp Negroes nothing is inanimate, incapable of being tricked. I have heard a swamp Negress talking about to her pot because it was slow about boiling. She begged it to boil, pointed out the advantages of boiling over not boiling, and when it remained obstinate she resorted to a trick which consisted of rubbing her belly. The pot promptly cooked faster" (383).

9. The story of Job, which is one of the most popular stories in the Old Testament, is of course an attempt to deal with exactly this problem: it suggests the Lord acts in ways which are not for man to question. The problematic nature of the solution put forth in Job is attested to by the fact that it is the most frequently analyzed book of the Old Testament.

10. Don Yoder, "Folk Medicine," in *Folklore and Folklife: An Introduction*, ed. Richard M. Dorson (Chicago: University of Chicago Press, 1972), 192.

11. George J. McCall, "Symbiosis: The Case of Hoodoo and the Numbers Racket," in Dundes, op cit., 420.

12. John S. Mbiti, *African Religions and Philosophy* (Garden City, N.Y.: Doubleday Anchor, 1970), 221–222.
13. Zora Neal Hurston, *Mules and Men* (New York and Evanston, Ill.: Perennial Library, 1970), 332–335.
14. Ibid., 340–343.
15. Ibid., 243.
16. Ibid., 245–246.
17. George Washington Cable, "Creole Slave Songs," *Century Magazine*, 11 (April, 1886); reprinted in *The Negro and His Folklore in Nineteenth Century-Periodicals*, ed. Bruce Jackson (Austin: University of Texas Press and the American Folklore Society, 1967), 237–238.
18. Hurston, op. cit., 332.
19. Ibid., 340–341.
20. Harry M. Hyatt, *Hoodoo-Conjuration-Witchcraft-Rootwork*, 4 vols. (Hannibal, Mo.: Memoirs of the Alma Egan Hyatt Foundation, 1970–1975).
21. See, for example, quoted material and reference in Dundes, op. cit.; Jackson, op. cit.; Richard M. Dorson, *American Negro Folktales* (New York: Fawcett, 1967); Newell Niles Puckett, *Folk Beliefs of the Southern Negro* (Chapel Hill: University of North Carolina Press, 1926); Georgia Writer's project of the Works Project Administration, *Drums and Shadows* (Athens: University of Georgia Press, 1940); Robert Tallant, *Voodoo in New Orleans* (New York: Macmillan, 1946).
22. Joel Chandler Harris, *Uncle Remus: His Songs and His Sayings* (New York: D. Appleton, 1880).
23. *Slave Songs of the United States*, ed. William Francis Allen, Charles Pickard Ware, Lucy McKim Garrison (New York, 1867; reprint ed., New York: Peter Smith, 1951).
24. See Jackson, op. cit., 134ff.
25. John Dollard, *Caste and Class in a Southern Town* (Garden City, N.Y.: Doubleday Anchor, 1957), 265.
26. Guy and Candie Carawan, *Ain't You Got a Right to the Tree of Life?* (New York: Simon and Schuster, 1966), 45. The photograph on the opposite page (44) shows an old woman (who may not be Mrs. Hunter, since the photos and interviews were arranged separately) sitting in a wooden chair before an old iron stove. The walls beyond her are papered with pages of newspapers. It may be that the newspapers serve because nothing else is at hand—but anyone from that area knows full well that *hants* (spirits, ghosts, demons), who sometimes possess people at night, are compulsive counters, and grains of salt or pages of a newspaper will serve as adequate protection because it takes so long to count the grains or the letters in a newspaper article that dawn comes before the hants can do any harm.

I am reminded of a visit to the Massachusetts Hospital for the Criminally Insane at Bridgewater about ten years ago. A guard tried to prove to me how batty one particular old Black inmate was. He called the man over and asked him about the devils in his room at night. The man said there weren't any devils in his room; "The devil's in your army, not mine." That seemed rational enough a position. The guard urged the man to tell me how he kept the devils out, and the man said it wasn't devils he kept out.

"Is it hants?" I asked.

He said it was hants and looked at the guard, who at that point was starting to look oddly at me.

"Tell him what you do," the guard said, "about the newspapers." "You put newspapers on the floor to keep them out?" I asked.

"That's right."

"Where are you from? South Carolina? Georgia?" He named a coastal town in northern Florida.

I asked the guard just what it was about the man that was supposed to be so batty. He scowled and asked, "How'd you know where he was from?"

"Because of the hants." I pointed out that no Southern doctor would consider that sort of superstition adequate grounds for incarceration. "Lots of the old people there used to do that." The guard, obviously no student of folklore, looked at me as if I were as batty as the inmate and walked way, shaking his head.

27. Leonora Herron and Alice M. Bacon, "Conjuring and Conjure Doctors," in Dundes, op. cit., 360 (originally in *Southern Workman*, 24).

28. Ibid.

29. Dorson, op. cit., 187.

30. Carl Carmer, *Stars Fell on Alabama* (1934; reprint ed., New York: Hill and Wang, 1961), 218.

31. Ibid.

32. Whitten, op. cit., 409.

33. Loudell F. Snow, "'I Was Born Just Exactly with the Gift': An Interview with a Voodoo Practitioner," *Journal of American Folklore*, 86 (1973), 277–278.

11

Foreword to Lydia Parrish,
Slave Songs of the Georgia Sea Islands

(Folklore Associates, 1965)

Serious collection of American Negro folklore began during the first year of the Civil War.[1] Since that time, there has been a steady series of anticipatory obituary notices written by collectors, informing us that they were members of the last decade or generation privileged to hear and record Negro folksong and story. Mostly, they toiled in error, for the Civil War, which was to have ended slavery and ignorance and thereby remove many of the conditions producing the folklore, did not do very much for the lot of the average Negro in the South. As Robert Ezra Park has correctly observed, the Negro traded his role of slave in the Old South's feudal system for a similar role in the New South's caste system. Only the terms changed, not the conditions.[2] But when Lydia Parrish tolls that same death-knell during the first year of the Second World War, she does it with good reason, for she is dealing with a doomed vestige of a dying phase of civilization, and she knows it.[3] What had made the Sea Islands folkloristically important was what made them socially intolerable: they were one of the last places in the United States reached by the 20th century. The anachronism was maintained not by local whites dedicated to keeping local Negroes ineffectual and inarticulate, but by the islands' physical isolation from the mainland, which discouraged both casual travel and serious migration, and also let develop a style of living quite unlike the mainland's. Natives, white and black, were able for a long time to live in the past.

That quality of being a small chunk of the past was no doubt part of the charm the islands held for Mrs. Parrish. As is obvious from many of her comments, she rather enjoyed the security with which we like to envision yesterday. Most of us, however, must do that in imagination only; she found what appeared to be the real thing. The past is the safest place there is, but unfortunately it is not the most real, and for that reason it is usually an intolerable landscape.

∼

When Lydia Parrish first visited the Sea Islands in 1912, she not only found them tolerable, but familiar, for they shared many qualities with the sparsely populated region in southern New Jersey where she had been born forty years earlier. Both areas were notorious for their numerous and greedy mosquitoes, both were noted for their isolated clusters of people who managed to avoid having very much to do with residents of other such clusters. And both areas were, during her periods of residence, sufficiently far in travel time (though not in actual distance) from areas of political activity for them to develop a kind of cultural lethargy ideal for the preservation of forms of folklore that had elsewhere disappeared, gone moribund, or mutated.

She was born and spent her youth in Salem County, New Jersey, an area rich in local legend and vague in political identity. Even before the American Revolution, men who wanted to disappear would fade into the pine barrens inland from the Jersey coast, a tremendous area occasionally interrupted by isolated settlements and a few roads. The territory had been Lenni Lenape, but by the 19th century, according to Henry Charlton Beck, the barrens were populated by "descendants of the first settlers, bog ore miners, lumber-cutters, glassmakers, sailors and soldiers of Washington's time, Hessians who preferred to go amok in the woods to returning home, slaves who sought strange ways to celebrate their new-found liberty. The more intelligent set up hotels along the trails of the barren, fire-swept country, journeying to town for marriage or more formal business. The rest bothered with laws and ceremonies only when it was convenient."[4] Various religious groups found relative peace and isolation in South Jersey, among them Mrs. Parrish's Quakers, who settled in Salem in 1675, founding there the first English settlement in the Delaware Valley.

As Mrs. Parrish points out, the Quakers were receptive to runaway Negroes quite early, and by the 19th century the Friends had made numerous converts among the former slaves. One was Captain David Mapps, who, with a Negro Quaker crew, manned his own ship that operated along the coast. During the War of 1812, William Richards, who had been a colonel in the Revolutionary War and was now operating the Batsto iron works, offered to pay Mapps well if he would ferry to New York a desperately needed shipment of 50 tons of cannonballs. Mapps refused, saying, "I'd like to oblige thee, Colonel, but I cannot carry thy devil's pills that were made to kill people."[5]

When the Civil War began, South Jersey's peculiar location in regard to the Mason–Dixon line produced further additions to the variegated population. Though the line followed only the southern border of Pennsylvania, it took but a map and straightedge to extend it across the Delaware River and note that it cut off a section of New Jersey bounded by a line running from about 20 miles above Salem on the west to Manahawkin on the east. The area became a haven not only for runaway slaves, but also for deserters from the Confederate army.[6]

But the intellectual climate of the area was not completely moderate. Though the Quakers in Salem continued to operate their stations of the Underground Railroad,[7] their neighbors in nearby Alloway included many Copperheads. Beck notes that even in the 1930s feelings were mixed. He questioned natives about the initials "U.S.C.T." he found inscribed on tombstones in the ruined graveyard behind the Salem County Poorhouse; some said the initials stood for "United States Confederate Troops," others insisted they stood for "United States Colored Troops." Still current was the story of the 1775 murder of Recompense Sherry by one of his slaves under a tree that did not bloom for a hundred years, but under whose branches green grass grew the year around.[8]

Lydia Parrish tells us that her Quaker community filled her with the liberal spirit, but we shall see that there were other forces influencing her attitude toward the Negro, and it is not unlikely that some of them were also part of her South Jersey heritage.

∾

I have not been able to find out very much about her middle years. She married Maxfield Parrish, the well-known illustrator, and moved away. When she was 40 years old, she visited St. Simons for the first time.

Lorenzo Dow Turner met her several decades later, when he visited the islands in the early 1930s to do research concerning African survivals among the coastal Negroes. He says that she had been living on St. Simons for several years by that time. Dr. Turner made a number of recordings for her and interpreted the African lyrics in many of them. He says of her:

She was well liked by all of the people in that area—both white people and Negroes. She travelled extensively throughout the Gullah region of Georgia and South Carolina, calling the Negroes' attention to the value of their African heritage and urging them to preserve their music and other aspects of this heritage. She would frequently arrange for Negroes from different sections of the Gullah region to come to St. Simon Island and engage in singing and participating in religious services that revealed the African influence. She made available on her property a house where such religious services took place. Since she had no speech-recording facilities, I was happy to supply them and to record the entire services, after which I would give her a copy of such recordings and retain a copy for myself. I still have scores of such recordings which I haven't yet found the time to publish, but intend to do so soon. . . .

Throughout the years I knew her I found her to be a very enthusiastic and stimulating person, and she was highly respected and well liked by the many Negroes with whom she had dealings.[9]

She remained at St. Simons until her death on March 29, 1953; she was 81. She had ready for publication at that time a two-volume genealogy of the English families who moved, with their slaves, to Nassau at the beginning of the American Revolution.[10]

Lydia Parrish was an amateur folklorist of the most easily identifiable kind: her scholarly lacks are obvious, her pages are filled with a mixture of factual information, prejudices, enthusiasm and naivete. But—as an open-minded reading of her collection will quickly make clear—her faults do not matter very much. Her love of the material enabled her to produce a collection such as no one else has produced, from an area vitally important to the study of American Negro folklore. The folk among whom she recorded were a link between the Negroes of America, the West Indies and Africa. "The folk of the Sea Islands," writes Alan Lomax, "kept to the speech of their ancestors and, in some places, still speak dialects in which many African words and syntactical features survive. Their folk and animal tales show a rich admixture of European and African traits at an early stage of blending. Their funeral customs, their religious ceremonies, indeed, their whole way of life bear the stamp of ante-bellum days."[11] Lydia Parrish did not have the academic perspective needed for a full understanding of her material, but she did have the temporal perspective needed to gather it—years in the field (that no scholar could afford) getting to know the materials at least partly from the informants' point of view. Instead of textual headnotes rich in references to other collections, she refers us to the living contexts in which the material was found; instead of critics' comments on the words of a song, she is able to offer the unlettered opinions of former slaves and their children. None of her inadequacies are so opaque we cannot cope with them, and none of her wrong-minded excursions ever obviate the fact that she presents a collection of material that in itself is quite sufficient to justify the book. We might, at this point, consider some of the ways in which her problems manifested themselves.

For all her obvious affection for her informants and her Quaker breeding, she was too much a sentimentalist to be willing to jettison the nice ante-bellum image of the happy darky happily living on a happy ol' plantation. She could deliver, in all seriousness, paragraphs such as this:

> No one, least of all the descendants of the slave-owners, could wish for a return of the institution, but a system that could produce such fine characters as the Caters' Dembo, the Kings' Neptun', his son Clarence, the Butlers' Dan and Liverpool, and "Miss Sis" Clifton's Mary Covington—born soon after freedom—and many other Negroes I could name, must have had its redeeming features. I know it will be said the system had little to do with their development, that it was the individual. Maybe so, but after reading everything I can find concerning our ante-bellum Negroes I wonder why there are not more who are outstanding characters today. Perhaps it is true that certain plantation owners were of a superior type and provided a superior example; or was it that the education received by the slaves was better suited to their needs?

This defies argument; the entire experience of the Negro since the Civil War demonstrates why she is wrong. Slavery did not have *any* redeeming features (for the Negro) and the main reason Mrs. Parrish could not find any more "superior examples" was that so many whites in the North and South had dedicated themselves with vigor to making sure that as few as possible developed, survived, or ran around loose. And one rather doubts that Mrs. Parrish did much real looking. Living on the Sea Islands permitted her to gather folklore that had survived the passage of time far better than the mainland counterpart, but it also seems to have permitted her to remain untouched by the other intellectual concomitants of that passage. Her position in the above paragraph is strikingly anachronistic—at best it is turn of the century. Could one write that way a bare few years after the Harlem riots and the Scottsboro trials? One gets a feeling that the pressing demands of social consciousness were part of the world she rejected when she set up permanent camp on her island retreat. As Harold Courlander noted in his review of her book, "Even though she emphasizes her northern Quaker origin, Mrs. Parrish's point of view toward Negroes emerges as ultra-conservative, maternal, and southern. Though it is usually hard to take offense at her plantation attitude toward her black friends, one becomes a little weary of her referring to them as 'our Negroes.'"[12] The plantation attitude, one might say, is one which assigns the Negro a number of set roles, which permits the plantation owner to explain his Negroes' actions without reference to personality or intelligence—there are intuitive characteristics that control everything. She shares part of this, and demonstrates it when she tells us that, "like their African cousins, our colored people are born actors" (23) and they have an "intuitive knowledge of music" (9), etc. We can be fairly sure that, even though she resided on the islands for many years and had many real friends, there were areas of the inhabitants' folkloristic experience which were simply not open to her—some of which she was not shown and some of which she couldn't see. And the fact that she was a woman no doubt put much extant material out of bounds.[13]

She does not seem to realize that the situation of the Negro in the United States was abominable, that the people with whom she spent so much of her time grew up in a world in which they could be beaten or worked or starved to death without any legal avenue of escape, that they were growing old in a world only partially improved. As a result, she wanders into some ludicrous positions. At one point she writes,

> It is amusing to question Southerners as to the number of times they remember hearing Negroes volunteer information. Not one so far has recalled an instance in which something has been told that was not common knowledge.
> This inborn reticence, coupled with the fact that natives of Africa remember little about their forebears farther back than their grandparents, is undoubtedly responsible for the race's lack of a past in either the Old World or the New. (20)

Does this mean she assumes that if a Negro tells nothing to a white he has nothing to tell anyone? She doesn't realize that the slave and former slave might have been loath to offer the white southern plantation owner or manager information for the same reason a convict does not chat freely with the warden or a union organizer with the company lawyer. Moreover, how many southerners were interested in hearing a Negro talk when he wasn't responding to a direct question? or permitted a situation to develop in which the Negro could conversationally produce a casual comment? or bothered to think the Negro was capable of saying anything of interest that the white hadn't himself thought first?

Her knowledge of the writing in the field is rather sketchy, and she would better have confined herself to observation and quotation from primary sources. She has a tendency to non sequitur that sometimes produces unnecessary complications. More troublesome is her tendency to believe what she reads (because she hasn't read enough to know when her sources are wrong) except when she is reading about white sources or influence—those books and articles she assiduously ignores. Some of the items listed in her bibliography seem to have been used only when convenient. In her introduction to "Moonlight-Starlight," for example, she refers to a comment by Fanny Kemble about a burying, which is of tangential relevance, and ignores the excellent text in Higginson's *Atlantic* article.

Carl Carmer, in a generally favorable review that appeared in the *New York Times Book Review*, also noted her lack of familiarity with relevant material: "In her Afro-American Shout Songs she included (without remarking on the obvious parallel) one entitled 'Where was Peter When the Church Fell Down,' which in its first section is similar not only in language but in musical phrasing to that overwhelmingly popular minstrel coon-song of some decades ago; 'Where was Moses when the Light Went Out?' . . . Mrs. Parrish also presents without other comment than that a St. Simon's Negro called it a 'Cracker Dance' one of the most widely known fiddle-dance songs in America, 'Bile de Cabbage down.' "[14]

In part, her scholarly difficulties would not be so obvious had she not been so vocal on occasions when it simply wasn't necessary. As Courlander observed in his review, "Despite the rightness of Mrs. Parrish's enthusiasm for her work, it is nevertheless important to point out that the explanatory material is largely overwritten and studded with little straw men that she is constantly flicking down with her little finger."

Had she ever collected folklore among whites or talked with anyone who had, she might have realized that many of the characteristics she ascribed to her Negro informants were endemic among folksingers in general. "With the best intention in the world the Negro never speaks the words of a song as he sings them" (xiv–xv), she tells us. But few traditional singers can reel off the words of a song with much facility, that is why the framing device—melody—is so important. Negro song, of course, is so orally composed and so various (particularly the kind of song she collected) that the concept of a spoken version is meaningless, not only to an informant but in fact.

∼

Having voiced these objections and noted that similar ones might be raised, we must note that her book is nevertheless a field collection of major importance and as such is worthy of considerable attention. Her pseudo-scholarly comments and facile conclusions may be passed over, as may Olin Downes' adjectival introduction, but her comments regarding the parts of the informants' lives to which she was privy and her descriptions of the situations in which the songs were found are invaluable.

Though she was wrong about the extent of her knowledge of the people of the island and confused her maternalism for liberalism, she did get at least partway into the lives of the people, got some idea of the place of folklore in it, and recorded a considerable body of authentic song, speech, custom, and dance lore, much of which had not previously appeared in print in any form, hardly any of which had appeared in print in this form.

She is best when she observes rather than infers—observation takes only sensory apparatus and interest, but inference requires a frame of mind quite unlike hers. But in this she is not out of keeping with many other white collectors of Negro folklore.

Her plan for a society of singers, presenting an incentive to those who could perform in the old way, is not quite so simple as it might appear. There are dangers in such a project: people will make up folklore to fit what they think the collector thinks folklore is, or they will offer only those parts of their repertory in which the collector seems to show an interest. Part of that effect may be neutralized by recording over a large period of time numerous people from different areas. The problem is to keep the focus on the informant's interests rather than the collector's. It is obvious that Lydia Parrish found some real success here.

When Alan Lomax visited the islands in 1959 and 1960, he found her group, now the "Spiritual Singers of Georgia," still active at the Cloister Hotel on Sea Island.[15] The singers still perform traditional material, but they are undoubtedly far more removed from their roots than they were just a few years ago. When Lydia Parrish first visited St. Simons, the only outside influence on the folklore came from the servants who accompanied vacationing whites, and it is likely that their influence was not great. In 1924, however, the causeway opened up, increasing the number of visitors and facilitating inter-island communication. Since 1929, her groups have been singing for whites in the cabin on her property and the hotel at Sea Island, and surely the singers' knowledge of that audience's tastes could not help but influence the kind and style of musical material they chose to sustain. For these reasons, Lydia Parrish's first two decades on the island might very well have coincided with the last period during which one might have collected a reasonable sample of the range of traditional material indigenous to the islands. One can still collect, but the process of natural selection has been significantly altered or done in altogether.[16]

Slave Songs of the Georgia Sea Islands was pretty much ignored by the learned journals. We know about the hostility developing between amateurs and professionals in these recent days of folklore's academic respectability, but there shouldn't have been very much of that around when this was published twenty-three years ago. Perhaps her scholarly gaffes blinded readers to the very real virtues of her book. In any case, *Journal of American Folklore*, *Southern Folklore Quarterly*, and other publications that should have taken notice, did not bother to review the collection. *Tennessee Folklore Society Bulletin* announced publication;[17] but reviews seem to have been limited to newspapers and general interest periodicals. Was the silence a result of her failure to master the technique of academic advertising? Should she have read pieces at meetings and published sections in the journals? Whatever the reasons, attention was not paid. Even the publisher's original records have disappeared: "Manhattan would sink if everybody kept all those pieces of paper," the nice lady said when I inquired.

One gets a feeling that she laments the mortification of the old song traditions not only because she regrets the passage of the songs, but because she also regrets the passing of the accompanying way of life. But keeping something alive when there is no other reason for survival *but* the urge to keep it alive is an unnatural mode for folklore. If folklore cannot develop it goes rigid and we have museum specimens (which may be interesting and lovely and valuable—but as museum specimens only), items that are finely preserved, perhaps, but suffer nonetheless from ethnographic rigor mortis.

Although one deplores the necessary destruction of the quiet old society on the islands (for that destruction included parts of a body of folklore in which we are interested), one does not deplore the forces that are making it go: education, realization on the part of the southern Negro that there are better forms of life to which he is entitled, realization on the part of most southern whites that there are now forces strong enough to prevent their obstructing that entitlement.

There is yet much old Negro folklore on the Sea Islands, but not very much, just as there is yet old Negro folklore everywhere in the country, but not very much. Folklore is a dynamic thing, a piece of the world that changes as the world goes around and along. Though historical folklore is of historical interest and present importance (so we may better understand the present), it is nevertheless of only collateral current interest—unless our interest is sentimental only. We go to books, not the field, for historical folklore, and Mrs. Parrish has left us one of the last records documenting one of the vitally important areas in the development of American Negro folklore. And for that we should be grateful. But we should not join her in lamenting the demise of the order that produced it. Let it rest in peace. We have other work to do.

Notes

1. Y. S. Nathanson talked about Negro song in "Negro Minstrelsy, Ancient and Modern," *Putnam's Monthly* V (January 1855), 72–79; an unsigned article, "Songs of the Blacks," appeared in *The Evangelist* XXVII (October 23, 1856), 1, which advocated study by America's unmusical and joyless whites of "the only musical population of this country . . . the negroes of the South." But collection doesn't seem to have begun until about the time a series of letters appeared in 1861 and 1862 in *Dwight's Journal of Music*. They were written by "C.W.D.," XIX (September 7, 1861), 182; James Miller McKim, XXI (August 9, 1862), 148–149; and Lucy McKim, XXI (November 8, 1862), 254–255. The McKims learned about Negro song in the course of their work with the Port Royal Relief Society. Lucy was one of the editors of *Slave Songs of the United States* (New York, 1867); she married Wendell Phillips Garrison, managing editor of *The Nation* and son of the noted abolitionist William Lloyd Garrison. In 1867, Thomas Wentworth Higginson published his "Negro Spirituals" in *Atlantic Monthly* XIX (June 1867), 685–694. Other collections followed, but these two are of particular interest here because they were gathered on the South Carolina sea islands, a hundred miles north of the Georgia islands where Mrs. Parrish collected.

2. Robert Ezra Park, "The Etiquette of Race Relations in the South," in *Race and Culture* (Glencoe, 1950, paperback reprint 1964):

> The social order which emerged with the abolition of slavery was a system of caste—caste based on race and color. The plantation had been organized on the pattern of a familial and feudal, rather than of a civil and political society. Caste was the form which race relations took under conditions which the plantation imposed. . . .
> Slavery is dead, and no one now defends it. But caste remains, and is still so much a part of the natural and expected order that few people in the South either question its right to exist or discuss its function. (181)

This interesting article originally appeared as the preface to Bertram W. Doyle's *The Etiquette of Race Relations in the South* (Chicago, 1937), xi–xxiv.

3. And, as she not infrequently indicates, she is not particularly happy to see it go.

4. Henry Charlton Beck, *Forgotten Towns of Southern New Jersey* (New York, 1936, reprinted New Brunswick, 1961), 9.

5. Beck, 30–31.

6. Dr. Richard Racz, of New Brunswick, has been particularly helpful for information regarding population movements and early settlements in New Jersey.

7. The Quakers were one of the earliest forces in America for abolition. They published the first antislavery tract in British America, did much to keep the Underground Railroad running, made Pennsylvania the first state to abolish slavery in 1780, and greatly influenced Rhode Island's passage of abolition and slave education laws in 1784. See Benjamin Quarles, *The Negro in the Making of America* (New York, 1964), 42–43, 58, 78–80.

8. Henry Charlton Beck, *More Forgotten Towns of Southern New Jersey* (New York, 1937, reprinted New Brunswick, 1963), 112–114, 175.

9. Personal communication, March 13, 1965.

10. *Wilson Library Bulletin*, XXVII (May 1953), 684.

11. In his liner to the long-playing recording *Georgia Sea Islands, Volume I* (Prestige 25001).

12. "Negro Music on Georgia Islands," *Saturday Review of Literature* ("Deep South Issue"), XV, 38 (September 19, 1942), 24.

13. And she sometimes misses verses that would not pass without comment in these days of Freudian criticism, as, "Get up Dinah / You ain' sick / All you need / Is a hickory stick / An' I ball the jack on the railroad track," about which she comments, "the words are of no particular moment, only sounds for carrying the rhythm. A box and a stick would do as well" (117). They most certainly would, but not in the sense she intends.

14. July 5, 1942, 8.

15. He produced three records that are of interest here: *Georgia Sea Islands, Volume I* (Prestige 25001), *Volume II* (25002), and *Deep South . . . Sacred and Sinful* (25005). Several of the songs in Mrs. Parrish's book appear on these records, though the fact that Lomax imported some of the performers from Virginia and Mississippi should be warning that the performances cannot be taken as raw and real. But they are excellent performances and well worth hearing.

16. Fortunately, the tradition of the islands was documented in far more depth than most other areas of Negro folklore in this country. In addition to Mrs. Parrish's *Slave Songs*, we have Professor Turner's study of the language of the islands, *Africanisms in the Gullah Dialect* (Chicago, 1949), and an excellent collection of custom, belief, and story produced by the Savannah Unit of the Georgia Writers' Project, *Drums and Shadows: Survival Studies among the Georgia Coastal Negroes* (Athens, 1940). Many informants contributed to all three studies. As Mrs. Parrish's bibliography indicates, there were also several earlier studies and collections.

17. *VIII* (June 1942), 55–56.

12

Introduction to *The Negro and His Folklore in Nineteenth-Century Periodicals*

(American Folklore Society and
University of Texas Press, 1967)

In the late 1930s, when Herbert Halpert was coediting the Works Progress Administration's American Folk-Song Publications series, he had mimeograph stencils cut for a small book on Negro folksong in nineteenth-century periodicals. In June 1943, the man carrying the stencils to be printed heard that the WPA project had closed and celebrated by getting drunk. When he sobered up, he had no idea where he'd left the stencils; they were never found.

Halpert never lost interest in the project, but he didn't have the resources to start it all over again. In the mid-1960s, he suggested to Kenneth Goldstein, then secretary-treasurer of the American Folklore Society and editor of its publication series, that someone be found to redo the book. Kenny suggested it to me.

I think Kenny had three reasons for that suggestion. He knew of the work I was doing on Black convict worksongs, so a close look at nineteenth-century reports of Black expressive culture would both interest me and be of use to me. He also knew that, as a Harvard Junior Fellow, I could take time to engage any project that caught my interest. And, as a bibliophile, he knew that the Harvard libraries would have many of the rare periodicals I'd need to see to get the work done. I agreed to take it on, but only if I could expand the focus to include nonmusical folklore forms.

Kenny sent me Herbert's list of articles in the lost WPA volume. Benjamin A. Botkin suggested several more as did Henry David Shapiro of the

Ohio State University History Department. I found more looking through journals in the Harvard Library collections.

When I was done selecting the articles and writing introductory headnotes for each of them, I sent the manuscript to Halpert. He responded with a 6,000-word letter that demonstrated his astonishing skills as an editor and depth of knowledge. Many of the headnotes contain quotations from that letter or otherwise benefit from his suggestions about them.

Norbert Fuerst, who taught one of the first graduate seminars I took at Indiana University in 1960 (it was, I think, on German Romanticism), said something that's always stuck with me: "You must always remember, scholarship is a collaborative enterprise." That applies in science, literature, history, folklore, whatever. The collaborator might be down the hall or dead however many years. In scholarship, we don't start from zero. Just about everything we do is grounded in something someone did earlier, even if we disagree with it. The Negro and His Folklore in Nineteenth-Century Periodicals, *both in the reprinted articles and in the introductory headnotes, more than any other of my books, is evidence of that.*

~

The thirty-five articles, letters, and reviews in this anthology represent but a fraction of the literature on Negro folklore published in nineteenth-century periodicals. I have tried to present as wide a range of material and attitudes as possible; the intention has been to offer a representative group of articles that present basic folklore materials, without undue concern about the prejudices of the authors, except where the prejudice seems to have distorted the materials. The articles present and discuss folksong, speech, belief, custom, and story; the authors range from militant abolitionists to dedicated slaveholders, and their attitudes toward the Negro and his folklore reflect their positions.

Although I have taken stage minstrelsy to be outside the scope of this anthology—for that is another problem with its own controlling social framework—a few minstrelsy articles are included to give some idea of the confusion in terms facing anyone beginning to study Negro folklore in the nineteenth century. Just as today, a broad audience thought what it was getting from the popular stage was folklore or something like it, and its attitude is not without importance. "Negro song" did not mean the same thing in 1829 that it meant in 1827, for in the intervening period Daddy Rice had burst upon the Louisville stage with a stereotype that still hasn't quit twitching. The great achievement of the early collectors of Negro folksong and speech was not that they collected good material (they did), but that they were able to write down what they saw and heard instead of seeking to verify the image pictured by the minstrels.

Minstrelsy, remember, was immensely popular for more than a half century. By 1850 it was big business, and during the next two decades dozens of minstrel companies traveled wherever American roads or rivers or railroads struck a city. Printed versions of minstrel songs were everywhere available (even the pages of the *Southern Workman*, a monthly magazine published by Hampton Institute, the Virginia college for Negroes and Indians, carried mail-order advertisements for *Minstrel Songs Old and New* and similar titles). As bigtime minstrelsy went into its well-earned decline, blackface and banjo moved to the vaudeville stage, presenting still more excessive parodies of the real Negro. In the 1890s, "coon songs" compounded the image.[1] It is still difficult to evaluate the extent of influence exercised by these entertainments on collectors.[2] With a few exceptions, serious collecting did not begin until the Civil War, when for the first time many Northern abolitionists came to know the slaves as something more corporeal than a good cause. There were problems from the start. Many of the people taking down the folklore were white Yankees, new to the material and the dialect. But, as D. K. Wilgus has observed:

> Considering the sympathies and understandable ignorance of these collectors, their conclusions are surprisingly moderate. They were not folklorists, anthropologists, or musicologists. They knew little of the South, their acquaintance with the "Western and Southern Camp-meetings" must have been superficial, and they knew nothing of folksongs among the white population. But they recorded a body of song, religious and secular, that differed from any they knew. They discovered the shout and the work song. They described the non-part harmony of the singers. They heard irregularities, *slides*, and *turns*, and noted what they could. They recognized adaptations of camp-meeting hymns, such as "The Ship of Zion," and rejected some songs paralleled in Methodist hymnals. For the rest, they turned to the only authorities they knew, the Negroes themselves.[3]

We are not likely to discover how representative were the songs and stories the white man heard, or what proportion he decided to print. It seems peculiar that nowhere in any of the accounts do we find any mention of bawdry; even though such material could not be printed, it could have

Introduction to *The Negro and His Folklore* | 213

been referred to. There must have been non-group songs in circulation, but perhaps those whites who could record with ease while their informants were in church or at work could not do so in a more private situation. W. G. Allen wrote, in his preface to *Slave Songs of the United States*: "Our intercourse with the colored people has been chiefly through the work of the Freedmen's Commission, which deals with the serious and earnest side of the negro character. It is often, indeed, no easy matter to persuade them to sing their old songs, even as a curiosity, such is the sense of dignity that has come with freedom."[4] When collecting became more sophisticated the problem remained, for the friends of the freedman were not likely to put things in print that would show him in a bad light, and the enemies rarely bothered to put the Negro in print at all.

We must read the transcriptions with some care and occasionally wonder what the white men did when they were confronted by sounds strange to their ears. Some tried to transcribe the actual sounds, but others, assuming mispronunciation, made editorial corrections; others assumed African origins for some words and produced weird orthographies; and some, *expecting* alien sounds, misinterpreted and misheard. How much and what kind of errors occurred we cannot tell, but we should assume there were some. What is surprising is the relative absence of obvious gross errors from this source.

To get some idea of the kind of distortion that could occur, consider the following item printed by Thomas W. Talley, a Negro collector, in 1922:

> Shool! Shool! Shool!
> I rule!
> Shool! Shool! Shool!
> I rule!
> Shool! Shacker-rack!
> I shool bubba cool.
> Seller! Beller eel!
> Fust to ma tree'l.
> Just came er bubba.
> Buska! Buska-reel![5]

The line breaks are Talley's. He titles the item "Tree Frogs," and parenthetically remarks, "Guinea or Ebo Rhyme." With his spelling, one might easily assume a West African provenience, particularly if one were unfamiliar with West African languages and white American folksong. The song is, of course, the Irish "Shule Agra," well known in the United States as "Johnny Has Gone for a Soldier."[6]

Ironically enough, some of the most accurate text transcriptions in the nineteenth-century articles probably appear in those written by hostile observers, for the anti-Negro or anti-folklore writers had no desire to make the Negro's syntax appear neat or exotic.

The sense of discovery that pervades many of the essays may be somewhat misleading. These writers were by no means the first to notice that slaves sang and told stories; they *were* the first to take such practices with much seriousness. Although earlier accounts described happy dancing throngs of carefree blacks,[7] few writers bothered to write down more than a few lines, and most were content to stop with the observation that the slaves did on occasion sing; few realized that they were observing phenomena more complicated than simple manifestations of uncomplicated happiness. A Southern slaveholder would no more have thought of publishing his slaves' songs than he would have considered paying them a salary or acknowledging his mixed progeny.

It was fashionable, in the early part of the nineteenth century, to say the Negro had a natural sense of rhythm and a natural ear for music; he wasn't particularly bright, but he sure did swing. The epitome of this notion was poor Blind Tom, the ugly and idiotic child pianist from Georgia.[8] Tom could not carry on a conversation, but he could repeat anything he ever heard—anything. One night he found his way to a piano and amazed his owners; later he amazed audiences and critics who came from all over the world to hear him play extremely complicated duets, either part, after one hearing. Blind Tom: musical prodigy and physical horror rolled neatly into one grotesque attraction. And everyone *knew* that every old slave could pat time and dance and sing and . . .

That passed, but parts of the fiction lasted until quite recently. Now, everything seems to have gone to quite the other extreme and it is gauche to say the Negro is musical at all. Some moderation is in order. American Negroes, particularly those who grow up in rural communities or first-generation urban ghettos, are generally more musical than whites. Not all of them—but many. There is nothing racist in that kind of comment, and a visit to a few Negro storefront or rural churches will supply empirical support. The reason is environmental, not genetic. If anyone matures in a milieu in which music exists as a participant activity, he has an excellent chance of at least sharpening latent abilities; in a milieu in which music is a passive activity, such abilities atrophy or never come to maturity. Certainly at this late date we need no justification for admitting the influence of environment. In this regard, articles such as "The Persimmon Tree and the Beer Dance," "A Georgia Corn-Shucking," "Creole Slave Songs," and many of the others here recorded are particularly valuable, for they give us rare contemporary accounts of the folklore in its own context.

If we are to appreciate the articles presented here both as historical documents and as folklore reports, we must note some of the attitudes toward the Negro current in the nineteenth century, for though all our writers use the word "Negro," they mean by the word quite different things: serf, chattel, stage caricature, human being.

II

Gunnar Myrdal has observed that captured Indians and imported Negroes originally were kept in much the same status as white indentured servants. When later the Negroes gradually were pushed down into chattel slavery while the white servants were allowed to work off their bond, the need was felt, in this Christian country, for some kind of justification above mere economic expediency and the might of the strong. The arguments called forth by this need were, however, for a time not biological in character, although they later easily merged into the dogma of natural inequality. The arguments were broadly these: that the Negro was a heathen and a barbarian, an outcast among the peoples of the earth, a descendant of Noah's son Ham, cursed by God himself and doomed to be a servant forever on account of an ancient sin.[9]

There is an obvious conflict between this view of the Negro and the views of humanity expressed in the basic documents of the American Revolution. For the Northern abolitionists, there was no conflict; to them, "human slavery was an offense against the fundamental moral law. Their spiritual ground was puritan Christianity and the revolutionary philosophy of human rights."[10] The antebellum Southerner solved the dilemma by accepting the American Creed only

> as far as whites were concerned; in fact, they argued that slavery was necessary in order to establish equality and liberty for the whites. In the precarious ideological situation—where the South wanted to defend a political and civic institution of inequality which showed increasingly great prospects for new land exploitation and commercial profit, but where they also

wanted to retain the democratic creed of the nation—*the race doctrine of biological inequality between whites and Negroes offered the most convenient solution.*[11]

Ironically, the belief in equalitarianism held by both the North and the South created the great intellectual schism between the two areas. In the North, equalitarian beliefs negated the arguments of racial inferiority, but in the South equalitarianism

> indirectly calls forth the same dogma to justify a blatant exception to the Creed. The race dogma is nearly the only way out for a people so moralistically equalitarian, if it is not prepared to five up to its faith. A nation less fervently committed to democracy could, probably, live happily in a caste system with a somewhat less intensive belief in the biological inferiority of the subordinate group. *The need for race prejudice is, from this point of view, a need for defense on the part of the Americans against their own national Creed, against their own most cherished ideals.* And race prejudice is, in this sense, a function of equalitarianism. The former is a perversion of the latter.[12]

Once the illogical leap required by this perversion is made, the rest of the Southern argument follows logically. Before the Civil War, the Negro was regarded legally and socially as mere chattel. If he is satisfactorily dehumanized, as he is by the racist argument, this is easy, and there are no complications. Frederick Olmsted, who visited the South in 1853–1854, wrote that "as a general rule, the larger the body of negroes on a plantation or estate, the more completely they are treated as mere property, and in accordance with a policy calculated to insure the largest pecuniary returns."[13]

We see, even before the Civil War, several major changes in the Negro's status in this country. He begins as something like an indentured servant, then approaches freedom when there is a weakening in the proslavery forces as the institution becomes unprofitable. Manumission requirements in the South are made easier and many Northern states legislate complete abolition at this stage. Then industrial innovation, such as Whitney's cotton gin, again makes slavery profitable and there follows a sequence of rationalizations which forces the Southern Negro into a role of dehumanized chattel, a role affirmed by the Dred Scott decision in 1857.

With the Negro's subordinate role expounded in philosophical theory and ratified by judicial process, the time was ripe for scientific treatises to explore the implications. A Dr. Cartwright, professor at the University of Louisiana, "thought that running away from slavery was a peculiar mental disease, called by him *Drapetomania*, to which Negro slaves were subject. He described the symptoms as follows: 'Before negros run away, unless they are frightened or panic-struck, they become sulky and dissatisfied. The cause of this sulkiness and dissatisfaction should be inquired into and removed, or they are apt to run away or fall into negro consumption.' "[14]

Reconstruction and awarding the Negro civil rights struck the South a greater blow than had military defeat in the war. One explosive reaction was voiced by the Fairfield *Herald* (South Carolina), which opposed "the hell-born policy which has trampled the fairest and noblest States of our great sisterhood beneath the unholy hoofs of African savages and shoulder-strapped brigands—the policy which has given up millions of our free-born, high-souled brethren and sisters, countrymen and countrywomen of Washington, Rutledge, Marion, and Lee, to the rule of gibbering, louse eaten, devil worshipping barbarians, from the jungles of Dahomey, and peripatetic buccaneers from Cape Cod, Memphremagog, Hell, and Boston."[15]

The editor did not have to rave for long. Negro enfranchisement survived in the North but it died quickly in the South.

There were several reasons why the South won, some political and others economic. Unlike most European serf-freeings, there was no land reform after our Civil War, and the Negroes found themselves without property, power, or function. The North, after the heavy costs of the war, did not feel up to compensating the landowners of the property that might have been confiscated and redistributed. "Under these circumstances," writes Myrdal, "the road to the national compromise of the 1870's was actually well paved from the beginning. Except for a Republican party interest in the Negro vote and the general craving for revenge against the Southern rebels, there seems not to have been much interest among most Northerners in helping the Negroes."[16] He says also:

> For a decade after the War, the aim of protecting Negro freedom retained its importance in Northern ideology. It gained strength by its capacity to furnish a rationalization for Republican party interests. After the national compromise of the 1870s, the Negro problem dropped out as a national issue. The great majority of Southerners have an interest in keeping it out as long as possible. On the surface, there seem to be no signs that the dominant North will break the compromise and start again trying to reform the South.[17]

When the Supreme Court in 1883 declared unconstitutional the Civil Rights Bill of 1875, the Negro's gains were all gone, and he found he had exchanged his status as chattel for the lowest role in a rigid caste structure.[18]

Against this background, the articles relating to Negro culture and folklore in the nineteenth century form a coherent pattern. Early in the century the Negro is a curiosity to be described with humor or paternalistic condescension, such as we find in "The Persimmon Tree and the Beer Dance" and "Uncle Sam's Peculiarities . . ." Minstrelsy was for many Northerners a way to shelve the problem posed by the free Negro: hide him in a caricature. But by the middle of the century a reaction to this had set in, and Kinnard and Nathanson published articles suggesting they have realized that the Negro may have a very real contribution to make. Just before, during, and immediately after the war, the Northern Abolitionists—C.W.D., the McKims, Spaulding, Higginson—comment on the Negro's spirituals. It is not surprising that they should find this one aspect of his culture most worthy of public attention, for it helped make their point that the Negro is a human being, one with a soul. Later, during Reconstruction days, there are several "discovery" articles—for the first time the Negro is regarded as a bearer of culture, and we are given accounts of his church services, his speech, his superstitions, and, finally, his stories.

During this period, America was still digesting the European Romanticism and the notion of the Noble Savage. As had the Europeans a short while before, the Americans included folklore in their romantic reaction. "Suddenly important literary figures (Cable, Harris, Thomas Nelson Page, etc.) started writing about the Negro and his folklore. In the past, the only important figures were socially and politically oriented, not literarily."[19] The interminable love affair between the American reading public and the image of the antebellum South was taking hold at just about the same time the Negro was demoted from freedman to serf. A chattel is not a fit subject for literature, but a serf, it seems, is. The old attitudes, safely distant in theory in the North and safely operational in the South, formed the matter of a new literature of nostalgia, and in that literature the folksy plantation Negro had his place. That nostalgic view was helped along by groups such as the Fisk and Hampton singers, who sang nice old plantation songs in palatable white harmonies.

With the last decade of the century we move into modern times. The Negro discovers the value of his folklore himself and, as the Folk-Lore and Ethnology series in *Southern Workman* indicates, begins to take seriously his own cultural heritage. This discovery was helped by scholarly attention, such as found in the articles that appeared in *Journal of American Folklore* beginning with its first volume in 1888, and the great psychic boost supplied by Dvořák, whose praise and use of Negro folk music helped make it fully respectable. This anthology ends with an article that is modern in intent, if not in method: Jeanette Robinson Murphy's serious attempt to identify—without opprobrium—cultural links between American Negro and African folklore.

Notes

1. See Paul Charosh, "Slander in Song," *Listen*, I (December 1963), 3–7.

2. For a demonstration of how fruitful a careful examination of the old minstrel collections might be, see the annotations to the songs in Newman I. White, *American Negro Folk-Songs* (Cambridge, Mass., 1928; reprinted Hatboro, Pa., 1965).

3. *Anglo-American Folksong Scholarship since 1898* (New Brunswick, N.J., 1959), 34.

4. (New York, 1867), x.

5. *Negro Folk Rhymes* (New York, 1922), 168.

6. Some versions by whites are easily as corrupt or were as strangely transcribed. In the *Frank C. Brown Collection of North Carolina Folklore* (II [Durham, 1952], 362) one finds for instance, the following:

Scheel-di-scheel-di scheel I ru
Sche-li-schackle-i-lack-i
Schil-i-bal-i-coo
The first time I saw my il-li-bil-i-bee
This come bib-ie-lapie slowree.

7. See Dena Epstein, "Slave Music in the United States before 1860, A Survey of Sources," *Music Library Association Notes* (1936), 195–212 and 377–390.

8. See *Dwight's Journal of Music*, XIX (May 18, 1861), 55. An article by the "author of 'Margaret Howth'" offers a lavish description of Tom's extraordinary career; see "Blind Tom," *Atlantic*, X (November 1862), 580–585, reprinted in *Dwight's Journal of Music*, XXII (November 8, 1862), 250–252. Tom, the semi-pseudonymous author tells us, could repeat verbatim a fifteen-minute speech, without understanding a word (much as John Steinbeck's Johnny Bear). Because Perry Oliver, his owner, did not want to risk Tom in the free states, he never performed north of Baltimore.

9. *An American Dilemma* (New York, 1964), 84–85.

10. Ibid., 87.

11. Ibid., 87–88. Italics in original.

12. Ibid., 89. Italics in original.

13. *A Journey in the Back Country* (New York, 1907), I, 64, quoted in E. Franklin Frazier, *The Negro in the United States*, rev. ed. (New York, 1957), 48.

14. Frazier, *The Negro in the United States*, 94.

15. Quoted in ibid., 138.

16. Myrdal, *American Dilemma*, 226.

17. Ibid., 431. The twenty-five years that have elapsed since Myrdal wrote this have seen great charges in both the attitude of the North and the status of the Negro, but this time the Negro himself has been largely responsible for the changes.

18. Robert Ezra Park sees the change as one from a feudal state to caste structure. See his article "The Etiquette of Race Relations in the South," in *Race and Culture* (New York, 1964), 177–178, especially 181. The article appeared originally as the introduction to Bertram W. Doyle, *The Etiquette of Race Relations in the South* (Chicago, 1937), xi–xxiv.

19. Dr. Roger D. Abrahams (private communication).

13

Prison Worksongs

The Composer in Negatives

(*Western Folklore*, 1967)

Both legally and artistically, the composer of prison worksongs functions in a depersonalized milieu. His song is never considered as an item to be *performed*, it is functional only; there is no audience posited for a prison worksong, a characteristic almost unique in American folk music. No one will credit the author with composition because no one cares if he is good or bad at it. Usually, he confines his creative activities to slight restructurings of old stanzas or the occasional introduction of a new one into an old song. If the stanza should catch his colleagues' fancy it might survive, otherwise it will be as ephemeral as breath.

The situation exemplifies splendidly the well-known passage from T. S. Eliot's "Tradition and the Individual Talent": "Poetry is not a turning loose of emotion, but an escape from emotion; it is not the expression of personality, but an escape from personality. But of course only those who have personality and emotions know what it means to want to escape from these things."[1] Eliot was talking about a far more formal kind of poetic composition, but his remarks are equally applicable to the prison situation. The prison composer really cannot turn loose his emotion, for if he did song would be too inappropriate, too lilliputian for his needs; song for him can serve only as a ritual form of exorcism, not exercise of emotion. He cannot express his personality because there is no one to express it *to*, no one cares, and the singing about his situation really places him in a ritualized third-person context and therefore for a time outside his own situation, an escapee if you will.

The most poetic of the prison worksongs are those used for untimed work, such as picking cotton or cutting sugar cane, which are often sung alone or in small groups (like "Go Down," "Old Hannah" and "No More Cane on the Brazos"). The worksongs that accompany axes and hoes have to be fairly simple and straightforward because the pace is rapid and there are many men involved. Because the cotton songs are often sung alone, they tend to have not only the most complex lyrics but also the most complex melodies—the singer doesn't have to worry about confusing other people and he is free to experiment and develop.

While doing fieldwork in the Texas Prison System I met an inmate, J. B. Smith, who had one melody he used for his solo cotton songs, and to it he sang about 130 different stanzas.[2] Both the melody and the words are fascinating, and they are the subject of this article.

When I first met Smitty he was in the eleventh year of a 45-year sentence for murder. He had been in three times previously, for burglary and robbery by assault. He said about his murder charge:

> I got out of here on those ten-year sentences, that robbery by assault. I lost my people while I was in here and I just felt like I was kind of in the world alone. I wanted to find me a pretty girl to settle down with and marry. I was 35 years old then. And I just wanted to marry and settle down. I left my home down at Hearn, Texas, other side of Bryant, and went to west Texas, out in the Panhandle country, to Amarillo. And I married a beautiful girl. She was about three-quarters Indian, I guess. A lot of mixed-breed girls out there, 'specially around Mexico and Oklahoma and Amarillo. I found me that pretty girl, the girl of my dreams I thought, and I had good intentions. But now, I fell in love with her, was what I did, and I got insane jealousy mixed up with love. So many of us do that. Lot of fellas in here today on those same terms. I was really insane crazy about the girl and I had just got out of the penitentiary and I was working, just trying to make an honest living and to keep from coming back. But I couldn't give her all she wanted and she'd sneak out a little. That went to causing trouble. I was intending to get in good shape, but I hadn't been out there long enough, not to make it on the square, you know. She wanted a fine automobile, she liked a good time, a party girl, she liked to drink, she liked to dress nice. So did I, and so I was living a bit above my income. And she would sneak out to enjoy these little old pleasures and that caused us some family

trouble. On a spur of the moment I came in one day, we had a fight, and I cut her to death. And regret it! Because I loved her still and still do and can't get her back.

So Smitty came back to Ramsey with a 45-year sentence, which looked to him pretty much like life because of his age (he was wrong: he was paroled this year). While working in the prison he began putting verses to his melody. He said about composition:

> Now these songs, we can, you know, you stay here so long, a man can compose them if he want to. They just come to you. Your surroundings, the place, you're so familiar with them, you can always make a song out of your surroundings. I read about some great poetry, like King David in the Bible, he used to make his psalms from the stars and he wrote so many psalms. A little talent and surroundings and I think it's kind of easy to do it.

Smitty's talent is considerably more than "a little." Working within a traditional framework and using some traditional elements, he has woven an elaborate construct of images that brilliantly details the parameters of his world. The songs were taped on several occasions and he sometimes gave them titles, but he meant them as part of *one* song, considered them that way, and we shall do the same here.

The song:

No More Good Time in the World for Me
(Nov. 17, 1965; 414.1)[3]

Prison Worksongs | 225

(1) No more good time, buddy, oh man, in the wide, wide
    world for me,
'Cause I'm a lifetime skinner, never will go free.
Well a lifetime skinner, buddy, I never will go free,
No more good time, buddy, in the wide, wide world for me.

(2) Lifetime skinner, skinner, hold up your head,
Well you may get a pardon if you don't drop dead.
Well you may get a pardon, oh, man, if you don't drop
    dead,
Oh well lifetime skinner, partner, you hold up your head.

(3) I been on this old Brazos, partner, so jumpin' long,
That I don't know what side a the river, oh boy, my home is
    on.
Don't know what side a the river, oh man, oh boy, my home
    is on,
'Cause I been down on this old river, man, so jumpin'
    long.

(4) Well I lose all my good time, 'bout to lose my mind,
I can see my back door slammin', partner, I hear my baby
    cryin'.
Yeah, I'm a hear my back door slammin', man, I hear my
    baby cryin',
I done lose all my good time, partner, I'm 'bout to lose my
    mind.

(5) You can go 'head on, an' marry, woman, good girl don't
    wait on me,
I got from now on, baby, to eternity.
Well I got from now on, woman, poor girl, to eternity,
You can go 'head on and marry, don't you wait for me.

(6) If I ever get lucky, man, pay the debt I owe,
Whoa, boy, I won't be guilty of the charge no more.
Hmmm and I won't be guilty of this charge no more,
If I ever get lucky, pay the debt I owe.

(7) If I ever go free, buddy, just goin' walk and tell,
'bout this lowland Brazos, it's a burnin' hell.

Well this lowland Brazos, partner, sure a bumin' hell,
Ever go free, man, just goin' walk and tell.

(8) "Little boy, why you keep on a runnin', just keep runnin' on your mind?"
Captain, I never had nothin' but that old runnin' time.
Well I ain't never had nothin', captain, this old runnin' time,
That's why I keep on runnin', just keep runnin' on, on my mind.

(9) Little girl make your bed up higher, higher woman, let your hair grow long,
Oh I be by to see you if I don't stay long.
Well I'll be by to see you woman, if I can't stay long,
Make your bed up higher, woman, let your hair grow long.

(10) Well if I ever make it, rider, ever make it to the danger line,
I'm goin' be long gone, partner, goin' be hard to find.
Well I'm goin' be long gone, rider, sure be hard to find,
If I ever make it 'cross that danger line.

(11) If you lookin' for heaven, lookin' for heaven, you getter go 'head by,
But if you lookin' for trouble, you can stop and try.
Well if you lookin' for trouble, oh man, you can stop and try,
But if you lookin' for heaven, you better go 'head by.

(12) Got your piece a pistol, rider, you know you playin' half bad,
Gonna be mine in the mornin', if you just make me mad.
Well it'll be mine in the mornin', rider, you just make me mad,
Got your piece a pistol, goin' 'round playin' half bad.

(13) Had my thirty-two-twenty, rider, just one round a lead,
I wouldn't leave enough livin', oh man, to bury the dead.
Oh wouldn't be enough livin', rider, oh man, to bury the dead,
Had my thirty-two-twenty, and a round a lead.

Prison Worksongs | 227

(14) What you do, buddy, get so jumpin' long?
"Man, I kill Roberta, my woman, in the high sheriff's arms.
Well I kill Roberta, oh man, in the high sheriff's arms."
What you do, oh partner, get so jumpin' long?

(15) Well if I never no more to see you woman, oh black gal, do the best you can,
I got a home on the river for a sundown man.
Well I got a home on the river, on the river, for a sundown man,
If I never see you no more woman, do the best you can.

(16) If you see my woman, buddy, buddy, please tell her for me,
I'm a longtime skinner, never will go free.
Well I'm a long gone skinner, man, and I never will go free,
If you see my woman, oh man, tell her for me.

Too Much Time for the Crime I Done: I
(Aug. 23, 1965; 406.1)

(17) I got too much time, buddy, oh lord, for the crime I done.
Whoa, I got too long, for the crime I done.
If I just had a knowed it, could a broke and, and run.
Well if I just had a knowed it, I'd a broke and run,
Hmmm, got too long, partner, oh, for the crime, crime I done.

(18) Well I don't mind doin', buddy, no two, three year,
Hmmm, hate like hell, partner, hmmm, do these ten or twelve. . . .[4]

(19) Well the time a gettin' better, better, everywhere but here,
Devil got religion, no more, no more hell. . . .

(20) Little boy, you ought a been here, been in here, back in nineteen oh four,
Mmmm, you could find a dead man, partner, on every turn row. . . .

(21) Sometime I wonder, ohh, where all the good men gone,
Mmmm, some in the building, poor boy, some gone home
Mmmm some in the building, some gone home,
Sometime I wonder where the high-rollin' men gone.

(22) If I don't get drownded, don't get washed away,
Mmmm, goin' to see my woman [if I] have to swim the Mobile Bay. . . .

Spoken: Yeah, if I don't get washed away or don't get drownded. Man behind me got a double-barreled shotgun loaded with double-ought buckshot. If I don' get washed away or don't get drowned I'm goin' to see my woman. When I get there, girl, I'm gonna take a long chance to get to you, get back to ya. I want you to be good to me. I'm riskin' my life tryin' to make it back home.

(23) If I call you woman, [and] you refuse to come,
Mmmm, Hot Springs water, girl, won't help you none.
Well the Hot Springs water won't help you none,
If I call you, black gal, and you refuse to come.

Prison Worksongs | 229

Too Much Time for the Crime I Done: II
(Nov. 17, 1965; 414.1)

(24) I done too much time, buddy, whoa man, for the crime I've done,
Well if I had a knowed it, oh, I'd a broke and run,
Well, I just had a knowed it, oh boy, I'd broke and run,
I got way too long, buddy, for the crime I done.

(25) "What you do, buddy, get your great long time?"
Whoa, man, they accuse me a robbin', poor boy, with a fire iron. . . .

(26) Well, wasn't I lucky, please 'sider me lucky, now when I got my time,
I got it cut from one hundred, oh boy, down to ninety-nine. . . .

(27) Oooo, well I soon have one hundred, whoa boys, as ninety-nine,
Whoa, man, ain't no difference, partner, for they both lifetime. . . .

(28) Well I been here rollin', buddy, so jumpin' long,
But I be here rollin' when the boys all gone,
Well I be right here rollin', hamin', when the boys all gone,
Well I been on this old river, partner, so jumpin' long.

(29) I done lose all my power, captain, out a my right arm,
'Cause I'm way overloaded for the crime I done.

(30) Well ain't no more loud hollerin', hey man, you may's well mumble low,
You'll find hell on the river, partner, everywhere you go. . . .

(31) Would you take money, hmmm, from a boy like me?
"I take money, partner, from the blind [who] can't see . . ."

(32) Well they hung my partner, oh man, shook the chain at me,
Double-crossed Kilroy Junior, framed poor Stagolee. . . .

(33) If I had my German Luger, oh my Luger, just one round a ball,
Man, I'd leave here walkin', I wouldn't run at all. . . .

(34) Rider, your two-barrel derringer, yeah, your derringer, it don't worry my mind,
Oh, the way I'm a lookin', that's the way I'm goin'. . . .

(35) Well I never got worried, never got worried, 'till I cross the line,
Got to thinkin' about dog sergeant and the twelve bloodhound. . . .

(36) Well, she told me not to worry, not to worry, but I got to worry some,
'Cause I'm way overloaded for the crime I done.

I Heard the Reports of a Pistol
(Aug. 23, 1965; 406.2)

Prison Worksongs | 231

(37) Well, I heard the reports of a pistol, whoa man, down
     the right-a-way.
Hmmm, must a been my partner, hmmm, tryin' make a getaway.
Whoa, they killed my partner, tryin' to get away,
Mmmm, just heard reports of a pistol, a down the right-a-way.

(38) If I leave here runnin', don't you follow me,
Mmmm, I'm a longtime skinner, mmmm, want to be free.
Well I'm a longtime skinner, oh, sure want to be free,
I hate to be charged with murder in the first degree,
Mmmm, hate to be charged with murder, oh, in the first degree,
Now if I leave here runnin' don't you follow me.

(39) If you don't believe, partner, that I killed a man,
Send and get my record, buddy, from Sugarland.
Well you can see my record, buddy, in Sugarland,
If you don't believe, partner, I have killed a man.

(40) Old Boothill over yonder, strictly belong to me,
Partner, a cold-blood murder is my pedigree. . . .

(41) I got a red-eyed captain, squabblin' boss,
Oh, work in the mud and the water, but he won't knock off. . . .

(42) Well, I asked the captain, did my money come.
"What the hell you care, don't owe you none.
What the hell you care, mmmm, don't owe you none,
Better get to rollin', get my levee done."

(43) I done lose all my good time, buddy, 'bout to lose my mind,
Mmmm, the way I'm a lookin', that's the way I'm a goin'. . . .

(44) Mmmm, everybody is talkin', mmmm, 'bout Mary Blair,
Mmmm, the poor girl is crippled, mmmm, and the clothes
     she wears.
Oh nothin' to the black gal, just the clothes she wear,
Everybody talkin', talkin' 'bout Mary, Mary Blair.

(45) If I go west Texas, drop in Abilene,
I got the cutest little woman, huh, you ever seen. . . .

(46) Well I don't want to be here when the last man die,
I don't want no trouble out a Marble Eye,
I don't want no trouble, oh, out a Marble Eye
I don't want to be here, partner, when the last man die.

Ever Since I Been a Man Full Grown
(Nov. 17, 1965; 414.6–415.1)

(47) Ever since I been a man, oh boy, a man full grown,
I been skippin' and a dodgin' for old farmer Jones.
Well I been skippin' and dodgin', hey man, for old farmer Jones,
Ever since I been a man, I mean a man full grown.

(48) Well my lead mule's crippled, partner, whoa, my wheel mule's blind,
Was the best in the country, but done been drove down. . . .

(49) Well I done a been all around, partner, in the whole corral,
Couldn't find a mule, buddy, with his shoulder well. . . .

(50) All you long line skinners, you better learn to skin,
Man comin' here in the mornin', want a hunderd men. . . .

(51) Well talkin' 'bout your hamestrings poppin' them old leather lines,
Ought heard the back bands stretchin', partner, and the collars cryin'. . . .

(52) I done worked old Rhody, hey man, I worked old Moll,
But I ain't gon' stop rollin' till I work them all.

(53) Little boy, little boy, if you can't hold 'em, you can't hold 'em, don't let 'em fool you here,
'Cause old Jesse James Seefus, partner, a walkin' 'lectric chair. . . .

(54) Well, but me and my partner, oh rider, and my partner's friend,
We could pick more cotton in the country than your gin can gin. . . .

(55) When I get up the country, hey, goin' tell all the boys,
"Don't you come no further south, buddy, than Illinois . . ."

(56) I want some missionary woman, oh woman, please pray for me,
Don't pray that I go to heaven, just pray that I go free. . . .

(57) Sometimes I wonder, oh, can I get my long time done,
Oh, boy, I prayed for better, man, but worser come. . . .

(58) If I had the good luck, buddy, oh like I had bad,
I'd win a barrel a dollars and keg a halves. . . .

(59) Life been a long lone gamble, I just can't seem to win,
If you don't believe I'm a sinkin', look what a hole I'm in. . . .

(60) Long lane, buddy, it's a long lane, buddy, that ain't got no end,
You may call me lucky, but I'm goin' up again. . . .

(61) "What you want me to tell your mama, tell your mama, oh boy, when I go home?"
Tell her you left me rollin', buddy, but I ain't got long.

(62) I got a high yella woman, woman, man, in the world somewhere,
She got three gold teeth, long black curly hair. . . .

(63) Well if you don't tell her, tell her, man, she will never know,
I got a home in Pocatella, oh man, Idyho. . . .

(64) Well I'm goin' to Oklahoma, marry a Indian squaw,
When I get her daughter, I be her son-in-law. . . .

(65) If I beat you to the Brazos, sergeant, oh man, you can blow your horn,
Well I done got worried, I'll be gone 'fore long. . . .

(66) Captain, captain, captain, you can count your men,
Well it's some goin' to the building, and it's some gone in,

Well it's some gone to the bushes, some gone in,
Well it's cool kind captain, you better count your men.

(67) Everybody talkin', talkin' man, 'bout old Danger Blue,
If I had my big horse pistol, I'd be dangerous, too. . . .

(68) Had my big horse pistol, buddy, just one round a ball,
I would leave here walkin', I wouldn't run at all.

(69) "Mornin', mornin', captain." He said, "Good mornin', Shine."
"I don't want no trouble, captain, I want that gal a mine."

(70) Man, they accuse me a murder, oh murder, and I ain't raised my hand,
They accuse me a forgery, I can't write my name. . . .

(71) Now I'm further up the river, oh man, than I ever been,
Me and my partner, nothin' but a walkin' gin. . . .

(72) Well I been here rollin', partner, ever since nineteen and ten,
But if you keep on gamblin', partner, I know you bound to win. . . .

(73) It's gonna rain, rain, rain, partner, oh boy, then turn cold,
But I don't mind the weather if the wind don't blow. . . .

(74) Saddest word in history, buddy, that I ever read,
"You got to do one hundred for the life you led . . ."

(75) Well you may be a bully, but you no bad man,
Uncle Bud will get you, put you on the ball and chain. . . .

(76) Man, wasn't I lucky, wasn't I lucky, when I didn't get killed?
Got in a Saturday night ruckus, partner, with old Trigger Bill,
Whoa, Saturday night ruckus, mean old Trigger Bill,
Wasn't I lucky that I didn't get killed?

(77) Rather been in Loosiana, partner, down with the whippoorwill,
Than to be here in Texas treated like a eel. . . .

Prison Worksongs | 235

(78) Due to be in Butte, Montana, oh man, oh boy, this very day,
If I ever get lucky, I goin' be on my way.

(79) But it ain't but one thing, partner, oh boy, I done wrong,
I stayed in Texas just a day too long. . . .

Woman Trouble
(Nov. 17, 1965; 415.2)

Spoken: Here's a little short one here, titled "Woman Trouble." He's worried about some old woman in the free world. Guy down here, if he's thinkin' about anything at all, he's thinkin' about his freedom and his woman.

(80) She left me this mornin', never said a word,
Whoa man, nothin' I done partner, just on somethin' she heard.
Well wasn't nothin' done, buddy, just somethin' she heard,
Woman left me this mornin', never said one word.

(81) "What you do partner, with your summer change?"
Man, I spent it all on the women for a great big name. . . .

(82) Waterboy, waterboy, waterboy, won't you bring your water 'round,
I got a great big notion to lay the hammer down. . . .

(83) I don't see no fire, oh man, but I'm burnin' down
Hmmm, don't see no fire, partner, but I'm burnin' down.

(84) Well you hear a shotgun a blastin', oh man, know somebody's lost,
Jumped in Big Muddy, whoa, and tried to cross. . . .

(85) Said she'd be back tomorrow, partner, but she carried her clothes,
She don't be here tomorrow, she will the next day sure. . . .

(86) You don't feel like a hollerin', oh rider, you wave your hands,
It's the man at the crossin', he gon' let me by. . . .

(87) Well my mama, heard her call me, poor boy, answered, "Ma'am?"
"Ain't you tired a rolling for Mister Cunningham?
Well ain't you tired a haming, poor sonny, for Mr. Cunningham?"
Poor boy, my mama she call me, and I answered, "Ma'am?"

(88) Well my papa he called me, "Sonny," so I answered, "Sir?"
"If you tired a rollin' what you stay there fur?
Mmmm, if you tired a haming, sonny, what you stay there fur?"
Poor boy, my papa called me and I answered, "Sir?"

(89) Well my woman finally called me, she called me, oh I answered, "Hey."
"If you tired a rolling, why don't you run away?." . . .

(90) Can't run away, woman, tell you the reason why,
They got a man at the crossing, he won't let me by. . . .

(91) Well I ain't tired a rollin', hmmm, I just got so long,
Just to keep down trouble, guess I'll go 'head on. . . .

(92) She got a hole in her belly, boy, and it won't get well,
And the more you rub it, well the more it swell. . . .

(93) Every time, buddy, every time, partner, man, I go to pee,
Mmmm, chills and fever come down on me.

(94) I went to see my doctor, boy, he said "I can't tell,
You may get better but you can't get well"

(95) Long as I live, partner, long as I live, poor boy, never die,
No more lovin' will I have to buy. . . .

(96) I know you're gonna murder me, rider, rider, why don't you set a day?
I don't have religion, I need time to pray. . . .

(97) Ain't nothin' but Tom Devil make a man do wrong,
Well I'm gonna do better, man, from this day on.

Prison Worksongs | 237

(98) I believe that lead row bully, rider, got a mojo hand,
He's a seven day roller, captain, and a sundown man. . . .

(99) I got a free transportation, oh man, in the world somewhere,
Been a long time a comin', but you welcome here. . . .

(100) If you stay in Huntsville, partner, oh boy, you may get by,
You come down on the Ramsey, you got to rise and fly. . . .

(101) "When you get your big old money, hey man, whichaway you goin'?"
I'm goin' a way up the country, oh boy, around Des Moines. . . .
Spoken: That's about the end a that.

No Payday Here
(June 12, 1966; 463.2)

(102) I used to weigh two hundred, two hundred, now I'm skin and bone,
Ever make a payday, captain, Hot Spring I'm goin'. . . .

(103) Well I asked the captain, asked the captain, "Did the payroll come?"
"What the hell you care, partner, I don't owe you none."

(104) If I never make a payroll, captain, if they never call my name,
Can't see the healing water, never make Hot Spring. . . .

(105) [They] tell me in Louisiana, big Louisy, oh boy, the murder[er]'s home,
Hmmm, may be a cemetery, partner, that's where I belong.

(106) Got a one more letter, one more letter, I got to go myself,
I done lose my woman, everything I have left.

(107) Well I heard a Winchester chargin', Winchester chargin', just a while 'fore day,
Hmmm, [if] you can't beat a bullet, partner, you can't get away. . . .

(108) Well don't let me catch you, rider, rider, see you foolin' round,
Lord I'd rather be shot to pieces, [than] stay here hobbled down. . . .

(109) Well the shotguns keep on blastin', just a blastin', somebody may be lost,
Sometime they shoot just to stop you partner, sometime where the [sus]spender cross,
Sometime they shoot just to stop you from runnin', man, sometime where your 'spenders cross,
When you hear the shotguns a blastin', somebody may be lost.

(110) You can tell 'em I'm a leavin', a leavin', you can tell 'em when,
Oh some goin' to the bushes, partner, and there's some goin' in. . . .

(111) Well you never know who be lucky, whoa boy, if you never try,
You may run on from under the gun, partner, you may be crossfired,
Well if you run from under the gun, partner, you may beat the crossfire,
Never tell who be lucky if you never try.

(112) Well when you wake up here every mornin', every mornin', then it's all day long,
Whoa boy, you can't hear nothing, buddy, but just "Roll 'head on . . ."

(113) Captain, he said, "Hurry, hurry, man," well the rider said, "Run."
Had my way, partner, wouldn't do neither one. . . .

(114) Ain't made a payday, captain, captain, since I been gone,
Rain or shine, buddy, got to go right on.

(115) Sure like to see the Governor, Governor Connally, I don't have my fare,

Prison Worksongs | 239

Hmmm, sure like to see you Governor, we don't have no payday here. . . .

(116) Governor John Connally, please Governor, if you see me as a man,
Please consider me in your working, working, release working plan.

(117) Hmmm if you hold 'em here, buddy, if you hold 'em here partner, you hold 'em anywhere,
But we just don't have no payday here.

(118) I'll make you this promise, oh this promise, to three or four reliable men,
Whoa, if you sign my release this time, Governor, won't have to do it again.
Well if you sign my release Governor, Governor Connally, won't have to do it again,
Oh I promise the good Lord above, Governor, three or four responsible men.

(119) Hmmm we never have had, oh, no payday here,
Talkin' 'bout your trouble, boy, I had my share.

The Major Special
(June 12, 1966; 463.3)

Spoken: This is mostly true. It sorta correlates with some of the past and the present. And it's sort of nice to think about him in his old age. We been knowin' each other a pretty good while.

(120) Oh you come down this Ramsey, partner, specially Ramsey Two,
Hmmm, fix it in your mind, buddy, you got your time to do. . . .

(121) Don't try to punch it, partner, you can't get away,
Under the supervision of Major McGauhy [Muh-gay-hay]. . . .

(122) No, you can't beat the rider, ain't no use to try,
He's a well-experienced river ranger with a eagle's eye. . . .

(123) Horse he used to ride was pretty, oh, I long remember Prince,
Tread water like old Rattler, jump a shallow fence. . . .

(124) Way back in the '30s, whoa, in the '30s, partner, I hooked up with then,
Whoa, he made me a roller, partner, I learned under him. . . .

(125) Well he raised plenty a watermelon, cotton a bumper crop,
Sugar cane don't you mention, boy, that's all he's got. . . .

(126) Major he know the river, oh he know the river, from the upside down,
Sandy land, old original, black land and the new ground.

(127) He's a man a law and order, ain't no doubt about it,
Please don't break the monopoly, you'll regret you ever started.

(128) If you come down to this old Ramsey, why you plannin' and a figurin',
Plan on leavin' legal, workin' for your livin'.

(129) Well the summer gone and a comin', keep a comin', I may be here to stay,
I got a home under supervision Major McGauhy.

(130) Now you talkin' about all your troubles, ho you troubles man, but, boy, I had mine,
Ho, workin' Moreland Brothers, got the best go here.

Glossing the Stanzas

1. *Good time* is a pun; the term means both "good time" in the ordinary sense of a pleasurable experience, and the time a man is given off his sentence for good behavior.

3. The Brazos River begins at the intersection of the White and Double Mountain Fork Rivers, about 60 miles north of Abilene; it runs north a little bit, then turns south, passes about 35 miles west of Fort Worth, goes through Waco, Navasota, Brenham, passes a few miles west

Prison Worksongs | 241

of Houston and reaches the sea at Freeport. The river winds through all the southern units of the prison system (Ramsey, Retrieve, Darrington, Sugarland, Central, and Harlem) and it serves as an important element in many of the prison songs.

8. *Running time* is an indeterminate sentence, such as 2 to 10 or 10 to 25 years. Modern penology favors it over a flat sentence because a man who shows great progress can be paroled early. Inmates often dislike it because, they say, they do as much time as before and are burdened with many years of uncertainty and unfulfilled hope. The argument is loaded: the inmates for whom the hope *is* fulfilled go home and aren't around to complain.

10. When the men work in the fields they are watched by at least one, and usually several guards on horseback, all of whom are called *riders*. In the songs, the *rider* is often addressed directly. When a large number of men are working in an area, there is an extra guard posted a short distance away from the workforce and riders, the *high rider*, who carries a rifle. He is often positioned on the *turn-row*, the elevated road surrounding a planted field. A *captain* will be in charge of a large work area. There are usually two day *majors*, one in charge of the building and one in charge of the entire field force. (In the old days, before shifting to the warden system, the prisons were each in charge of a major, the individual camps under a captain.) Accompanying the men to the fields is a pack of tracking dogs handled by the inmate *dog boy*, supervised by the guard *dog sergeant*.

"The *danger line*," Smitty says, is the dividing line between the state land and the free land, the penitentiary and the free world. "We always call that the danger line no matter whichaway you're goin'. 'Cause when you leave the state property you's in the free world, and so there's always somebody at the danger line to keep you, try to keep you from going, of course. The dog sergeant, high rider, dog boy, somebody. But now usually, if you beat them to the danger line you got a pretty good chance—there's nobody the other side to shoot at you right away."

15. "A *sundown man*," Smitty says, "is the way they used to work here years ago. They'd work right up to just about as long as they could, long as it was day. We'd often say we glad God made day and night, 'cause if it stayed day all the time they'd work a man to death the way we used to work here."

17. That is, "If I had realized how long the sentence would be, I would not have permitted myself to be captured and tried."

19. The only hell left, therefore, is here on Ramsey.

23. Hot Springs and its waters seem to have a fascination for Smitty. He has never been to the resort, but he regards it as a kind of promised land and mentions it several times in the songs.

26. This particular irony appears frequently in the inmate cotton and cane songs.

28. *Haming*: working. Derives from "hamestring": leather lines used to control mules pulling wagons.

32. *Kilroy Junior* and *Stagolee* are inmate nicknames.

34. *Two-barrel derringer*: the guard's shotgun (an anachronism—the riders carry .38 pistols now). Smitty says: "That's what we call 'down-talkin'' it, makin' it small."

35. *Line*: the danger line.

42. Obviously a levee-camp verse.

46. *Marble Eye*: guard's nickname.

47–52. These stanzas are all from levee-camp songs.

53. *Jesse James Seefus* has the reputation of being the fastest cotton picker ever to be an inmate in TDC. I had heard about him for several years and, when I was told that he was a participant at this year's prison rodeo, asked one of the inmates to point him out to me. The inmate said he would, but asked a favor: Seefus had for years told everyone he had been arrested by Sky King and had been brought in after his capture in Sky King's airplane; the inmate would introduce me to Seefus, but would it be all right if he said I was Sky King? I agreed and after one of the events he brought Seefus over to where I was sitting by the chutes and said, "Jesse James, here's the fella that wanted to see you. You remember him, don't you? It's Sky King."

Seefus looked at me, nodded, stuck out his hand, said, "Hiya, Mr. Sky King, nice to see you again," and walked away. The other inmate muttered and did the same.

About this stanza, Smitty said, "Jesse James Seefus, he claims himself a walkin' electric chair in the cotton patch. He say, 'I'll 'lexecute anybody that keeps up with me. Picks as much cotton as I do.'"

"He'll get them or picking that much cotton will?"

"Working. If you try to stay with him. He's a eight or nine hundred pound picker. I saw him in a two-man squad. Sergeant carried him and another boy from my home town, Johnny Thomas, he's in the free world now. He picked like Jesse James. Sometimes they'd take three rows together, sometimes they'd take one apiece, sometimes they take two, depending how they catch them, and the condition the cotton is in."

"How much cotton does a regular man pick?"

"The high squads, they pick 350 or 400. They don't have to pick that much now. You can get in on a couple of hundred pounds now."

67. *Danger Blue*: guard nickname.

75. *Uncle Bud*: Bud Russel was for many years the prison's transfer agent, the man who would travel around the state to bring prisoners from the county jails to Huntsville. Smitty said:

> He's the first man that brought me to the penitentiary. In nineteen and thirty-eight. He's the first man that rode me down from Dallas County Jail. Two years. Bud Russel. Put a chain on your neck and a lock—little Yale lock. Turn your collar up and say, "All right, boys, get ready to put on this necktie." A Yale lock and a chain and you had a throw chain he'd run through the whole line. If one guy run, he got to carry the whole bunch with him. You can't do it, he had you. Bud Russel, he worked here for quite a few years. I thought it was just talk when I first heard of Bud Russel, but there actually was one. Don't know what the Bud means, but he was a rustle.

Another inmate, listening, said, "The name is still used throughout the system. 'Well, let's go get Uncle Bud's Cotton,' or 'Let's get some a Uncle Bud's cows.' Whatever it might be, it's still used."

"Just like 'Uncle Sam,'" Smitty said.

87. *Mister Cunningham*: onetime general manager of the prison system.

87–91. This is an interesting sequence of relatives. He is first asked by his mother if he is tired, then the father asked why does he stay if he is tired, then his woman suggests he leave, and he answers in 90–91 with resignation.

92–93. These have to do with a vagina and gonorrhea, respectively. Verses like this—erotic or lightly obscene—are rare in the worksongs.

98. *Mojo*: Smitty says:

> Mojo hands: that's a boy gone to them witch doctors, hoodoo people, that believe in them. We use the term mojo hand for a guy that seems to have something extraordinary or can do something the other fellas can't hardly do, or he holds out longer. The lead row fellas here, the lead row bullies, is usually got long wind and they can work, work, and work, work you down. I been one a them a long time ago, I'm not one a them now. And it's hard for the pull-dos [bad or weak workers] to

keep up with them and so those songs fit in the fellas that's haming, trying to keep up with the lead rows.

100. Huntsville now has several prison farms around its perimeter, but in the old days the town held only the main unit of the system, The Walls. This is the oldest unit of all, the only one with a wall (the others all have cyclone fences surrounding the buildings), and duty there is relatively soft. Work is indoors, mostly in shops, and there is none of the seasonal pressure that is felt on the large farms.

102–104. His Hot Springs interest again. These stanzas are also probably from a levee song, but Smitty has used them as the basis for one of his own. The inmates in TDC are not paid, and the difference between a levee camp boss who won't come through with the payroll on time and a prison system that doesn't bother with one is slight enough to make the song transfer easy.

115–118. See Leadbelly's various songs to governors pleading for release.

120–130. This song expresses considerable respect for the Major, the officer currently in charge of Ramsey's No. Two Camp. This is not so surprising as it might seem to an outsider. Smitty has known McGauhy for thirty years, off and on, easily as long as anyone else he knows presently; they get along and understand one another. Inmate/warden relationships are peculiar in their symbiotic aspects. Warden C. L. McAdams, now running Ellis, the unit for difficult recidivists and escape risks, is the strictest and most highly respected warden in the system; many of the men on his unit are proud of that strictness, proud that they get along with "Captain Mac." That the keepers and convicts are both prisoners of the same system is an ancient insight. For a discussion of a similar kind of symbiosis among police and drug addicts, see my "Exiles from the American Dream," *Atlantic Monthly*, January 1967, 44–51.

121. *Punch it*: escape.

124. *Rattler* is the Ur-tracking hound, the one who can follow any trail, walk a log, swim the Big Brazos. There is a well-known song about him and he is frequently mentioned in other songs. I've been told that it is traditional to name at least one of the dogs on the various farms Rattler.

130. *Moreland Brothers*: Smitty says, "We call the 'Moreland Brothers' any man with a whole lot of land around this penitentiary. He don't have to be blood-related. Just if he's a big farmer, owns a lot of land. They yoke him in with all the farmers. They got more land than anybody else."

Commentary

Structure

Musically and verbally, Smitty's style is extremely ornamental. He frequently adds words, repeats phrases, and shifts the locations of stresses while maintaining the metric base. The most striking aspect of his verbal style is the device in most stanzas of making a quatrain of a couplet by reversing the lines. Sometimes the turn just fills out a four-line verse with what is essentially a mere couplet, or acts as a simple restatement (as 14), but on other occasions the turn is more functional. Consider,

> She said she'd be back tomorrow, partner, but she carried her clothes,
> She don't be here tomorrow, she will the next day sure,
> Mmmm, she don't be here tomorrow, oh partner, she will next day sure,
> Said she be home tomorrow, but she carried her clothes. (85)

The first line (A) reveals the situation with the woman and suggests mendacity; the second line (B) presents what appear to be the singer's conclusions about the meaning of (A). He repeats the line (B') and then, when he sings (A') we know, rather than suspect, that he is consoling himself merely, that no matter what he wants to think and what she said, the fact remains that she did take her clothes and that means she will not be back and he knows it quite well. The movement is: promise and evidence that the promise is untrue (A), statement of hope and restatement of hope (B and B'), then revelation of the futility of hope (A') (which suggests that the deeper thematic content of the stanza is not really different than the stanzas about his long sentence—there too hope is lacking or minimal or artificial).

The mode is statement and comment, as in blues, but instead of the statement being given three times and the comment once (AAAB), we have the comment repeated immediately (ABB'A'), as if to reconsider first the comment by visiting it twice, then to reconsider the original remark by viewing it in inverted order. This does more than affirm merely. We are able to see A and A' in light of the insight gained through B and B', a re-view lost in regular blues form. The hyperbata sometimes creates dramatic monologue out of stanzas that in the AAAB form would be scenic only.

The device even increases the intensity of stanzas that are more direct:

Sometimes I wonder, oh, where all the good men gone,
Mmmm, some in the building, poor boy, some gone home
Mmmm, some in the building, some gone home,
Sometime I wonder where the high-rollin' men gone. (21)

The touching sense of sadness and wistfulness, the sense of epigonity even in prison, isn't really apparent until A'. The first couplet is a simple query and answer, the second couplet, the inversion, shifts the focus to the sense of loss.

Rhyme

Except for about ten or so stanzas, all the stanzas in Smitty's songs rhyme; two of the non-rhyming stanzas were taken directly from other songs. There is considerable variation in the rhyme sounds (about 45 different sets), and, more important, there is hardly any repetition even with the sounds used frequently. The *e* sound is rhymed in eight stanzas; each pair includes "me," which is rhymed with five different words: Stagolee (32), free (1, 16, 38, 56), eternity (5), see (31), pee (93); each of the four "me/free" stanzas is different in content. Another common rhyme is *i*, which appears seven times, none of the pairs repeated: why/by (90), buy/try (11), die/eye (46), die/buy (95), by/fly (100), try/eye (122), try/crossfired (111).

It is difficult to talk about slant or partial rhyme in this kind of context. It is quite common in Negro folksong and I suspect that many singers do not distinguish between full and slant, or if they do, feel that both are equally acceptable. Smitty's mixture of "air" and "ear" illustrates this best.

Except for "rightaway/getaway" (37), all the rhymes are masculine. I think "try/crossfired" (111) is the only apocopated rhyme. *Rime riche* occurs twice (9, 83), but one of those stanzas is of two lines only, A and A', and probably shouldn't be considered. In one pair of stanzas that do not rhyme there is an interesting prosodic element. Stanza 18 is "year/twelve," and stanza 19 is "here/hell"; the two are not necessarily consecutive dramatically, but they are sung that way, and as a pair they happen to rhyme *abba, abba*.

The rhyming pattern displays considerable variation in terminal sounds and an obviously deliberate avoidance of complete repetitions. Considering that the author had no high school education and that his song is 260 lines long, I think one cannot help but admit that there is a tremendous natural talent being exercised.

Sources

Most of Smitty's verses are his own, but he frequently uses lines or parts of lines that are in the prison repertory. Twelve stanzas are in versions of other Texas prison songs in my collection (2, 3, 14, 16, 20, 26, 27, 48, 49, 50, 52, 66); in nine stanzas he has taken the first line only (9, 11, 25, 28, 39, 60, 69, 70, 82); and in seven stanzas he has used the second line only (1, 10, 21, 34, 43, 59, 110). When Smitty does use one of these lines more than once he tends to change the context and part of the word structure. The second line of each of the stanzas that follow is essentially the same (with some formulaic changes), but the first line is quite different in each case:

> Sometime I wonder, oh, where all the good men gone,
> Mmmm, some in the building, poor boy, some gone home (21)

> Captain, captain, captain, you can count your men,
> Well it's some goin' to the building, and it's some gone in (66)

> You can tell 'em I'm a leavin', a leavin', you can tell 'em when,
> Oh some goin' to the bushes, partner, and there's some goin' in (110)

A number of the stanzas appear in free world songs. The stanza "Man, they accuse me a murder, oh murder, and I ain't raised my hand, / They accuse me a forgery, I can't write my name. . . . (70)" appears in Texas Alexander's "Levee Camp Moan," recorded in 1928 and republished on RBF-9; Eddy Boyd's "Third Degree," recorded in 1950, Chess 4374; Skip James sings a similar verse in his "22-20"; another inmate sang it in partial form, in a song called "If You See My Mother" (on EKL-296). Most of the free world stanzas are from levee camp songs (the first six stanzas of "Ever Since I Been a Man Full Grown" 47–52, 42, 69, 81, 102–104, and possibly a few others).

Smitty also uses a number of phrases and partial lines from the traditional prison songs. One could make a fairly good case for the kind of oral composition, *mutatis mutandis*, Albert Lord describes in his *Singer of Tales*.[5]

Other Devices

Smitty is particularly skillful with oppositions and parallels pivoting around the caesura:

> Oh, boy, I prayed for better, man, but worser come (57)
> If I had the good luck, buddy, oh, like I had bad (58)
> Well she told me not to worry, not to worry, but I got to worry some (36)
> Well I lose all my good time, 'bout to lose my mind (4)

He occasionally sets up pun situations in which the fact of the pun is not revealed until the second line:

> "Little boy, why you keep on a runnin', just keep runnin' on your mind?"
> Captain, I never had nothin' but that old runnin' time (8)

> No more good time, buddy, oh man, in the wide, wide world for me,
> 'Cause I'm a lifetime skinner, never will go free. . . . (1)

In these stanzas the reversal and repeat serve an extra function: on one hearing one gets the sense, on the other a chance to appraise the word play.

When he does use a line more than once, he shifts the context in its mate:

> Rider, your two-barrel derringer, yeah, your derringer, it don't worry my mind,
> Oh, the way I'm a lookin', that's the way I'm goin'. . . . (34)

> I done lose all my good time, buddy, 'bout to lose my mind,
> Mmmm, the way I'm a lookin', that's the way I'm goin' . . . . (43)

> Well I lose all my good time, 'bout to lose my mind,
> I can see my back door slammin', partner, I hear my baby cryin'. . . . (4)

Prison Worksongs | 249

We see considerable rhetorical and prosodical skill and variety, and that the singer works in a traditional framework to fashion something within the tradition but still quite his own.

THEMES

I have saved for last what is really the most important aspect of Smitty's verse: What is he singing *about*? "Guy down here," Smitty said, "if he's thinkin' about anything at all, he's thinkin' about his freedom and his woman." That is quite true, and both Smitty's songs and the general repertory of prison song reflects those interests, but the themes he names are too broad to be of much use to us. The verses themselves reveal a slightly more atomized set of concerns, both in the themes directly revealed and the imagery used with sufficient frequency to draw our attention.

Smitty sings sixteen stanzas apiece about the length of his sentence (1, 3, 5, 8, 16, 17, 18, 24, 25, 26, 27, 28, 29, 36, 57, 74, 124) and his woman (5, 9, 14, 15, 16, 22, 23, 44, 45, 62, 80, 81, 85, 89, 92, 106). Of slightly more concern is the possibility of escape, which occurs seventeen times (8, 10, 22, 24, 34, 35, 37, 38, 43, 65, 66, 89, 90, 107, 111, 121, 122). Connected with this is concern with geographical locations; there are twenty-three mentions of places outside the prison: Mobile Bay (22), Hot Springs (23, 104), Boot Hill (40), Abilene (45), Texas (45, 79), Illinois (55), Pocatella, Idaho (63), Louisiana (77, 105), Butte, Montana (78), Big Muddy (84), Des Moines (101), unspecified river (3, 15, 28, 30, 71, 126), Brazos (3, 7, 65).

The guards, riders, major, etc., are mentioned thirty times (8, 10, 12, 13, 15, 29, 34, 46, 65, 66, 67, 69, 75, 86, 87, 96, 98, 102, 103, 104, 108, 113, 114, 121–124, 126, 127, 129). The two other important image and theme sets are sickness and death, cited twenty-four times (2, 13, 14, 20, 29, 32, 37, 38, 39, 40, 44, 46, 48, 49, 70, 76, 83, 93, 94, 95, 96, 102, 104, 105), and firearms, also cited twenty-four times (111, pistol 12 and 37, thirty-two-twenty 13, fire iron 25, German Luger 32, two-barrel derringer 34, horse pistol 67 and 68, shotgun 84 and 109, Winchester 107; men shot at 37, 84, 107, 109, 109, 111; firearm as equalizer 67, 68, 12, 13, 33, 34).

These lists tell us something about an interesting problem of composition, one that is thematically central to the entire song sequence. Smitty's concern is his relationship to certain institutions of the state, certain legal situations, certain interpersonal relationships, and he must somehow express these in his songs. Because of the rhetorical exigencies of the singing style, the songs must be as nearly a-syntactic as possible. Words are dropped and slurred, pronouns and conjunctions and particles are frequently omitted, so it remains for nouns and verbs to bear the burden of the thoughts, to imply the relationships. The metaphoric and analogic aspects of the lines are extremely concrete. But, in Kenneth Burke's words, "Sociopolitical institutions, with the personal and social relations involved in them, and the vast terminology of attitudes, acts, and motives that goes with them, do not enjoy exactly the kind of extraverbal reality we find in the commonsense vocabulary of the natural realm; yet they are not identical with the verbal order as such (the order of words-about-words)."[6] But the language of the songs is not abstract; it is highly imagistic, highly concrete. And this creates or reveals the problem: the themes are almost entirely negative or institutional: unfreedom, unlove, unvolition, unimportant. The natural world itself, the world from which the images derive, has no negatives, no un's: man makes those things in his head.[7] "The essential distinction between the verbal and the nonverbal," Burke says, is in the fact that language adds the peculiar possibility of the Negative" (420). "*For the negative is an idea;* there can be no image of it. *But in imagery there is no negative.*" "The negative is properly shown by a *sign*, not by an *image*. For a 'negative image' would be a contradiction in terms" (430). We see in this concept the dramatic necessity for the theme of Hell (mentioned four times in 7, 11, 19, and 30), which, Burke says, "is, to perfection, a function of the negative. . . . The notion of Hell involves a scenic reinforcement of the negative as a principle, the total or ultimate thou-shalt-not" (474–475).

The reason Smitty cannot dwell at any length on his woman or his freedom is that he does not really think of *them*, he thinks of their *absence*, he perceives the negative only, and in his imagistic song-world there are no terms to present these things directly. All he can do is deal with the devices of control: the number of years he has to do, the weapons of the guards, the simple presence of the guards, the existence of other places to which he has no access. To express both hope and longing, both his sense of self and his lack of control over its movements, Smitty is forced to utilize the presence of the enemy, the prison itself, because that is all that is concrete, and depend on rhetoric to return to his real themes. The singer needs the ugly.

And that—the dependence for expression on the loathed and ugly—is not so frustrating as one might suspect. Hazlitt puts it:

> Not that we like what we loathe; but we like to indulge our hatred and scorn of it; to dwell upon it, to exasperate our idea of it by every refinement of ingenuity and extravagance

of illustration; to make it a bugbear to ourselves, to point it out to others in all the splendor of deformity, to embody it to the senses, to stigmatize it by name, to grapple with it in thought, in action, to sharpen our intellect, to arm our will against it, to know the worst we have to contend with, and to contend with it to the utmost. Poetry is only the highest eloquence of passion, the most vivid form of expression that can be given to our conception of anything, whether pleasurable or painful, mean or dignified, delightful or distressing. It is the perfect coincidence of the image and the words with the feeling we have, and of which we cannot get rid in any other way, that gives an instant 'satisfaction to the thought.' This is equally the origin of wit and fancy, of comedy and tragedy, of the sublime and pathetic.[8]

Notes

1. T. S. Eliot, *Selected Essays* (New York, 1960), 10–11.

2. In 2015, Dust-to-Digital Records released a two-disc set of all of my recordings of J. B. Smith: *No More Good Time in the World for Me*. See Nathan Salzburg, "Sundown Man," *Oxford American*, January 27, 2015 (online at https://oxfordamerican.org/magazine/issue-87-winter-2014/sundown-man), and Max Nelson, "No More Good Time in the World for Me," *The Paris Review*, August 10, 2016 (online at https://www.theparisreview.org/blog/tag/bruce-jackson/).

3. Following each title are the date of the recording session (all of which took place on Ramsey Unit, Texas Department of Corrections, Otey, Texas) and my original tape number. Should anyone need to consult the original tapes (there are about 200 from the Texas prisons), they are on deposit in the archive of the American Folklife Center in the Library of Congress, and Folklore Archive, University of Texas. The musical transcriptions are by Norman Cazden.

4. The ellipses indicate the third and fourth lines are approximately the same as the second and first lines, respectively. Verses terminated by a period after the second line did not have the usual repetition.

5. (Harvard, 1960).

6. Kenneth Burke, *Language as Symbolic Action* (Berkeley, 1966), 375.

7. The discussion that follows was suggested by a conversation with John Gagnon and a reading of Burke's essay, "A Dramatic View of the Origins of Language and Postscripts on the Negative," *Language*, 419–479. The discussion is briefer than I'd like, but all that is really appropriate to this essay. In a later essay

I intend to discuss at some length the importance of problematical imagery in certain styles of folk poetry.

8. From "On Poetry in General," in Walter Jackson Bate, ed., *Criticism: The Major Texts* (New York, 1952), 306.

14

What Happened to Jody

(*Journal of American Folklore*, 1967)

Life in an army during wartime and life in prison anytime have a number of aspects in common, so it is not surprising when we find items of folklore shared by both camps. One mutual concern is who is doing what, with, and to the woman one left at home. In Negro folklore, this concern is personified in the songs and toasts about one Jody the Grinder—"Jody," a contraction of "Joe the," and "Grinder," a metaphor in folk use for a certain kind of coital movement.

Jody's activities and lifestyle are perhaps best described in the toast bearing his name. Roger Abrahams collected a version of "Jody the Grinder" in Philadelphia in the early 1960s.[1] I collected a longer and more detailed version in Texas in 1965. The toast is pretty well dated by its content and slang: *solid news* and *solid sender* were out of circulation by the early 1950s; Japanese war brides didn't start receiving much attention until sometime after the American occupation of Japan was well under way, probably around 1947. The atom bomb and fall of Japan are so central they supply an absolute early cutoff date. One would be safe in assuming somewhere between 1947 and 1950.

But Jody was around earlier. He is named in the brief blues "Joe the Grinder," recorded by John A. Lomax from the singing of Irvin Lowry in Gould, Arkansas, in 1939.[2] During the war years, Jody figured in the marching song "Sound Off," a version of which is printed in Alan Lomax's *The Folk Songs of North America*.[3] Lomax says, "In many variants this was sung by all Negro outfits in World War II." Abrahams notes that "This song is often called 'Jody's Song' and other similar ones 'Jody Calls.'"[4] Woody Guthrie, in an undated note included in *Born to Win*, says, "The best of marching I saw in my eight months in the army was to the folk words of a folky chant tune that went: Ain't no use in writin' home / Some joker got your gal an' gone. / Hey, boy, ya' got left, right? / Ho, boy, ya' got right."[5]

If Abrahams' version of the toast is at all representative of its current condition, it seems the toast is wearing down with age: younger performers have dropped the allusions and slang they don't understand, and, concomitantly, some of the narrative elements. The man who performed the longer version printed here was sixty-four and, fortunately, he is one of those uncreative folk performers incapable of destroying anachronisms in a text.

But the song has fared better. It was sung during the Korean War and I've been told that it is still sometimes sung in military camps. And it has gone to prison.

In 1965 I heard a group of inmates in a Texas prison sing a song they called "Jody's Got My Wife and Gone." The first regular stanza is similar to the one Guthrie quotes. Most of the verses have to do with conditions of prison labor: the singer describes his various tasks, the weather, the field captain, parole, his loneliness, the Jody theme. That recording session was in a room in the prison, late at night.

When I returned to the prison in March 1966, I asked whether anyone else around knew it. This time we were out in the woods and the men were clearing timber. Benny Richardson, who told me he had put the song together, offered to sing lead for the song "Jody's Got Your Girl and Gone" while a group of sixteen inmates chopped down trees.

It might be useful to attempt to visualize the scene. The workers group themselves about the trees. If the trunk is less than a foot thick, two men will work on it, alternating strokes. Four men work on the larger trees, with north and south swinging their axes at the same time; as they pull their axes back, east and west swing. If north swings from his left, so does south; both east and west will swing from their right. North and east will drive their axes into a cut on one side of the tree, the marks of their blades at an angle of about 15°; every other stroke or so a wedge of wood will fall out. The tree-cutting songs are faster paced than the other worksongs (which are used for hoeing, cutting up logs, and picking cotton or cutting sugar cane) for two reasons: each man hits on every other beat, and there is no real rest at the end of a stroke because the ax is always nearly horizontal.

Because of the rhythm supplied by the axes, melodies are usually better when the men are working than when they sing in an artificial indoor situation. The singers do not have to concern themselves with maintaining rhythm when they are working—their strokes let them know if they are starting to slip. Perhaps more important, they relax and are not conscious of the song as performance, but instead regard it as part of the work activity itself. Usually, the words are better in a work situation also, primarily because the lead singers, who are usually older inmates, have difficulty remembering many verses when they are not in a work situation. When they are working, the songs are considerably longer.

The version led by Richardson with the men at work, was, I think, much better in text and tune than the one recorded earlier indoors. He had obviously given the song some thought in the seven months between sessions. All the verses rhyme, as compared with only nine in the first version. The song has more structure: Richardson sings two verses about the work, one about his physical situation; the next three have to do with the guards, their severity, power, soft life: the captain sits in the shade and receives a salary, the inmates work all week (he does exaggerate here—they work a five-day week now) for two sacks of rolling tobacco and a movie; he thinks about going home and then is reminded of Jody, who got not only his girl, but his sister as well; he closes with a decision to avoid prison in the future. The song is important for several reasons. Esthetically, it is one of the best of the songs now being performed in the fields. Some of the stanzas have a haiku-like brevity and force; the rhymes are not contrived or strained; the melody is lovely. Unlike the sketchy World War II songs and their Korean counterparts, this "Jody" forms itself into several descriptive and thematic blocks, each covered or developed before the singer moves on. The song represents a survival of traditions: one is thematic and deals with Jody and the threat he has continued to represent in the folk culture; the other has to do with the genre: the song is one of the few that we can say are of obviously recent adaptation and incorporation, and the composer is a young man, still in his thirties, which suggests that the worksong tradition may yet survive a while even though many of the work situations that produced it are being replaced by modern machinery and the prison conditions that maintained it have been replaced by modern penology.

I: Jody the Grinder

Sam, Wynne Unit, Texas Department of Corrections, Huntsville, Texas, August 18, 1965.

Say, old Joe the Grinder was coppin' a snooze,
when the world got hip to some solid news.
Say, now, there was a no-good whore with a man overseas,
sayin', "Now get up, Jody, wake up please!"
Say, "I know you'd rather burn in hell,
but it's all over the headlines: Japan just fell."

Then old Jody turned over and his eyes all red,
he say, "I beg your pardon, baby, now what is that you said?"
She said, "I know you're high, motherfucker, and restin' fine,
and I know you heard me the first damned time."
He said, "Baby, I know that can't be right,
because I know those damned Japs just begin to fight.
And, anyway, I know those Japs they have to be invaded before they scrap."
She said, "No, no, Jody, back in Pearl Harbor the Japs had their day
but General Douglas MacArthur made a comeback play."
Say, "There may have once been a time when those Japs wouldn't quit,
but that atomic bomb has stopped all that shit."
Jody said, "I don't dig this play,"
said, "I'm goin' up on the cuts and see what the other cats say."
She said, "Jody, darlin', don't be mad,
but whilst you up on the cuts try to dig you up another pad."
Say, "I'm sorry, darling, but that's all she wrote,"
say, "my old man may be here on that next damn boat."
Jody said, "Don't front me with that shit because it's not anywhere,
and this is Joe the Grinder, and damn that square."
Say, "Now I'm not interested in your point of view,
now turn on the radio and get me the news."
Now the news he got, Jack, was a solid sender,
old Tojo was just signin' unconditioned surrender.
He said, "Turn it off, baby," say, "I don't want to hear no more,
and see who's knockin' at that motherfuckin' door."
He said, "Wait a minute, baby, before you answer that knock,
will you get me that bottle and pour me a shot?"
He [GI Joe] said, "That's all right, Jody, I'm already in," said,
"now let's *all* sit down and have a drink of gin."
Said, "Now I can tell by the look in both a your eyes
that I took this joint completely by surprise."
He said, "Hush, whore, I know what you gonna say before you even begin—
that you and Jody are just damned good friends.
But I'm gonna put you and Juanita wise,"
said, "there's lots a firepower in this forty-five."
He said, "And before some dreadful mistake is made,
Jody, will you kindly pocket that old rusty blade,"

258 | Folklore Matters

Say, "I heard you say you didn't give a damn,
but will you hip him, baby, to who I am."
She said, "Yes, daddy, if you want him to know.
Mr. Jody Grinder, meet Mr. G.I. Joe."
Said, "Now you people pull me up a seat
and I'll make my little story short and sweet."
He said, "Jody, ever since Pearl Harbor, back in '41,"
say, "you've played the cuts and had your fun."
Say, "You even shucked my old lady, and that ain't all,
You even carried her to the Allotment Balls.
You carried her to the park and you carried her to the zoo,
then you finally decided you'd just move in, too."
Say, "Now you know you and Juanita didn't play it fair,
but now you face to face with this same damn square."
He said, "Oh, yes, I picked up on your wardrobe as I came down the line,
and from what I hear about it, it's awful fine.
Now that's all right, babe, I'll get around to you;
I picked up on your wardrobe and it's foxy, too."
Say, "Now I have a little chick over across the way
and those togs may come in handy for her some day."
Say, "Now if you people will be cooperatin' and give me a helpin' hand,
we can soon have all this jive in my movin' van."
Boy, he took the rug off the floor, he took the mattress off the bunk,
he took the divan, cookstove, and the wardrobe trunk.
He took her shoes and stockings, her highest priced dress,
he took a combination Victrola and a cedar chest.
He said, "Load up, Jody, and load up fast,"
say, "I'm about ten seconds off your motherfuckin' ass."
Say, "Now when you load this van you don't have to be ashamed,
'cause lots of other Jodys are doing the same damned thing."
Say, "I know you people are interested in what I'm goin' to do,"
say, "I'm gonna open up a hopjoint on Cedar Avenue.
And you can pick up on me most any old day,
when me and my new old lady step out to play."
Now he made a military bow as he backed through the door
and he said goodbye to Jody and his dogassed whore.
He said, "Oh, yes, Jody, I want you to meet my Japanese queen—
and will you please hand me over that Longine?"

II: Jody's Got My Wife and Gone

W. Sandell and group, Ellis Unit, Texas Department of Corrections, Huntsville, Texas, August 12, 1965.
Tune transcribed by Norman Cazden.

260 | Folklore Matters

Leader: Yeah, yeah
Group: Yeah, yeah
Leader: Yeah, yeah
Group: Yeah, yeah

Leader: Jody's got my wife and gone
Group: Yeah, yeah, yeah, yeah
Leader: Jody's been here and now he's gone
Group: Yeah, yeah, yeah, yeah

Got me pickin' cotton and corn
A come on, fellas, let the hammer ring

And tell the waterboy to bring some water
I got to wash my hands one time

Cleaned my heart and left my feet

But Jody done got ya in my house
A come on, fellas, let the hammer ring

The hotter the day
The cooler the afternoon

Let the hammer ring
Drive on boys (*Spoken*: Drop 'em)

I think I see the captain' comin' around
He's fixin' to let us go down **(a)** (*Spoken*: Drop 'em)

Come on, captain, won't you raise your hat **(b)**
Talk for me and go to bat

Talk to the parole board and let me go
I got to drop this o-mighty hoe

I got a diamond **(c)** in my hand
Now you know I'm a lonesome man

Yeah, yeah
Yeah, yeah

Jody's got my wife and gone
I got to get some more cotton and corn

Listen here fellas, now listen to the song
Jody done got my wife and gone (*Spoken*: Oh drive 'em)

Come on, captain, a raise your hat
My heart is worried and I just got the bat (**d**)

I got to go, I can't stand no more
So here's your sack (**e**) and here's your hoe

Yeah, yeah, yeah, yeah
Yeah, yeah, yeah, yeah

262 | Folklore Matters

III: Jody's Got Your Girl and Gone

**Benny Richardson and group, crosscutting, Ellis Unit,
Texas Department of Corrections,
Huntsville, Texas, March 24, 1966.
Tune transcribed by Judith McCulloh.**

Leader: I've been working all day long
Group: Yeah, yeah, yeah, yeah
Leader: Pickin' this stuff called cotton and corn
Group: Yeah, yeah, yeah, yeah

We raise cotton, cane and a corn
'Taters and tomatoes and that ain't all

Back is weak and I done got tired
Got to tighten up **(f)** just to save my hide

Boss on a horse and he's watchin' us all
Better tighten up, [if you] don't you'll catch the hall **(g)**

Wonder if the major will go my bail **(h)**
[Or] give me twelve hours standing on the rail **(i)**

Yeah, yeah
Yeah, yeah

I see the captain sittin' the shade
He don't do nothin' but a he get paid

We work seven long days in a row
Two sacks a Bull **(j)** and a picture show

In the wintertime we don't get no lay **(k)**
Cuttin' cane and makin' syrups every day

When it get wet in the cane field
All the squads work around the old syrup mill

Yeah, yeah
Yeah, yeah

Two more months and it won't be long
I'm gonna catch the chain **(l)** 'cause I'm goin' home

Goin' back to my old gal Sue
My buddy's wife and his sister, too

Ain't no need of you writin' home
Jody's got your girl and gone

Ain't no need of you feelin' blue
Jody's got your sister, too **(m)**

First thing I'll do when a I get home
Call my woman on the telephone

Yeah, yeah
Yeah, yeah

Gonna settle down for the rest of my life
Get myself a job and get myself a wife

Six long years I've been in the pen
I don't want to come to this place again

Captain and the boss is a drivin' us on
Makin' us wish we'd stayed at home

If we had listened what our mama say
We wouldn't be cuttin' wood a here today

Yeah, yeah
Yeah, yeah

Yeah, yeah
Yeah, yeah

IV: Variant and additional stanzas, Richardson and group, March 22, 1966

Know old major won't go my bail
Standin' twelve hours on the mean old rail

Captain settin' over yonder under the shade
He don't do nothing but a he gets paid

Gonna settle down and get me a job
A pretty little girl and a great big yard

When a I get there the first thing I will do
Look up my old good girl Sue

When I go home I'm goin' to stay
Ain't gonna do no wrong for quite a few days

Don't worry buddy, I ain't comin' back
Don't want no fine clothes and no Cadillac

Get myself a wife and get myself a job
Anything but pickin' cotton and a parkin' cars

Don't you worry, fella 'bout a me
Won't steal no more, now you watch and see

Never been a place like this before
All they do is pick cotton and a use a hoe

Glossary

a. *Go down*: work to exhaustion.

b. *Raise your hat*: an old signal executed by the senior officer in a work area to signal that the workday is over.

c. *Diamond*: *double-bladed* ax.

d. *Bat*: a strip of leather about thirty inches long and four inches wide, used for corporal punishment until sometime in the 1940s.

e. Cotton sack.

f. *Tighten up*: work more closely together.

g. *Catch the hall*: When a man commits an infraction of rules in the field, he is told to "catch the hall" when he returns to the building that night, that is, wait to see the major for a summary trial.

h. *Go my bail*: "speak up on my behalf."

i. *Standing on the rail*: a punishment; the offender is made to stand for a number of hours on a narrow wooden beam.

j. *Bull*: Bull Durham, the tobacco issued in the prison.

k. *Lay*: from *lay-in*, permission to remain in the building during the day.

l. *Chain*: a group of prisoners being transferred from one institution to another. The singer here refers to the inmate chains sent from the farms to the main unit in Huntsville when men are about to be released.

m. This is a Dozen.

Notes

1. Roger Abrahams, "Jody the Grinder," *Deep Down in the Jungle* (Hatboro, Pennsylvania, 1964), 170–71.
2. Library of Congress Record AAFS 14.
3. Alan Lomax, *Folk Songs of North America* (Garden City, New York, 1960), 595.
4. Abrahams, 170.
5. Woody Guthrie, *Born to Win*, ed. Robert Shelton (New York, 1966), 22.

15

The Afro-American Toast and Worksong
Two Dead Genres

(In Günter H. Lenz [ed.], *History and Tradition in Afro-American Culture*, Zentrum für Nordamerika-Forschung [ZENAF], Universität Frankfurt, 1984)

In this talk at a Universität Frankfurt symposium, I described function and death of two genres of Black American folklore—the worksong and the toast. I was only partly right: the toast tradition didn't die; it morphed into rap, which has gained far greater currency than the toast ever had.

∽

My subject today is the decline and death of two genres of American Black folk poetry—the worksong and the toast. Before I can discuss either of them, I must first outline something of the nature of folklore and tell you about the peculiar history of the collection of Black folklore in America.

The genres of American Black folklore that have been collected and studied are: spiritual songs (except for self-conscious situations, such as concerts and folk festivals, these are rarely performed now), blues (recorded randomly and primarily for commercial purposes until scholars discovered the form some three decades ago), custom and belief (more and more rare as technology and education replace the functions documented in studies such as Harry Hyatt's massive *Hoodoo, Conjuration, Witchcraft, Rootwork* (1970–1978), sermon (studied only a little so far, still very much alive), folk tale (except for the personal anecdote, the memorat, rare these days), toasts (rarely told or learned by younger performers), and the worksong (completely dead). Some of the genres—worksong, *marchen*, some beliefs—have documentable African antecedents. The history of the others is a matter of speculation only.

There is no history of any genre of North American Black folklore. There are only occasional collections—the equivalent of potsherds from occasional digs at uncoordinated archaeological sites. What we have of Black American folklore is like an elementary archaeology. There isn't a coherent body of recorded material that permits anything more.

At best, there are collections and analyses based on a point in time (such as Newman White's *American Negro Folk-Songs*, 1925), specific examinations of a genre in a specific context (there are many of these), or historical essays based on and incorporating the intermittent observations of various collectors (such as Lawrence Levine's *Black Culture and Black Consciousness*, 1977).

There are no intermediate documents. The study of folklore isn't like the study of government or insurance or steel production, it isn't like the study of any subject in which critical information was and is continually recorded. We can't go back and pick up what we missed before: what wasn't recorded before is gone forever.

Works of literature have fixed texts. Verbal folklore has no fixed texts: it has only the text uttered at a certain place and a certain time by a certain person. Each edition of a work of literature is accurate insofar as it matches a real and specific original; each performance of a work of oral folklore is unique and as legitimate as any other. A book may have editions, a film may have versions; these differ from one another, but each is specific and fixed: we can refer to a certain edition of *Leaves of Grass* or *Finnegans Wake* or the 128-minute version of Peckinpah's *The Wild Bunch* and other scholars will know our referent exactly. But no performance of verbal folklore is exactly like any other performance. Even when the same singer or storyteller performs the same item on different occasions, there are almost always variations. A written text exists on a page; verbal folklore exists only at the moment of performance.

A folk text—a story or song, say—varies for several reasons. A teller may make deliberate changes so the text will better fit his or her location: place names and character names change frequently. Some performers make changes for aesthetic reasons. Some changes result from faulty hearing or bad memory. An enthusiastic audience elicits a performance very different from that of an audience that is barely responsive. (See Albert Lord, *The*

Singer of Tales, 1960.) When items have been in the tradition for a while, variations accumulate.

For a literary scholar, a perfect text of any literary object consists of nothing more than an accurate reproduction of the author's own words in the author's medium; for a folklorist, a perfect text of a folkloristic event includes not only the words said or the melodies incorporated, but also the specific context of the event.

Folk texts survive in tradition only when there is interest in them. When people are no longer interested in a particular item, no one learns it, no one performs it, and it disappears from the active repertory. When people are no longer interested in or served by a particular genre, it, too, disappears from the repertory. Here, again, folklore differs significantly from literary texts. When William Faulkner won the Nobel Prize in 1950 all of his novels but one were out of print; *Don Quixote* and *Moby-Dick* were unread for long periods of time. No one in the Renaissance knew the story of Gilgamesh or the tale of Marduk's defeat of Tiamat told in the *Enuma Elish*. So long as a text of a book—on paper or carved in stone—exists anywhere, we have it, and it is always potentially available whenever a public is ready to utilize it. Not so with folklore.

Different publics have different needs, different demands, different concerns. Publics seek out the texts that most fit their needs, that most suit their times. We may read back into fixed texts new interpretations, we can map them in ways appropriate to our culture, to our time. We don't assume that fifth century Athenians liked Aeschylus for the same reasons we like Aeschylus. The text we have of the *Oresteia* is extremely close to what Athenian theatergoers heard in the year 458, but we will never know what folk tales or songs those theatergoers sang or heard in the cafes later the same day.

Some students of folklore fancy themselves "functionalists." Their concern is with folklore texts and genres that have a demonstrable function in the world. In a real sense, all literature—folk or written—is functional. If it serves no need, it gets no use. The need may be merely one of entertainment, but since Freud it has been impossible to speak of "mere" anything, let alone something as serious as entertainment.

One group whose needs folklore serves is the collectors of folklore. Collectors have not, in America, been much studied, and I think that is unfortunate. They are our major source of information about folklore genres long dead, and we rarely know much about their motives. They are almost always outsiders who, for various reasons, chose to document a tradition or group of traditions not their own.

Black American folklore has been collected in fits or waves of special interest. The collectors were mostly Whites. The concerns of those White collectors were based on changing political concerns, changing images of the slave, the Negro, the Afro-American, the Black.

Before the Civil War, as Gunnar Myrdal and others have observed, the Black in America was a chattel; one no more looks at a chattel's culture than at a mule's culture or a fence post's culture. There were occasional reports of Black verbal art, but until the Abolitionist movement these were usually incidental to something else or they were caricatures. The Abolitionists began to look at slaves and ex-slaves as people who owned the kinds of cultural baggage all people own. Those first lookers weren't interested in simple documentation, however, they weren't scholars and they didn't pretend to objectivity: they were political activists anxious to convince others of the humanity of the slaves and former slaves.

Slave Songs of the United States (1867), by William F. Allen, C. P. Ware, and Lucy McKim Garrison, consisted almost entirely of spiritual songs, which is hardly surprising given, that the collectors were ministers, children of ministers, or workers affiliated with religious organizations. "Our intercourse with the colored people has been chiefly through the work of the Freedmen's Commission," Allen wrote in his introduction to the volume, "which deals with the serious and earnest side of the negro character. It is often, indeed, no easy matter to persuade them to sing their old songs, even as a curiosity, such is the sense of dignity that has come with freedom." In the same year, Thomas Wentworth Higginson published in *Atlantic Monthly* a widely-read article about songs of the Blacks, later reprinted as a chapter in his successful autobiographical work, *Army Life in a Black Regiment* (1869). Until well into the twentieth century, there was little interest in any kind of Black folk song except spirituals.

The worksongs existed, but they are mentioned only occasionally and quoted rarely. Surely the Blacks had secular songs—dance songs, game songs, perhaps even blues songs. But these were rarely collected and almost never published. The White collectors knew what they wanted and they avoided the rest. We will never know what and how much they were able to avoid.

A similar self-limitation occurred after the publication of Joel Chandler Harris' *Uncle Remus: His Songs and Sayings* (1880). The animal tale became for collectors *the* Black folk tale, and even though there were in existence tales about humans (such as trickster stories about John, the clever slave and farmworker, and numbskull stories about Irishmen), only a few were recorded and fewer were published. Collections published in the United States reflect the bias toward animal tales well into the 1920s.

In the American scholarly and semi-scholarly communities, the 1920s and 1930s were decades of Proletarian Romance. Robert Winslow Gordon published in the *New York Times* in 1927 and 1928 a series of articles about folksongs of American ethnic and occupational groups; his categories were later adopted by the well-known collectors and authors, John A. and Alan Lomax. Sociologists Howard Odum and Guy B. Johnson published *The Negro and His Songs* (1925) and *Negro Workaday Songs* (1926), the first important studies of Black secular songs by social scientists.

The most important development in the collection and examination of Afro-American folklore in that period was the work done under the auspices of the Federal Writers' Project of the Works Progress Administration (the WPA was established by the Roosevelt administration to make work for the millions of unemployed) from 1936 to 1939. Among the studies resulting from the FWP's field collection were *Drums and Shadows: Survival Studies among the Georgia Coastal Negroes* (1940) and *Lay My Burden Down: A Folk History of Slavery* (ed. B. A. Botkin, 1945). For the first time, there was a concerted effort to find out what was there rather than continuing exercises in ratifying what was already assumed.

In the twenty-five years after the end of World War II, many of the most important workers in the Black folklore field were Jewish academics. Some members of that group were B. A. Botkin, Richard Dorson, Roger D. Abrahams, and me. I'm not sure what to make of that, but I do know that the particular interests we brought to our work continued the outsiderness of the collection and analysis. Botkin was probably the most eclectic of the group. Dorson was anxious to prove that Black American folk narrative was based on European traditions rather than African traditions; he was uninterested in music. Abrahams was interested in performance styles—in the rhetoric of complex social events. My concern was sociological: how culture helps people survive.

Through the century or so of Black folklore awareness, it was largely the awareness of Whites that controlled the published information. A few Blacks did a few articles, a few collections—but only a few. Some folklore research and publication by Blacks was extremely important—such as the studies and novels of Zora Neale Hurston. Much of the Black interest in folklore was political and theatrical and came long after the major traditions had been heavily influenced by modern electronic culture. There are folklore elements in much nineteenth- and twentieth-century literature, but folklore itself was rarely the subject of the writing.

What we have, then, is primarily a record of what interested outsiders, not a record of what Blacks actually did.

Folklore is conservative in nature: it consists of things learned from others and performed more or less the way they did it; folk communities repress radical departures from traditional ways of performing and uttering, they encourage consistency and coherence. But folk culture is also enormously volatile. Brief spaces of time can make enormous differences. Folk culture is not only conservative, it is also highly reactive. Its reactions sometimes lead to the disappearance of great masses of material when, as I noted above, those materials no longer serve a vital function.

I will discuss briefly two Black folklore genres that illustrate the process of consistency and then sudden disappeared: the Toast and the Worksong.

The toast was not noted or studied until it was already mature, already decaying. The worksong was noted, but it wasn't studied in America until a short time before it died, and when it went it disappeared quickly.

The toast was missed by White collectors for a long time. The first notable publication of unexpurgated toasts was in Roger D. Abrahams *Deep Down in the Jungle* (1964). No one knows when the toast began or what it was like when it began. Whites didn't hear toasts for a long time because they didn't have access to situations in which toasts were performed; many collectors didn't hear toasts because they didn't want to hear them. Toasts are often obscene, violent, misogynistic, and vulgar. They were important social documents, but until the mid-1960s they were unpublishable in America. Scholars, like anyone else, tend to focus on what they can sell. The few versions of toasts that did find publication before Abrahams' work were heavily edited and bowdlerized (e.g., the versions of "Stackolee," "Signifying Monkey," and "Titanic" in Langston Hughes and Arna Bontemps, *The Book of Negro Folklore*, 1958, 359–367).

The toast was a social genre, the folk poetry of poor Black men. There were situations in which toasts were told and women were present, but women seem rarely to have told them, which is not surprising given the misogynistic character of so many of the poems. Toasts were performed at parties, bars, streetcorners, and in county jails. They lasted in county jails longer than anywhere else because in county jails there was little to do and few other forms of amusement. (In America, prisoners awaiting trial or serving short sentences are held in county jails; prisoners serving long sentences go to state and federal prisons, where there are often work requirements, school programs, and other activities required or permitted. Since county jail time is usually brief, few such diversions exist, hence the prisoners spend most of their time hanging around, waiting for something to happen.)

Many of the poems depict street roles of hustler, badman, pimp, and drug addict—street characters and threatening types, generally treated at a comic distance. Some of the poems are homiletics—advice in poetic form. Some come from hobo tradition. Some come from once-popular poets like Robert W. Service. And some are written about local well-known characters. I once heard in Texas a poem about a transvestite, "The Voodoo Queen," and a few months later met Voodoo, the real subject of the poem. Voodoo said, "That wasn't a nice poem. I tried to buy it back, but they wouldn't sell it to me." Some of the toasts collected by Abrahams in the early 1960s were about the street life of the Philadelphia youths he was studying; many others were obviously from earlier decades. When I collected toasts in the 1960s and 1970s, I found only a few that seemed of recent vintage. Many had anachronistic slang that marked them as having been written in an earlier time. Students who collect toasts now rarely discover any texts that weren't in the tradition twenty years ago, and only rarely are their informants young men.

No one knows where and when the toast entered Black tradition. There is no documentation of Black American folk narrative poetry in the nineteenth century and there is precious little documented in the first half of the twentieth century. No one even knows where the name *toast* comes from. The recitations are only occasionally linked to drinking situations. (Not all tellers call them "toasts," by the way. Some tellers refer to them as "stories," even though they are metered and rhymed, or as "lies.")

So far as I can tell, the three best known toasts were "Signifying Monkey" (about a jungle trickster who manages to get his archenemy the Lion severely beaten by Elephant), "Stackolee" (about a psychopathic badman), and "Titanic" (about Shine, presumably the only Black aboard the ill-fated ship, and who, in the poem, is the only person aboard smart enough to swim to safety).

This is a version of "Titanic" I collected in Texas in 1966:

All the old folks say the fourth a May was a hell of a day.
I was in a little seaport town and the great Titanic was goin' down.
Now the sergeant and captain was havin' some words
when they hit that big iceberg.
Up comes Shine from down below,
he said, "Captain, captain,"—say, "you don't know,"

say, "we got nine feet of water over the boiler-room floor."
And the captain said, "Go on back and start stackin' sacks,
we got nine water pumps to keep the water back."
Up come Shine from down below,
he said, "Captain, captain," says, "You don't know,
we got forty feet of water over the boiler-room floor."
He said, "Go on back and start stackin' sacks,
we got nine water pumps to keep the water back."
Shine said, "Your shittin' is good and your shittin' is fine,"
say, "but there's one time you white folks ain't gonna shit on Shine."
Now a thousand millionaires was lookin' at him
when he jumped in the ocean and began to swim.
Rich man's daughter came up on deck
with her drawers around her knees and underskirt around her neck.
Like a noonday clock Shine stopped
and his eyes fell dead on that cock [=cunt].
She says, "Shine, oh, Shine," says, "save me please,"
say, "I give you all the pussy that your eyes may see."
He said, "I know you got your pussy and that's true,
but there's some girls on land got good a pussy as you."
She said, "Shine, oh Shine," say, "please save my life,"
say, "I'll make you a lawfully wedded wife."
He said, "Your shittin' is good and your shittin' is fine,
but first I got to save this black ass of mine."
Now was another fella by the name of Jim,
he jumped in the ocean and he begin to swim.
Another girl ran up on deck
with her drawers around her knees and underskirt around her neck.
Like a noonday clock Jim stopped and his eyes fell dead on that cock.
Now she had long black hair that hang from the crown of her head to the nape of her belly,
she had a twenty-pound pussy that shook like jelly.
Say, "Shine, oh, Shine," says, "save me please,
I'll give you everything that your eyes may see."
And before the last word could fall from her lip,

Jim climbed his black ass back up on that ship.
Up come a shark from the bottom of the sea,
said, "Look what godalmighty done sent to me."
Shine bowed his neck and showed his ass,
"Get out the way, let a big shark pass."
And after old shark seen that Shine had him beat,
he said, "Swim, black motherfucker, 'cause I don't like black meat."
About four-thirty when the Titanic was sinkin',
Shine done swimmed on over in Los Angeles and started drinkin'.
But now when he heard the Titanic had sunk
he was in New York damn near drunk.
He said, "Ladies and gentlemen," say, "when I die, Don't y'all bury me at all.
Soak my balls in alcohol
and lay my old rod up across my breast,
and tell all the people old Shine has gone to rest."

The social function of the toast has been replaced by transistorized electronics: all those streetcorner, barroom, and party situations in which toasts were performed now have high-fi and high-volume music delivered by portable tape recorders, portable FM radios, stereo record players. It is difficult to recite rhymed verse when the ambient noise is penetrated by a continuing disco beat.

The location in which toasts were most often told in the past—county jails—is where they are still probably told most often. But that frequency has declined significantly. One important reason for the decline is that jails in America are now integrated and Black performers are less likely to recite the poems in racially mixed situations.

That means potential performers have far fewer opportunities to learn texts and styles, or to practice their own recitations. Other social factors have contributed to the decline of the toasts: the misogyny in them became unfashionable, and many of the street roles—pimp, drug dealer, hustler, and psychopath—lost much of their former folk romance.

Toasts are rarely told nowadays. Friends and students who do fieldwork tell me that few young men seem to learn them. The toasts served a need in another time, but now they are anachronisms, now they exist primarily in books by scholars, on a few phonograph records, and in occasional barroom performances by a fellow named Rudy Ray Moore. The toasts have become the matter of scholarship and art. The transition from vigorous tradition to moribund artifact took less than a decade.

The Black worksong in America disappeared even faster, and when it went it didn't attenuate into a murmur as did the toasts: the worksongs died quickly and completely.

Worksongs are not songs about work; they are songs used to help people do work. The songs are used, they are functional in the most obvious sense. Greeks sang while drawing water, treading grapes, pulling ropes; Hebrideans had songs for working tweed; West Africans had songs for nearly every kind of group activity; American slaves had worksongs for fieldwork; railroad workers had chants for moving rails and loading ties; laborers at docks used worksongs to coordinate body movements on unsteady gangplanks; sailors used worksongs to raise sail and turn winches. For all those groups, the worksong was a matter of participation, not performance. Unlike all other folksongs, work songs have no audience.

In the United States, the worksong had all but disappeared by the 1920s. There were no more sailing ships, loading was done by machines rather than by muscles. The only place the worksong survived in the United States was in the southern prisons. That was because southern prisons were the last places they were needed. Those prisons maintained the physical world of the southern plantation nearly a century after the Civil War ended.

The images and themes of the convict worksongs are directly related to the prison situation: guards, escape, sentence length, things remembered, sickness, death, guns, the work. The songs are about control and impotence.

There is a scale of metrical, melodic, and textual complexity. The songs that kept large groups moving together while doing rapid work (such as cutting down trees with axes) generally consist of brief unrhymed verses sung by a leader and brief simple choruses sung by the group; only rarely do the leader's verses rhyme and even rarer yet are there any narrative sequences in the verses. Melodies, meter, verses, and the extent of group involvement get progressively more complex as the pace of the work slows: there is more variation in work done cutting up trees on the ground (which has a slower axe cycle) and even more variation than that when working with the long-handle hoe. The most complex songs, in all regards, are the songs used when working with a cane knife or while picking cotton. That is because in those tasks the individual singers pace their own body movements to the song's meter, but they are not also paralleling the movements of other singers.

The psychological function of the songs is obvious: they gave men a regular outlet for emotions that had no other legitimate outlet. A convict could not very well sit in a prison cell and say, "I hate being in prison" or "I miss my woman." Everyone within earshot knows those things quite well and announcing them is like announcing that water is wet. Neither could one insult the guards: punishment would be swift and certain. But those things could be included in song and no one listening would object at all. Worksong lyrics are in some ways like opera lyrics: they are sometimes poetic and interesting, but even when they are banal and stupid they are legitimized by the musical context.

The songs also served two direct physical functions.

The first had to do with cutting down large trees. When Black convicts cut large trees, they would work with as many as ten men around a single trunk (Whites, to my knowledge, never worked with more than two). Imagine ten men around a tree, and imagine them numbered in order: 1, 2, 3, 4 . . . All the men with odd numbers would swing from the left, all the men with even numbers would swing from the right; when the odd men were swinging in, the even men would be swinging out. There would be five notches in the tree, each being struck by one left and by one right axeman. So long as all the left axemen swung in while all the right axemen were swinging out, there was no problem. But if a left axeman was moving in at the same time his partner (the right axeman hitting the same cut) was swinging in, the results could be very bloody indeed: severed fingers, a severed hand, a split skull. The songs kept those axemen moving in perfect rhythm, the songs gave them the timing to keep their bodies away from their partners' axes. (The reason the Whites worked only two men to a tree was they could never master the technique. "Those white boys just don't have the rhythm," one Black convict said.)

The second physical function was less direct, but equally violent. Prisoners who worked too slowly were singled out for punishment by the guards. Punishment in Texas in the 1930s and 1940s consisted of ten or twenty strokes of the "bat." The bat was a strip of leather twenty-four inches long and four inches wide mounted on an eighteen-inch wooden handle. With each stroke of the bat, the victim's body would snap off the ground; after a beating, a man couldn't sleep on his back for weeks; some men died. But the songs prevented anyone from being singled out for punishment. The songs kept everyone together: no one was far ahead, no one was far behind. The simple worksongs, which the White guards looked upon as "old-time nigger stuff," kept many convicts alive.

Leaders were not selected for having a pretty voice or for being particularly creative in their lyrics. What was most important in a leader was the ability to sing loudly enough (over the noises of the work and the ambient sound of the forests or swamps or farms) and the ability to keep perfect time (so those men with the axes wouldn't get confused and accidentally be in the wrong place at the wrong time). Most leaders were tenors: the higher voices required less power to travel a fair distance than did lower voices.

This is a version of "Grizzly Bear," a song used for cutting down trees. The words in capital letters were sung by the group, everything else was sung by the leader. The word "grizzly" is sung with three syllables: *grizz-a-ly*.

> Oh well that grizzly, grizzly, GRIZZLY BEAR,
> Oh well that grizzly, grizzly, GRIZZLY BEAR.
> Oh everybody keeps talkin' 'bout the GRIZZLY BEAR
> Oh everybody keeps talkin' 'bout the GRIZZLY BEAR
>
> (Leader continues to sing each line twice and group sings "Grizzly Bear" refrain after each line.)
>
> Oh everybody keeps wonderin' who the . . .
> Oh if I tell you don't you tell it to the . . .
> Oh Jack O Diamonds ain't nothing but a . . .
> He come walkin' and talkin' like a . . .
> I heard Mama tell Papa 'bout the Well Lordy . . .
> Oh well I b'lieve I go to lookin' for the . . .
> I looked all in Loosiana for the . . .
> Well Lordy that grizzly . . .
> He makes a track in the bottom like a . . .
> Oh everybody keeps a talkin' 'bout the . . .
> Oh Jack O Diamond ain't nothin' but a . . .
> He got two white tushes like a . . .
> He make a echo in the bottom like a . . .
> Wo Lordy that grizzly . . .
> Oh everybody keep wonderin' who the . . .
> Well Stormy Weather ain't nothin' but a . . .
> He makes a track all in the bottom like a . . .
> He comes a-reelin' and rockin' like a . . .
> Well Boss Rainey ain't nothin' but a . . .

He come walkin' and talkin' like a . . .
He make a track all in the bottom like a . . .

There are no longer any Black convict worksongs in prisons in the American south. The worksong is gone forever in those institutions. Few convicts now incarcerated in those prisons ever heard a worksong; no convict now incarcerated in one of those prisons will have occasion to use or learn one.

Two things—both of them socially laudable—destroyed the tradition: racial integration of the prisons and termination of the physical brutality that was so much a part of their design for so many years. Integration put Whites into the same work gangs as Blacks; the Whites still "don't have the rhythm," and that means the gangs cannot do the songs even if they want to. The ending of the physical brutality abolished the physical necessity for the songs: it was no longer necessary for everyone in a work group to keep perfect pace with everyone else in order to save the lives of the weaker members of the group.

The worksongs served physical and psychological needs. The physical need for the worksong disappeared when the field brutality was stopped; the physical possibility for the worksong disappeared when Whites and Mexicans and Blacks worked in the same gangs. The information we now have on the Black worksong in America is probably all we ever will have.

When items of folklore no longer make sense, they disappear. And when whole genres of folklore—like the Black worksong and toast—no longer make functional sense they disappear, too.

The folklore of the American Negro was the only immigrant tradition specifically singled out as being worthy of study in the organizing document of the American Folklore Society in 1888. Much collection has been done. But that collection remains, and always will remain, like a board on which bits and pieces of an enormous jigsaw puzzle are only here and there filled in. The brief period the toast was available for study—a decade or two—and the rapidity with which the worksong disappeared—a year or two—testify to the fragility of the folkloric moment.

Part V
People

16

Benjamin A. Botkin (1901–1975)

(Journal of American Folklore, 1976)

Ben Botkin died July 30, 1975, after a long and disabling illness. He was seventy-four years old.

More than any other folklorist of his generation, he was content to let his sources tell their own stories. What set him off from his professional colleagues was his consistent refusal—often in the face of violent attack—to limit those sources to things academics could find more or less respectable. Ben was a scholar, not an academic, so he never suffered that limitation of apparent respectability: he was willing to admit equally the voice of someone he met on the road and the copy on the back of a cereal box. What got him in trouble with the academic folklorists was the simple and sadly elusive fact that his vision was so much broader than theirs: they were looking for texts that could be properly annotated and indexed; Ben was trying to document the soul of a land.

His quest was poetic at heart, as he was. He sensed that when, in 1940, he abandoned his university position to devote himself to writing about the things he loved. Few professors have nerve for such a leap.

University people are not awfully good at dealing with poets. They sometimes hire them for a while and give them jobs as pets in English departments, but they are always more than a little uncomfortable about them, and rarely very unhappy when they revert to form and move on. It's not just that those poets insist on dancing to their different drum, but that they have the arrogance of refusing to tell us how to interpret it. They just keep saying, *Listen, listen, listen.*

Ben's youth was spent in the Boston area. Scholarships and a variety of part-time jobs enabled him to do his undergraduate work at Harvard (BA, magna cum laude, 1920). He took his MA in English at Columbia in 1921, working under John Erskine, Clayton Hamilton, Brander Matthews, and Carl and Mark Van Doren; his thesis was on Thomas Edward Brown, the Manx poet. He taught English at the University of Oklahoma for two years, then in 1923 returned to New York where he attended classes at Columbia University, worked in settlement houses, taught English to foreigners, and spent as much time as he could manage seeing plays. In 1925, while visiting Quincy, Massachusetts, he met and married Gertrude Fritz.

When he returned to Oklahoma, Ben began collecting folklore among students and townspeople and involved himself with the Southwest "renascence." He was founder and editor of the annual, *Folk-Say* (1929–1932), and a monthly, *Space* (1934–1935); he was also contributing editor of the *Southwest Review* (1929–1937) and book reviewer for the *Sunday Oklahoman*. He took his doctorate in English and anthropology in 1931 under Louise Pound and William Duncan Strong at the University of Nebraska. His association with the University of Oklahoma continued until 1940, but his turn from a local to a national approach to regionalism began when he went to Washington on a Julius Rosenwald Fellowship in 1937 to do research at the Library of Congress in southern folk and regional literature. From 1938 to 1941 he was successively national folklore editor of the Federal Writers' Project, co-founder and chairman of the Joint Committee on Folk Arts of the WPA, and chief editor of the Writers' Unit of the Library of Congress Project; in 1941 he became Library of Congress Fellow in Folklore (Honorary Fellow 1942–1956). In 1942, he was named head of the Library's Archive of Folk Song. *A Treasury of American Folklore* was published in 1944; the following year, while still president of the American Folklore Society, Ben resigned from the Library and moved to New York. About that time, his interest shifted from rural to urban folklore; that work was helped by a Guggenheim Fellowship in 1951.

> The most important advance in my thinking [he wrote in 1970] came in the fifties through my work with the Workshop for Cultural Democracy in the field of intergroup understanding and community integration. This was the reaffirmation of my applied folklore concept (folklore for understanding and creating understanding), first enunciated in 1939 . . . and first published in 1953. . . . "Whereas," I wrote, "a pure folklorist

might tend to think of folklore as an independent discipline, the applied folklorist prefers to think of it as ancillary to the study of culture, of history or literature—of people." Of all my folklore concepts this gives me the most satisfaction because of its multidisciplinary broadening and deepening of my perspective and insight. If I have any further contribution to make, it will be by way of the integration and crystallization of all my folklore thinking, beginning with my interpretive work in progress, *American Social Myths and Symbols*, made possible by a Louis M. Rabinowitz Foundation grant (1965) and a National Endowment for the Humanities Senior Fellowship (1967).

He was concerned with folklore in its broadest and most social sense and in that his work was something of a contradiction, for Ben was both quiet and shy. Though he taught for many years and sometimes gave lectures after he left teaching, the major role he chose was not that of public speaker but of writer, perhaps the loneliest job of all, one that involves locking oneself away from the world in order to make some sense of it.

The second floor of his Croton-on-Hudson house was a place visitors would leave awed and tantalized: when you told Ben what you were working on he would go to the shelves or piles or stacks and haul out copies (often signed) of the appropriate classics, a dozen other things you'd never heard of but knew immediately you needed absolutely, as well as sheets of ephemera no one but Ben knew about any more, let alone owned. The floors and shelves bulged with scholarly treatises, fictions, fictions posing as fact, guidebooks, magazines, Sunday supplements, handbooks, manuscripts, pamphlets, reference works, and all the other printed forms that have served to document or present or analyze or eulogize or indict those verbal artifacts of the complex of high and low and mass and pop and folk culture we sometimes call the American Experience: Ben's field.

He was always interested in the ways people negotiated and documented their lives, and he refused to draw a line—when it seemed to him a certain kind of informing idea was involved—between something uttered in a traditional conversation and something locked in print. (That was a concept that didn't get a name until a folklorist wrote a paper a few years ago on "folk ideas," a folklorist's attempt to come to grips with the curious and annoying reality that there is a lot of stuff out there that fits no genre we know or permeates too many we know, but seems traditional nevertheless, beyond genre and beyond performance, a notion that would have been perfectly clear to Ben Botkin.)

His work covered a multitude of subjects; his focus was always on people and their genius of expression. *The American Play-Party Song* (1937), a revision of his doctoral thesis, is still a classic collection and analysis; *Lay My Burden Down* (1945), one of the most moving demonstrations of slavery as an experience, is a work of verbal choreography more than history; the several *Treasuries—American Folklore* (1944), *New England Folklore* (1947, rev. 1964), *Southern Folklore* (1949), *Western Folklore* (1941), *Railroad Folklore* (1953, with Alvin F. Harlow), *Mississippi River Folklore* (1955), and *New York City Folklore* (1956)—have, because of Ben's enormous range of interest and his consistent belief in the virtue of inclusiveness rather than airy exclusiveness, taught millions about the legitimate place of folklore in the American cultural continuum. That those books were long eschewed by professional folklorists perhaps tells us more about the ideological tunnel vision inculcated by grim professionalism than it does about Ben's work.

He did not look lightly on the work of making books. Not long before he died, when he was very ill and very tired, he asked me what I was up to. I told him I'd recently had a couple of new books published and I was now at work on two others.

"*Why* are you still writing books?" he said.

It was, for me, a very spooky question, because I often think about the arrogance of putting things to print, and fear it. We'd never talked about that before, but I knew, in that winky moment, that he was fully aware of it, had more than once wrestled with it himself, and that he had, in that moment, done the sort of thing he always did: threw something out and by implication said, "Here's something you might think about if you want to. You should." Then he got very tired and we talked of it no more.

In 1966 I edited a festschrift for him on the occasion of his sixty-fifth birthday. The preface concluded, "In presenting Ben with this small collection of essays, we acknowledge the work he has done for and in the field of folklore and, more personally, our pleasure in having him as colleague, teacher, and friend." I would add nothing to that now, because the one thing I would like to name—my sadness and the sadness of Ben's family and friends that all that must now be relegated to the past tense—is not expressible. The magnitude of absence is named only by the locus of what was.

Ben's last project was that book he called *American Social Myths and Symbols*. He saw it as the fulfillment of his long career as teacher, poet, critic, folklorist, and social historian. Ten years ago, he described the project this way:

> In nearly a score of volumes I have explored the relation of folklore to folksay (a word which I coined in 1928 to designate unwritten history and literature in particular and oral, linguistic, and floating material in general); the folklore of regions and cities—New England, the South, the West, the Mississippi River region, New York City, "Sidewalks of America"; the folklore of occupations—railroading; the folklore of slavery and the Civil War; the folklore of play and leisure time. In *American Myths and Symbols* I intend to integrate and culminate my thinking on applied folklore in an analysis of folk and popular assumptions and their symbolic expression in heroes, idols, butts, scapegoats, archetypes, stereotypes, totemic creatures and objects, fictitious personalities, cliches, catchwords, shibboleths, slogans, phrases, historical traditions, legends, myths, fables, anecdotes, jests, codes and rituals.
>
> The project had its inception in the present revival of folk singing and song-making (ballads, blues, Freedom songs) and folklore in literature and education. By centering attention on folklore utilization and folklore values, the revival has raised basic questions as to the relevance of the past to the present, the uses and abuses of tradition, and the relation of folklore to the folkways and mores.
>
> My own conception of the reciprocity of folklore and the folkways in the diffusion of myths and symbols has a theoretical basis in Sumner's neglected but still pertinent theory of *Folkways*, which I have extended as follows:
>
>> Like folklore, the folkways rest on assumptions with the backing of tradition and group acceptance. Like all tacit assumptions, the folkways (and the mores growing out of them) can be harmful when used as a substitute for or an obstacle to thinking. As the strength of folklore lies in its imaginative appeal, so the folkways are reinforced by the "instrumentalities of suggestion," or myths, symbols, and tokens in which outmoded folkways and mores are embodied. In a changing society with concomitant rapid

> growth and mixture of disciplines, a folklore study of socio-historical myths and symbols should help us to reassess old and new values and to understand the present in the light of the past and *vice versa* by providing a new approach to the positive or negative role of myth and symbols in unifying or separating people and promoting social progress or reaction. In the last analysis we may discover that whatever affects our values has symbolic meaning and whatever has symbolic meaning affects our values.

It seems odd to read that now, for much of what Ben had to say has become part of the working vocabulary of folklorists, many of whom know or recognize or admit nothing of the legacy involved.

Ben never finished *American Social Myths and Symbols*, which is hardly surprising, since he intended it to be a descriptive and theoretical compendium of everything he'd learned in all those years. There is no way for one book to report all that. But there was another reason he couldn't finish it: he'd done it already, he'd been doing it for forty years, he'd got a lot of other people doing it too, and what was needed now was commentary. But commenting never interested Ben half so much as simply saying, *Listen, listen, listen.*

17

Remembering Alan Lomax
(January 31, 1915–July 19, 2002)

(*Buffalo Report*, July 26, 2002)

Not long after this was published I received an email from the editor of Journal of American Folklore *saying she really liked the piece and asking permission for her to publish it in the* Journal. *I wrote back immediately saying she was welcome to reprint it. I didn't hear from her for a while, so I wrote and asked when it might appear. She responded that she wanted to thank me for submitting my article but the editorial board didn't think it was appropriate for* Journal of American Folklore. *Why do you think the feet got cold? I bet anything it was the "squoze" in the last sentence that did it.*

John and Alan

In the 1930s, when most academics interested in folklore spent their waking hours in libraries looking for printed versions of the 305 ancient British and Scottish ballads certified as authentic forty years earlier by Harvard scholar Francis James Child, John and Alan Lomax were ranging the countryside looking for people singing their own songs about their own lives. They recorded scores or hundreds of those Child ballads; they also recorded thousands of songs of cowboys, convicts, miners, farmers, railroad workers, hobos, cotton pickers and other folks none of those library-ferrets gave a hoot about. The Archive of American Folk Song in the Library of Congress took its shape under their hands, and millions of Americans first learned about the great range of American folk music because of their work.

John Pareles, in his excellent obituary for Alan in the July 20 *New York Times*, wrote that "Mr. Lomax was a musicologist, author, disc jockey, singer, photographer, talent scout, filmmaker, concert and recording producer and television host. He did whatever was necessary to preserve traditional music and take it to a wider audience."

Alan was also a huge presence in the American musical and broader cultural scene. His contribution to our heritage, to our understanding of ourselves, was incalculable.

Much of the music urban participants in the folk song revival of the 1960s played came from recordings Alan and John had made thirty years earlier, recordings published on red vinyl by the Library of Congress. The most important performers the urban folksingers in those years were emulating—Lead Belly, Woody Guthrie, Muddy Waters—had been recorded by the Lomaxes. Pete Seeger is indebted to the Lomaxes' work, so is Bob Dylan, so was John Lennon. If you've listened to the six-times-over platinum CD *Oh Brother, Where Art Thou?* you've heard one of Alan's recordings from the 1930s: the very first song on the album, James Carter and a group of convicts singing "Po' Lazarus."

There was a time when, if you were out studying traditional music in America, you could not help but cross a path Alan Lomax and his father had blazed. You probably still can't.

"That other feller"

In the summer of 1964 I was recording traditional singers and instrumentalists in Saltville, Virginia, a small mountain town north of Bristol, Tennessee. Someone I met in Saltville's gas station sent me to see Alec Tolbert, who lived in a place called Poor Valley.

According to my notes from that trip, you get to Alec Tolbert's house in Poor Valley by going out Route 91 about four miles to McReady's Gap, then you turn left at the red brick church, go three-quarters of a mile to the top of the hill, turn right, go about two miles to a little store. Then you go in the store and ask anyone where Alex Tolbert's house is. It was the most out-of-the-way place I had, to that time, been. Alec Tolbert and I talked for a bit and then he said, "That other feller had one a those machines."

"What other feller?"

"The one who had that machine like yours. He was here a while back. He was doing the same thing you're doing. His name was Lomax."

A few weeks later, I was down a red dirt road outside of Marshall, a small town in the Arkansas Ozarks, visiting Barry Sutterfield, a 73-year-old ballad singer, and his wife Nellie. The three of us sat on the porch talking for a while, after which Uncle Barry sang old ballads like "Cole Younger," "Barbry Ellen," and "The Little Rebel."

Then Uncle Barry said, "You know that other feller?"

"Which one?" I said.

"The one who was doing the same thing you're doing. Only he had a beard." Alan Lomax.

In a very real way, I owe my academic career to Alan and his father, John. One of my earliest books was *Wake Up Dead Man: Afro-American Worksongs from Texas Prisons* (Harvard University Press, 1972). That book never would have come about had it not been for the prison worksong fieldwork by the Lomaxes in the early 1930s: I heard and was entranced by their recordings, got interested in the music, went off to see what was still around, then moved from the studies of music to studies of prisons themselves, and from there to studies of the criminal justice process. A few years ago, it all came around when Alan's daughter Anna asked me to do the booklet for *Big Brazos: Texas Prison Recordings, 1933 and 1934*, one of the 150 CDs in the astonishing Alan Lomax field series being produced by Rounder. While annotating those recordings I realized for the first time that Alan and his father had recorded some of the same men I'd recorded in Texas in the mid- and late sixties.

Newport

I met Alan in 1965, when Pete Seeger got me elected to the Newport Folk Festival board of directors. We used to meet every month at jazz producer George Wein's Riverside Drive apartment to plan the four-day festivals that took place in July and to figure out ways to give away the money left over from the previous year's concert.

Newport was based on a concept developed by Pete Seeger, George Wein and Theodore Bikel. Their idea was that if people came to hear music they already liked, they'd also listen to music they hadn't known existed, and the way to make that happen that was to let the popular performers underwrite the unknown performers. So everybody got $50 a day. If you were famous, like Pete or Joan Baez, you got $50 a day. If nobody outside your town or village ever heard of you, you got $50 a day. The Foundation rented several of the big Newport mansions and put everybody up in them. (A few people, like Peter Yarrow and Bob Dylan, were fancy and stayed in their own suites in the Viking Hotel in town, but they paid for that themselves.) Most of the famous singers never collected their payments; they just performed for the fun of it.

Everything that was left over each year was donated to folk music performers and to support folk music projects.

I remember Ralph Rinzler, Mike Seeger, Pete and Alan coming up with really interesting performers and projects. Most everybody was pretty calm, but Alan would often get really agitated if the rest of us didn't get enthusiastic about some plan or project he thought was absolutely necessary. He'd tell us that if we didn't see the necessity for this or that we could not claim to take ourselves seriously. Sometimes Alan's projects were great, sometimes they were balmy. In my first year or so, when I was new kid on the block, I'd mostly sit quietly while Seeger and Brand and Rinzler worked it out with him. They were wonderful discussions to watch and hear.

Resurrection City

In 1968, after Martin Luther King was killed, Ralph Rinzler got the Newport Foundation to underwrite and help staff the music and children's programs at Resurrection City, the tent and shack camp next to Washington's Reflecting Pool. Resurrection City housed the participants in King's last project, the Poor People's Campaign.

Ralph started setting things up and I went down to Washington to help him. Alan heard about what we were doing and caught up with us at a meeting we were having with Jim Bevel and other members of the Southern Christian Leadership Conference staff. Ralph (who was later founding director of the Festival of American Folklife in Washington and then the Smithsonian's assistant secretary for public service) was one of the most tactful people I ever met. He was saying to Bevel and the others, "Here are the resources we have. How can we help you?" when Alan jumped up and gave everybody a lecture on the power and importance of folk music, black folk music in particular.

It was a good lecture, but that was neither the time, place nor company for it. Bevel and the others listened to Alan in polite, stony silence, then went on to other business. When the meeting was over, Bevel beckoned Ralph and me to the side of the room and said, "You guys ought to do something about him."

"I wish we could," Ralph said. "He means well, and he knows a lot."

"I guess," Bevel said.

That night was, I think, the first night of real activity in Resurrection City. A thousand or so of the six thousand people who would eventually inhabit the place had arrived. Bevel and several others made rousing speeches in the big community tent and Frederick Douglass Kirkpatrick gave a great performance, followed by some other musical groups.

Alan and I were standing at the back of the seats, listening to the music. When one group finished, Alan said, "Are there any academic studies of the high tenor in black male vocal music?" I said I had no idea. "I'm wondering where it comes from. Do you think it has to do with repressed homosexuality?"

He said that much more loudly than I would have liked. Several heads turned and stared. Another group sang. Alan tapped the shoulder of a woman in the back row and said, "Those boys sure do sing good, don't they, honey?"

I don't think he meant anything ill by it. It's just how he was. Several young men nearby had heard both his remarks and were looking at him hostilely. I was feeling more and more uncomfortable, and rather than have an argument with him about it, I just left the tent and started walking up the Mall toward the Capitol.

He caught up with me a few minutes later and said, "Why did you leave like that?"

"I didn't want to be there when you got them *really* pissed off."

"Ah," he said, seeming to find that a reasonable answer.

We walked along in silence, then I said, "Alan, why are you like that?"

He was quiet for a while. Then he said, "You don't know what it was like, growing up in the Library of Congress." For some reason, I thought I knew exactly what he meant.

I guess he *had* grown up in the Library of Congress. He joined his father in the pursuit of American folk music when he was seventeen, and that set the arrow of his life. Alan was a boy from Austin, Texas, who became the man who was more driven than anyone else I know for the world to understand and honor its own music. In the decades when academic folklorists in America and Great Britain were desperately seeking survivals from bygone centuries, Alan was insisting, "Listen to what people are singing now."

That night, walking along the Mall, the sounds from the tent fading out behind us, Alan talked about his early years in the Library, about being on the road with his father, about the thrill of finding and preserving bits and pieces of a musical world he knew was vanishing even as he recorded it.

I was staying at Ralph Rinzler's house, the other side of the Library of Congress. I don't remember where Alan was staying. I remember that when we reached the place where he went one way and I went another we stood there for a while, while he finished telling me something.

Nashville

I heard him talk like that one other time.

In 1983, Diane Christian and I were in Nashville for a meeting of the American Folklore Society. Saturday night we got on the hotel elevator to go downstairs for the plenary session, the big speechifying meeting of the Society. I had just been elected the Society's president for the following year, so I was supposed to be at that plenary session. In the elevator, we met Alan's sister, Bess Lomax Hawes, who was director of the Folk Arts Program of the National Endowment for the Arts, which meant she was supposed to be at that plenary session too.

Bess said she was stopping at Alan's room to fetch him. "Come on along," Bess said, "and we'll all go down together."

I hadn't seen him for a while, so we joined her. It was one of those hotel rooms with two beds and one chair. Alan was sitting on one, talking on the phone, and all his stuff was on the other. There was an almost-full quart of bourbon next to the telephone. Alan motioned for us to sit down. We moved the stuff on the other bed around and one of us sat on the bed, one on the floor, one in the chair. When Alan was done with the call he said, "Let's have a drink before we go down." We all had some bourbon, which I hate.

Then Alan started telling stories. It was astonishing. I've known a lot of great storytellers, but I remember no one ever doing anything like that. Alan talked for maybe three hours.

Occasionally Diane or Bess or I said something, but almost entirely it was Alan, telling stories. Stories about working with his father, stories about people we all knew, stories about people only he knew, stories about doing the work. Three hours of it. It was just magnificent.

I remember one sentence out of all the sentences he said that night. He had gotten onto the subject of academic folklorists and he pointed down to the floor, toward the place however many stories below us they were doing their speechifying.

"They squoze and they squoze," he said, "and they produced another generation of pedants just like the generation of pedants they wanted to replace. But without the beautiful manners."

How can you not love somebody who can summarize a generation of ambitious and competitive pedants like that?

The four of us emptied that bottle of bourbon. None of us made it downstairs that night. After the bourbon was gone and Alan had wound down—or maybe it was we who had worn down—Bess, Diane and I went back to the elevator and went upstairs. Diane and I got off at our floor and Bess went on to hers. That was the best evening I ever had at an American Folklore Society or any other academic society meeting.

"They squoze and they squoze and they produced another generation of pedants just like the generation of pedants they wanted to replace. But without the beautiful manners." Goddamn!

18

Legman

The King of X700

(*Maledicta 2: Festschrift for G. Legman*,
ed. Reinhold Aman, 1977)

This special number of *Maledicta* is dedicated to the furious American emigre who knows more about this stuff than anyone else: Gershon Legman. Few American scholars would admit that Legman knows more about erotica than anyone else. That is because he has for many years with great skill, wit, scholarship and occasional perverse glee attacked most of their sacred cows and revealed them to be dry and moth-eaten skins.

Legman would right now probably consider me masochistic: I've just reread all his books except *The Guilt of the Templars*; I even skimmed the little bibliography of Ricardo he seems to have authored but does not list among his publications. I'm not totally masochistic: I did skip some of the jokes in *Rationale of the Dirty Joke* and *No Laughing Matter*. But I'm worn out anyway: my head swims at the awesome display of magnificent information he draws before the reader like a line in sand accompanying a bellowed dare: *Here are the facts, the references, the connections: go do something intelligent for a change.*

He is one of the few humanistic scholars still writing whose work makes the publications of most academic folklorists seem a trail of failed charlatans, which is one of the reasons many of them are so pissed off at him. He makes them look like dilettantes, not very stylish dilettantes at that. The range and density of information in his books is rarely matched. There is more solid (hard core?) scholarship in *The Horn Book* and the two volumes of *Rationale of the Dirty Joke* than all other scholarly studies of Anglo-American erotic literature and folklore combined. His frequent angry remarks about the state of current scholarship and the trajectory of American culture are a bonus: they give the reader something to argue with and think about, often both at once.

Some scholarly reviewers complain that he sometimes wanders from his stated subjects. In *Rationale of the Dirty Joke*, for example, he complains about the American government's "insincere and mock-religious official stamp-cancellation: 'PRAY FOR PEACE'—meanwhile assiduously making war" (I, 31). He says things like that because, for him, the goal of scholarship *isn't* the safe and elegant isolation and expansion of an unassailable aperçu; rather, it is the considered reintegration of apparently disparate things so they can be seen as existing in a complex political and social and psychological continuum, a world in which *everything counts*.

All his books are richly annotated; they all contain enormous masses of direct information. The two volumes of *Rationale* would have been major folklore documents even if he had not offered a word of interpretation: the jokes and the sources and parallels would have placed those books in a rank with the major collections.

One disagrees with opinions, not facts. Legman is usually careful to first lay out a rich carpet of facts. He is not a good writer for a stupid reader. One must be willing to argue many of the things Legman asserts, work through in one's own mind the anger that rises suddenly at many of his apparently outrageous remarks. Few scholars force that kind of work. *Makes you think* doesn't have to mean *gets you to agree*. Few folklore books of recent years—hardly any since the comic arguments about communal composition in the silly early days of modern ballad scholarship—have been contaminated by ideas at all.

He does it all from his home in the tiny village of Valbonne, near the southern tip of Alpes-Maritimes, not far by auto from Cannes. Legman doesn't have an auto, so the trip to the city is always a difficult affair. He lives with his wife and three children in a moderately old stone barn about fifty meters from a two-story frame house. The barn is crowded and disorderly; it has only two rooms and they are constantly in use by the family. Books and clothes are everywhere.

Legman keeps his larger world over in the house. Every morning he walks the winding path through the weeds and trees; every night he comes back to the small converted barn. An anachronistic intercom connects the two buildings. The house is very neat. There are thousands of books, ranks of file cabinets, many shelves of neatly-arranged LP recordings of classical music, stacks of index cards. There is a grand piano, in tune, and three speakers.

When Diane Christian and I visited him there in June 1975, he had just completed *No Laughing Matter*, the second half of *Rationale*. He showed me the jacket, which had just arrived; it was wrapped around three inches of blank pages. "It gives a feel of what the book will look like," he said. I had been in Paris for an exhibition of my photographs and the French publication of one of my books. We talked about publishers. Legman had suffered enormous problems with the publishers of *Rationale*: they kept moving his contract around, not telling him what they were doing, not doing things they promised. I told him about a former New York publisher of mine who had a few years earlier gone to San Francisco to run *Rolling Stone*'s book division. The publisher, when I first met him, had told me about his books: "I did this book and then I did that one," he said, and I thought him a famous writer I had missed entirely. I sat in his office uncomfortably, feeling naive in the hip New York literary scene. Then the publisher told me his most successful book had been *Manchild in the Promised Land*. The publisher was slim and very white; he was obviously not Claude Brown, who was neither. I mentioned this to him. "Ah," he said, fluttering his hand, "Claude Brown. He wrote it, but *I* . . ." I no longer remember how he finished the sentence, but I shall always remember the look of complacent superiority he put on his face when he hit the first person pronoun.

"Those people," Legman said, "they're like midwives and gynecologists who do it six times a day: for them, the women are nothing. Those publishers think the same thing of writers: they're nothing. But, you know, those guys rarely stay in a job more than three years, they're always moving and quitting and getting fired. A productive writer works fifteen or twenty-five years, maybe more. He can outlast six sets of them. You have to ignore those people. That's what you have to do if you want to stay sane." He hefted the empty book and said he thought such publishers were like guards in a harem: "They know what to do and they know how to do it. There's just one little thing missing: they *can't* do it."

Legman, of course, *has* done it. The list of books bearing his name on their spines is deceptive. The two volumes of *Rationale* consist of over eighteen hundred pages and four thousand stories; they could make a half-dozen of the kinds of book Legman so often complains about, the usual compilations. He doesn't think much of books that come into existence merely because a collector stumbled upon a certain batch of material. Most of them, he often says, have little or no real analysis, and the authors often suppress obscene and erotic material because such material isn't seemly in a "serious" publication. Those books, Legman says, are really presentations of the collectors'—not the folk's—sensibilities. He is equally upset by American collectors' knee-jerk obeisance to the *Motif Index of Folk Literature*, which ratifies their erotic and obscene lacunae by having no categories for any narrative elements dealing with fucking, sucking, and other kinds of carnal enterprise. The folk would find the deliberate omission as bizarre as Legman does if they read such books. (The *Motif Index* has a slot for erotic and obscene items—X700—but the category has no entries except for a few non-erotic elements dealing with old maids.)

Legman finds the decision to delete the obscene on grounds of taste, while including sadism and violence, bizarre. "Another culture than our own," he wrote, "might prefer to include the obscene motifs, and omit the hundreds of descriptions of horrible murders and sadistic mutilations" (*Rationale*, I, 33–34). It's a complaint he has voiced for decades. In *Love and Death* (1949) he asked why it was permissible to show children adults destroying one another with a dazzling array of secular weapons (in comic books, movies, television), but impermissible to show them adults tenderly stroking one another into orgasmic ripples.

He does his work without foundation grants, university sinecures, research assistants, free offices, free xerox machines, free telephones or free postage meters. He operates under a set of financial strictures most American academics would find totally disabling. Those who have bothered to read his work carefully know he hasn't gotten the barest bones of support and gratitude, which he has at great personal cost earned.

There are three important American folklore scholars who have done magnificent work and have given great aid to other scholars, but who have remained cut off from the academic mainstream dollar-teat: B. A. Botkin, Vance Randolph, and Legman. All three, I think, elected not to join the academic procession into a well-funded old age and none of them, so far as I know, ever regretted the freedom resulting from that choice. But all of them suffered miserably because of it.

Botkin was viciously attacked during much of his career because he insisted folklore studies should include everything the folk learn through non-academic means, a recognition of folk culture's workings that has only started manifesting itself in the *Journal of American Folklore* in the past few years. The change occurred in an article by Alan Dundes, of the Berkeley anthropology department, in an article about "folk ideas" that didn't mention Botkin at all, though it essentially restated a position Botkin had taken thirty years previously. Botkin was excoriated in the folklore press for being a "popularizer"; Dundes was praised for his expansion of folklore study objects.

I suspect ideas have little to do with these affairs. What matters is whether or not one is a member in good standing of the Club. Botkin wasn't. And neither is Randolph or Legman. All members of the American Folklore Society received subscription options for prepublication orders for *No Laughing Matter*: only *two* bothered to respond. Three years ago, I asked a member of the American Folklore Society's self-perpetuating Fellows group why neither Legman nor Randolph had been elected to membership; I asked that after several scholarly lightweights had been, with all due pomp and applause at the banquet, initiated. "Nobody suggested either of them," the Fellow said. I asked if a nonFellow might suggest a Fellow-candidate. "Anyone can suggest," he said. I suggested Legman and Randolph. A year elapsed and still Legman and Randolph were passed over. I asked another Fellow why. "They're not paid-up current members of AFS," I was told, "and the Fellows are all paid-up members of the Society." I said some vile things and reminded the Fellow that Legman lives on nickels and that Randolph was waiting to die in a miserable old-folks home. I suggested that both men be made honorary life members. He looked at me as if I were crazy. Maybe this year. Maybe next year. Maybe it will be moot by then.

Maybe Legman has offended the profession too profoundly for such recognition. It was he who in print pointed out the curious arrogance and inequity noted behind the title pages of almost all twentieth-century American folklore collections: the folksongs and stories, even though collected with the help of public monies by people often on public payrolls, are copyrighted in the names of the collectors and/or their publishers. Only rarely are the materials copyrighted in the names of the people from whom they were collected, or noted as being from the public domain. The copyrights protect the financial interests of people paid to go out wandering with their Japanese tape recorders.

Few get as rich on the royalties as Legman's rhetoric suggests, but many do get nice jobs. After two copyrighted collections of other people's traditional possessions, one can get tenure, which means a guaranteed (usually adequate, sometimes lush) salary for life, a salary that can't be lost unless one performs some outrageous moral violation upon the academic community. Off-campus behaviors don't count, which is fair, but neither do being a bore or an incompetent teacher or intellectually inert, which isn't.

Legman's rage about professors who fund one another's projects isn't entirely wrong either. Grants may not often go to people who are total dodos, but when it comes to a decision between a reasonable insider and an equally reasonable outsider, the insider gets the bucks every time. Nothing wrong with that, I suppose: the reason people seek power is so they can exercise it. The thing is, most of those people don't admit that that is what they are in fact doing.

On the whole, the professors treat one another well, for they know who sits on which foundation's evaluation committees and they also know that they will have their own turns to sit in judgment. The wheel of academic fortune rotates to favor all the players who participate in the game with proper style and grace. I think of two incidents from the 1976 American Folklore Society meeting in Philadelphia.

The first involved two teachers of folklore and it happened immediately after one of them, a woman in her early thirties, had disagreed in the course of a public meeting with the other, a man in his mid-forties. The man got her alone in the hall after the meeting and said, "You've committed suicide. Political suicide."

"What are you talking about?" she asked. "Political suicide? You're just a goddamned folklore professor."

"Ah," he said, waving his hand to include the people mulling about in the hallway. "But I'm *Carter's* folklore professor!"

The other incident was more disheartening and probably more common. It happened at the same meeting. A professor from a West Coast university said to me that a book recently published by a prestigious university press was truly an embarrassing affair, one that did neither the author nor the Press any good. He didn't think the positions taken in the book did "the Profession" much good either.

"But Max," I said, "you were one of the two outside readers the Press relied on for that book. You must have approved it, else they wouldn't have published it."

"Of course I approved it," he said, "what else could I have done? I've known Alberto a long time and he's very important in the field."

I looked at Max with an expression I'm sure revealed my sincere disapproval. I wouldn't have behaved so irresponsibly; I would have told the people at the Press the truth. Of course, I notice when I tell the story to you, I'm not up to telling you the real name of either author or reader or the real institutional affiliation of anyone involved. There are grant applications on my desk and . . .

Legman, I assume, has no grant applications on his desk and he says what he damned well pleases whenever he damned well feels like it. And that is another thing that gives scholars fits when they read his work.

302 | FOLKLORE MATTERS

We aren't used to competent scholars who are also passionate polemicists; unembarrassed commitment is sometimes frightening. Most scholarly argument stops far short of where it might be caught wrong. That is because of the way scholarly reviewing works: one first goes after the conclusions, and second for the methodology; if one draws no blood at either stop, then one gets to the more difficult job of picking at the body, the content. In such an enterprise it is probably foolish for an ambitious author to stain his conclusions with speculations, spot his methodology with insight, or to include as part of the substance the ideas the job has gotten his mind thinking or raging about.

I said earlier that Legman was not a good writer for stupid readers. He has too much to say and the dummies get exhausted early on. None of the reviewers of *Rationale of the Dirty Joke*, for example, seems to have understood the title, though Legman several times in his introduction explained it clearly enough: "What is meant is that these stories and individuals do personify what the tellers and singers well know to be real but inexplicable peculiarities of human behavior, which they are attempting somehow to fit into a rational view of the world, whether as horror or as humor" (I, 22). He wasn't trying to *explain* the dirty joke, which is a complex psychological event requiring analysis of the teller and understanding of all the parameters of the telling context; he was trying to see what the dirty joke itself seemed to be trying to explain. His concern in those two volumes is how the dirty joke seems to make rational something not apparently rational. There are a lot of things in the world that don't seem rational and there are a lot of dirty jokes.

He gets assaulted in print from time to time because of his rants about the various conspiracies he thinks afoot in the world. He thinks, for example, there are a number of malevolent homosexuals generating women's fashions. Fashion designers and non-malevolent homosexuals respond in anger to such remarks, but no one answers the question he is really putting forward—if not malevolent homosexuals, then who *is* responsible for that horrid stuff? Could anyone with affection for a female body at all have designed that draped Edsel of yesteryear's clothing industry, the Sack? Legman gets attacked for having attacked the wrong malfeasants, but no one answers his basic questions: Who the fuck is responsible and why are they doing it to us? No one is responsible, is the lame answer, it's just how things are. Bullshit, Legman responds. Legman abandons the fine distance that makes such dangerous discussions comfortable and safe.

A person named Charles Rycroft reviewed *Rationale* for the *New York Review of Books*. He was extremely upset by the experience. He was annoyed that Legman occasionally "turns aside from his stated theme to take swipes at somebody or something he dislikes or to ride off on some totally irrelevant hobby horse. He also takes a delight in impugning the sexual normality of literary figures who are so recently dead that the allegations, even if true, can only cause offense." Aw, darn, one should wait a few decades before taking up the sexual proclivities of people like D. H. Lawrence and Ernest Hemingway, who themselves displayed it day after day and created killing models for the readers who happened to take their works seriously. Charles Rycroft was offended that Legman didn't tell us that dirty jokes were only about dirty jokes, he was distressed because Legman dragged into his discussion everything else that seemed to him relevant, and he was more offended because Legman kept offering *evaluations* of behavior, which scholars should not do. One example: "In [Legman's] view, hysterectomies and mastectomies are performed by men who enjoy castrating women and 'never have and never will save any women from dying of cancer,' while 'psycho surgery and sterilization of the insane are available for physicians more interested in men.'" Rycroft found that vile; Legman's anger was inappropriate. Rycroft should have checked the data: hysterectomies are the second most common surgery procedure done in America, and the death rate from hysterectomy complications is *many* times the death rate from the uterine cancer they are supposed to prevent; recent reports indicate that many radical mastectomies (which is removal of not only the lump and the breast surrounding it, but also the muscle and lymph tissue a half-foot away) are unnecessary, and that only 30 percent of the women who suffer them survive anyway, which is not a great deal better than those who survive mere removal of the little deadly lumps. Legman's rhetoric about surgeons may be excessive, but it hardly compares to the very real atrocities done to many women's bodies.

Legman scampers around the groves of academe screaming, "You assholes: you left out the best parts!" He finds the incompetence infuriating, the deliberate betrayal of the informants unforgivable. He writes of

> the great peace of non-understanding that comes when scholars funk their responsibility to interpret in a human way the materials they have studied and collected; and, instead, pour their materials into adding-machine jukeboxes, and wait for the insights to slide out on a perforated tape into their palms.
>
> The curse of folklore and folksong publication, as everyone knows, has been this endless doodling with the unimportant and

> nonsignificant paraphernalia of form—once the textual form, now the musical form—without any matching concentration on meaning and function; with no study, until barely yesterday, of *what the material means to the people who transmit it*, and not to the outsiders who collect it; what it tells us about their inner aspirations and their response to the lives they live. As far as sexual folklore is concerned, this complete overlooking of the essential, and concentration solely on the form, is tantamount to spending the entire wedding night examining the bride's trousseau. (*Horn Book*, 285)

Legman's asides, the correct and brilliant ones and the outrageous and bizarre ones (the difference being whether or not one agrees with the aside in question), introduce *his own* consciousness into the scholarship. Little wonder the academics take flight.

Anyone who writes Legman for help receives—usually by return mail—detailed references, commentaries on the references, and suggestions regarding the project described. He is very good at discovering the level of competence of people who write him, and his letters sometimes adopt an appropriately tutorial—rather than collegial—tone. A couple of years ago, for example, a graduate student I knew wrote him for help on a dissertation on English and American proverbs. The student had gone through the usual folklore sources and found them lacking sexual proverbs he knew were there. Legman wrote him, in part:

> Taylor's *Proverb*, and everything else he did (as on riddles, nose-thumbing, etc.) is expurgated to the hilt in the old, Child-ballad, DEATH-yes-SEX-no style. (Compare also "Jaws," "Towering Inferno," etc. at your local playhouse—billed as "Bake & Quake," whereas two pornos billed as "Cream & Scream" would be IN BAD TASTE.) My advice to you is simple: *Buy* a copy of Morris P. Tilley's *Dictionary of the Proverbs in England* in the 16th & 17th centuries, and read it from cover to cover, *marking marginally* the unexpurgated items, which Tilley does not evade, and being sure to read all the *quotations* for the items that interest you. This should take you about two years. Write to me again then.

The student was shell-shocked by the letter. He was used to professors who chatted a while, then made an appointment to chat some more a week or two hence. He asked me if I thought Legman were serious. I asked him if he were an idiot. He went away and didn't bother either of us again.

One prominent folklorist I know, a man whose early work was heavily indebted to detailed criticism, commentary, and suggestions Legman sent after reading the man's unpublished manuscripts, told me he had recently motored from Paris to Rome. I asked if he had stopped off at Valbonne to visit Gershon and Judith. He looked at me oddly: "No. Of course not."

"How come?" I asked.

"It wasn't on the way. It's very far out of the way."

I said I thought that odd. If I were in a foreign country and a friend lived a hundred or so miles from where I was passing, a friend I hadn't seen for a long time, one who wasn't very well, I'd take the detour to say hello. Especially if it were someone like Legman, with whom one cannot have an extended conversation without learning a great deal: he teaches constantly. The speed limit in France is now about 160 kilometers per hour; the roads are very good; it would use up a morning or an afternoon at most. One could take in some movies in Cannes on the way back or go for a swim at Antibes. The beaches are very good in the area.

"Legman's not a *friend*," the scholar explained. "We've never even met."

"Oh," I said.

"We've just corresponded."

"For how long?"

"Ten or twelve years."

This was a guy who was in Europe almost every *year*.

Diane Christian heard that conversation. "If Gershon were on the Guggenheim committee," she said to me later, "George would have managed the drive."

I think if Legman were on the Guggenheim committee—or Rockefeller or NEH or NEA or NIH or APS or ACLS or whatever—George would have walked. Or run. They all would. All those Georges. But Legman is not on any of those committees, nor will he ever be; he isn't even a Fellow of the American Folklore Society.

Someone told me Legman wouldn't function well on such committees anyway: he is not good about finding felicitous ways for describing work he thinks dreadful. He has perhaps been infelicitous too many times to be forgiven now.

Legman is perfectly well aware of which opinions he might have suppressed so the academics would look at him with safe affection. He knows which asses are out there waiting to be obediently kissed. He has elected to kick them. He is a driven man, a serious man, a knowledgeable and opinionated man. But for all his cranky attacks on everything in motion and his unambivalent opinions regarding any behaviors under consideration, Legman remains one of the very few American humanistic scholars who is truly fun to read.

For him, jokes, and the other kinds of folk and written narrative he explores, aren't little pieces of tale floating through the verbal interactions of the romantic and demotic folk. They are a living aspect of a complex social organism. And the scholar's job isn't simply to isolate those little verbal events, there is a further responsibility: the responsibility to say—or try to say—what it all means and does.

Because of that concern, he has long been a keen critic of American life. Fourteen years ago, for example, he accurately predicted the present trend of popular narrative forms: "The purely sadistic content of mass-appeal fiction and electrically broadcast spectacles is still incredibly high, and increases unremittingly, despite all wishful theories that it cannot possibly rise any higher, and that it will soon 'level off' to at least an approximate normality. No such levelling off has been observable over the last fifteen years, or is really expected. It is the opposite that is to be expected: an increasingly larger dose" (*Horn Book*, 307).

The power of the media to give reality to violence, and the willingness of editors and reporters to exploit it, became so great in the past several years that terrorists have come to rely on the press to deliver their graphic messages to the world—the Hanafi Muslims in Washington, the PLO at the Munich Olympics, the SLA in Oakland. New York's multiple murderer, the psychotic who called himself "Son of Sam," sent cryptic letters to the press, which printed them alongside of the photographs of the young women Sam shot to death. A recent pornographic film became a success not because of the sexual activity it displayed, but rather because a rumor went around that the young girl apparently killed in one scene was *really* killed in that scene, hence the film's name, *Snuff*. When Legman wrote about the sadistic matter presented to the public, he was writing about fictive forms; in recent years, the sadism has become part of the evening news. As Legman has so often said, the mimetic representations really matter, people really need them. The problem is knowing why, understanding how, seeing how things link and lock and knowing what one might do when the intersections become deadly.

I just found a postcard he sent me ten years ago. "Please understand," he wrote, "that I can't fix things, from *here*, that you are letting it happen, *there*. It is time for SOMEbody to bloody well *do* something." He's still out there trying to show us what we see, and we're still over here, letting it happen.

The postcard closed with Cyrano's closing line: " 'Je sais bien que c'est inutile, mais C'EST BEAUCOUP PLUS BEAU QUAND C'EST INUTILE . . .' No pasaran!"

D'accord.

Legman's Books

David Ricardo and Ricardian Theory, 1949
Love and Death: A Study in Censorship, 1949
The Horn Book: Studies in Erotic Folklore and Bibliography, 1964
The Guilt of the Templars, 1966
The Fake Revolt, 1967
Rationale of the Dirty Joke, First Series, 1968
Oragenitalism: Oral Techniques in Genital Excitation, revised and enlarged, 1969
The Limerick: 1700 Examples, enlarged edition, 1970
Rationale of the Dirty Joke: An Analysis of Sexual Humor, Second Series (*No Laughing Matter*), 1975
The New Limerick: 2750 Unpublished Examples, American and British, 1977

19

In Prison with Pete Seeger

(FolkStreams, 2006)

When FolkStreams added our 1966 film, Afro-American Worksongs in a Texas Prison, *to its website—https://www.folkstreams.net/films/afro-american-work-songs-in-a-texas-prison—they asked each of us to write something about how the film came about. Pete remembered the project as my idea; I remembered it as his. Here's my version of the film's genesis and what happened when Pete, Toshi, and Dan Seeger joined me at Ellis prison farm in Texas in March 1966.*

∽

In early winter 1966, Pete said to me, "There aren't any films of those black convict worksongs you've been working on in Texas. Somebody should make one before it's too late, before they're gone."

I told him that I didn't know anything about making movies and nobody was going to give us any money to do it anyway. NEH and NEA had just been established and weren't giving money to people making movies about folk music yet, let alone people like us—me, who nobody knew, and Pete, who was still persona non grata in Washington because of his politics. We couldn't wait, Pete said. Those songs would not be around much longer and it was important to document them now. He said he would pay for the film himself.

So, in mid-March 1966, Pete, his wife Toshi, and his son Dan came with their film equipment to Huntsville, Texas, where I was doing research at Ellis prison farm, then the place Texas put multiple recidivists serving long sentences. When I met them at the motel, I saw Pete unloading from their rented station wagon his guitar and banjo cases.

"Why did you bring them?" I asked.

"They're going to sing for me," he said, "so I'll sing for them."

"You don't have to do that," I said.

"Yes I do," he said.

We spent several days in the Ellis live oaks with a group of convicts who sang tree-cutting and logging songs while they cut down trees and chopped them into pieces with axes, and then we went to a field where they sang flat weeding songs while they worked with hoes. Pete reminded me about him singing for the convicts.

I went to the warden and said, "He wants to do a concert for the convicts."

"Why?" the warden said.

"That's what he does," I said. "Okay," the warden said.

The next night several hundred convicts marched into the Ellis prison gymnasium and sat in folding iron chairs. I was certain it would be a disaster. These guys didn't know from folk music. These guys didn't know from Pete's kind of politics. These were very tough guys. These guys would eat Pete Seeger alive.

I didn't know a damned thing about anything.

I don't remember what song Pete opened with, but within five minutes he had just about every convict, white and black, in that huge room singing along. And the guards. And the warden. I stood at the side of the stage astonished. It was like a Saturday afternoon workshop at the Newport Folk Festival. The next night Pete gave another concert at the Wynne Farm, another prison at the edge of Huntsville, and exactly the same thing happened.

A day or two after we finished the filming and Pete, Toshi, and Dan had gone back to New York, a convict I'd been seeing for several years but who had never talked to me stopped me in the Ellis corridor and said, "How come you never recorded me singing any of them river songs?" River songs is what they called them because nearly all the Texas prisons in those days were in the rich bottomland along the Brazos and Trinity rivers. They were nineteenth-century plantations hiding in the twentieth century.

"I never knew you knew any," I said.

"Well, I never knew you knew Pete Seeger," he said.

When he said that line to me I was really tickled by it because I was certain that until Pete got up there in the gymnasium a few nights earlier he had never heard of Pete Seeger and his long-neck five-string banjo and twelve-string guitar, and neither had most of the men incarcerated or working in that penitentiary. I told the story a lot of times over the years and always thought that when I told it: how amusing that that guy said that thing about Pete about whom he knew nothing before the concert in the gymnasium.

But now I have come to realize there is something far more important and substantial in what that man said to me in the Ellis corridor. He was perfectly serious and he was telling me what Pete Seeger had accomplished in Ellis prison. It was because he felt he was a friend of Pete Seeger, because he felt he knew Pete Seeger, and that was something we shared, so he and I weren't as total strangers to one another after all.

How many musicians do you know who can do that? How many people do you know who can do that? Go into a perfectly strange place and perform music in a style hardly anybody in the room ever heard before, and before the evening is over, they're all your buddies? Singing songs about things that really matter and thinking about those things?

Maybe that's Pete's great gift to us: his ability to join a group of people who might not only be strangers to him but to one another as well and to leave them, however many hours later, with some feeling, some knowledge, that transcends the moment entirely, a feeling and knowledge about the things that bond rather than the things that rend, about what it means to be human rather than what it means to be brutal, about how we must and can get on together by conspiring in the best and most basic sense of that word: breathing together.

Part VI

The Folklore Business

20

Things That from a Long Way Off Look Like Flies

(Journal of American Folklore, 1985)

> [Borges] quotes a "certain Chinese encyclopedia" in which it is written that "animals are divided into: (a) belonging to the Emperor, (b) embalmed, (c) tame, (d) sucking pigs, (e) sirens, (f) fabulous, (g) stray dogs, (h) included in the present classification, (i) frenzied, (j) innumerable, (k) drawn with a very fine camelhair brush, (l) *et cetera*, (m) having just broken the water pitcher, (n) that from a long way off look like flies." In the wonderment of this taxonomy, the thing we apprehend in one great leap, the thing that, by means of the fable, is demonstrated as the exotic charm of another system of thought, is the limitation of our own, the stark impossibility of thinking *that*.
>
> —Michel Foucault, *The Order of Things*

Folklore studies, like any other kind of studies, don't just happen. Fields of scholarship occur because specific technological and economic and institutional resources are available and because specific individuals utilize those resources in specific ways. Whatever measure of intellectual or academic freedom we enjoy takes place in a grid defined by preexistent theoretical and social models which we accept or with which we must contend, with machines that help us deal in specific ways with the implications of those models, and with rewards available to those of us who use both models and machines in ways that seem valuable to the payers of salaries and the givers of grants. The American Folklore Society will soon be a century old. This seems a good time to consider where we've been, where we are, and the character of the forces modulating the changes in direction and concern that will define our future.

Models and Methods

No folklore collection can ever, without a great deal of independent information, be assumed to be representative of what was out there to be collected; scholarship based on fieldwork is based on scholarly artifacts, not on facts themselves.

Fieldwork collections, published or unpublished, reflect what individual collectors found, preserved, and selected, based on their own personal idiosyncrasies, the facts of the moment, and their ideas of what folklore was, what folklore information could be used for, and what recording technology was at hand. This applies equally well to a trained scholar who has been collecting folklore materials for thirty years and undergraduate students taking an introductory folklore class. No one collects everything that might be collected, and no one publishes every fact recorded and every observation made. I don't know any honest folklore collector who won't admit that somewhere in the work he or she redirected the conversation because of the creeping feeling that articulates itself as "there's no way I can use this."

Scholars of literature have far more security than any folklorist: the objects of literary study are uniformly and equally available; we can all buy a copy or travel to the library holding a copy of whatever it is we wish to read. If the literary document exists anywhere, it potentially exists everywhere. Xerox technology is the new Gutenberg: it has freed us from the daydreams of the copy clerk. But folklore is available only to those present when it happens. It is, in the computer technician's term, an online activity; everything after the moment is forever commentary. We are not even saved by doing our own fieldwork, for the condition applies to our own work as well as it does to the work of any stranger. Once out of the field, we can see and hear only selected artifacts. The observer forever defines and limits the text to which the rest of us shall have access, and our access to the basic materials of our discipline, therefore, is always secondary. Whenever our work involves primary material reported to us by others, we are not studying folklore so much as we are studying scholarly *reports* of folklore.

We deal with objects in terms of our sense of the boundaries of objects. At dinner, we eat the food on our plate but not, normally, the food on the plate of the person next to us. Our sense of boundaries influences how we negotiate conversations. If the person sitting on your right says to the person sitting on his or her right, "I love you," you do not, normally, respond with, "And *I* love *you*." All of us are encyclopedias of codes about boundaries of things that apply to us and things that do not apply. We have codes for our social behavior, our occupational behavior, and our intellectual behavior. Our ideas of what is and what isn't folklore, what is and what isn't meaningful, are dependent on our ideas of where things belong and where things are, where things begin and where things end.

When does an event start and when does it end? Does a formal dinner begin when you receive the invitation, when you change from street clothes into what you will wear for the dinner, when you arrive at the house where the dinner will occur, or when you lift your fork? Does it end after dessert, when you go out the host's door, when you reach your door, when you pay the babysitter, when you change into comfortable clothes, when you get up at 3 a.m. for an Alka-Seltzer, when you weigh yourself the next morning and swear never, never will you do that again? You can describe the dinner well enough in any of those time frames, within any of those temporal contexts, but you cannot make the same sense of it.

If our goal in collecting songs is to get tunes and texts, the material that matters begins when the music starts and ends when the music stops. If our sense of boundary is the performance event, our information collecting begins before the first song and ends after the last song. If our sense of boundary is the place the music occupies in the performers' lives, then our collecting must include enough information on those lives for us to be able to locate music within it. Once our boundary includes specific people, we must begin providing specific, rather than generalized, tunes and texts.

In that set of alternatives is the history of fieldwork in our discipline: the boundaries have steadily broadened, the role of the item has narrowed, and the legitimacy for generalization has become ever more tenuous.

Our models control the information we bring home from the field, the information we elect to analyze, the analyses we think deserving of publication and teaching others. We often pretend that our systems of classification are derived from the raw facts of our research, and that our theoretical models are in turn derived from our analysis of the systems. In fact, the process works quite the other way around: we have our models, and from them we derive our systems of classification. That is why the systems of classification always make such perfect sense. And it is why the facts we find fit our systems of classification so well: the system tells us what bits of the world are facts and what bits are inconsequential fluff or clutter. The difference between *meaningful* and *meaningless* in any analytical context has to do only with whether and how something fits the analytical structure—with whether or not the analytical structure has a way to use the information.

The definitions of what is or what isn't folklore and the categories of behavior those definitions imply—the stuff on which the discipline is based—are very much our invention. We don't make up the facts, but we make up the boxes in which they are carried home. No definition has universal acceptance, nor have any of the definitions been constant in time.

The relation of folklore scholars to whatever makes a moment or event or utterance or object or action folklore has become less, rather than more, clear as the literature has expanded, the scholarship increased, the institutional bases expanded. I remember twenty years ago regularly hearing older scholars make snide remarks about the twenty-one varying definitions of "Folklore" in the Leach *Dictionary* (Leach 1949–1950). No one makes such jokes anymore. If we could settle on twenty-one definitions we'd be on a roll of consensus unseen in this Society since it had only twenty-one members. At a recent meeting in Washington of folklore department and program heads, several respectable and responsible individuals said without a trace of doubt or irony in their voices that we would have no difficulty agreeing on what was the core of the discipline, what was the set of facts and books and ideas and skills that set folklore off from everything else. And then, as anyone with a whit of good sense could have predicted, all subsequent discussion and argument about this point showed nothing of the sort obtained. If there is a central image to which we all refer it is like the figure outside Plato's cave—only we all seem to be receiving differing quantities and qualities of incident light. There's nothing wrong with that—I rather like and enjoy the ambiguity and freedom of it—but it's good to acknowledge the condition.

In his essay on photography, Roland Barthes wrote: "Photography evades us. The various distributions we impose upon it are in fact either empirical . . . or rhetorical . . . or else aesthetic, or in any case external to the object, without relation to its essence" (1981:4). The stuff of folklore, like Barthes's photograph, has an existence independent of any of us, and the classification we impose likewise depends on the use we wish to make of it, on the kind of discourse we intend to mount about it.

Classification—whether the divisions of labor imposed by the departmental structure of universities or the differences in focus and concern imposed by the opportunity structure of the disciplines—serves our needs, not the needs of the objects we study; they reflect our concerns, not the natural order of the world. "Nothing really exists in nature except individuals," argued the eighteenth-century French naturalist Buffon, "genera, orders, and classes exist only in our imagination" (Foucault 1970:147). Had Darwin's interests been a little different, he might have given us lists of animals in terms of those that are soft and fuzzy and those that are hard and slick. Had Stith Thompson been a little less Victorian, *The Folktale* (1946) would have some delightfully different stresses. The facts are always out there; the variables are our needs, our uses, and whatever colors and organizes our perceptions of the facts.

We need our systems of classification. Without constant reference to our own systems of classification we could not negotiate a day. Our understanding of the system of highway designations permits us to translate the abstraction that is a roadmap into practical and specific decisions when we steer our automobiles. We are dependent on alphabetical classifications to find words in dictionaries and to find useful numbers in telephone books. Our knowledge of categories of foodstuffs permits us to find specific products in the long aisles of a large supermarket. The decimal system of book classification directs us to the physical location of a single volume in a library holding a million volumes. The system of temporal classification lets us know when to go to work and when to leave off work, when to go to class and what day class will be held, when to meet people we have said we would meet, and when there are holes in time for activities yet unplanned. We use classification systems to help us find things, to help us get places, to help us understand structures. We constantly negotiate the world in terms of models of organization and systems of classification that admit to or lock out of consciousness all the facts we encounter. Things are meaningful or not meaningful in terms of the structure we have for holding and utilizing information.

In recent years, folklore studies have incorporated methodologies from a half-dozen distinct disciplines. Some scholars see this as a sign our discipline isn't still a field seeking its intellectual home. Most of the external models are easy enough to spot: we know when the psychoanalytic or linguistic jargon is rolling by and we can decide whether the folkloric data are being informed by the external model or, in Diane Christian's phrase, are merely being plundered by it.

The problem is not unimportant. As Tzvetan Todorov has argued in another context, those other disciplines have their own questions to ask, their own answers to pursue; their technologies and methodologies are keyed to those perceived questions and desired answers (1981:5–6).

Northrop Frye wrote of the skewing of value that can occur in the parallel situation of a sociological examination of literature: "Horatio Alger and the writer of the Elsie books may well be more important than Hawthorne or Melville, and a single issue of the *Ladies Home Journal* worth all of Henry James" (1957:19).

The larger models of an age are far more difficult to know. They are what Marshall McLuhan called the fish's water and Ruth Benedict called the film's lens. They are so basic to our conception of the universe we neither see nor sense them. They are like the particulate matter in air that so scatters the sun's light we think the sky at high noon on a clear day is blue; nothing from our position here on earth will tell our senses that the sky in fact is black. Only the astronauts who are outside our air get to see the job it does on our vision. Daylight is the illusion, night is the truth; the symbolism runs backwards because of dust. We never approach a moment or a fact with no prior model of organization or value; we never confront the world in full innocence; we never perceive anything without the diffracting genius of our own invisible dust.

Have you ever heard the sound of nothing? I don't mean the absence of sound suffered by the totally deaf; I mean what happens when all the sounds that are part of our lives are taken away—the sounds of traffic, of people's movements, of machines, of electricity humming in the wires, of air moving against objects. John Cage was dazzled when, in Harvard's anechoic chamber, the quietest room in the world, he heard two sounds—a high-pitched whine and a low steady rumble. Cage told the technician that the chamber was defective; sounds came in. No, the technician told Cage, the sounds are your own, you brought them with you. The high-pitched whine was Cage's nervous system; the rumble was his bloodstream (1966:8).

And we, in any situation, bring our noise, our concepts, with us. The most important set of concepts for the development of folklore studies in the early nineteenth century had nothing to do with linguistics, nothing to do with ethnology, nothing to do with literature, nothing to do with history or nationalism. Rather it had to do with physics and mathematics, specifically with Newtonian mechanics, which for the first time posited an order in the universe completely independent of any intelligent agency whatsoever. Newton provided a rationale for collecting specific observed information, and for honoring it on its own terms. That was followed by a social corollary: Comte's positivism. Higher knowledge, Comte said, lurked in ordinary objects perceived by ordinary senses. And that led to a biological corollary: Darwin's natural orders, a history of life determined from the apparent scheme of present life and the detritus of prior life. The Newtonian model posited order, reversible order, mathematic order, coherent order. The Darwinian model postulated social process directed in time: things got better, things got more organized, things got more complex in functional ways. Newton gave us economy, Darwin gave us the hope of purpose.

The early folklorists saw folklore as revealing earlier, simpler states of social organization; they collected words and tunes and stories and proverbs as biologists collected buds and fish, and as the social positivists sought social facts. Discrete objects were extracted from their trajectories in the world, neatened up, and catalogued. Like William Graham Sumner, that positivist sociologist whose *Folkways* (1959) remains curiously absent from nearly every recommended folklore reading list, they believed the specific natural facts of ordinary life would themselves reveal the character of ordinary life. The nineteenth-century vision of folklore as item was perfectly in tune with both the Newtonian and Darwinian visions of the world, and it bridged the contradiction in those visions.

There was always *some* kind of context explicit or implicit in folkloristic definition. Our genre definitions, for example, have never been verbal only. It was never ballads or stories as such folklorists found of interest. Wordsworth's *Lyrical Ballads* and Blake's *Songs* and E. T. A. Hoffmann's fantastic tales never found a place in folk ballad or lyric or narrative seminars or collections. Literature is defined by a text; folklore is defined by a text *and* a context. The context licenses the text for folklorists. Without the context, the text—be it a group of words or a process or a behavior or an object—is of little folkloristic concern.

Not so long ago, the proof of an item's presence in tradition was adequate to enter the item into folkloric discourse, and the folkloric consideration could therefore focus on the item itself; nowadays, proof that *events* are of a folkloric type is adequate to enter whatever occurs in them into folkloric discourse, and the scholarly analysis is more likely to focus on the events themselves. This often produces interesting results, but it is useful to keep in mind that this discourse is a matter of current choice and preference and fashion, not a natural fact of the universe or a slice of ultimate truth. To "see" a story in the context of performance is per se no more noble or true than "seeing" it in the context of other such songs. The word "context" means nothing more than the events bracketing or embedding the event or moment we have defined as being of concern.

Blackbirds

Folklore studies lean either toward the humanities or toward the social sciences. A few folklorists have been entranced with a model drawn from the physical sciences—the "scientific method." The scientific method is attractive, it promises a kind of certitude, but I think it is finally useless for folklore and folklife studies. It might be reassuring if it could be shown that folklore information profited from the kind of manipulation central to the scientific method, but I know of no such evidence. No folklorist who has argued for a scientific model of folklore studies has ever done more than *assert* a connection.

The scientific method consists of developing a hypothesis, collecting data in a replicable way (that is, the report of research done includes sufficient information for another researcher to carry out exactly the same experiment), analyzing the data in a replicable way (the report of analysis includes sufficient information for another researcher to carry out the same analysis), and proceeding to a conclusion. The reason for the replicability is so other scientists can check the data and the computations.

Experiments do not reveal what we did not think we knew previously. Experiments confirm models, they do not generate them. Hypothesis is central to the scientific method *not* because hypothesis leads to a better or more efficient understanding of the world, but because hypothesis ensures that the experiment will be performed in terms of the science we have already determined to be "true." The experiment then proves or disproves the hypothesis, but always in terms of the model we had going in.

The heart of scientific inquiry is not getting answers to questions; rather it is in knowing what questions to ask and how to ask them. In science, once the question is posed the answer is structured. Physics, Martin Heidegger observed, "requests nature to manifest itself in terms of predictable forces, it sets up the experiment precisely for the sole purpose of asking whether and how nature follows the scheme preconceived by science" (Prigogine and Stengers 1984:33). Experimental science, as Nobel-laureate Ilya Prigogine and Isabelle Stengers wrote, is "the art of choosing situations that are hypothetically governed by the law under investigation and staging them to give clear, experimental answers. For each experiment certain principles are presupposed and thus cannot be established by that experiment" (1984:88).

The scientific method is useless in humanistic studies exactly because of its structural purity. The scientific method takes us only where we thought we were in the first place. It speaks with the voice of the first and last lines of Eliot's "East Coker": *In my beginning is my end* and *In my end is my beginning.*

The facts of the humanities are not the same kinds of things as are the facts of physical scientists. A poem or a song or a drawing or a carving is not the same kind of object or event as a cloud or a boulder or a subatomic particle emitted from a nucleus. The facts collected and studied by folklorists and other humanities are the products of human intelligence and imagination; they are idiosyncratic; they are made up. A poem is made up, a painting is made up, a symphony is made up, a joke is made up, a jumping jack is made up. Being made up doesn't make those things any the less true or valid or useful—but we know we must deal with them differently than we do with an isotope or a sparrow. We use a different rhetoric and have different expectations when we set out to describe or understand what seem to be their natural histories.

There is another, equally important difference in the ways scientists and humanists work. The world of the physical scientist is perfectly located in the foreground; the world of the humanistic scholar is ever deepening in time and space and range and complexity. In the physical sciences, new work occurs beyond the edge of all previous work; new work in science builds on the most immediate step, and it can safely ignore everything else. One correct insight in science renders forever useless all previous insights in its line. Not so in the humanities. The humanities have none of that linearity of the physical sciences; the past, for the humanities scholar, remains forever present. And that past, as Stanley Cavell has observed, "may at any time come to life, not merely as the recovery of certain neglected problems within the field but as a recovery of the field's originating, or preserving, authority" (1983:185n). Our job never gets simpler: we need to know it all, and more is being put on the table all the time. If the behavior of the physical scientist is best characterized by the experimental method, the behavior of the humanist is probably best exemplified by Wallace Stevens's "Thirteen Ways of Looking at a Blackbird."

Folkloric inquiry never has the kind of certitude and simplicity to which physical science aspires. Science tends to be complicated in getting there; the *conclusions* of science tend to be uncomplex. The humanities offer us complex conclusions that immediately force us along to more complex inquiries. No folklorist presumes to conduct the kind of inquiry that would reduce the analysis of a myth recitation to the unambiguous certitude a physicist expects from his analysis of a physical process. The humanities reveal to us the complexity of human experience and they give us intellectual tools that help us take comfort in that complexity;

the sciences reveal to us the simple relationships that describe the most complex sequences of events and interactions. The two are not the same kind of thinking, nor are they the same kind of quest.

The scientific method is useful only for investigations that are absolutely replicable, and no folkloric investigation requiring fieldwork is *ever* replicable. Chemists can do spectrographic analyses of tiny bits of material, then check themselves or have their work checked by other chemists a dozen times. If the material sampled is homogeneous, if the process is followed exactly each time, and if the equipment functions correctly each time, the results will be exactly the same each time. Not approximately or nearly or more-or-less. Exactly the same. An American chemist or physiologist will, if the work is done properly, produce exactly the same results as a Russian or Israeli or Italian chemist or physiologist.

That never happens in a folklore field study because nothing of importance is ever exactly the same. The researcher and the informant are changed by, among other things, each of their previous encounters. Folklore fieldwork is personal work. It isn't neutral and it isn't objective. It is too much subject to such factors as the unique chemistry between people at a specific moment in time, by the presence or absence of indigestion that day, by a slight memory of someone who had exactly that color eyes, by the response to the fabric and hue of the shirt one of you happens to be wearing, to a faint odor there just below the edge of consciousness. And those are the simple factors influencing what goes on. The ideas about the material and the world are far more deeply hidden, far more pervasive in their influence.

Perhaps the most important change in folklore studies in the past century has been in our sense of significant moment. The moment comprised by the folklore event or incorporated in the folklore process has lengthened significantly. Few folklorists nowadays would consider responsible the mere presentation of texts with no information other than the nouns associated with the performance: this was performed by so and such at such and such a time and place.

We want to know more. To talk of breaking into performance we have to know what performance is being broken into from. To know when performance starts we have to identify the behavior that is not-performance or, more accurately, behavior that is some other kind of performance. (All expression is directed at some audience and all conversation is modulated for some perceived intelligence. There is no shift from a baseline of normal discourse to a special plane of performance discourse; there are instead only kinds of performance in which kinds of discourse occur.)

This expansion of desiderata doesn't occur merely because some of our colleagues found wanting the scope of information provided by their predecessors and neither does it occur because of the appearance of the various external models folklorists have adopted, adapted, embraced, embellished, or championed. That is because none of those models has yet in itself modified in any basic way the way we work. Freudianism, structuralism, performancism—these have each in turn become little machines into which the basic data of the field have been thrust or through which the data have been cranked. In the hands of thoughtful and intelligent scholars, these machines have shed light on the objects and the contexts; in the hands of mechanics these machines have served merely to validate the models that were antecedent to them.

Machines

More important than models, I think, were two sets of factors that are not ideas at all. One set was technological; it increased the amount of information any collector could capture in any single moment or group of moments. The other set was social and economic; it increased the contexts in which *scholarly* performance could occur and the financial rewards for doing it. One put at our disposal great masses of information, the other provided us great numbers of jobs and great amounts of money.

We no longer have to fret about capturing words and tunes; we no longer have to depend on a rich vocabulary and a grand literary style to let others know what we saw. Since Edison's invention of the cylinder recorder, our field of vision has expanded exponentially. Each new technological innovation freed us to examine more, to broaden the context. Recording devices permitted for the first time specific comments about words and tunes and utterance style. The recording instruments permitted, in Dennis Tedlock's words, the scholar to "hear the *music* of the voice, the rises and falls of pitch and amplitude, the tone and timbre, the interaction of sounds and silence . . . precisely all the dimensions of the voice that the spelling ear tunes out" (1983:3–4). The disc recorder and microphone permitted far more accurate renditions of dynamic range and pitch than were possible with the cylinder recorder. The tape recorder permitted capture of lengthy performances rather than bits and pieces of performances or performances limited to the brief memory of the 78 rpm disc recorder. The battery-operated tape recorder freed the recordist to capture information anywhere and at great length, and the inexpensive high-fidelity battery-operated cassette recorder made that option available to nearly everyone. Film and video technology permitted the capture of complex physical events, along with the sounds they created, and portable video technology, which has developed largely as a result of the space program and the Vietnam War, has made possible low-cost and high-fidelity recording of sounds and images.

The machines make no choices; they do not capture everything and they never capture anything realistically. Every documentary device represents some measure of compromise. No film has the sensitivity of the human eye; no unadjusted audio system has the auditory sensibility of the human ear. Machines may hear things we cannot hear, but they cannot select among things making noises; we can hear a single conversation in a noisy subway—no recording device can do that without distorting significantly all the other sounds going on. We can shift our gaze from bright sunlight to dark shadow; no film emulsion can handle that range.

We respond to our machines. We ask questions they can answer well. The invention of machines for measuring small-particle interactions resulted in the best physicists of the time studying small-particle interactions; the invention of the microscope changed the focus of concern of biologists from the macroscopic social world of animals to the microscopic chemical world of cells. Our relationship with our machines is exactly the same as our relationship with our structuring models: we see with and through both of them. The relationship is collaborative or symbiotic, not one of lowly service.

Money

Only thirty years ago there were in America no graduate programs in or departments of folklore. A few academic amateurs—amateurs in the sense of lovers of something—managed to crank a folklore course now and then into their regular loads as professor of English or anthropology. The half-dozen folklore journals ranged in style from the amateur—amateur in the sense of naive and unprofessional—to the dryly academic. The American Folklore Society was then as now a loose confederation of individuals whose relationship to folklore ranged from passionate dedication to mild and benign amusement. The American Folklore Society was, as now, as close to a disciplinary center as anyone might find.

Twenty years ago, Indiana University had the only North American PhD program in folklore. Only one member of its faculty had been trained in folklore—Jerome R. Mintz (who two years earlier had been appointed to the first full-time folklore position in the country). The others—Stith Thompson, Richard M. Dorson, W. Edson Richmond, Warren Roberts, John Messenger, Thomas A. Sebeok, and George List—had been trained in literature, history, anthropology, linguistics, and music.

There are now four North American PhD departments of folklore and at least a half-dozen more semiautonomous programs that award the MA, the PhD, or both. Graduate students in several other universities can develop concentrations in folklore studies within other disciplines. At least three hundred colleges and universities now offer folklore courses, and most of those courses are taught by men and women with a significant amount of training in—if not MAs or PhDs in—folklore. Within only two decades folklore has gone from a field taught by autodidacts who were solidly grounded in older disciplines to a field taught by specialists nearly all of whose post-baccalaureate training has been in folklore itself.

Meetings of the American Folklore Society in the pre-PhD days were not so much meetings of a professional society as the annual reunions of an interest group, many of whose members happened to have college jobs. One middle-aged folklorist ten years ago lamented that the Society had changed—much to his dissatisfaction. "It used to be that I came to these things and I knew everybody. Now I don't know everybody. There are all these students from other places. It's getting like the MLA." It didn't get like the MLA and I doubt it ever will, but the Society indeed is too large now for anyone to keep up with the membership, for anyone to ever again know everyone. (Since I never knew everyone in the old days, I am less disturbed by this fact than was my friend.)

Not only are there more strangers in AFS, there are far more jobs for those strangers to obtain. The baby boom following the Second World War and a rising standard of living for certain segments of the American population produced the terrific expansion in American universities that resulted in the creation of the jobs most of us hold or hope to hold. That expansion in the universities led to an expansion in research and scholarly publication—job requirements the preexistent university structure had in place. The increase in working folklorists and in regular folklore programs created a new market for folklore books, so there was a concomitant increase in folklore book production. I know of no adequate folklore book in the last ten years that has not found a publisher, and I can point to a lot of real trash that has been published by otherwise respectable presses.

The federal government's involvement in folklore work, which had, except for the NDEA fellowships, been dormant since the end of the WPA, has also expanded enormously. The Folk Arts program was created at NEA. NEH never developed a folklore program but it has funded folklore projects through all of its divisions. Most states now have state folklore programs. The Folklife program at the Smithsonian Institution developed and expanded rapidly. And the American Folklife Center was established in the Library of Congress.

More people are trained as folklorists than have ever been trained as folklorists before. More trained folklorists are employed than have ever been employed before. Folklorists are employed in a wider range of occupations by more institutions and agencies than ever before. The subjects of inquiry folklorists take on range further than they ever have before. More folklore journals are now published than have ever been published before. As the job markets expanded, folklorists proved themselves as adept as anyone else at expanding the work they might do.

Had things remained as they were in the early 1970s, things would be fine indeed. But things did not remain the same and things are not fine. Along with all the fine employment I just described, there are more trained folklorists without folklore jobs than ever before, and more academic folklore positions at risk than ever before, and more folklore programs near a state of collapse or at risk of being absorbed into older departments than ever before.

Times are hard in the academic world and they will continue to be hard until the children of the Baby Boom generation themselves begin passing through college. Colleges and universities have not yet reversed the faculty cutbacks of the past five years, nor will they for at least another decade. Most academic jobs for new folklore PhDs, like academic jobs for other humanities PhDs, will not be tenure track jobs. Many of our students will float from temporary appointment to temporary appointment. Those who hang on until the real hiring starts again will find themselves in direct competition with whatever new PhDs may be coming along at that time. If it hadn't been for the creation of a new job market for folklorists in the public sector in the past ten years, several of our graduate programs would have a difficult time justifying their continuing existence at all.

NEA has not increased folklore funding in the past several years and only dedicated congressional opposition has so far thwarted the Reagan administration's attempts to slash the operating and funding budgets of both Endowments. Further, the administration has attempted to introduce partisan and ideological politics in the grantmaking process to a degree unprecedented previously. Access to humanities dollars is becoming increasingly difficult for anyone dealing with modern life or for projects having to do with non-mainstream-Anglo culture. And it is becoming increasingly difficult for smaller organizations and ethnic organizations to get any of that money.

Humanities and arts programs are not the only casualties of the past four years of federal cutbacks, and neither are they the programs that have suffered the greatest hurt. Social Security benefits for children between sixteen and twenty-two were wiped out two years ago, Medicare benefits were greatly reduced, school lunch programs were radically cut back. The constant-dollar amount of federal aid to public education has dropped 25 percent in the past four years. The states have less money for higher education than they did a decade ago, and next year they will have less than this year, and the year after will be even worse. The cuts in federal aid to social and educational programs have a direct influence on nongovernmental funding for scholars in the arts and humanities: many foundations and corporations that previously gave significant amounts of money for arts performances and humanities projects have redirected their giving to provide for many of those crippled human services programs. To make matters worse, the 1981 tax reform bill significantly reduced the incentives for corporations and wealthy individuals to make philanthropic contributions at all.

Federal funds—for research, performances, and educational programs—are far more likely to go for the naive notion of what folklore is than what educated folklorists are likely to think folklore is. Things that are American and safe and which seem to reinforce homey values will get support. Funds will be available for square-dance festivals; they will not likely be available for breakdance festivals. Funds will be available to study high art done in seventeenth-century Florence; they will not be much in abundance to study verbal art in twentieth-century Detroit. The problem of having an American Folklife Center was not solved when the legislation went through Congress eight years ago; each year the budget fight is more and more difficult.

Few scholars are rich enough to do what they want when they want. Most are dependent on university positions and grants to fund their research. Whatever abstract needs are discovered by the profession, the actual projects undertaken by actual people will be in some measure conditioned by the dollars available to underwrite projects and the academic and government positions available for those who do them well. One of the great and cynical discoveries of the Kennedy administration was exemplified in what came to be called Project Camelot. Kennedy's men realized that it was not necessary to pressure scientists to do research in areas the government wanted researched, and neither was it necessary to force scientists to avoid research in areas the government thought unimportant. All that was necessary was to say, "Funds are available for people doing this kind of work." The best scientists—who more than anything want to work—immediately designed splendid projects within the administration's guidelines. The scientists thought they were free and the government got exactly what it wanted. The resources available to us are changing and so is the government's sense of what matters and what doesn't, what is worth supporting with public monies and what isn't.

We cannot know beforehand what will be the effects on our profession of recent political and economic changes but surely they will be significant. Introducing folklore to the university changed the discipline significantly, the Baby Boom expansion of the universities changed the discipline significantly—and there is no reason to expect we will stop responding to the changing structures of opportunity.

Real People in Real Gardens

In the early years of self-conscious folklore study, the field was occupied by individuals who were political or belletristic in orientation. They valued folklore largely because of what it illustrated about something else or because of what other and more acceptable thing it might be turned into. Neither Chaucer nor Joel Chandler Harris was concerned with preserving for later readers great moments in Oral Tradition: they were, like any good artist, simply scooping up whatever was around and modifying it in the service of their own vision. Other collectors had more political ends: Lucy McKim and Thomas Wentworth Higginson wrote about slave songs not because of what the songs were as music or poetry, but rather because of what the songs said about the slaves and former slaves. The *Kalevala* was inspired not by a vision of the glories of narrative art, but rather by passionate feelings of Finnish nationalism. You can adduce as many other political examples as I.

The attention to minutiae—such as Child's devotion to contextless ballad variants and Newman Ivey White's diligent accumulation of thousands of song fragments—develops only when folklore enters the academy. Few nonacademic nineteenth-century collectors had the time or interest for that kind of work. And the academy always had its mannered notions of what aspects of folklore were fit for serious study. At Harvard, for example, George Lyman Kittredge was as uninterested in the folk- part of the -lore as was his teacher, Francis James Child. When John Avery Lomax paraded Leadbelly through Harvard in 1934 and had him put on a concert there, Kittredge sat through it politely, then later told one of *his* students that he thought it was the most unpleasant and vulgar musical performance he had ever endured and Leadbelly was probably the most unsavory individual he had ever met. Lomax was encouraged to continue his collecting and his writing; he was not encouraged to repeat the show and tell. You *know* what kind of folklore got taught at Harvard.

Disciplines are nothing more or less than individuals acted upon or acting in the presence of ideas and movements and larger events and changing technologies. We are influenced by the ideas and politics of our times and the technologies and the economic and occupational resources at our disposal, but such influence works upon and through specific individuals. Ideas are abstract, but behaviors are not. They are carried out by specific people with real names in real places. Only from a distance in time or space are we restricted to notions of movements and trends. It is like the difference between standing in the shade of a specific oak and looking from a great distance at the forest in which the oak lives. *Forest* is an outside observer's notion; forests behave according to general principles, but this tree in this place develops according to what happened to this tree in this place.

For better or for worse, this discipline would not be the same had it not been for the interest of the Grimms in language as spoken rather than language as written and had not Dvořák made respectable nonwhite and non-European folk music in America. It would not be the same had not the missionary abolitionists "discovered" the sacred music of the blacks the same way a geographer "discovers" a continent or an astronomer a star: the music and continent and star were quite perfectly in place all along. The discovery has not to do with them; it has to do with the discoverer's former ignorance.

Our discipline, for better or worse, would not have been the same without the narrow mechanical vision of Francis James Child. It would not have been the same without the organizational genius of William Wells Newell or the nearly limitless energy and money of Elsie Clews Parsons. It would not have been the same without the drive to discover and tailor folksong for wide public consumption of John A. Lomax or the controlled and studied popularization of B. A. Botkin or the paranoid missionary zeal of Richard M. Dorson.

It would not have been the same had it not been for the vision of the organizers of the WPA's various folkloric enterprises. It would not have been the same had it not been for the grand range of interests and designs motivating the nineteenth-century European and American artists and scholars who for whatever reason found worthy of collection and preservation the congeries of materials we now claim as the roots of our discipline. It would not have been the same had not Edison invented the cylinder recorder. It would not have been the same had it not been for the popular folk music fad of the 1960s, which led so many people now teaching folklore and chairing folklore programs into a discipline far more complex and ranging than their innocence had led them to expect.

And it would not be the same were it not for the political and economic structure of opportunity in the academic and public sectors that have steadily and efficiently caused a reconsideration of what graduate education, hence research, in folklore is all about.

Scholarship is a communal activity. We build on the work of others and our work provides the materials for others yet to come. But the community that makes our work necessary or desirable or possible ranges far beyond those individuals we need to identify in the footnotes or bibliographies to our own work. We are all children and victims and beneficiaries of our shared political and economic and technological and intellectual past, a past so much a part of our present we hardly ever glimpse its real shadow.

So, bless the models and the model makers and luck to the users of models and long life to the institutions in which the models are cast and filed and polished and displayed. In proper service, they can serve us well, those models and model makers and institutions. In their own end the models and machines become solipsisms, grand technical tautologies that have no purpose but their own ratification, and the institutions become masters we serve like blind pit ponies. We need them, but we likewise need ever to confront them, to challenge them, to stand back from them and wonder what specific knowledge of the world the models really impart, what secrets the machines really have to tell, and what use our work really has. We need to know whether we are looking at sirens or sucking pigs or things that are frenzied or things drawn with a very fine camelhair brush or things that just broke the water pitcher or things that from a long way off look like flies. We must continually interrogate our own vision to discover what matters enough to be worth the work.

I have discussed the forces structuring the information with which folklorists deal, the technological innovations that have liberated folklorists' vision, and the economic and political conditions that provide the economic base for the discipline most of us more or less inhabit. I have said why I think recent tendencies to refer to folklore studies as if they had much in common with the physical sciences are either misdirected or wooly-minded. And I have said something about the kind of humanistic inquiry we do. This discussion has to do with the very real forces that put and keep us in our place. I end with Walt Whitman on the need for us now and then to regain perspective, on our very real need to ground our vision in the world itself:

> When I heard the learn'd astronomer,
> When the proofs, the figures, were ranged in columns before me,
> When I was shown the charts and diagrams, to add, divide, and measure them,
> When I sitting heard the astronomer where he lectured with much applause in the lecture room,
> How soon unaccountable I became tired and sick,
> Till rising and gliding out I wander'd off by myself,
> In the mystical moist night-air, and from time to time,
> Look'd up in perfect silence at the stars.

Acknowledgments

I am indebted to Diane Christian (State University of New York at Buffalo) and Henri Korn (Institut Pasteur, Paris) for their astute critical readings of earlier drafts of this essay. The essay benefited from discussions about its central issues with Christian, Korn, and the late Michel Foucault. Carl Fleischhauer (American Folklife Center) provided useful detailed information on the development of documentary technology. Richard Bauman and Jerome R. Mintz clarified my hazy memory of faculty alignment at Indiana University twenty years ago. Ellen Stekert reminded me of the importance of the shift away from item-centered folklore studies. Foucault's *The Order of Things* (1970) and Prigogine and Stengers's *Order Out of Chaos* (1984) inform more of my thinking in the section on models and methods than is indicated by the specific citations.

References

Barthes, Roland. 1981. *Camera Lucida: Reflections on Photography*. Translated by Richard Howard. New York: Hill and Wang.

Cage, John. 1966. *Silence*. Cambridge: MIT Press.
Cavell, Stanley. 1983. "Politics as Opposed to What?" In *The Politics of Interpretation*, edited by W. J. T. Mitchell, 181–202. Chicago: University of Chicago Press.
Foucault, Michel. 1970. *The Order of Things: An Archaeology of the Human Sciences*. New York: Pantheon.
Frye, Northrop. 1957. *Anatomy of Criticism*. Princeton: Princeton University Press.
Leach, Maria, ed. 1949–1950. *Standard Dictionary of Folklore, Mythology, and Legend*. 2 vols. New York: Funk and Wagnalls.
Prigogine, Ilya, and Isabelle Stengers. 1984. *Order Out of Chaos*. New York: Bantam.
Sumner, William Graham. 1959 [1907]. *Folkways*. New York: Dover.
Tedlock, Dennis. 1983. *The Spoken Word and the Work of Interpretation*. Philadelphia: University of Pennsylvania Press.
Thompson, Stith. 1946. *The Folktale*. New York: Dryden Press.
Todorov, Tzvetan. 1981. *Introduction to Poetics*. Translated by Richard Howard. Minneapolis: University of Minnesota Press.

21

Folkloristics

(Journal of American Folklore, 1985)

- A friend calls from the heart of the country. He has just come from a conference in Washington, DC, and he feels fine things were said and done there. "It was a great moment for folkloristics, Bruce, it really was."

- A grant proposal arrives from NEH for review. The applicant lives and teaches in the deep South. The title of the project includes the term "folk narrative," the abstract describes the applicant as a "folklorist," the blank space after "Major Field of Applicant or Project Director" is completed: *Folkloristics.*

- A student in my traditional narrative graduate seminar brings to my office a copy of a page from a recent *JAF*. She points to two circled words. "I want to know what is the difference between the American word 'folklore' and the American word 'folkloristics.'" I look at the page, consider the context, and tell her there is no difference. "Then why do you have two words?" she asks.

When I first saw "folkloristics" in print in 1964, I was sure it was a gag mounted by Richard M. Dorson. Later, as the word began to appear in works by some American folklorists, I thought it was merely bad taste and a failed sensitivity toward the language. Lately, as I see and hear it more and more, I worry that "folkloristics" may actually become a word thoughtful people use without thinking, and that it may one day ooze on over into the general vocabulary. The word sounds scientific to some people, but it isn't a scientific word; the word seems an improvement over "folklore," but it isn't an improvement at all.

"Linguistics" is the field name closest to "folkloristics" and it is, I suspect, the model for the American neologism. The similarity of the constructions—"linguistics" and "folkloristics"—is probably more than coincidental. Folklorists for the past twenty years have adopted their most-used (and on occasion most-useful) models from linguistic studies, so at first the parallel may even seem logical: folkloristics/linguistics, folklorist/linguist. It works fine until we back up to the first step: folklore/language.

"Folklore" and "linguistics" entered the English language about the same time. William Thoms's suggestion that "folklore" replace "popular antiquities" was published in 1846; the first English usage of "linguistics" noted in the *OED* is 1837 (1971:1632). "Linguistics" and "folkloristics" share something else: both nouns of field are derived from nouns of person. "Linguist" and "folklorist" were both in use before the words "linguistics" and "folkloristics." The root for "linguistics" is the Latin *lingua* (tongue), from which are derived the French stem *lingu-* and the French *linguiste, linguistique*, and *la linguistique*; the English "linguist," "linguistic," and "linguistics" seem to have been derived from the French (Partridge 1958:335; see also Onions 1967:530).

Why should the word for the study of language seem to derive from the word for *students* of language rather than the word for language itself? The source is a word that in English and French presents curious ambiguities in adjectival and other derivative forms. It is itself a metaphor, albeit a common one: tongue as language, with the image grounded in what the tongue helps the body utter. The older and literal meaning of "lingual" is still very much present in our language: it means "having to do with the tongue." The phrase "lingual act" can mean "an act of language" and it can mean "an act done with the tongue." "Linguistic act" has none of that ambiguity. "Linguistics" makes sense for the same reason "criminalistics" makes sense: because other words are in the way.[1] But no words are in the way of "folklore," the word upon which "folklorist" and "folkloristics" are built, and neither is there any crippling ambiguity.

"Folkloristics" is an adjective decorated to look like a substantive noun by the addition of the plural "-s." If the word is consistent with other nouns made adjectival by the addition of single and double adjectival suffixes, it means "the measurement of folklorists."[2] Except perhaps for the few scholars who study folklorists rather than folklore, the word is almost always used incorrectly. I believe that "correctness" in language should be a matter of description rather than prescription, which implies that if everyone does it, *it* becomes right. But everyone does not yet describe our field as "folkloristics," no departments in the field are yet named "folkloristics," no successful texts are yet named "folkloristics"—so there is yet time for us.

Most academics whose self-identification is a word ending in "-ist" do not then try to name the field after themselves (which is what happens with "folkloristics"). Botanists study botany and their field is botany; literary historians and critics study literary history and works of literature and their field is literature. Many other fields also do perfectly well with the name of the subject: medicine, dentistry, Chinese, French, Spanish, German, history, English. Making a doubled adjective of those words would be bizarre: Chinistics or Sinistics (sounds left-handed and dangerous), Francistics, Spanishistics or Iberistics, historistics, Englishistics.

So far as I know, all words ending in the double-suffix "-istic" are adjectives. The usual process is for an abstract noun or adjective (absolute, real, fatal) to be attributed to a person (absolutist, realist, fatalist) and thereby made into a noun of another order, and then for that noun to be turned into an adjective (absolutistic, realistic, fatalistic). The adjective in such cases refers to person: "absolutistic" means to be absolutist-like, "realistic" means to be realist-like, "fatalistic" means to be fatalist-like. The derivation is the same for most other -istic words: agonistic, anabaptistic, animistic, artistic, fetishistic, etc. Sometimes the derivation is slightly more complex: the idea "-ism" becomes the person "-ist" and the adjective "-istic": altruism/altruist/altruistic, optimism/optimist/optimistic, monotheism/monotheist/monotheistic, euphemism/euphemist/euphemistic, masochism/masochist/masochistic. These adjectives too refer to person: "masochistic" means "like a masochist," not "like masochism." And it is the same for us: the person who studies the class of things called "folklore" is a "folklorist," and the adjective meaning "folklorist-like" is "folkloristic." "Folkloristic" as an adjective is correct when it refers to *work done* by folklorists; the adjective for the *material examined* by folklorists is "folkloric." "Folkloristic research" means "the kind of research folklorists do," but *not* "research into folklore."

No one in any other profession tries to turn any of those "-istic" adjectives into nouns by making them seem to be the plural of something that doesn't exist in the singular. Two persons who are each fatalistic are not "two fatalistics"—they are two fatalistic persons; two persons with artistic proclivities are not "two artistics," and neither are two persons who do not believe in a supreme being "two atheistics." "Journalistic" is an adjective referring to a style of writing favored by individuals who call themselves "journalists"; the profession of people doing that kind of writing on a regular basis and the field of scholars who study and teach matters having to do with that profession is "journalism," not "journalistics."

So why "folkloristics"? Why not simply *folklore*?

Jan Brunvand[3] suggests that a possible source for "folkloristics" was the adjective in the title of Kaarle Krohn's *Die folkloristische Arbeitsmethode* (1926). The title of the English translation was *Folklore Methodology* (1971), but, writes Brunvand, "in the foreword to that 1971 AFS publication Archer Taylor used 'folkloristic' several times in the first paragraph, and it also crept into the dust jacket copy." Brunvand is correct: Taylor did use "folkloristic," but only as an adjective: "folkloristic materials," "folkloristic texts," "folkloristic text," and "folkloristic method" (1971:ix). In fact, words similar to "folkloristics" occur in several European languages, but all of them are declined languages, so the English cognates have very different meanings. To scholars who know Finnish, German, Russian, and other such languages, the differences are obvious; to scholars who do not know those languages, the terms might seem equivalent. I suspect that may be what happened to the Americans who may have thought "folkloristics" was legitimized by Krohn's *folkloristische*.

Alan Dundes, Brunvand notes in the same letter, had advocated using folkloristics

> for the study of folklore in his 1965 anthology of that name. . . . I did not use the term in my 1968 *Study of American Folklore* but in the 2nd edition (1978) it entered Chapter One in quotes, and then was scattered around in other places too. (I also included it as an occasional term for folklore study in my 1976 *Guide*.) But Toelken has gone all the way: he has it in the title of his introduction in *Dynamics of Folklore*, and his index lists all twenty-one pages of that chapter under "folkloristic." He does not seem to use the word in the chapter itself, though he does use "nonfolkloristic" in his notes. Bronner seems to have accepted it wholesale, as in the latest issue of *NYF* I have seen.

Simon Bronner, who uses the word more than anyone else I've read recently, writes that he "thought it was Dundes's term. My source is [Roger D.] Abrahams' review of *Analytic Essays in Folklore* in *Folklore Forum* (Spring 1977) where he states '*Folklorics* and *folkloristics* (a Dundes coinage, I believe, one of many)' (32)."[4] "As far as I know," Abrahams told me, "Alan Dundes *did* invent 'folkloristics,' as a joke that was picked up on. The explanation was that folklorics would refer to the attributes of folklore-in-general, folkloristics to the theory authored by folklorists-in-general. Like most gobbledygook, I don't like the term, but find myself resorting to it all the time."[5]

The 1965 Dundes line to which Brunvand refers is: "To avoid confusion it might be better to use the term *folklore* for the materials and the term *Folkloristics* for the study of the materials" (1965:3). That, however, was not the first appearance of "folkloristics" in an American publication.

The word appeared prominently a year earlier in the first issue of the *Journal of the Folklore Institute* in an article by L. Zemljanova, "The Struggle between the Reactionary and the Progressive Forces in Contemporary American Folkloristics" (1964). (No translator's name or original article title was given, but since the article first appeared in a 1962 issue of *Sovetskaja Etnografija* it is unlikely that the original appeared in English.) Zemljanova's article attacks most establishment American folklorists and praises almost any folklore writer on the far left. (The hero of the piece seems to be Irwin Silber, then editor of *Sing Out!*) Zemljanova attacks Dorson several times in the article. I long assumed the reason Dorson printed it was that it was one of those frothing attacks that needed no response because in translation it came off just as silly knee-jerk posturing. The final paragraph gives a sense of the article's tone: "Contemporary progressive folkloristics in the United States is developing in difficult conditions. It is not easy to overcome the ossified traditions of bourgeois scholarship, the influence of bourgeois ideology, the obstacles of censorship. But on the side of progressive folkloristics are the creators and performers of folklore creations themselves, and the people; and this is the best guarantee of the successful development of a science of folk creation" (Zemljanova 1964:144).

The jargon is so thick that focusing on the issues is impossible. "Folkloristics" appears at least twenty times in the sixteen-page article. Without getting into the merits of the article and its arguments, I can tell you that the diction made it *seem* extremely silly. Whether that was a function of the author, the translator, or both, I cannot say.

I am grateful to Robert Georges for bringing to my attention two quotations from papers by Kenneth Laine Ketner that contain what is probably the kinkiest approach to the problem of naming the field that folklorists inhabit.[6] Georges quotes a passage from a ditto copy of "A Preliminary Survey of the Grammar of 'Folklore': An Introduction to Hominology," which Ketner presented at the 1973 meeting of the American Folklore Society. Ketner argues that since there is no determinate subject matter named folklore . . . and since there is no folklore, there is no discipline of folklore or folkloristics. There has been, however, a discipline that came to call itself folklore. That discipline, so it seems to me, has been studying universal human behavioral patterns and interactional processes. As I use it here, the term "universal" means "distributed throughout the human species." Some examples of human universals are storytelling, singing, and believing. Therefore, the message of this paper is, I think, that we could get on with this task so much better if we stopped wasting so much valuable talent and energy upon folklore, upon finding out what folklore is, upon studying folklore, and instead simply realize that we are studying various universal human processes because they tell us something about what it is to be a member of the human species. It would seem that the most important conceptual problem in folkloristics is to stop studying folklore, thus ceasing to be as folkloristicians.

"Ketner goes on to propose," writes Georges, "that our field change its name to *hominology* and that we call ourselves *hominologists*." The second quotation is from Ketner's contribution to a 1978 colloquium on semiotics: "Scholars of folkloristics basically wish to avoid the word 'folklore' whenever possible because of its unfortunate associations with class prejudice, especially in countries that have been associated in past years with British colonialism. If forced to employ the term 'folklore,' students of folkloristics will insist that by it they only mean 'the lore or learning that is universal in homo sapiens,' and that 'folk' simply means 'any human being whatsoever in their [sic] capacity as human'" (1981:130–131).

This is sillier than "folkloristics," and even less useful. Ketner, who received an MA in folklore and a PhD in philosophy, trivializes the work done by folklorists, even the ones who call their field "folkloristics." Ketner may find it rhetorically useful to deny the existence of something called "folklore," but nothing in his argument tells us what we should now do with all those books on our shelves that seem very much filled with samples or analyses of materials several thousand scholars seemed perfectly content to refer to as "folklore." Reality isn't undone merely by saying "We're abolishing that word now." Emerson insisted that words were symbols of natural facts; he would also have insisted that the natural facts remained even if the words were changed, but he didn't have occasion to make that argument because no one presented him with Ketner's logic. Alice's Humpty-Dumpty dissolved categories by denying the words that named them; academics (Ketner teaches philosophy at Texas Tech) are held to a more responsible standard.

After reading the two Ketner quotations, I examined several dozen recent publications and tried to discern which writers using "folklore" represent the old colonialist ideal and which writers using "folkloristics" are telling me about universal "lore or learning." Practice does not uphold Ketner's assertion: some authors use one word and others use the other, but there seems little political sensibility separating the two; several authors use either word interchangeably. Whatever colonialistic connotation developed around "folklore" developed in the period when many folklorists *were* colonialist, and the period immediately after that when the discoverers of the new field were trying to identify the mode of expression they had discovered. The non-colonialist character of most recent folklore scholarship will do far more to undo that anachronistic connotation than any prescriptive name-changing. (That kind of name change makes me think of those stores on Forty-Second Street in Manhattan: "Under New Management." Sure.) Furthermore, I don't know of *any* "lore or learning that is universal in homo sapiens." People everywhere have sex, but they do not all have sex the same way or think of it the same way; people everywhere eat and tell stories, but they do not eat the same foods or tell the same stories, and neither do they ascribe the same significance to their eating or storytelling acts. The things that do not vary from place to place or time to time or group to group—our need for air, food, and sleep, the ineluctable facts of birth and death—are so general that concentration on them avoids everything that makes culture fun. Finally, "hominology" is a noun meaning "study of hominids." The category includes everything from us back to the sivapithecines, small apelike animals that inhabited the Siwalik Hills of India and Pakistan some fourteen million years ago. That turf is too expansive even for Ketner's neologism.

What puzzles me now is this: given the burlesque introduction of the word to American scholarship by Dorson and his colleagues on the editorial board of the *Journal of the Folklore Institute*, why did Dundes, Abrahams, Bronner, and so many others embrace "folkloristics"? I know several folklorists who like "folkloristics" because it sounds to them more abstract and technological than "folklore." (*Folklore*—what does that word conjure up for you? If it's "what the folk do and know," do you fear it won't sell in a modern English or anthropology department?) They don't like "folklorics," the substantive noun built on the adjectival form of "folklore," because it sounds too simple, and it's too close to the noun they're trying to flee. And perhaps "folklorics" was too much like "Dianetics" and "numismatics": no respectable and professional folklorist would want to be associated, even through a weak half rhyme, with a field that smacks of pop psychology and crank religion or one identified primarily with archiving and cataloging small samples of transient coinage. And maybe "folklorics" didn't catch on because it sounds too much like the adjective it really is: "I study folklorics," the young man says. "Folkloric what?" asks his mother, dropping the "-s" that has no business there anyway. "Folkloric dance? Folkloric story? Folkloric fiction?"

Folklore is a field of adjectival modification: folk song, folktale, folk cooking, folk dance, folk community, folklife, and folklore itself. Perhaps that eased the way for *folkloristics*, a noun with a double-adjective suffix and no existence as a noun in the singular, a word now used to indicate what folklorists do as distinguished from what the folk have. *Folkloristics*—four big syllables. No other discipline has a word quite like it. It's even a syllable longer than "linguistics."

Some colleagues warn that it may be too late to get rid of "folkloristics." The word has been used by a few scholars regularly for more than a decade, and some of them have been teaching it to younger people. A decade of tradition props up that ugly and useless word. For folklorists, the mere fact of tradition is often enough to legitimize among those we study the most curious and vulgar behaviors, so there is no reason to assume we won't apply the same tolerance to our own perversions of the language. I would prefer to find my colleagues wrong in this instance.

"Folkloristics" brings us no respectability we don't have anyway. Surely the field has become well-enough established in the past few decades so most other academics can now differentiate between someone with a PhD to sell and someone with a tale to tell or song to sing. The American Folklore Society approaches its Centennial and I think it appropriate to suggest an easy homage to the ancestors that will be of value to the inheritors: let's abandon this neologism with its pompous and misleading suffixes, this clumsy construct that doesn't propel us into the modern age but instead only makes us appear slightly silly to anyone who knows the English language well. Our predecessors in this profession spent well over a century bringing academic respectability to the word *folklore*. Why flee a battle that's already won?[7]

Acknowledgments

My thanks to Marta Weigle, Diane Christian, Ellen Stekert, Jan Brunvand, and especially Robert Georges for their comments on an earlier draft of this essay.

Notes

1. The academic fields whose names end in the double-suffix "-istics" include statistics, ballistics, criminalistics, and linguistics. Scholars whose fields are statistics and ballistics study subjects named statistics and ballistics, so the field names are hardly surprising. "Criminalistics" was invented because the words "criminology" and "criminologist" were already used by people who studied and analyzed criminal behavior and the relationships of such behavior to society at large. The people who would call themselves "criminalists" and their field "criminalistics" were not concerned with theories of behavior; they were concerned instead with facts of evidence. Criminalists testify in court about the caliber of the bullet that did the damage and the reliability of the latent fingerprint found at the scene; they are also the people who teach those subjects in colleges and junior colleges with police training programs. "Criminalistics" is a misnomer, one that came about by default. The people who made measurements at crime scenes or who taught other people how to make measurements needed *something* to set themselves off from the scholars who studied more abstract and social matters, something that nonetheless sounded technical and scientific. "Criminal-" was taken to be the same kind of structural entry as "stat-" and "lingui-." It isn't, but we can sympathize with those measurers of criminal events who longed for an adequate title to put on their business cards and office doors and program diplomas, those specialists who needed something impressive to say when the prosecutor asked, "Occupation?"

2. The names of several academic disciplines end with "-ics" but no preceding "-ist": physics, classics, and economics. These names don't concern us here because they don't parallel our problem: I know of no attempt to foist upon the world "physicistics," "classicistics," or "economistics," and if anyone did use such words the referents would have to do with measuring classicists, economists, and physicists rather than considering the work they do or the subjects they study.

3. The quotations from Brunvand in this paragraph and the one following are from his letter of 22 February 1984.

4. Letter from Bronner of 25 January 1984.

5. Letter from Abrahams of 8 February 1984. I don't know what Dundes remembers as his source for the word, since he has not responded to any of my queries about the matter.

6. Letter from Georges of 9 May 1984.
7. A 2023 PS: I lost this one. "Folkloristics" is all over the damned place now.

References

Dundes, Alan. 1965. *The Study of Folklore*. Englewood Cliffs: Prentice-Hall.

Ketner, Kenneth Laine. 1973. "A Preliminary Survey of the Grammar of 'Folklore': An Introduction to Hominology." Paper presented at the 1973 annual meeting of the American Folklore Society, Nashville, Tennessee.

Ketner, Kenneth Laine. 1981. "Semiotic and Folkloristics." In *Zeichenkonstitution: Akten des 2. Semiotischen Kolloquiums Regensburg*, 1978, 129–132. Berlin: Walter de Gruyter.

Krohn, Kaarle. 1926. *Die folkloristische Arbeitsmethode*. Oslo: Institute for Comparative Research in Human Culture.

Krohn, Kaarle. 1971. *Folklore Methodology Formulated by Julius Krohn and Expanded by Nordic Researchers*. Translated by Roger L. Welsch. Introduction by Archer Taylor. Austin: University of Texas Press for the American Folklore Society.

Oxford English Dictionary, Compact Edition. 1971. New York: Oxford University Press.

Onions, C. T., ed. 1967. *The Oxford Dictionary of English Etymology*. Corrected ed. New York: Oxford University Press.

Partridge, Eric. 1958. *Origins: A Short Etymological Dictionary of Modern English*, 2nd ed. New York: Macmillan.

Zemljanova, L. 1964. "The Struggle between the Reactionary and the Progressive Forces in Contemporary American Folkloristics." *Journal of the Folklore Institute* 1:130–144.

22

Arctic Silence

Icy Terror in the Heart of the Smithsonian

(*Counterpunch*, May 2003)

The Smithsonian Institution has decided to move the exhibit of Subhankar Banerjee's highly-acclaimed photographs of the Arctic National Wildlife Refuge from a main floor rotunda to a smaller, lower room and to cut the text out of most of his captions. The photographs are from Banerjee's book, *Arctic National Wildlife Refuge: Seasons of Life and Land; A Photographic Journey*, which, according to *New York Times* reporter Timothy Egan, "advocates preservation of the refuge. It features quotations from President Carter, the writer Peter Matthiessen, and the nature poet and essayist Terry Tempest Williams. Some of these quotations were to be in the exhibit; they have all been deleted."

Interior Secretary Gale Norton has referred to ANWR as "an area of flat white nothingness." Hardly. During last month's Senate debate on opening ANWR to drilling, California senator Barbara Boxer held up some of Banerjee's photos and urged her colleagues to look at them so they would have an idea what they were arguing about. The drilling bill failed, 52–48, after which Senate Appropriations Committee chair Alaska senator Ted Stevens promised personal revenge: "People who vote against this today are voting against me. I will not forget it."

Smithsonian officials say there was no political pressure behind the sudden and unexplained downgrading of what was to have been a major exhibition, that it was just "routine."

And why were the captions censored? According to Timothy Egan, Smithsonian spokesman Randall Kremer said, "Some of the captions bordered on advocacy."

Banerjee's caption for a picture of the Romanzof Mountains, for example, "The refuge has the most beautiful landscape I have ever seen and is so remote and untamed that many peaks, valleys and lakes are still without names," was changed to "Unnamed Peak, Romanzof Mountains." A caption that included the quotation, "Here there still remain elements of mystery in the unknown which in themselves have great value in the human perception of wilderness" was changed to "Rock lichens."

"There was another caption on the buff-breasted sandpiper," Egan told NPR's Liane Hansen on Sunday's *Weekend Edition*. "Mr. Banerjee had a caption saying that this species was remarkable because it traveled from Argentina to the Arctic coastal wildlife refuge to nest up there. They've removed all that. They now just say, 'Coastal plain of the Jago River and Sandpiper.' So they've taken out any sort of interpretive stuff about what these animals do, what this wildlife does in the Refuge."

A Smithsonian spokesman told Egan, "There was no pressure whatsoever, either from the White House or anyone else."

Silent Pressure

A lot of people don't believe that. They think Ted Stevens called over there and said, "If you don't cancel that exhibition I'm going to be all over your ass at budget time," as he promised the world in general after the 52–48 vote.

I don't think anybody had to call the Smithsonian to tell them to gut the Banerjee show. It doesn't work like that in Washington. It's not that calls aren't made. They're made all the time when someone wants to get something, like having a friend appointed to this or that, or wants to be sure a lucrative contract goes to a pal or a big contributor.

But calls don't have to be made when powerful people want to destroy something they don't like. For that to happen, all the powerful people need do is make their position known and the civil servants and bureaucrats further down the line will do the dirty work quite on their own.

That way, whatever happens is indeed just "routine."

Black Dust

I've seen this happen in government many times. I remember especially the National Endowment for Humanities during the Bill Bennett and Lynne Cheney years, when solid grant applications that received positive recommendations from peer review panels started disappearing somewhere after they left the program directors' desks, after which the program directors and program officers began counseling applicants to stay away from anything political or unpleasant.

"The humanities," Bennett famously proclaimed, "are in the past," and there ended all NEH support for documentary films any closer to the political and social complexities of the modern world than the hugely expensive and politically innocent Burns Brothers productions. Nobody told the peer panels not to vote in favor of proposals with political substance and nobody told the program officers to tell applicants not to develop such applications. No one had to.

I first saw this process close-hand in the Library of Congress 35 years ago in an event involving some cylinder recordings made during the first quarter years of the 20th century.

Edward D. "Sandy" Ives, an anthropologist friend who taught at University of Maine in Orono, phoned to say he'd recently learned that someone in the Archive of American Folk Song in the Library of Congress had opened the boxes containing several old cylinder recordings and discovered that many of them had turned to powdered carbon. The binder had decomposed and all that was left in the cardboard tubular containers was very fine black dust. Every year, Sandy said, more and more of the cylinders were disintegrating. Nobody knew how long it would take for them all to go, but at some point, they would all be gone. The Archive, he said, didn't have funds to pay for transferring the cylinders to tape.

He wasn't calling me in the abstract. I was then on the board of directors of the Newport Folk Foundation and Sandy knew that after all the bills were paid for each year's festival we gave the rest of the money away to folk music connected projects.

He told me how much he thought the transfers from cylinders to tape would cost. I no longer remember the number, but it didn't seem like a great deal of money and I was surprised that the federal government wouldn't come up with it to preserve so obviously important a part of our musical heritage. I presented the proposal at the next Newport board meeting.

Everyone—Pete Seeger, Theo Bikel, Judy Collins, Fred Kirkpatrick, Jean Ritchie, Oscar Brand—said yes immediately. They said Newport would pay for the transfers, whatever they cost.

I told Rae Korson, then head of the Archive of American Folk Song (she held the job from 1956 through 1969), about the grant. Rae was the widow of George Korson, who had done two important books about coal miners' songs. I liked her; everybody liked her. She was a nice person. She seemed very enthusiastic about the Newport grant to transfer the cylinders to tape. She said it was such a good thing to do because the material on the cylinders was so valuable, it was unique, and so forth.

"How do we do it?" I asked her.

"What do you mean?" she said.

I told her that we didn't know how to give money to a government agency. Newport had an accountant who would write the check, but how should it be made out and to whom should it be sent? We know how to give money to people or businesses or nonprofit corporations or the IRS, but we didn't know how to give money to a small specific agency deep within the Library of Congress. Rae said she'd get back to me with that information.

But she didn't.

I wrote her a few more times. She didn't respond to any of the letters. When I saw her at meetings, I'd remind her that we needed that information before we could send a check and she'd always say, "Oh, gosh! I'll do that as soon as I get back to the office, Bruce." She never did.

After about three years we couldn't justify sequestering the money anymore and it went for some other project. There were always more worthy projects than we had money for.

Does Money Have Politics?

Then, some years after that (I don't remember how many; across this expanse of time the years telescope), I saw Rae at another meeting. I said, "Rae, how come you never told me how to give the Archive the Newport money to save those cylinders?"

"Oh, we couldn't take that money, Bruce."

"You *couldn't* take it?"

"No."

"Why not?"

"Pete Seeger was on the Newport board. We just couldn't have taken that money."

It quite took my breath away. Rae was in charge of protecting those archive holdings, she was the official responsible for finding ways to make the material they had accessible and gathering under the Library's roof material that needed protection, and she had, knowingly, permitted recordings that were unique in all the world to turn to powdered carbon because Pete Seeger was on the Newport Folk Foundation board of directors.

The reason Rae was so terrified of Pete Seeger was because in 1956 Pete had refused to provide names to a congressional witch-hunting committee. He had been called because professional informer Harvey Matusow had named him as a communist. Instead of claiming the Fifth Amendment protection against self-incrimination, Pete claimed the First Amendment's protection of freedom of speech. He had nothing to hide about his own acts or beliefs, he said, but he wasn't going to be forced into saying things he didn't think it was right to say. Along with playwright Arthur Miller and seven other people, Pete was cited for contempt by a House vote of 373 to 9. He was tried, convicted, and sentenced to a year in prison in 1961. His case was thrown out by the US Court of Appeals on technical grounds, but mostly because the whole thing was stupid.

By the time the Newport board offered the Archive of American Folksong the money it needed to preserve those unique recordings, Pete was just about respectable again. He was no longer blocked from performing in major concert halls, he appeared regularly in concerts around the country, he was for many people an American hero. The communist witch hunts were over and the House and Senate committees that engaged in them had few defenders, even on the right. The Newport Folk Festivals, the source of the money, were hugely popular affairs, as American as apple pie. Pete would eventually be awarded the National Medal of the Arts, one of a grateful nation's highest honors.

But Rae Korson, a decent person of no particular political ideology that I ever saw, wouldn't touch Newport's money. Because Pete Seeger was on the board.

Years later, the American Folklife Center, which incorporated the Folklore Archive, did find money to begin rescuing those disintegrating cylinders. Some of the cylinders Sandy Ives had called me about were copied to tape in the mid-1970s, a decade after Rae Korson didn't accept the Newport Folk Foundation money. By the time Tip O'Neill appointed me to the board of trustees of the American Folklife Center in the Library of

Congress (a larger unit which grew up around and then incorporated the old Archive of American Folk Song) in 1990, a project was underway to transfer to tape the surviving recordings of Native American performances on cylinder and to give them to the tribes. I was never present for any of the returning ceremonies, but one staffer told me that at one of them an old woman listened to the tape, burst into tears, and said, "That is my grandmother. I haven't heard her voice since I was a little girl."

Calls That Don't Have to Be Made

I am sure that no one ever told Rae Korson to avoid accepting the Newport check. No one had to. It was just routine. I doubt anyone from the White House called over to the Department of Education last week and told them to scrub their web sites of anything that might controvert White House policy or party line. That purging of uncomfortable information was just routine too. And so was the downgrading of Subhankar Banerjee's Arctic National Wildlife Reserve exhibit and the censoring of his captions.

The Senate oversight committee is going to have a hearing to find the smoking gun in the Banerjee affair. They won't find one. There's no need to find one. In these affairs, no gun is needed. The victims do it all themselves. And the bullets never miss.

23

"Only the Sailor Knows the Archipelago"

(For the colloquium Terre Humaine,
une aventure éditoriale et scientifique,
Bibliothèque national de France, March 31–April 2, 2005)

Seeing

First, some words on the work of observation and documentation.

It is far easier to describe in detail the aspects of and feelings occasioned by the face of a stranger sitting across the aisle in the metro than the face you have seen every day of your adult life in your bathroom mirror. When we look at our own faces, the defects we have always ignored and the strengths that are interesting to others but merely ordinary are to us are equally invisible. It doesn't matter that you are a man who carefully trims his beard and moustache every day or a woman who carefully applies makeup to her face every day. You will not describe your own face the same way that you will describe mine, or the face of a stranger, or of your lover.

That is because, except by accident, we never encounter ourselves in a close mirror unprepared: by the time our eyes focus on our image, we have composed our face to be one we are willing to encounter. It is impossible to do otherwise. Remember the shock of recognition you felt when you briefly glimpsed a stranger's image in a taxi's rearview mirror that turned out to be your own face, not expecting and therefore not ready to be seen by you, or when you caught a view of your face from an unexpected angle when you passed between two mirrors not quite parallel to one another. Looking and seeing, at oneself or anything else, are always acts; they aren't passive, like getting rained on.

In the US there is a proverbial expression about the very familiar: people say, "I know it like I know the back of my own hand." In fact, most people know *nothing* of the backs or the fronts of their own hands and could do no better a job describing either of them than they could describe the soles of their feet. That is because, unless they have had a special reason for doing so, they've never looked at either the backs of their hands or the soles of their feet with the intensity and curiosity and commitment to memory even superficial description would require.

One reason we look at the hands of others is to learn things they may not have told us with their words. Hands may reveal the kind and amount of work a person does, and perhaps even the person's station in life. Hands may provide information about age concealed in the face by plastic surgery or makeup. We don't need to look at our own hands for such information; we already know everything they might have to tell.

Likewise with space. The perfect order or horrible clutter of our own kitchen or bedroom or workshop is transparent to us, a mere fact of life, while the order or clutter of the stranger's kitchen or bedroom or workshop we enter for the first time is immediately noted and remembered, and the owner or occupant is judged or evaluated on the basis of it. Are you a beggar or a king? Let me see your hands, your kitchen, your bedroom, your workshop.

Every ethnographer and police detective knows that it is far more difficult to describe the immediate and familiar than the strange and new. Most of us, if we visit in a foreign land a family that eats with knife, fork, and spoon exactly as people eat with those implements in our own country, will not make detailed notes about how they eat, nor will we take photographs, or make drawings of them doing it. Why bother?

It is not just a matter of observing and documenting. There is also the matter of why observation and documentation are taking place. If you are looking at the glacier as part of a vacation trip to the Arctic you see and note and remember different things than if you are looking at it as geomorphologist or ethnographer.

Once we know that we are making something of this moment rather than simply being here now, we see with two sets of eyes, hear with two sets of ears, interpret in two distinct places of the imagination: our own in the moment, and those of the persons we hope to reach later with what we are learning now. For the writer, it is the readers; for the photographer, it is the lookers; for the talker, it is the listeners.

This is the key insight of all travelers who in the moment of experience, however difficult or painful that moment might be, are already partly in the future looking back at themselves telling their tale of this moment to an as-yet-unencountered and perhaps as-yet-unimagined audience. This is the lover who knows the affair will end, already looking back, though the moment of passion is still going on. This is Aeneas, after the killing of the three stags and shortly before he will arrive in Dido's Carthage, famously saying to his men on the coast of north Africa "forsan et haec olim meminisse iuvabit": *Some day it will perhaps be good to look back on these things.* And not just look back, for there is one characteristic courtly Virgil and wandering Aeneas share more than any other: they are both storytellers. Some day it will perhaps be good to look back on these things—and to tell the story of them.

We look far more than we see; we see far more than we understand; we understand far more than we know. It is the ethnographer's task to look, to see, to understand, and then to go one critical step further: to tell the story in a way that is meaningful and useful and honest. To tell it in a way that the readers know and feel something significant of a life they did not know and feel before, and could not have known and had feelings about otherwise.

Without those four discrete acts—looking, seeing, understanding, and telling—the experience is a moment lost in time. It may have been horrible or it may have been sublime, but in either case it is gone forever. That is, it is merely travel. Ethnographers travel, but travel is not what they do. What they do is tell.

As ethnographers, we go elsewhere—whether halfway around the globe or to a street in our own city to which we have never before ventured, let alone let ourselves be immersed—to come to know the world and experience of the Other, that person who is Not Us. But there is a key fact or irony to this enterprise which all ethnographers at some point learn: the only "other" in that distant place or on that street in our own city never before visited is the ethnographer. Everyone else is at home; everyone else is natural; everyone else is doing what there is to be done. It is only the ethnographer who is the stranger, the outsider, the alien. If the ethnographer travels in order to understand the other, then at least one purpose of all ethnography is understanding oneself.

The task is differentiating and knowing the other-who-is-the-stranger and the other-who-is-oneself, and preserving enough of that difference to be able to write about it later. Lose the distance entirely and you never come home; bridge it inadequately and you've understood nothing and have no story to tell.

Science, After a Fashion

Before the telling of the story there is the experiencing of the event and before that there is the choice of what event or place will be experienced, the decision about what is valuable to be experienced.

There is a fork in the road of studying human knowledge where those of us who write the kind of books that find their way into the company of Terre Humaine go one way and those who write "social sciences" books primarily composed of numbers and charts and language few, if anyone at all, in this room would take any pleasure in reading aloud go another. As soon as you decide that the most important thing or most reliable thing is what can be counted, you thenceforth see as important only things that can be counted. Once you make that choice, things that cannot be counted do not count.

That is a necessary and essential choice in the experimental sciences. The experimental sciences need replicable procedures with specific results utilizing models that make enough apparent sense to be worth proving or disproving, worth applying or not applying. "*This* is done; *that* does or does not happen; it is so big or weighs so much or happens in this many seconds. Next!"

In the human sciences, however, experimental modeling has the great danger, perhaps the great likelihood, of leading to a trivialization of the human experience, of leading to *scientism*—putting on the garments of experimental science without having earned the right to wear them.

In the early 1990s, when I was editor of *Journal of American Folklore*, I began receiving more and more articles that referred to the field of study as "folkloristics." "Folkloristics" was the term used for the field of study in the Nordic countries, but in the US and in Great Britain, the name of the field had long been "folklore." That word no more covered what all folklorists did than the term "English" covers what is done in the departments in American universities that have that title. Those words are just what those fields and departments are called; they are names, not behaviors. What is actually done in the fields and departments is determined by what people in them are doing at any time. So why was I seeing so many articles with "folkloristics" where only a short time earlier I had seen the word "folklore"? Because, I was told, "folkloristics" was far more "scientific" a word and the authors were certain they would be taken more seriously if they were regarded as being more scientific than they had been previously. I refused to publish articles with the word "folkloristics" where the word "folklore" would have served perfectly well. A few authors got very angry and withdrew their submissions; most accepted my suggestion that they use the word "folklore," as people had for years. Mine was a hollow victory, however: as soon as my successor took over, the pages of *Journal of American Folklore* were awash with "folkloristics-this" and "folkloristics-that." Did people in other fields thenceforth take them more seriously? Of course not. Nothing changed except the word.

I talked about this foolishness with editors in other disciplines. They were experiencing the same thing. Different words were at issue, but the same process was taking place. What we were seeing wasn't science. It was *scientism*, pretending to the certainty of the experimental sciences where it did not exist and never would exist.

The only place in the human sciences where the certainty of the experimental sciences exists is where the researchers have limited themselves to inquiries that look like experimental science. Sometimes that produces useful results; just as often, perhaps more often, it does not. It also produces truly abominable prose, like this passage from an award-winning essay which I discovered in the American Anthropological Association's ethnographic journal, *Ethos*:

> Specifically, we are interested in the construction of deviance as a rhetorical device and in the dialogical possibilities that this construction opens for reaffirming or changing the boundaries of symbolic-moral universes (Ben-Yehuda 1990; Berger and Luckmann 1966). Our focus is thus on the transactional process between center and periphery through which deviance is confronted, appropriated, and remade by powers representing (or aspiring to represent) the society's core values. In the case under discussion the system of local knowledge that informs the cultural construction of deviance, and the moral-symbolic universe that is consequently reaffirmed, are not biomedical but mystico-religious.

Why would anyone want to write like that? Who can read language like that? For whom is language like that written? Who cares about language like that? Language like that calls to mind a wonderful passage in filmmaker Luis Buñuel's autobiography, *My Last Sigh*.

I must state my hatred of pedantry and jargon. Sometimes I weep with laughter when I read certain articles in *Cahiers du Cinéma*, for example. As the honorary president of Centro de Capacitación Cinematográfica in Mexico City, I once went to visit the school and was introduced to several professors, including a young man in a suit and tie who blushed a good deal. When I asked him what he taught, he replied, "The Semiology of the Clonic Image." I could have murdered him on the spot.

The authors of the psychological passage I quoted are probably no better or worse than anyone else doing similar work. I could have skimmed other issues of *Ethos* and found many similar passages, as I could have found them skimming the pages of *American Anthropologist* or *Journal of American Folklore*. You could find them skimming the pages of equivalent French journals in the same fields.

I don't usually read work like that because I don't like it. So far as I can tell, the sentiment is reciprocated: people who cherish process and prose like that rarely cherish the kind of process and prose found in Terre Humaine. They say we're not scientific enough, they say we're *literary*.

Languages

They are right, and a good thing it is. What else *could* we be? Of *course* we're literary. That doesn't mean that we're not doing good ethnography, good "social science." All it means is that good social science, good ethnography, unlike good experimental science, can be literary. There's nothing complicated about that concept. Words are as valid and precise a language as is scientific notation—if the author and reader know how to use them correctly and take the trouble to do so. Neither language is inherently better than the other; neither is more privileged than the other. If something in either is bad, it's bad; if something in either is good, it's good.

They each have things they do better than the other. The language of scientific notation is the best language we've got for describing, say, the interaction of subatomic particles or the curve of airfoils or the architecture of a microprocessor. You just can't do those things well or usefully with words, no matter how good a writer you are.

If you want to describe the human condition, however, you've got to opt for the tools of literature. There's no way around it. That's what literature is for; that's what literature does. Literature is a machine for describing the human condition. Everybody who works in literature knows that. If the proponents of scientism cannot understand or accept that, too bad for them. We can't save them; we can only do our work and hope they sometime learn how to read it.

Jean Malaurie knew this perfectly well when, in 1955, he published as one of the two mottos of the first book in Terre Humaine, his own magnificent *Les derniers rois de Thulé*, this quotation from Jean Giono's *L'eau vive*:

> On ne peut pas connaître un pays par la simple science géographique. . . . On ne peut, je crois, rien connaître par la simple science; c'est un instrument trop exact et trop dur. Le monde a mille tendresses dans lesquelles il faut se plier pour les comprendre avant de savoir ce que représente leur sommme. . . . Seul le marin connaît l'archipel.
>
> (We cannot know a country merely through the science of geography. . . . I do not believe that we can know anything merely through science; it is too precise, too rigid a tool. The world has a thousand nuances into which we must lean so that we may understand them before we learn what the sum of their parts represents. . . . Only the sailor knows the archipelago.)

This Truth and That Truth

But saying something is literature is at once saying too much and not enough; we must refine the term further if we are to know anything useful. Some literature is prose, some is poetry, though some prose is so good we honor it by calling it poetic. Some prose is called fiction, or made up; all the rest is called nonfiction, or not made up. Fiction and nonfiction use the same writing techniques. There is only one important difference in fiction and nonfiction. Sometimes it matters a great deal; sometimes, it matters not at all. It is an external, not an internal difference, a difference you might feel but cannot ever fully know by looking only at the work itself.

The difference in the two kinds of prose is this: nonfiction is always accountable to things outside itself, while the fictional work owes no allegiance to anything other than its own internal narrative integrity.

The novel by Jonathan Swift that recounts the several voyages of Lemuel Gulliver reads like a perfectly good, albeit highly fantastic, autobiographical travel account, but none of it ever happened anywhere except in the brain of Jonathan Swift. Franz Kafka's Gregor Samsa awakens one morning as an insect, feet in the air, carapace against the sheets. We never know him as anything other than an insect, so there is no reason for us to question it. Likewise, it matters not a bit whether or not Flaubert was, in *Madame Bovary*, faithful to his models—his father and mother, his friend Ernest Chevalier, his mistress Louise Colet, poor sad misguided Delphine Delamare, Flaubert himself. What matters in the realm of fiction is how real the author's characters and places *seem* to us, not how real they *are* or *were* in the world. You and I can talk about Emma Bovary as if we knew her, and perhaps we do, but that knowledge is the mark of Flaubert's narrative genius, not a reflection or evidence of the fact of her life.

Fiction that works, that makes us feel we are reading something real even though we know what we are reading is not real, is fiction that has what some critics called "authority." Exactly the same thing is at work in nonfiction. The best writers of nonfiction convince you that you can take what they say as true without your having to consult anyone or anything else.

Authority exists in fiction and in nonfiction, but not in the same way. Not only do you and I know Emma Bovary, but we both know *exactly* the same things about her. Indeed, we know *everything* there is to know about her, everything anyone knows about her. There may be things written about Flaubert's sources or Flaubert's words, and there may be notes and letters from Flaubert explaining this or that, but the object is itself fixed: it is the novel that bears his name as author and her name as title. Emma does not exist outside that novel. Her affair with Rodolphe is inside that novel; her grave is inside that novel.

A work of fiction is referential only by coincidence or convenience. But a nonfiction work—whether one of experimental science or biography or ethnography—is referential of necessity. It does not exist without that referent, and the further it strays from that referent the less useful or meaningful it is to us, no matter how well written, how craftily it is designed or wrought.

Every work that claims to bear witness is an individual encounter with something far more resonant and complex than the individual doing the encountering. The several editions of *Les derniers rois de Thulé* give physical testimony to that: each new edition of the book is one hundred pages longer than the previous edition. The book is organic, responding to the external world it is about and to changes in the author himself. The Jean Malaurie who wrote *Les derniers rois de Thulé* was not the Jean

Malaurie who arrived in Greenland in 1951, knowing little about the place but confident that his earlier experience would see him through. And neither was the Jean Malaurie who wrote the fifth edition the Jean Malaurie who wrote the first edition in 1955. It could not be otherwise.

No one put difference between fiction and nonfiction better than James Agee in one of the most important theoretical passages in *Let Us Now Praise Famous Men*:

> In a novel, a house or person has his meaning, his existence, entirely through the writer. Here, a house or a person has only the most limited of his meaning through me: his true meaning is much huger. It is that he exists, in actual being, as you do and as I do, and as no character of the imagination can possibly exist. His great weight, mystery, and dignity are in this fact. As for me, I can tell you of him only what I saw, only so accurately as in my terms I know how: and this in turn has its chief stature not in any ability of mine but in the fact that I too exist, not as a work of fiction, but as a human being. Because of his immeasurable weight in actual existence, and because of mine, every word I tell of him has inevitably a kind of immediacy, a kind of meaning, not at all necessarily "superior" to that of imagination, but of a kind so different that a work of the imagination (however intensely it may draw on "life") can at best only faintly imitate the least of it.

Why Are Some True Stories Novels while Other True Stories Are Not Novels?

A few years ago, Jean Malaurie published in Terre Humaine something he'd previously said he would never publish in Terre Humaine: a novel, Claude Lucas's *Suerte*. Claude Lucas was sufficiently concerned by the question of genre to append a note to his book explaining why he chose to cast his life in terms of what he called a novel rather than a memoir. His book is interesting for many reasons, not the least being how it forces us to rethink our distinctions between "fiction" and "nonfiction" and the kinds of truth each can represent, the kind of accountability to which each is subject, and the kind of authority each has.

I thought of *Suerte* recently when I was reading one of the classic American proletarian novels of the 1930s, Jack Conroy's *The Disinherited*, a first-person narrative about coal miners, factory workers, and other people suffering from the Great Depression. The book received a flutter of attention when it was first published in 1933, then disappeared until the early 1960s when it was rediscovered at exactly the same time and perhaps for exactly the same reasons James Agee's and Walker Evans's *Let Us Now Praise Famous Men* was rediscovered.

The Disinherited is a novel the way *Suerte* is a novel, which is to say, in the thinnest possible sense of that generic word. Conroy began writing his book as a first-person autobiography then shifted to fiction. He was never comfortable with the category. He told an interviewer in 1963: "Novel or not, just so it tells the truth. I describe myself as a witness to the times, not as a novelist. And that's what I prefer to be known as." In another interview he said, "I wanted to be a witness to the times, to show how it feels to be without work and with no prospect of any, and with the imminent fear of starvation, to move people to think about these things, and, what was more important, to do something about it."

A witness to the times. That is perhaps the simplest definition I have ever read of the mission and accomplishment of the writers who form the companionship of Terre Humaine. Conroy's phrase has two components: *the times*, the human reality out there; and *a witness*, a specific person experiencing that human reality and finding a form and a language with which to tell the rest of us about it in a book that has not only specificity, but also meaning and passion.

One can only bear witness to the times in the first person. You cannot bear witness to the times in the passive voice of science, let alone the hollower and even more passive voice of scientism. No statement beginning "It was observed that . . ." can ever bear witness; the best such statements can do is report that someone with another voice entirely saw (and perhaps experienced) something.

There is delight and vitality to the process of becoming less a stranger, less an outsider, whether as explorer and writer, or as reader. The great achievement of Terre Humaine, the reason it continues to grow in books and readers, the reason it has lasted half a century in a time of increasing velocity and obsolescence, is that it continues to allow strangers to tell us what they saw and learned, it continues to let them tell us not about our world's uniformity but rather its differences. We are not the same, nor would we want to be. What we want is the ability to know and understand and cherish the differences that make us who and what we are.

24

From the Editor

The Humanities at Risk

(Journal of American Folklore, 1989)

Lawrence W. Levine's "Jazz and American Culture," in this issue of the *Journal*, explores the way jazz transcended the barriers created by the professional arbiters of taste and propriety. In addition to being a fine essay on one of the world's major music forms, Levine's article reveals a condition perhaps better known to folklorists than to any other group of scholars: vital aspects of living culture get on perfectly well despite the provincial vision and behavior of the official arbiters and brokers of culture. When the arbiters and brokers shut the doors and windows, they don't stop the music; they merely limit their own vision.

Lest anyone think that similar battles are no longer necessary or in progress, consider *Humanities in America: A Report to the President, the Congress, and the American People*, by Lynne V. Cheney, chairman of the National Endowment for the Humanities. (The report was reprinted in full in *Chronicle of Higher Education* 35:4 [21 September 1988], A17–A23.)

The humanities, the report tells us, are the canon, and we tinker with that canon at our peril. It is wrong, Chairman Cheney says, to focus on the political, social, and economic aspects of "great books"; these books should be studied for their beauty (assumed to be a constant throughout time) and their value (assumed to be independent of all social meaning).

The report is astonishingly ethnocentric and elitist. The only black writer quoted, Maya Angelou, is brought in to tell us why Shakespeare is a great black poet. The two Spanish-speaking writers mentioned are from

South America, and no Native American is mentioned at all. Modern poetry is characterized as among the "unlikely humanities subjects" (A21). Alexis de Tocqueville is quoted at length.

The report attacks specialization and says that "To counter the excesses of specialization and to strengthen the contributions the academy can make to society, those who fund, publish, and evaluate research should encourage work of *general* significance" (A23, emphasis added). (There are other views about the relative merits of specialization and generalization. To Edmund Burke's assertion that Sir Joshua Reynolds "was a great generalizer" and that "this disposition to abstractions, to generalizing and classification, is the great glory of the human mind," William Blake responded, "To Generalize is to be an Idiot. To Particularize is the Alone Distinction of Merit. General Knowledges are those Knowledges that Idiots possess.")

Cheney three times points with admiration to the "PBS series of conversations with Joseph Campbell which recently propelled a book of those conversations and two books of Campbell's writing to the best-seller lists" (A17). Best-sellers they may be, but few, if any, competent folklorists, anthropologists, or ethnologists regard Campbell's facile generalizations about mythology with any seriousness at all.

To go by Cheney's report, the primary, if not the sole, function of the humanities presenter or scholar is to deliver down: *we* know what culture really is, *they* don't, we bring it to them so they know about beauty and the past. Cheney's report is perfectly consonant with the prescriptive dictum of her predecessor, William J. Bennett: "The humanities are in the past." There is no sense at all that the information of the humanities is ever-developing, or that humanities scholars have as much to learn as they have to tell and instruct. It is a vision that has the stuff of the humanities very much in place.

NEH is the principal purveyor of all government grants for humanistic research. The more NEH accepts the notion that humanities are in the past, the more it closes off funding to scholars dealing with the uncanonized present and scholars who attempt to see the past in new perspectives or with new knowledge and sensitivity. (Our word "revise" derives from the Latin *revidere*, to look at again; for scholars and artists the word and concept apply as much to ideas in the mind as to words on the page.)

Walter Berns, a member of the NEH Council (the Endowment's governing body; it sets policy and has final approval on all grants), and chairman of the Council's Committee on Research, recently argued *against* funding projects dealing with cultures lacking a written language. Leon Kass, another Council member, said that the studies of a language without a written literature are of interest only to the linguist, not to the humanist. An NEH policy holding that languages without literatures are too insignificant for funding has serious implications for folklorists, anthropologists, and ethnologists. It is, at heart, a political rather than just a scholarly position. There is, Dennis Tedlock points out, a bizarre irony here: the same Council members who would foreclose funding projects involving cultures without writing endorse the notion of the great canon. That canon includes the works of Homer. Homer, like much ancient poetry, existed for centuries only in oral tradition. Under the guidelines proposed by Berns and implied by Cheney's report, study of a living Homer or vital Homeric tradition would be unacceptable to NEH.

There are profound secondary effects to this parochialization of the NEH field of view. NEH is a flagship organization; many state humanities agencies and many private foundations take their cues from NEH. Many foundation directors really don't know what they're doing (who can know the disciplinary subtleties in all the project proposals that seem reasonable?) but they want to do the right thing—whatever it is. Documents such as Chairman Cheney's will tell them what the "right thing" is.

The jazz musicians Lawrence Levine writes about wouldn't have been the losers had the arbiters of taste succeeded in keeping jazz outside the official musical canon. The jazz musicians were going to go on playing their music anyway. The losers would have been the rest of us. The same is the case if the current NEH vision of humanities is allowed to prevail: traditional artists will continue doing what they do, but the rest of us will have ever-decreasing access to that art and insight.

Levine's article details how the jazz battle was pretty much won; Cheney's report reminds us that the war goes on.

25

From the Editor

Dead Soldiers and the Arctic Night

(Journal of American Folklore, 1990)

Since the late 1960s I've had on my office wall a photograph of a dead soldier in a trench. Even before you notice the puckered bullet hole above his left eye you know he's dead. His right hip twists too far to his left and his head bends back too far to his right for him to be asleep or even unconscious. A coat, wool on one side and slick on the other, is bunched in a backward "S" from his left shoulder, across his chest, to the underside of his right arm. His weapon lies across his abdomen where it probably fell when he rolled down the trench; the muzzle hovers just above his right calf. A few feet beyond him is another weapon, its muzzle propped delicately upon a rock; this weapon points in the opposite direction, toward the place from which the bullet that killed the young man probably came.

Not long after I hung the picture, a student asked me if I'd taken the photograph myself or if I got it from a combat photographer. I had no idea what he was talking about and told him so. "That picture there. The one of the dead guy in Vietnam."

"That's not Vietnam," I said.

"It isn't?" he said. He looked at the picture. "Where is it, then?"

I told him to look at it closely. After a while he said, "There's something weird about this." I told him that the man in the photograph had been dead over a century, that the picture had been taken in 1865 in Petersburg, Virginia, by Thomas C. Roche. "Yeah," he said, "I knew there was something weird about it."

It would have been a silly conversation but for one thing: over the next six or seven years something like it occurred again and again and again. Men, women, students, faculty, some of them Vietnam combat vets, glanced at the photograph and connected it to Vietnam. At first I thought the responses showed how carelessly people looked at pictures. After all, how could anyone who really *looked* at that photograph mistake the cap and ball musket for an M-14, or the dead man's clothes for the uniforms worn by American troops in Southeast Asia? Then, about 1976 or 1977, the misreadings of the photograph stopped: the few visitors to my office who noticed it at all spoke about the Civil War or the history of photography.

The content of an icon isn't inherent in the icon: we deliver the content, every single time, and as our ideas and narratives change so do the meanings of images. Images are frozen, but their meanings remain ever in flux. We read facts in terms of ideas. Without ideas, facts are gibberish, clutter, noise. Ideas organize our facts, prepare us to receive or ignore them, tell us how to manage them when they appear. Our knowledge of childhood's first searing burns forever conditions our understanding of bright dancing flames.

And our stories, therefore, aren't just *what* we know; they're *how* we know. The makers of stories take the things of our lives and create or shape things that take meaning only insofar as they relate back to our lives. Leslie Fiedler writes, in his article in this issue, about the 12-point buck in *The Deer Hunter*: "that impossible animal is the iconic embodiment of a deep wish, like the images which possess our dreams." If there ever was a time when folk, pop, and art culture were truly separate, that time is probably long past: the distinctions are valid, but the borders are ambiguous, porous, protean.

Academic practice is to take things apart so we can examine them with a single glass—the glass of the folklorist, historian, psychologist, which- or whoever. Such visions are illuminating, informing, and often necessary, but so is the vision that transcends disciplinary inquiry and rhetoric and instead applies whatever perceptions are necessary to achieve broader understanding. All complex events in our world are polysemous. The icons of the mass media are drawn from and feed back into folk and art culture, hence our publication in this issue of cultural critic Leslie A. Fiedler's splendid essay on the mythologizing of modern war in film.

If film is a kind of public myth to which anyone may ascribe, personal narrative is a private myth by which individuals may describe or attempt to circumscribe themselves. My own contribution to this issue of the *Journal* focuses on the character and implications of such personal narrative practice. Factual truth in either mode is a contingent matter only. Individuals shape their narratives in ways that please audiences and fit whatever images they are attempting to construct. The extreme of this process comprises those individuals who cloak themselves with the narratives of others' lives in order to re-create themselves. Such personal creation, which is fully dependent on heard and tuned oral narrative, is perhaps the far end of scale that has at its other extremity the resonant kinds of film work analyzed by Fiedler.

I'm writing these last editor's notes near the Arctic Circle on Midsummer's Night. From up here, looking toward the top of the world, I offer my thanks to the many individuals who, during the past five years, have served as the *Journal*'s associate editors, editorial assistants, and manuscript readers; to the consistently friendly and superbly competent editorial staff at the American Anthropological Association; to the State University of New York at Buffalo Department of English and Faculty of Arts and Letters for financial support and countless courtesies that made this job easier. And thanks most of all to the contributors, whose creative endeavors are the point of all this labor.

A few yards from the stony shore where I'm sitting, two graylings have for some time been almost perfectly motionless in the crystal water. Not long ago and a half-mile or so upstream, a beaver swam silently from one side of the river to the other, its dark snout barely breaking the water. We tried to remain motionless but the beaver noticed our canoe anyway, slapped the water with his tail and disappeared, whereupon the radiating vee of his swimming wake was overtaken and replaced by the concentric circles of his slap and dive. Earlier in the evening we came upon a moose cow with two calves; as we drew near, they melted into the scrawny black spruce tilting eccentrically above the permafrost. The dragonflies are out, so the June mosquitoes have for a while gone elsewhere. It's a few minutes after 1 a.m. and the sun is a brilliant cool white ball 15 degrees above the horizon. The air is flawless. It's a magical time and everything seems possible.

Index

Abrahams, Roger D., 1, 28, 144, 151, 221, 255–256, 266, 271–273, 338, 341, 343
Adnopoz, Elliott (Ramblin' Jack), 162
Aeneas, 353
Aeschylus, 269
AFS: *see* American Folklore Society
Agee, James, 359–360
alcohol, 64, 69, 75, 76
All the News that's Fit to Sing (Ochs), 161
"All you tough guys that thinks you're wise" (toast), 19
Allen, W. G., 214
AMCC: *see* Prisons: Anvil Mountain Correctional Center
American Folklore Society, 9, 161, 191, 211, 279, 284, 294, 295, 301, 302, 306, 327, 326, 327, 328, 342, 339
American Services Association (con game), 83–84
Amundsen, Roald, 57
Angelou, Maya, 361
Angola (prison), 108, 118
ANWR: *see* Arctic National Wildlife Refuge
Appalachian Volunteers (AVs), 35, 39–41, 44–47, 49–50

Archive of Traditional Music (Indiana University), 2
Arctic National Wildlife Refuge, 345
argot, 10, 19, 22–24
Art Worlds (Becker), 152
Asbury, Bishop Francis, 172
Atlantic Monthly, vii, 30, 126, 175, 191, 205, 208, 220, 245, 270
AV: *see* Appalachian Volunteers

Banerjee, Subhankar, 345–346, 350
Barnett, Governor Ross, 146
Barrow, Clyde, 102–103
Barth, Bill, 157
Barthes, Roland, 318
Batista, Fulgencio, 146
Battered Women's Shelter (Nome), 55, 61
Bauman, Richard, 333
Bay of Pigs, 146
Beck, Henry Charlton, 200, 209
Becker, Howard S., 3, 27, 152
Belafonte, Harry, 145
Ben Botkin, 2–4, 211, 283–286, 288
Bennett, William, 347, 362
Bennett, William J. (Bill), 362
Berkman, Alexander, 12, 23, 28
Berns, Walter, 362
Bevel, James, 292–293

Bibb, Henry, 183, 193, 196
Bikel, Theodore, 291
Black lung, 35, 37–38, 47
blackface, 213
Blake, William, 321, 362
Blues: Skip James, 153–159; in Folksong Revival, 143, 144, 148, 150, 165; *passing mention,* 255, 267, 279, 287
Board of Trade (Nome), 61
Bonanza Channel (Nome), 70
Botkin, Benjamin A., 2, 3, 150, 211, 271, 283–288, 300–301, 331
Boxer, Barbara, Senator, 345
Brand, Oscar, 152, 166, 348
broadform deed, 43
Bronner, Simon, 338
Broonzy, Big Bill, 144
Buckley, Bruce, 144, 152
Buckley, William F., Jr., 166
Bunhart, Jerry, 63–64
Buñuel, Luis 355
Burke, Kenneth, 252
Bybee, Hilton, 102–104

Cable, George Washington, 197
Cage, John, 320
Campbell, Joseph, 362
Canned Heat, 148, 159
Carawan, Guy and Candie, 192, 197
Carmer, Carl, 194, 198, 205
Castro, Fidel, 146
Catch-22 (Heller), 146å
Cavell, Stanley, 323
Charles Rycroft, 303–304
Charles Seeger, 145
Charles Wesley, 177
Charlie Patton, 155
Charters, Sam Charters, 154
checks (forged), 84, 96–98, 128–129, 134–135
Cheney, Lynne V., 347, 359, 361–373
Child, Francis James, 289, 331

Chilingarov, Artur, 58, 69
Chirac, Jacques, 53
chock, 26
Christian, Diane, 30, 69, 126, 294–295, 299, 306, 319, 333, 343
Clemmer, Donald, 24, 28
Coetzee, John, 126
Cohen, John, 145
Coles, Robert, 30
con games, 83–84, 93, 96–98
confessions, extorted (Texas Rangers), 131–134
conjure, 182–198
Conroy, Jack, 359
convict code, 9, 13–14, 28, 91–92
convict guards,: 105, 109–110
Corpus Christi, 130–131, 133–134
cotton gin, 217
Council (Alaska), 39–40, 59, 70–72, 152, 362–363
Crabtree, Will, 156
Cressey, Donald, 27
criminal code, 91–92; refusing to snitch, 100–101; killing snitches, 105
Cuban Missile Crisis, 146
cylinder recordings (Archive of Folksong), 347–349

Darwin, Charles, 319, 321
Davidson, Bruce (photographer), 30
Davis, Slew Davis, 98–99
Diehl, Rick, 46, 50
Disinherited, The (Conroy), 359–360
Dolby-Stahl, Sandra, 151
Dollard, John, 192–193, 197
Dorson, Richard M. (Dick), 2–3, 28, 81, 144, 151–152, 194, 196–198, 271, 327, 331, 335, 339, 341
Dr. Strangelove (Kubrick), 146
Dred Scott decision, 217
Dundes, Alan, 151–152, 196–198, 300–301, 338–339, 341, 343–344

370 | Index

Mintz, Jerome R., 327, 333
mojo, 196, 238, 244
Monroe, Marilyn, 146
Morris, Willie, 29–30
Mules and Men (Hurston), 189, 197
Mulloy, Joe, 42–43, 45–48, 52
Mulloy, Karen, 45
Myrdal, Gunnar, 216, 270

National Endowment for the Humanities, 347, 361
Newport Folk Festival, 3, 144–149, 154, 159, 161, 164–165, 291, 310, 347, 349; performer parties: Janis Joplin, 165, Jerry Rubin, 166, Phil Ochs, 165–166; William F. Buckley, Jr., 166
Newport Folk Foundation, 292, 347–349, 350
No Laughing Matter (Legman), 297, 299, 301
Nobile, Umberto, 57
Nome, 53–59, 62–63, 65–73, 75, 77–78; homeless people in, 65

O'Connor, Hugh, 39
O'Diamonds Jack (prison guard), 14–15, 278
O'Neill, Tip, 349
Ochs, Alice, 164
Ochs, Phil, 161, 167
Odum, Howard, 271
OEO (Office of Economic Opportunity), 40, 47, 49
organizing rural poor, 34, 39–47

Paramount (recording company), 156–157, 159
Pareles, John, 290
Park, Robert Ezra, 199, 209, 221
Parker, Bonnie, 102–103
Parrish, Lydia, 199–203, 205–207, 209
Parrish, Maxfield, 201

Pigeon Drop (con game), 84
Pike County (Kentucky), 33–34, 37, 43–45, 51–52
Pikeville (Kentucky), 29–52
pimp, 21, 84–87, 92, 273, 275
Polaris Hotel (Nome), 54, 60, 78
Pound, Louise, 284
Prigogine, Ilya, 322, 333–334
prison: argot, slang, nicknames, 22–25; code, 13–14; escapes and escape attempts: Texas, 99–108 *passim*; Louisiana (Angola), 111–112, 114–115; Louisiana, 113, 117–120; prisoner self-mutilation: Texas, 102; sex, 16–18; society, 11–13
prisons: Angola (Louisiana), 108–123; Anvil Mountain Correctional Center (Nome), 63–65, 75; Darrington (Texas), 101, 242; Death Row (Texas), 126; Ellis (Texas), 9, 245, 260, 263, 309–311; 126 Eastham (Texas), 99–103, 105; Missouri Penitentiary, 20–21; Ramsey (Texas), 9, 24–25, 102, 125, 225, 238, 240–242, 245, 252; Retrieve (Texas), 9, 25, 98, 101, 105, 242; Texas Department of Corrections, 9, 28, 243, 245, 252, 257, 260, 263; Texas Prison System, 224; The Walls (Texas), 9, 102, 105, 245; Walpole (Massachusetts), 14
Project Camelot, 329
Puckett, Newbell Niles, 195, 197

Quakers, 200–201, 203–204

racism, 216–219
Racz, Richard, 209
Rangers: *see* Texas Rangers
Rationale of the Dirty Joke (Legman), 297–298, 303, 308
Ratliff, Thomas, 40, 47, 49

Ray, Jink, 43, 51
Reconstruction, 218–219
Redwine, 98–100, 107
Resurrection City, 292–294
Reynolds, Sir Joshua, 362
Richardson, Benny, 256, 263
Richmond, W. Edson, 327
Rinzler, Ralph, 149, 151, 292, 294
Roberts, Warren, 327
Rosenberg, Ethel, 145
Rosenberg, Neil, 144, 152
Rubber Soul (Beatles), 162
Rubin, Jerry, 166
Russell, Bud, 235, 244

safecracking, 126–140 *passim;*
    keisters, 137, 139; peeling, 138–139;
    punching, 137, 139
Scott, Roy, 132
Sea Islands (Georgia), 147, 199–210
Sebeok, Thomas A., 327
sedition, 44–48
Seefus, Jesse James, 233, 243
Seeger, Charles, 145
Seeger, Dan, 309–310
Seeger, Mike, 292
Seeger, Pete, 145, 147–149, 166,
    290–292, 309–311, 348–349
Seeger, Toshi, 309–310
Service, Robert W., 273
shamans, 58–60, 76, 77
Shapiro, Henry David, 211
Silber, Irwin, 339
silicosis, 35, 37–38
Simmons, Lee, 106–107
Sing Out!, vii, 145, 148, 152, 339
Skip James/Today!, 153, 155, 157–158
Sky King, 243
Slave Songs of the United States,
    176–177, 191, 197, 208, 214, 270
slavery, 171, 172, 176, 181, 189, 209,
    209n7, 216–218, 270, 271, 281, 287
Smith, J. B. ("Smitty"), 224–252

Smithsonian Festival of American
    Folklife, 149
Smithsonian Institution, 149, 328, 345
Smitty: *see* Smith, J. B.
snitch, 13–14, 24, 91, 105
Snow, Loudell F., 194, 198
South Jersey, 201
Southern Christian Leadership
    Conference, 292
Southern Workman, 193, 198, 213, 219
spirituals, 171–181, 206, 213–214,
    219–220
St. Simons (Georgia), 201–202, 207
Stekert, Ellen, 2–3, 144, 152, 333, 343
Stengers, Isabelle, 322, 334
Stevens, Ted, 345–346
Stevens, Wallace, 323
Stranger in a Strange Land (Heinlein),
    146
strip mining, 31, 43–44, 52
Swift, Jonathan, 357–358

Talley, Thomas W., 214
TDC: *see* Prisons: Texas Department
    of Corrections
Tedlock, Dennis, 325, 363
Teller (Alaska), 10, 56–57, 59, 72, 268,
    303
Terre Humaine, 53–54, 351, 354, 357,
    359–360
Texas Monthly, 81
Texas Rangers, 91–92, 131–133, 136
The Spy Who Came in from the Cold
    (Le Carré), 146
Thompson, Stith, 319
Thoms, William, 336
Thule, 53, 58, 69, 77
"Titanic," 272–273
toasts, 18–22, 26, 255–256, 267–279
    passim
transaction, 29–31
Treasuries (Botkin), 286
truck mining, 33–37

Dvořák, Antonín, 220, 331

Easterling, Edith, 39, 41, 50
Eliot, T. S. 223, 252, 323
Elliott, "Ramblin'" Jack, 162
Ellis, A. B., 185, 196
Ellis, O. B., 106

Fahey, John, 153, 157
fakelore, 2
Federal Writers' Project, 271
ferret (Nome), 73
Fiedler, Leslie A., 366
Fieldwork, 2, 68, 147, 149, 195, 224, 275, 290–291, 316–318, 324
Fisher, Miles Mark, 181
Fisk University, 177
Flaubert, Gustave, 358
Fleron, Frederic, Jr., 29–30, 34
Folk Arts Program (National Endowment for the Arts), 149–150, 328
Folklore Institute (Indiana University), 2
folklorismus, 151
folkloristics, 335–344, 354–355
Folksong Revival, 143–152, 161–167
Fort Davis roadhouse (Nome), 73, 77
Foucault, Michel, 315, 333
Frye, Frye, 320

Gagnon, John, 252
Gambling: card dealing (casino), 94; craps (dice), 92–93; shilling (casino), 94
Garrison, Wendell Phillips, 208
Gator, Judge Bradley M., 63
Georges, Robert, 339, 343
Giono, Jean, 357
Goffman, Irving, 10, 14, 27–28
Great Revival, The, 171
Greenway, John, 11, 27
"Grizzly Bear," 278

Grossman, Albert, 145
Guralnick, Peter, 158
Guthrie, Woody, 266, 290
Guthrie, Arlo, 148
Guy, Buddy, 165

Halpert, Herbert, 211
Hampton Institute, 178, 213
Hand, Wayland D., 183, 191
Handlin, Oscar, 9, 27
hants, 197–198
Harper's Magazine, 29–30
Harris, Joel Chandler, 197, 330
Harvard Society of Fellows, 3
Hassler, Alfred, 20, 28
Hatfield, Big Ellison, 33
Hawes, Bess Lomax, 149, 152, 294–295
Hendrix, Jimi, 148
heroin, 87–90
Herskovits, Melville, 10, 27
Hickerson, Joseph, 144, 152
Higginson, Thomas Wentworth 175, 177, 191, 205, 208, 219, 270, 330
Hoffman, Abbie, 166
Holcomb, Robert, 34, 52
Hoodoo-Conjuration-Witchcraft-Rootwork (Hyatt) 191, 197
hoodoo, 187, 191, 193–194, 196–197, 244, 267
Horn Book, The (Legman), 297, 308
Horowitz, Irving Louis, 30
House, Son, 155, 158–159
Howell, Peg Leg, 158
Hughes, Langston, 272
Hummocks (Malaurie), 54, 69, 75
Hunter, Mrs. Janie, 192
Hurston, 189–190, 197, 271
Hurston, Zora Neale, 189, 271
Hurt, Mississippi John, 148, 153–155, 159

"I was sittin' in the jail to do a stretch of time" (toast), 21

Index | 371

Irwin, John, 27
Ives, Edward D. "Sandy," 32, 34, 40, 144, 152, 241, 347, 349

Jackson, George Pullen, 174
James, Nehemiah "Skip" 148, 153–159, 162, 248, 339, 162, 248
James, Willis, 154
Jefferson Airplane, 148
"Joe the Grinder" (toast and worksong), 19, 255–266
Johns, Jasper, 146
Johnson, Guy B., 271
Johnson, James Weldon, 181
Johnson, Lyndon, B., 146, 148
joke, 62, 297–298, 303, 308, 339
Jones, Ernest, 98, 107
Joplin, Janis, 165
Journal of American Folklore, 9, 151, 196, 198, 207, 219, 255, 283, 289, 300, 315, 354–335, 356, 361, 365
Jubilee Singers, 177

Kafka, Franz, 358
Kass, Leon, 362
Kennedy, John F., 146
Kennedy, Robert, 42, 148
Ketner, Kenneth Laine, 339
King, Martin Luther, 146
Kingston Trio, 145
Kirkpatrick, Rev. Frederick Douglas, 348
knives, 26, 105
Korn, Henri, 333
Korson, George, 2
Korson, Rae, 348–350
Krassner, Paul, 166
Kremetz, Jill, 31
Krohn, Kaarle, 338

language: call-and-response in, 173; camp meetings, 171, 213; folklore studies, 331, 335–336, 338, 342, 355; Gullah dialect, 210; in the Arctic, 59, 61, 76; lining out, 172–173; missionary suppression of, 61, 76; NEH and, 362–363; prison, 9, 22–25; science and ethnography, 356; spiritual songs, 171–181; spirituals, 171, 174; worksongs, 251
Lay My Burden Down (Botkin), 271, 286
Lead Belly (Huddie Ledbetter), 245, 290, 331
Legman, Gershon, xii, 297–308
Les Derniers rois de Thulé (Malaurie), 53, 70, 357–358
Leveau, Marie, 189
Levine, Lawrence W., 268, 361, 363
Library of Congress, 27, 252, 266, 284, 289–290, 293, 328, 347–348
List, George, 2, 327
Lomax, Alan, 145, 149, 202, 206, 255, 266, 271, 289–291, 293, 295
Lucas, Claude, 359

Madame Bovary, 358
Malaurie, Jean, 53–55, 57–61, 63, 65, 67–77, 348, 357–359
Maledicta, vii, 297
Manning, Robert (Bob), 30
Marrowbone Creek (Pikeville, Kentucky), 32, 39
Marrowbone Folk School, 40
material folklore, 25–27
McAdams, C. L., 245
McCarthy, Eugene, 148
McCulloh, Judith, 2, 275
McKim, Lucy, 176, 197, 208, 270, 330
Mcluhan, Marshall, 320
McSurely, Al, 44, 46, 52
Mencken, H. L., 23, 28
Meredith, James, 146
Merton, Thomas, 46
Miller, Arthur, 349
minstrelsy, 208, 212–213, 219

372 | Index

tundra: Jean Malaurie and, 53, 57, 70, 75; train in (Nome), 70–71; change in, 76
Turner, Lorenzo Dow, 201
Tuskegee Institute, 178
TVA (Tennessee Valley Administration), 47, 50
two-head, 194

UMW: *see* United Mine Workers of America
United Mine Workers of America, 34–35, 41, 47
University of Chicago Folk Festival, 145

Vestine, Henry, 157
Vietnam, 146, 148, 326, 365–366
Virgil, 353
VISTA, 40
voodoo, 182–198, 244, 273

Walton, Mary, 38, 50
War on Poverty, 34
Warhol, Andy, 146
Waters, Muddy (McKinley Morganfield), 290
Weavers, The, 144–145

Weigle, Marta, 343
Wein, George, 145, 147, 165, 291
Wells, Junior, 165
Wesley, John, 172, 174
White, Bukka, 158
White, Newman I., 174
Whitman, Walt, 143, 333
Whitten, Norman, 194
whorehouse, 81–83, 135
Wild River, 50
Wilgus, D. K., 145, 181, 213
Williams, Robert Pete, 154, 159
Wilson, Al, 159, 162
Woodstock, 148
worksong, 223, 257, 267–269, 271–273, 275–277, 279, 291
worksongs, convict, 23, 223–253, 256–257, 267–272, 276–279, 291, 309
WPA (Works Progress Association), 211, 271, 284, 327, 331

Yarrow, Peter, 292
Yeltsin, Boris Nikolayevich, 54
Yippies, 166
Yoder, Don, 172, 174, 181, 186, 196

Zemljanova, L., 339
Zinberg, Norman, 162

www.ingramcontent.com/pod-product-compliance
Lightning Source LLC
Chambersburg PA
CBHW022033020325
22763CB00019B/428